PATTERN

1. Detail of the Façade, Notre Dame de Dijon, *c.* 1240

PATTERN

A STUDY OF ORNAMENT
IN WESTERN EUROPE
FROM 1180 TO 1900

By JOAN EVANS

B.LITT. (OXON.), D.LIT. (LOND.)

VOL. I

A DA CAPO PAPERBACK

Library of Congress Cataloging in Publication Data

Evans, Joan, 1893-
    Pattern.

    (A Da Capo paperback)
    Reprint of the 1931 ed. published at the
Clarendon Press, Oxford.
    Includes bibliographical references and index.
    1. Decoration and ornament — Europe.   I. Title.
NK1442.E8 1976   745.4'49'4   76-10682
ISBN 0-306-80040-3 (v. 1)
ISBN 0-306-80041-1 (v. 2)

ISBN 0-306-80040-3

First Paperback Printing 1976

This Da Capo Paperback edition of
*Pattern: A Study of Ornament in Western Europe
From 1180 to 1900, Volume I,*
is an unabridged republication of the first edition
published in Oxford, at the Clarendon Press, in 1931.

Published by Da Capo Press, Inc.
A Subsidiary of Plenum Publishing Corporation
227 West 17th Street
New York, N.Y. 10011

TO
THE MEMORY OF
MY FATHER
JOHN EVANS
1823–1908

PREFACE

AS soon as I began to write this book it became evident that a bibliography of the subject complete enough to be of real use would be of a size to demand a volume to itself,[1] and that it would not be possible to attempt to give a complete set of references for each monument or building cited. I have therefore contented myself with giving references in the footnotes to books that I have consulted on special points.[2] I should like to express a general indebtedness which cannot there be noted to certain books of reference, notably to Michel's *Histoire de l'Art,* to Venturi's *Storia dell'arte italiana,* to Guilmard's *Les Maîtres ornemanistes*, and to the series of books on Renaissance and later decoration in England by Miss M. Jourdain.

My work has been lightened by much kindness from many friends and many courteous strangers.

My thanks are due to all those who have taught me; to all those who have opened to me their own collections and the collections in their charge; to those who drew my attention to relevant books; and to those who have answered my importunate questions on points of detail. I should like to express my gratitude to the staffs of the libraries of the Musée de sculpture comparée at the Trocadéro, of the Reading Room of the British Museum, of the Library and the Department of Engraved Ornament in the Victoria and Albert Museum, and of the Bodleian Library, for their ungrudging service.

Sir Henry Maxwell Lyte, Mr. Samuel Gardner, Mr. J. R. H. Weaver of Trinity College, and Mr. Stokes of Exeter, have generously given me photographs of their own taking and have freely allowed me to publish them; Lady Victoria Manners, Professor de Zulueta, and Dr. G. C. Williamson have given me photographs in their possession with permission to reproduce them; and Mrs. Olive Edis Galsworthy has taken photographs for me at Holkham under conditions of considerable difficulty.

Permission to reproduce objects in the collections in their charge has been granted me by the authorities of the British Museum, and the Victoria and Albert Museum; of the Ashmolean Museum and Bodleian Library at Oxford; of the Whitworth Institute at Manchester; of the Louvre, the Musée de Cluny, the Musée des Arts décoratifs, the Musée de sculpture comparée (Trocadéro), and the Bibliothèque Nationale at Paris; of the Musée des Antiquités de la Seine Inférieure at Rouen and the Musée de l'ancien Evêché at Angers, of the Musées Royaux du Cinquantenaire and the Bibliothèque Royale of Brussels; of the Rijksmuseum of

---

[1] The subject catalogue of the Library of the Victoria and Albert Museum will be found invaluable by London readers.

[2] Where the place of publication is not given it may be assumed that English books have been published in London and French in Paris.

Amsterdam; of the Stadtliche Porzellän Sammlung of Dresden; of the Uffizi Galleries and the Laurentian Library of Florence, and of the Museo Nazionale of Ravenna.

The Provost of Oriel, the Warden of New College, the Warden of All Souls, the authorities of Winchester College and Stonyhurst, and the Corporation of Brighton have allowed me to reproduce objects in their possession. Among private owners I have to thank the Duke of Devonshire, the Duke of Rutland, Lord Leicester, Sir Henry Bedingfeld, the Dean of Westminster, Dr. Forrer, Miss C. A. E. Moberly, and Mr. E. R. Roberts Chanter. Mr. Dyson Perrins has been so good as to allow me to have a page from one of his manuscripts specially photographed for reproduction in this book, and to reproduce another from his Gorleston Psalter. Messrs. Morris & Co. have kindly allowed me to reproduce their *Fruit* paper.

For help on points of detail I owe sincere thanks to Miss Hope Emily Allen, Mr. C. F. Bell, Professor R. W. Chambers, Mr. R. G. Collingwood, the late Monsieur Camille Enlart, Dr. R. T. Gunther, Dr. C. R. S. Harris, Dr. G. F. Hill, Miss M. Jourdain, Monsieur Jacques Meurgey, Professor Daniel Mornet, Mr. C. C. Oman, Professor Rudler, Mr. G. McN. Rushforth, Dr. and Mrs. Charles Singer, the late Professor Paul Studer, Mr. A. Van de Put, Mr. A. J. B. Wace, Mr. W. W. Watts, and Mr. J. R. H. Weaver. To Monsieur J. J. Marquet de Vasselot, Conservateur au Musée du Louvre et du Musée de Cluny, I owe an especial debt of gratitude: he has given me every facility for study in his two museums, he has made me free of his important manuscript bibliography of French decorative art,[1] he has answered innumerable questions, and throughout the writing of the book has helped me by constant encouragement and occasional friendly and constructive criticism. Professor Tancred Borenius has not only acted as supervisor for those chapters of the book that were offered as a thesis for the Doctorate in Literature of the University of London, but has also been so kind as to read the whole book both in manuscript and in proof; I am greatly indebted to him for encouragement and information most generously given.

Finally, my thanks are due to my Mother and to my friends Mrs. Murdo Mackenzie and Miss Agnes Conway, who have done me the great service of reading and criticizing the book in manuscript; to Mrs. E. M. White of Somerville College, who has undertaken the labour of the Index; and to the officers of the Clarendon Press, who have seen the book through all the stages of printing and publication.

LONDON, *March* 1930.   J. E.

---

[1] The section dealing with goldwork and enamel has been published by the Société française de bibliographie, 1925, *Bibliographie de l'orfèvrerie et de l'émaillerie françaises.*

CONTENTS

VOLUME I

LIST OF ILLUSTRATIONS

VOLUME I

VOLUME II

INTRODUCTION

FOR almost a century pattern has been studied by archaeologists, anthropologists, and mathematicians. Students of the history of the human race continue to study its origin and evolution; historians of art year by year produce monographs on some of its aspects, and mathematicians and designers alike calculate the mathematical bases of complicated repeating units of design. But the anthropologist does not usually do justice to the arts of Europe in recent times; the archaeologist is as a rule too much occupied with points of technique, provenance, and documentation to study the development of pattern apart from these; and neither the mathematician nor the designer is concerned with tracing the history of the past. I have therefore thought it well to trace the development of the motives of ornament in western Europe from the time of the rise of Gothic architecture to the dawn of the present century; and in doing so I have found them to be a *speculum minus* of human life, darkly reflecting the web of man's thought and feeling.

Anthropologically, Europe[1] is a field in which there is a confusion of races and cultures; artistically, it is less rich than Asia both in the creation and the tradition of ornament; but from the point of view of analysis and comprehension it is for us the only perfect field of investigation, since we ourselves belong to it and inherit and understand its traditions. Moreover, the seven centuries of European history here studied represent the most continuous epoch of intense living and thinking in the history of the world.[2] In the course of these centuries the activities of intellect have defended their freedom; and tradition, whether of religion, art, or learning, has not held them captive. Alien influences from the Near and the Far East have been felt from time to time; but though such oriental styles have been appreciated for their novelty and their intrinsic beauty, they have soon been modified, and have eventually been transformed beyond recognition by the influence of national tastes inspired by direct observation.

Therefore with relatively abundant knowledge of a relatively untrammelled development we are able in this limited sphere to study cause as well as effect. We can recognize almost any form of European artistic creation during this period as the reaction, conscious or unconscious, to a stimulus of interested perception.

The history of civilization is the history of the development of humanity, wherein the study of the evolution of the human faculty of perceiving beauty takes its place. The influence of environment lies not in those things which do in

[1] I have not scrupled to omit any consideration of the purely Arab arts of Spain or of the oriental arts of eastern Europe, since they do not really form part of the European tradition.

[2] Only in amusements has there been comparatively little change; and thus hunting scenes are the only genre of decoration continuously represented from 1180 (and of course before) until the time of Horace Vernet and his imitators.

fact surround us, but in that part of them of which our perceptions make us aware. Outside the houses and the cities the world has hardly changed; mountain and torrent, forest and heath, the folded plain beneath the serene or stormy sky; rain and sunshine, snow and wind, the beauties of fire and water are as they have ever been. Even everyday human activities—the farmer's sowing and harvest, the woman's weaving and needlework, the craftsman's mastery of gold or clay—are older than history. It is still the oldest beauties that move us most; but we who see them belong to our own day, and we see them differently from the generations before us; are blind, it may be, to what they saw, and find instead fresh interest, fresh significance, fresh beauties that have hitherto remained unseen. So we change our man-made surroundings to make them congruous with the world we see; and these, too, as they change from year to year are more or less seen as habit or appreciation or distaste makes us more or less conscious of their quality. Our perceptions make our world; and our artistic expressions of those perceptions are that world's truest history.

New interests, whether arrived at by intellectual progression or by fortuitous circumstance, may thus change the current of human sensibility. Some of these interests are trifling alike in character and influence; others, since they remain vital for more than a day, perhaps for more than a generation, find more than ephemeral expression in art, and so long as they form a part of the intellectual heritage of man continue to be a living part of his artistic tradition. All, whether trifling or noble, influence in some degree the course of the development of human sensibility; and their reflection in art, even if it may seem ugly or unimportant, is not unworthy of our study.

Regarded from this angle the criticism of art, and the aesthetic theories based upon it, are chiefly significant as expressions of sensibility. Consequently they are most valuable when they are nearly contemporary, and are parallel expressions of similar perceptions. In this study I have confined myself as far as possible to contemporary criticisms and contemporary descriptions, and have considered aesthetic theories only in relation to the art known to those who advanced them.

Within the limits of time and space set for this book it can, I think, be proved that the styles of ornament current at any date are conditioned by the perceptions of the aristocracy of the time, whether that aristocracy be one of taste, of learning, of birth, or of mere wealth. Those outside this privileged class, in so far as they use ornament, inherit it from the aristocracy at second hand. Like discarded clothes, it reaches them a little out of date; and as they might cut down court dresses for everyday use, so they modify and simplify it to meet their needs. On the other hand, there is at all times another aristocracy of great artists; and these, out of the decorative material created to satisfy the needs of others, will take themes and schemes to modify and enrich for their own use. For it will be found, I think, that it is in the commonplaces of the decorative arts that the great artist finds the genres and the types that he transmutes into creations at once nobler and more personal. Indeed, up to the end of the fifteenth century there was no distinction between 'fine' and applied arts in men's minds. The same man painted the king's banners, his castle walls, and his devotional pictures; the same carver worked at the architectural details of his chapel and the great recumbent effigy on his tomb.

For this reason I think that a study of the conditions of creation in the decorative arts should precede a study of the psychology of beauty in arts of a more advanced and more personal kind. Such a study gives the key alike to the peasant arts and to the 'fine' arts, that derive from the same source, though the one be distorted by simplification and multiplication, and the other stamped with the imprint of genius and turned from the service of the many to the spiritual expression of those whose perceptive spirit transcends that of the rest.

I have found it difficult to draw a clear line between decoration on the one hand and the Fine Arts of painting, sculpture, and architecture on the other; and have contented myself with an arbitrary division for the purposes of this book. I have included the decorative details of architecture, while omitting the study of the architectural whole, and I have omitted any free-standing sculpture. In decoration representing human figures it has been easy to set aside religious iconography, closely though this may be connected with decorative schemes; but in civil iconography it has proved impossible to draw a hard and fast line between decoration and representational art. I have therefore adopted the *via media* of recording the subjects of sculptured and painted figures forming part of decorative schemes, and of figured tapestries and embroideries, without illustrating them or considering them as fully as other genres of ornament.

The first essential of decoration is a defined and limited space. It is the absence of a limiting frame in the rough and undefined spaces of a cave that accounts for the absence of decoration from Palaeolithic and Bushman art.[1] Once civilization has reached a point where it can define and limit an empty space, the decorative arts are created in response to its appeal. So pattern, even if a technique of relief is employed, is essentially two-dimensional; its ornament is surface ornament in relation to the structure, however plastic its expression may be. Pattern is an art not only of representation, but also of rhythm; it tends to exclude illusion in favour of symmetry. But paradoxically, just because of this stylization, the relation between the perception that inspired its creation and the pattern created is often more obvious than it can be in the more representational 'fine' arts.

The study of decorative art is concerned primarily with progress and change, and therefore can be confined, broadly speaking, to the arts of the countries which as

[1] See R. Fry, *Vision and Design*, p. 58. He notes further: 'children's drawings are never decorative when they have the whole surface of a sheet of paper to draw on, but they will design a frieze with well marked rhythm when they have only a narrow strip.'

leaders are initiating such changes. The centres of intellectual thought are the centres of decorative creation, and it is their influence that spreads over those at a lower stage of development. Consequently, the study of pattern must be based on a study of the *beginnings* of each of its manifestations. Therefore, since the decorative art of the whole of Europe cannot be studied simultaneously, the ornament of the countries that at any given moment are imitative and not creative will only receive incidental consideration in this book.[1]

Pattern in the wide sense exists in everything possessing mass and proportion, form and colour, that is seen in relation to a defined space. The leaves of a plane-tree make a pattern against a rectangle of London sky; the daisies make a pattern on a plot of grass; ripples on water, veining on marble, frost-crystals on a window, all in their repetition and their formal beauty make a pattern within their frames. So with the works of man: a colonnade of Doric pillars makes a pattern with the wall behind it, and the gable of the Parthenon makes a pattern with the gabled lines of Pentelicus. In this sense pattern is essential to beauty; but if it is taken in the restricted sense of applied ornament beauty can well exist without it, since proportion of mass, of form, and of colour can have their being in the actual structure of any creation, independently of any added diversification. On the other hand, pattern itself must rely for its beauty on this essential balance of mass, form, and colour, so that in pattern as well as in structural design the principles of harmony can be expressed, studied, and revealed.

---

[1] Similarly the Romanesque survivals in the more backward countries, though they may fall within the chronological limits of this book, are not discussed.

I
THE MISTRESS ART

I

THE last half of the twelfth century was one of the great creative epochs of the world. Feudalism passed from existence as a military institution established to meet the necessities of a dangerous age into existence as a political system blessed by the Church, standing on its own merits in peace as in war, with codes, obligations, an honour and a loyalty of its own. The life of the Church little by little became centred not in the cloisters and cells of monasticism, but in the cathedrals where the people of God prayed and worshipped alike as individuals and as citizens. Leadership in learning gradually passed from the regular to the secular clergy. The monastic schools were outshone by the rising cathedral schools of Laon, Tours, Chartres, Orleans, and Paris. Then European learning, strengthened by a revival of classical studies at the end of the eleventh century and by a revival of scientific legal studies in the middle of the twelfth, found a fresh centre in the newly founded universities, where study in common created the characteristic art of dialectic.[1] Everywhere a new corporate spirit was abroad; even the trader and the craftsman in their guilds were conscious of their identity as units among many men of like skill with themselves.

Inevitably such a stirring of new life, and especially of new corporate life, alike in social organization, religion, and the sphere of intellect, brought to men a new idea of human potentialities. With a single ideal and a single plan what might not man accomplish? The seven arts lay within the compass of his mind; he stood, as Bernard of Chartres said, on the shoulders of the giants of antiquity; and thanks to them he could see farther than they. He had to examine tradition afresh, and to create it anew, in the light of logical reasoning; already Berengar of Tours was proclaiming that 'it is the part of courage to have recourse to dialectic in all things, for recourse to dialectic is recourse to reason, and he who does not avail himself of reason abandons his chief honour, since by virtue of reason he was made in the image of God'.

All this stirring of the human spirit had its centre in France. It was in the royal domain of France that the feudal system became a system of civilization, that the cathedrals became centres of religious thought and education,[2] that the first great philosophic university became a centre of logical thought, that the guilds of merchants and artisans were established, and that the vernacular literature of the

---

[1] This was firmly established before the death of Berengar of Tours in 1088.

[2] I do not wish to minimize the importance of the monasteries, but their *creative* epoch is rather the Romanesque than the Gothic age.

B

citizens was created. In France too, and in the royal domain of France, a new architectural style had its birth and rose to its maturity.[1]

We are apt to forget, in an age in which we take the achievements of the intellect for granted, that the rediscovery of the principles of logical thinking was so fresh and exciting that it had the emotional force that projects intellectual conceptions on to the artistic plane. In other fields than that of dialectic, logical sequence and construction became an ideal of creation; and in Gothic architecture a new system of construction was evolved—logical, dynamic, and living.

The essential characteristic of the style is the rejection of the classic column-and-lintel structure and of the Roman arch and barrel vault in favour of a system of ogival vaulting in which the stress is taken by the crossing ribs that serve to support the stones of the roof. The corresponding arches themselves have a pointed form, in harmony with the ogival vault;[2] while the necessity for countering the lateral thrusts leads to the development of systems of exterior buttresses, of which the flying buttress is the most original and characteristic. Naturally the creators of Gothic shared in the French Romanesque tradition; but the significance of their system lies in the fact that it is a new creation, a pure feat of the intellect, the crowning achievement of a creative age. Since the first perfect maturity of the Periclean age, the artists of civilized Europe had never ceased to look backward. The archaism of Pasitelean sculpture, the classicism of early Christian art, the decadent traditions of the ornament of the Migration period, the massive splendour of Romanesque architecture, had all sought to recapture the glories of a past epoch. Even Byzantine magnificence had owed much to an element of retrospection. But at the end of the twelfth century the chains of tradition were loosed and visual art once more came round in the cycle of time to a point when a more original creation was possible. A new style was achieved in which European art found its expression for centuries. The style, like every marked style of art, finds its best literary exponents in the thinkers of the generation immediately succeeding its creation. Just as the Doric and Ionic orders of Greek architecture, with their symmetry, unity, and proportion, were the mirror in which Aristotelian and Platonic thinkers unconsciously saw visual beauty, so Gothic architecture, with its logical construction, its symbolic sculpture, and its religious aim, was the mirror

[1] See F. de Verneilh in *Ann. Archeol.*, xxiii. 1 and 115; R. de Lasteyrie, *L'Architecture religieuse en France à l'époque gothique*, i. 7. Exactly the right stone for such construction is quarried in the district between Noyon, Soissons, Mantes, Paris, and Senlis.

Note the great number of churches built in the royal domain under Louis VII between 1150 and 1180: Noyon, Soissons, Sens, Arras, Cambrai, Laon, &c., and the less important movement under the Plantagenets in Anjou, Touraine, Maine, and Poitou. In England itself the force of monastic conservation was the chief impediment to the progress of the French style: 'it is the continuance of monastic direction in our English style which really gives the explanation of its want of sympathy with the French'. (E. S. Prior, *A History of Gothic Art in England*, p. 21.) Up to the end of the twelfth century the monks of Ely and Peterborough were finishing their naves in pure Romanesque style.

[2] It must not be forgotten that this pointed arch was in common use in central France in Romanesque architecture of the late eleventh and of the twelfth centuries.

3. The roof of the Nave, Exeter Cathedral. Begun *c.* 1280

2. Detail of the Lantern, Cathedral of Coutances, *c.* 1230

4. Town canopies on the Portail Royal, Cathedral of Chartres, 1145–55

5. Town canopies on the West Front, Notre Dame d'Étampes, c. 1200

6. Town canopies on the South Door, Cathedral of Rheims, c. 1240

of beauty for the scholastic philosophers. In the scholastic view the elements of beauty were *ordo, magnitudo, integritas, debita proportio, aequalitas numerosa, commensuratio partium elegans*;[1] and it would be hard to find a better summary of the characteristics of early Gothic architecture.

Aquinas reduces these elements of beauty to three essentials: integrity, since intelligence likes wholeness of being; proportion, since intelligence likes order; and, last and above all, brilliance and clearness, for intelligence loves light and comprehensibility.[2] Even in detail, the scholastic view, however traditional it in fact may be, reads like the thought of one who has passed long hours of meditation in a Gothic cathedral: *Ratio pulchri consistit in resplendentia formae super partes materiae proportionatas.*[3]

The medieval civilization of France, having its centre in Paris and the royal domain, spread over all the land whether under French or English domination; and similarly Gothic architecture created subsidiary schools of Gothic[4] in Normandy, Burgundy, Champagne, Languedoc, and the south-west. Nor was it only on French soil that it flourished; in Plantagenet England it enjoyed a development almost as rich (if not so logical) as that followed in its own country. In the middle of the thirteenth century the area of Gothic building extends roughly from Dijon to Dryburgh and from Troyes to Dublin. Outside this area it is never completely at home. The Church might have unity of ritual and belief through all Christendom, but the level of its intellectual quality and its emotional force varied from country to country and from province to province; and it is these which set their stamp on the style of the cathedral builders.

In Spain, until the fifteenth century, it had to fight its way as a definitely French style against an indigenous half Arab system of decoration and a deeply rooted local Romanesque architecture; in Italy the classic tradition, however decadent, was too strong for it. The Cistercians brought the style into Italy at the end of the twelfth century,[5] but its constructive principles were never really accepted. Almost the only pure Gothic structures in Italy, in construction and in ornamentation, are S. Andrea at Vercelli, 1219–25, S. Francesco at Assisi, 1236, and S. Fran-

[1] See M. de Wulf, 'L'histoire de l'esthétique et ses grandes orientations', in *Revue Néo-Scolastique*, Louvain, xvii, 1909, p. 245.

[2] *Summa Theologiae*, i. 39, a. 8 c.

[3] This quotation, generally ascribed to the non-existent *Opusculum de Pulchro* of Aquinas, is really drawn from a fragment of Dionysius the Areopagite *de divinis nominibus*, published separately by the Abbate Pietro Antonio Uccelli in 1869. See J. Maritain, *Art et scolastique*, Paris, 1920, p. 34.

[4] It seems hardly necessary to state that 'Gothic' is a term of opprobrium invented by the critics of the Renaissance. In France 'style ogival' or 'style français' is preferred; but, as de Lasteyrie points out (*Architecture religieuse à l'époque romane*, p. 323), *ogival* is true only of the late form, and *français* can hardly be applied to English Decorated. I have therefore preferred to keep the familiar designation. The English reader must distinguish between the French use of *ogival* to indicate the curve of a Gothic arch, and the English use of it to indicate an arch with curve and countercurve: this is the French *accolade*.

[5] Fossanova, consecrated in 1208, is in the Cistercian style of Burgundian Gothic. On the whole subject see A. L. Frothingham, 'Introduction of Gothic Architecture into Italy by the French Cistercian Monks', in *American Journal of Archaeology*, 1890, vol. vi, p. 10.

cesco at Bologna, 1236–40. Even when, in the fourteenth century, Italian figure sculpture and painting were dominated by Gothic line, the soaring quality of Gothic in Italian construction and ornament was conditioned by the national instinct for lintel construction.[1] Farther to the south-east, it is true, a purer Gothic is found; but such buildings as the cathedrals of Nicosia and Famagusta in Cyprus and the churches, castles, and markets of the Latin kingdoms of the East are only a colonial architecture planned by alien craftsmen and have no real roots and little independent development.

Nor was the Gothic style much more fruitful in the northern countries. In Germany the Rhenish school of Romanesque continued active and dominant long after the creation of Gothic architecture in France, and, though ogival vaulting might be used, the character of the whole remained Romanesque.[2] Not until the middle of the thirteenth century was it possible to build such Gothic churches as the Cathedrals of Trier and of Limburg on the Lahn, which were modelled on the churches of Champagne and Picardy. Farther to the south, Burgundian influence was strong at a rather later date. In the Low Countries a lack of fine stone and a consequent tradition of building in brick soon modified the Gothic style into a provincial architecture of little distinction. In Sweden, though the Cathedral of Upsala may be based upon Notre Dame de Paris, the style never progressed beyond the imitative stage.

The first edifice which can be considered a Gothic whole is the Abbey of St. Denis, begun under Suger about 1137.[3] Thenceforward the great monuments of the style follow in quick succession: Noyon was begun about 1150, Senlis about 1156, Laon about 1160, Notre Dame de Paris about 1163. But while the increasing influence of naturalism[4] was beginning to modify the Romanesque capitals, friezes, and pilasters that the early Gothic architects used to adorn their buildings, it can hardly be said that any system of Gothic architectural ornament is to be found much before 1180. Even then Gothic ornament arises rather from the austerity consequent on the rejection of irrelevant Romanesque decoration than from the deliberate adoption of a decorative scheme.

In the age of its creation, too, religious iconography passes in a great measure out of the sphere of decoration. In Romanesque ornament religious themes are used with a symbolic appropriateness that gives them not only intellectual significance but also decorative value. But such use, natural when the finest minds of the age were devoted to symbolic interpretation, and when decorative art still

[1] In France, too, the balance between sculptured figures and their architectural background was maintained, and the architectural element often even preponderates, whereas in Italy the figures gradually encroach upon the architectural frame.

[2] e.g. in the Church of Andernach, *c.* 1206.

[3] The earliest English church with ogival vaulting and pointed arches would seem to be Malmesbury, built later than 1140. On the relation between Norman and Gothic vaulting see Royal Institute of British Architects, *Journal*, 3rd series, vi. 259, 289, 345; ix. 350; x. 19.

[4] See Chapter II.

7. Detail of the South-west Porch, Saint Jean des Vignes,
Soissons, *c.* 1220

8. Detail of the West Front, Cathedral of Bourges, *c.* 1220

9. Detail of the Apse, Church of Chars, Seine et Oise, *c.* 1210

10. Capital in the Nave, Notre Dame de Semur-en-Auxois, *c.* 1230

11. Crocketed mouldings of owls and monkeys, Cathedral of
Bourges, *c.* 1280

12. Detail of the Portail de la Vierge Dorée, Cathedral of Amiens, *c.* 1220–88

13. Piscina at Jesus College, Cambridge, *c.* 1220

found its chief home in the learned shelter of the cloister, gradually ceased to be natural when decoration fell into lay hands.[1] Certain great iconographic schemes created in the Romanesque age were perpetuated; but Gothic iconographic use does not aim at a symbolism, only comprehensible to the learned, peculiarly adapted to the purpose of that which it adorns, but at the illustration of scenes of the life of Christ and the Saints that have a didactic value and significance for the ordinary layman. As a consequence it is far easier to delimit iconography and decoration in Gothic architecture than in Romanesque. Moreover, in the earlier style figure sculpture sometimes played its part as a structural element in the architecture itself, whether as a caryatid figure or as the ornament of a capital; whereas Gothic figure sculpture performs no structural function[2] and however much it may enrich and adorn the whole, and however beautifully congruous it may be with the architectural scheme, it is yet, like the sculptures of most classic temples, a part of the whole that can bear consideration apart.

Gothic architecture, indeed, was in its beginning essentially a style of constructive architecture and not of decoration. Even the elements that in Romanesque architecture had fulfilled a function that was chiefly decorative were given a new structural significance.[3] The ribs of the vaulting had become the key to the whole structure; string courses, cornices, and archivolts had all a part to play in strengthening the walls at the points of greatest strain. The Romanesque capital had borne an almost negligible load; the Gothic capital was no mere classical survival, but performed a real structural function in adjusting the load of the archivolts to a slender shaft. The Gothic capital consequently developed along structural lines. With the progress of the style the load became heavier and heavier, and consequently the abacus and the base alike thickened in compensation. Up to the first quarter of the thirteenth century the section of the load was usually square, and the abacus retained its classic shape; but with the advance of Gothic style the section of the archivolt became polygonal, and the classic tradition of a square abacus was renounced, since a round or polygonal abacus was structurally needed. With the square abacus the tradition of Corinthian foliage came to an end. In France a feeling for the lines of growth kept an architectonic form for the new capital, however naturalistic its decoration; in England a greater freedom of treatment resulted in a certain shapelessness, first evidenced in St. Hugh's work at Lincoln about 1195. In England, too, perhaps in reaction against this loss of form, a plain moulded capital of purely structural form like an inverted and elongated Attic base was evolved as an alternative. This was used at Winchester in 1204, and was perpetuated by the austere traditions of the Cistercian builders. A similar if less

[1] Cf. Bernard's distinction between the aims of the art of the cloister and of the cathedral. (Coulton, *Medieval Garner*, p. 70.)

[2] The exception that proves the rule is the use of caryatid figures on the pier buttresses of the nave of Rheims. Another exceptional caryatid is the late Gothic figure of a beggar in the Cathedral Museum of Mainz.

[3] The point is well brought out by A. Kingsley Porter, *Mediaeval Architecture*, ii. 97.

exaggerated simplicity is evident in much early Gothic work alike in France and England. The most common decorative features of early Gothic churches are the triforium and the arcade, features inherited from the Romanesque style; and their use in such schemes as that of the interior of Laon Cathedral shows how far the elements of the decorative scheme are yet structural, columns and arches playing their part in the distribution and endurance of the weight of the whole. This is equally true when the arcading is applied to the exterior: for instance, in the beautiful and severe arcadings of the buttresses of Chartres even the circular piercings in the spandrels have a structural justification in that they lighten the structure without weakening it.

Yet inevitably, with increased facility in the use of Gothic structural forms, an increasing freedom in their use led to decorative elaboration. The Gothic style itself was passing out of its first stage of architectural grammar and logic into a further stage when its architects had mastered the art of rhetoric as well. The double columniation of the Romanesque style was applied to an arcade within arches, as on the early thirteenth-century triforium at Beaumont sur Oise; the mouldings of the archivolt tended to become more complicated,[1] the shafts more lofty; the style remained constructive but it more frankly confessed a decorative intention. It would be hard to better the effect of the interior treatment of the lantern of Coutances[2] (fig. 2) or the nave clerestories of Sens and Ripon, but their structural purpose could have been more simply achieved. The same is true of the interior of Salisbury Cathedral, begun in 1220, and of the contemporary choir of Southwark; their style is remarkable for its purely architectural quality and for the absence of applied ornament, yet the design shows a search for aesthetic effect far more sustained and intense than that evident in many more ornate buildings.

It is with this end in view that the ribs of the vaulting tend to become more numerous; at Lincoln the vaulting of the nave has six unnecessary ribs—four tiercerons and two liernes—in each of its compartments. The system of imposts and capitals, elaborated to take these more complex vaults, had to be harmonized; at Sens the tripartite vaulting imposts are set at an obtuse angle, to receive the thrust of the vaulting ribs direct; in the choir of Notre Dame de Paris they are juxtaposed in line, with differing capitals, while in the nave they are beginning to be fused, and have their capitals carved alike; at Laon the imposts are united and the capitals multipartite. The form of the columns on which the vaults rested afforded another problem of which almost every cathedral offers a different solution, each more complex and accomplished than the last.

The tendency in England was to multiply colonnettes, ribs, and mouldings like

[1] For an excellent study of English arch-moulds see E. S. Prior, *History of Gothic Art in England*, pp. 114 et seqq. For French arch-moulds see R. de Lasteyrie, *L'Architecture religieuse en France à l'époque gothique*, i. 295 et seqq.

[2] Professor Prior considers that Coutances shows some English influence in its round abaci and rich mouldings: *History of Gothic Art in England*, p. 306.

14. Detail of the North Porch, Wells Cathedral, *c.* 1185

15. Detail of the base of the Portail du Sauveur, Cathedral of Amiens, *c.* 1250

16. Detail of the base of the West Door, Cathedral of Auxerre, *c.* 1230

the monorhymed *tirades* of Anglo-Norman verse. At Wells, though the piers are relatively complex,[1] the vaulting is simple, with three necessary ribs rising from corbels formed of three little colonnettes; at Exeter, begun some forty years later, there are sixteen colonnettes to the piers, eightfold mouldings to the archivolts and eleven ribs to the vaulting (fig. 3). This splendid multiplicity gives a peculiar breadth and richness to the fifteen bays of the nave, though purely decorative detail is confined to the comparatively small corbels and to the remote bosses of the roof. A similar decorative use of a multitude of ribs gives their characteristic charm to the English chapter-houses with vaulting springing from a central pillar; there is a hidden fallacy in the logic, but the most is made of the artistic significance of structural form.

Again, by the middle of the thirteenth century the parapet crowning the cornice was receiving considerable decorative elaboration. Generally the parapet was pierced with a lancet arcade either plain or trefoil-headed, and a crocketed pinnacle over every buttress served at once to support the parapet and to enhance the soaring lines of the architectural whole. The corresponding development of waterspout gargoyles resulted in their being in their turn transferred from structural to decorative use, notably on the double arcade of the façade of Notre Dame de Dijon (fig. 1: Frontispiece). It is this same enjoyment of architectural motives that makes a continuous moulding, set to emphasize the line of structural form, the most common and most characteristic motive of Gothic ornament.

There is, too, a gradual tendency upwards: Notre Dame de Paris, begun about 1163, measures 32 metres up to the keystone of the vault; the choir of Beauvais, begun little more than a century later, soars up to 47 metres. The English churches do not attain such proportions, and average but two-thirds of the height of the French: our country seems always to retain its taste for breadth and low pitch,[2] as against the soaring quality of French medieval building. But if England did not raise such lofty vaults, she equalled and indeed excelled France[3] in the use of elongated lancets, especially in her northern counties;[4] the aperture is lengthened until it is sometimes from fifteen to twenty feet in height to a foot in width.[5] In

[1] It is noteworthy that the central colonnette in each angle has a marked rib down its centre that helps to preserve the architectonic form of the whole. An interesting comparison with these piers is provided by those of the easternmost bay, built by Bishop Reginald de Bohun between 1186 and 1191. The plan is similar, but the whole is more slender in proportion and slighter in relief. The abacus is not continuous and the clusters of colonnettes are not fully fused into the pier.

[2] In the nave of Wells, for instance, no upward line runs for the whole height, but the horizontal line at the base of the triforium runs for the whole length and is further emphasized by a continuous plain roll moulding.

[3] An extreme example of height in arcading is, however, provided by the exterior of the south transept of Chartres.

[4] An exceptional, and less marked, southern instance is on the west front of Romsey, c. 1200.

[5] The tendency appears before 1150 in the presbytery of Buildwas, and recurs on the west front of Tynemouth, the transept of Hexham, and the west front of Byland about 1190. Even as late as 1240 such work as the front of the south transept of York Minster depends for its rhythmic beauty almost entirely upon such simple lancet forms, either blind or fenestrated.

England, too, the use of shafts of Purbeck marble and kindred stones made possible an effect of slightness, alike in triforium and arcade. Such shafts as those of the west front of Wells, and of the Chapel of the Nine Altars at Durham, both of about 1240, would be almost over-slender were they not visually held together by the bracelet-like mouldings at the junction of the shorter Purbeck shafts.[1] In fact in all early Gothic there is a great delight in economy of mass, that is like the dialectician's enjoyment of a cognate economy in argument: *Ubicumque invenitur aliquid superfluum per quod a bono rationis receditur, hoc est vitiosum.*[2]

With such elaboration of structure, structural forms entered the minor arts of decoration that they might endow even lesser things with the dignity of greatness.[3] The 1245 inventory of St. Paul's[4] describes a cope 'de albo diaspero, opere triforio mirabiliter in ipso panno contexto quasi in orbicularibus'; a four-tile pattern on the floor of the Westminster chapter-house represents fairly accurately one of the great rose windows of the transept. A whole building might even be mimicked on a lesser scale; the metal shrine of the relics of St. Taurin at Evreux, made between 1240 and 1255, follows the model of a church in all its details. So, too, with the parallel if rather slower development of the art of castle building, such architecture entered the minor arts of secular decoration. The inventories of Louis d'Anjou include an immense amount of 'œuvre de maçonnerie' in gold-work: for instance, a 'tabernacle' made like a castle with double crenellated walls, with two gates and two towers in the first wall and four in the second,[5] and a gold cup, its cover crenellated and adorned with eight gates of masonry and a postern, all with turrets to guard them, and in the middle a four-square donjon with a double gate.[6]

2

Nor was the slow elaboration of structural elements the only form of Gothic architectural decoration. However logical and original it might be, it naturally

---

[1] A recognition of the decorative importance of these bracelets is shown on the pillars of the Westminster nave, where they survive although the shafts they ring are in one with the piers. They are much rarer in France than in England; an example of the second half of the twelfth century is the vaulting piers of Laon, which have five such bracelets between their capitals and those of the columns on which they rest. They also appear on the west door of the Church of Condé en Barrois, Meuse. They are found in Spain, for instance in the clerestory of Toledo Cathedral and in the external cloister of S. Vicente at Avila, and in the Rhineland, as at St. Cunibert's at Cologne. Their use together with a bell capital of English type at Avila and together with a window with a central light of English type at Cologne suggests English influence on both countries. The thirteenth-century door leading from the north transept of Mainz Cathedral to the Chapel of St. Gotthard has the English system of bracelet shafting applied as a moulding to a round arch, a use that occurs at Strata Florida, Kilkenny Cathedral, and Boyle Abbey. See Champneys, *Irish Ecclesiastical Architecture*, p. 141.

[2] Aquinas, *Summ. Theol.* ii, a 2 ae, qu. cliii, art. 2.

[3] The tendency is evident in late Romanesque metal work, such as the Shrine of the Three Kings at Cologne.

[4] *Archaeologia*, l. 477; the description continues: 'nova est'.

[5] Laborde, *Glossaire des Émaux*, ii. 2.

[6] Moranvillé, *Les Inventaires de Louis I duc d'Anjou (1379–80)*, p. 74. Cf. the Castle patterns found on fourteenth-century Lucchese brocades. O. v. Falke, *Decorative Silks*, 1922, p. 36.

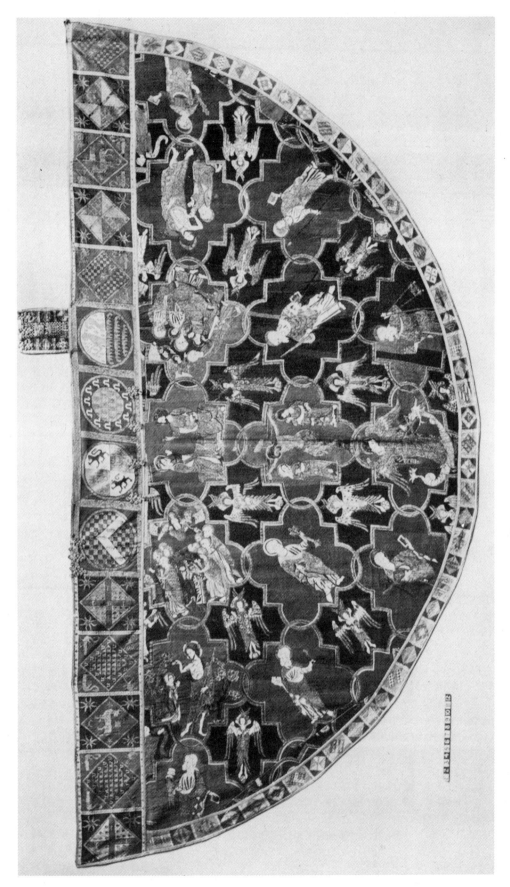

17. The Syon Cope, English, *c.* 1280, the orphreys, *c.* 1330

18. Detail of the South Porch, Abbey of
Saint Denis, *c.* 1235

19. The Western Rose Window, Cathedral of Chartres, 1220-5

inherited certain uses and motives without structural purpose from the preceding style. These, however, were not long used as decoration merely applied to the Gothic structure. The motives remained, but they were modulated in key to bring them into harmony with the architectural whole. Anything as structurally significant as a pointed arch must affect the ornament of the whole building; just as the rectilinear frames of classic ornament had been in sympathy with the classical column and lintel construction, so the Gothic decorative elements had to become congruous with Gothic construction. The Romanesque 'town-canopy' was early modified; clearly the logical sense of the Gothic builder was not altogether satisfied with so irrelevant an ornament, and was seeking to make it a more integral part of his structure. On the twelfth-century façade of the Cathedral of Le Mans town-canopies are adapted to form capitals; while on the 'Portail royal' of Chartres (fig. 4) they not only appear under the acanthus moulding that serves to link the storied capitals of the many columns, but are repeated a little way down such columns to serve as a background to statues. The effect is one of almost Oriental richness and irregularity; in some of the upper canopies attempts are made to show the town in perspective, while on the lower canopies buildings of as many as three stories of the most varied types are shown in high relief, with every window and inter-columnation duly fretted and chased. Such richness and freedom of detail were not architectonic enough to satisfy for long; and by the end of the century the builders of Notre Dame d'Étampes, while content to follow the general scheme of the neighbouring Cathedral of Chartres, reduced the elaboration of its town-canopies to an arcading, itself decorated with a plain arcading of long narrow arches with schematic towers at intervals (fig. 5). When a simpler and stronger architectural scheme was adopted it was again possible to elaborate the details of the town-canopy; those of the south portals of Rheims (fig. 6) and of Chartres and of the west portal of Le Mans show at once greater simplicity of line and greater complexity of detail. The same instinct for form is evident in the use of a battlemented coping to divide the 'town' from the architectural arcading, such as appears on the capitals of the Porte de Blé at Semur en Auxois.[1] But when, as on the portal of the Gilded Virgin at Amiens, town-canopies were used to crown not only the statues of the façade but also the little grotesque groups that serve as their pedestals, the detail of the 'town' was once more schematized and the type would hardly be recognizable did we not know its history.[2] Thenceforward the town-

[1] Others appear on the capitals of the Church of Ambronay, Ain, of the porch of Notre Dame de Dijon, and on the façade of the Church of Germigny l'Exempt, Cher.

[2] Other town-canopies may be studied on the Porte royale of the Cathedral of Bordeaux, on the Church of Longpont, Seine et Oise, on the Church of St. Martin at Candes and on the portals of Notre Dame de Paris (the latter much restored), and on the twelfth-century glass of Le Mans Cathedral. Except for very early painted examples (e.g. the wall painting at Kempley) they are not found in England. One of simple and regular form appears above a double arcade on a Templar's tomb of the late thirteenth century in the Church of the Magdalene at Zamora; others, rather of the Amiens type, on the west door of the Baptistery of Toro.

canopy passed out of use in architecture; it was too childish and irrelevant to form a part of the logical scheme of the Gothic cathedral.[1]

The 'foiling' of arches to give a polylobed outline was one of the few features of Romanesque decoration that was neither structural nor sculptural; and, perhaps as a consequence, it survived the transition into the Gothic style. On the south-west porch of Saint Jean des Vignes at Soissons the arches are enriched by a double row of such foiling, with foliated finials, divided by a moulding of rosettes in quatrefoils (fig. 7); while polylobed foiling of the arches is one of the character-istic features of the architecture of Bourges (fig. 8). But naturally the cusps have undergone a transformation to make them congruous with an architecture at once more civilized and more elegant; their edge is chamfered and set with lines of flowers, their finials are carved with little human heads, gracious or grotesque; and, especially when they foil an open arch, the projections at the junction of the lobes are both slighter and longer, so that the effect is one not of heaviness but of delicacy. At Amiens, again, lobing with leaf finials is used as a moulding around the arches of the main arcade of the eastern façade, giving an effect of great lightness.

The element of Romanesque decoration that proved most congenial to the Gothic builder was the crocket. Even in the magnificently austere interior of Coutances crockets not only spring from the capitals but also appear as a moulding below the arcade that supports the dome. At Brie Comte Robert they rim the rose window and form a frieze above; in the apse at Chars they are used everywhere [2] (fig. 9). Their form was early modified by the prevailing naturalism. At first they were tipped with leafy buds, and eventually they were merged into the naturalistic foliage. At Saint Père sous Vézelay such leafy crockets spring sparsely from the capital; at Semur [3] (fig. 10) they are more thickly set; while at Saint Yved de Braisne the capitals of the choir have four rows of bristling leafy crockets. On English capitals they were transformed into such free trefoil foliage as that of the capitals of Ely Choir. On string courses and as arch moulds they were replaced by

---

[1] It occasionally survives on incised tomb slabs as late as the fifteenth century: e.g. on that of Robert de Dreux (d. 1478) formerly in the Church of the Jacobins of Rouen. (Bodley 18346, Gaignières, p. 90). It sur-vived long enough in glass painting to appear (in a strictly symmetrical form) on the windows of the lower part of the Sainte Chapelle; but it does not occur in the slightly later glass of the upper Chapel, dedicated in 1248. In goldsmith's work it had early been adapted for the decoration of censers, but again eventually fell into disuse. E.g. 1295 Inventory of St. Paul's: 'duo turribula argentea . . . cum ecclesiis et turribus . . . duo turribula argentea . . . cum ecclesiis et thurellis rotundis'. Dugdale, *History of St. Paul's*, 1818 ed., p. 311.

[2] At Bourges a double row of crockets springing frondwise from a central rib encircles the windows of the façade (fig. 65); at Rheims rather more leafy crockets surround the rose of the south transept; at Amiens they emphasize the ridges of the pinnacles and the lines of the gables; at Notre Dame de Paris they are the most important decorative element in the whole façade. In the Sainte Chapelle they are imitated in glass as a border to some of the windows. In England they appear first at the backs of shafts, as in St. Hugh's work at Lincoln of about 1190 and on the west porch at St. Albans, and thence are transferred to the corbels of the English vaults.

[3] Almost exactly similar capitals occur in the thirteenth-century Pauluskirche at Worms. Another in the Cathedral Museum at Mainz still has its blue painted background to emphasize the lines of the crockets.

21. Bay of the Triforium and Clerestory of the Angel Choir,
Lincoln Cathedral, c. 1270

20. The Choir and Presbytery, Ely Cathedral, c. 1240

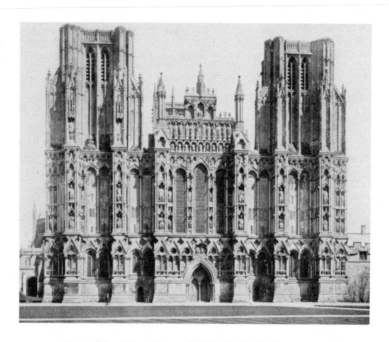

22. The West Front, Wells Cathedral, *c.* 1240

23. The West Front, Salisbury Cathedral, begun *c.* 1230

naturalistic foliage with projecting buds, as at Rampillon; or, as at Bourges and
Le Mans, were formed as beasts and birds (fig. 11). Even as gable ornaments they
were formed as leaves, though keeping their original curves. After the middle of
the thirteenth century they were little used except for such gable mouldings;[1] but
their development, the crocketed finial or 'fleuron', first found on the Church of
Guarbesques, Pas de Calais, about 1160, had a longer career before it. Gothic
architects, too, did not despise the Norman arcade of interlacing arches. It appears
as an interior wall-decoration in the early thirteenth-century nave of Séez. On the
Portal of the Gilded Virgin at Amiens it is modified by a frieze that links the sculptured capitals, and by the recessing and consequent emphasizing of the narrow
lancets formed at the intersection of the arches (fig. 12). In England the interlacing
was elaborated; in the piscina at Jesus College, Cambridge,[2] the mouldings are
plaited together (fig. 13), and at St. John's, Devizes, three arcades are interlaced in
similar fashion. At Lincoln a rich and rather Oriental effect is achieved in the
lower arcading of the aisles by the use of two trefoil arcades, not actually interlaced, but superimposed. On Bishop Jocelin's western tower and the north porch
at Wells a graceful derivative of the interlaced arcade is employed, in an arcade of
arches of which the archivolts spring from the farther side of the capital and
intersect above it[3] (fig. 14).

The ceramic revetments of the Spanish and Oriental mosques, with their
mosaic of many-sided tiles, formed the model whence the sculptured revetments
of the bases of some of the Gothic façades drew their inspiration.[4] Yet the polygonal panels of different shapes fitting into one another that decorate the lowest
stage of the façade at Auxerre (fig. 16) seem alike too exotic and too unplastic to
frame the delicate reliefs of scriptural scenes. The scheme was more happily applied
to painted decoration, or to such less architectural work as the panels of the
Westminster retable or the embroideries of the Syon cope[5] (fig. 17). For architectural use, indeed, such ornament was early modified into a form more harmonious
with the Gothic style. It was simplified into such quatrefoils as those of Amiens
(fig. 15) and Notre Dame de Paris, or it was reduced to a frieze and took the form
of quatrefoils with angles between the lobes, such as appear on the sides of the

[1] In England a delight in decorating the hollows of the mouldings kept them (in a modified form) in use
for a longer period. In Italy they were flattened into conventional curl forms to decorate gables, e.g. on
Arnolfo di Cambio's tomb of Adrian V at S. Francesco, Viterbo, c. 1280.

[2] Exactly similar work, except for the use of plain capitals, is to be found in Histon Church,
Cambs.

[3] A similar use occurs in the thirteenth-century church of Noirey in Normandy.

[4] Similar decoration appears also on the ceiling of the Cappella Palatina at Palermo, c. 1132. Such ornament
was freely adapted to use in stone and brick in the Mudejar architecture of Spain, for instance on the exterior
wall of the Cathedral of Saragossa. A similar decorative scheme is also to be found on Oriental ivories after
the tenth century.

[5] A similar scheme is also employed on late thirteenth-century Italian damasks and on an early fourteenth-
century tapestry with figures of birds and beasts, some grotesquely and some naturalistically treated, in the
Museum of Freiburg im Breisgau.

towers of Notre Dame.[1] As a diaper its place was taken by a form of ball flower decoration—another Gothic survival of Romanesque detail [2]—flattened and arranged as a rosette-like diaper. This appears in a simple form on the stone chair in the Church of St. Etienne at Toul, traditionally called that of St. Gérard, and on the Eleanor Crosses; it is elaborated on the lowest line of decoration on the base of the north porch of Chartres, and appears in many different forms to decorate the spandrels of the arcading of the chapter-house at Westminster.[3]

3

Town-canopies, crockets, and tile patterns had relatively short careers before they disappeared from the Gothic scheme; but arcading and cusping were more structural in their character and were susceptible of development that followed the lines of Gothic progress. The interlaced arcade of round arches was soon superseded by a simple arcade of pointed arches, that in the narrow width of the arches to some extent reflected the ponderation of the interlaced type.

At Bourges and on the door to the Angel Choir at Lincoln pointed arches are foiled with semicircular lobes; but this transition stage was soon passed, and pointed arches were foiled with pointed cusps ending in sharp points, graceful leaf finials, or in little sculptured heads.[4] A little before 1230 cusping of the plain sort began to be applied to the shafted arcade that is the foundation of the decorative system of the thirteenth century. The lancet-arcade was the first to be so decorated, as at Chalons-sur-Marne and Saint Denis (fig. 18). The lancet window followed; at Christ Church, Dublin, built about 1220, a curiously elegant effect is obtained by setting a trefoil cusping in the central light of a triple lancet and leaving the side lights plain.

Soon, however, the pointed lancet ceased to be so emphatically slender and lofty, and tended to spread out into breadth and fullness of form. The cusping of its head, which gave it a more decorative quality, may have been a contributory cause of this widening; at all events the progress of such decoration depended on the wider arch, such as appears in the lower chapel of the Sainte Chapelle and in the triforium of the nave at Nevers. Thus widened, the arcade formed an admirable frame for a seated figure, whether in stone, as on the shrine of the heart of Thibault V of Champagne, who died in 1270, in the hospital of Provins, or in such

[1] In Italy stronger eastern influences and a different architectural tradition kept such patterns longer in use. In a modified form they are used in Giotto's decorative bands on the arches of the Cappella dell'Arena at Padua, painted in 1305, and on Orcagna's mosaic tabernacle in the Church of Or San Michele, Florence, erected between 1349 and 1359.

[2] It is particularly characteristic of western English work of the first half of the fourteenth century, e.g. on the south aisles of Gloucester and Leominster and on the niches of St. Mary's, Oxford.

[3] It is a common ornament of English fonts. It occasionally appears in Italy, e.g. as a moulding on the loggia of the Palazzo Ducale at Venice.

[4] As at Billom, Puy-de-Dôme.

pictorial work as John of Thanet's panel of *opus anglicanum* of some fifty years later.[1] In England the decorative treatment of the spandrels of such arcading came to play as important a part in the decoration of the whole as did the decoration of capitals in France. At Worcester, as at Notre Dame de Paris, miscellaneous grotesques, chiefly of fabulous beasts, were used to fill them; at Stone Church, Kent, and at Mont Saint Michel, scrolling leafage; but with the progress of the century the English sculptors evolved a more gracious form of ornament. A spandrel decoration of purely decorative figures of angels appears at Lincoln about 1200; the famous series of the 'Angel Choir' there—exquisite figures of which one holds a little soul, one plays the viol, one drives Adam and Eve out of Eden, and one, wearing hawking gloves, holds a falcon on a lure[2]—were begun in 1237.[3] The Winchester Angels are of about the same date, while others, with their wings spread to fill the spandrels, adorn arcading of about 1250 in Westminster Abbey.[4] Such angels reappear to enrich the embroidered arcading of English thirteenth- and fourteenth-century vestments; a thirteenth-century cope in the Museo Civico of Bologna, embroidered with scenes from the life of St. Thomas of Canterbury, has angel musicians worked in the spandrels of its arcades,[5] while on the

---

[1] In the V. and A. M. Such arcading was later used in Italy; three tiers of it decorate the upper part of the façade of San Michele in Borgo at Pisa, c. 1304. Occasionally the line of the true arch was suppressed and that of the cusping emphasized to give a tri-lobed arcading. The type is found in Spain in the twelfth century, e.g. in the cloister of San Pablo del Campo at Barcelona. It was later used in Germany, for instance on the tomb of Engelbert von der Mark, d. 1368, in Cologne Cathedral. At Beverley Minster the triforium is formed of such a trefoil arcade with a second plain arcade behind, of which the arches reach only to the capitals of the trefoil arcade. Other instances occur on the balustrade of the south porch at Chartres, the interior wall decoration of the west end of Rheims Cathedral, the richly moulded arcade of Fountains Abbey, the sides of the tomb of Adelaide de Champagne at Joigny, the Cantilupe Shrine in Hereford Cathedral, and the later arcading of the chapter-house at Westminster.

[2] It is difficult not to regard these figures as the ecclesiastical equivalent of the 'esbattements' of civil decoration: see p. 60. Indeed in lay decoration the angels' place was sometimes taken by human musicians; e.g. 'Un trepié, d'argent doré, dont les jambes sont faites de maçonnerie en manière de piller ... et en chascun piler a un homme dont l'un joue de la vièle, l'autre de la guiterne et l'autre de la cornemuse, et dessus les testes desdiz hommes a un chapitel de maçonnerie.' Inventory of Louis d'Anjou, 1360, ed. Laborde, *Glossaire des Émaux*, ii. 13.

[3] Professor Coulton suggests (*Art and the Reformation*, p. 205) that the fact that the figures have been set up with the wrong wings attached shows that they were carved in London and set up by local masons.

[4] Half figures of angels holding crowns adorn the spandrels of the thirteenth-century arcaded woodwork behind the stalls of Poitiers Cathedral. Many angels appear on the vaulting bosses at Tewkesbury and Gloucester, c. 1350. A vaulting boss of about 1300 at Notre Dame, Étampes, has magnificent figures of angels radiating from it. Angel figures, no longer in spandrels but in canopies, appear on the musician's gallery of Exeter, c. 1316, and above the high altar of Gloucester, c. 1350; while angel cornices, as in St. George's Chapel at Windsor, come in at the end of the fifteenth century. On the English use of angels in decorative sculpture, see Prior and Gardner, *An Account of Mediaeval Figure Sculpture in England*, pp. 84, 260, 329, 515 et seqq.

[5] Cf. the Italian orphreys described by de Farcy (*La Broderie*, p. 125) with angels in the arcading spandrels carrying scrolls with the names of their orders: *Serafini, Cerubini, Potesta, Angiolo, Arcangiolo*, and the 'dossier' of green velvet elaborately embroidered with figures 'dedans tabernacles de maçonnerie, et sur les pillers desdiz tabernacles a plusieurs angeloz tenens rouleaux' ... described in the 1402 inventory of Jean duc de Berry (Guiffrey, *Les Inventaires de Jean duc de Berry*, ii. 160). The subject was eventually carried over into civil decoration; the Maison du Grand Pignon at Paris, built for Nicholas Flamel, d. 1418, was decorated with figures of angel musicians. Some Florentine damasks of the late fourteenth century are brocaded with figures of angels bearing censers and instruments of the Passion. (Examples in Bock Collection, V. and A. M.)

fourteenth-century English copes of St. John Lateran and of the Bowden family of Pleasington, the zones of arcading are multiplied and the angel musicians are promoted to the lesser arcadings.[1]

The use of arcading as a wall decoration, and the gradual increase of the ratio between window and wall, brought the development of decorative arcading into close relation with the development of Gothic fenestration.[2] Such early 'wheel' windows as the western rose of Chartres (fig. 19) and those above the gables over the arches of the west front of Peterborough show a scheme based on an arcade radiating from a central point. The use of lanceolate arcading within an arch in triforia, as at Coutances (fig. 2), naturally resulted in the analogous use of double and triple lancet windows within an arch;[3] and in English examples of the second quarter of the thirteenth century these lancet windows are often decorated with plain cusps.

The course of the development of window tracery is entirely dependent on that of the triforium. This begins with the decoration of the 'shield' space above the arcade and within the arch with simple cell-wise piercings ('plate tracery'), as in the triforium of the south transept at York. By a natural analogy a similar decoration was applied to the clerestory of Chartres. Then the piercing was continued right through and the background removed, leaving it outlined on space. Trefoils of this sort decorate the shields of the triforium of Noyon, finished about 1185, and the spandrels of the arcade that shelters statues of standing figures above the south porch at Chartres;[4] similar quatrefoils appear above the double windows of the south-east transept of Beverley Minster,[5] and on the shields of the trefoil arcade in the Chapel of the Nine Altars at Durham.

The full development of such work was accomplished in the treatment of the English triforia. These had rapidly been elaborated from the comparatively simple Romanesque type. A good transitional example is the eastern triforium of Chichester, built about 1190; a round outer arch, resting on a pier surrounded by five colonnettes, encloses a double pointed arcade resting on double columns, cusped with circular foiling; the 'shield' above is not pierced but filled with sculptured figures and foliage. In the north transept at Ripon the scheme is similar, but the shield is pierced by a quatrefoil, and the outer arch is flanked by a blind pointed arch on either side. The next stage is represented by the ruined choir of Whitby,

[1] It is probably from such medieval sources that the inspiration was derived for the lovely angels bearing bells of flowers who stand ready for the dance round the cupola of the Cappella Portinari at S. Ambrogio in Milan, begun in 1462. The use of winged figures for spandrel decoration was revived in the sixteenth century; see vol. II, p. 37.

[2] The classic reference for the subject is still E. Sharpe, *A Treatise on the Rise and Progress of Decorated Window Tracery*, London, 1849. Good modern summaries will be found in E. S. Prior, *A History of Gothic Art in England*, and A. Kingsley Porter, *Mediaeval Architecture*.

[3] At Cherry Hinton Church, Cambridge, a row of lancet windows of about 1220 has every third blind to take a buttress, thus combining window and arcade in a single series.

[4] Cf. similar usage at Tours and Le Mans.

[5] About 1230, but noticeably conservative in style.

24. The South Porch, Cathedral of Chartres, begun soon after 1194

26. Detail of the interior of the Porch, Saint Père sous Vézelay, c. 1240

25. Detail of the West Door, Cathedral of Auxerre, c. 1250

some twenty years later in date: the circular arch enclosing a double pointed arcade is the same, but each arcade has two subsidiary lancets; and these subsidiary shields, and the shield of the greater arcade, are pierced with circular apertures decorated with trefoil cuspings. At Rievaulx, about 1230, the scheme is the same, but the outer arches are pointed and quatrefoils have taken the place of the cusped circles. Soon these apertures, and the window cuspings, were completed with simple mouldings, such as appear at York. At Ely about 1235 these simply moulded apertures were multiplied;[1] there is a trefoil on either side of the corbels on the spandrels of the arches, with quatrefoils to correspond on either side of the vaulting shaft in the storey above, and quatrefoils in the shields of the triforium (fig. 20). In the nave of Lincoln about 1240 two quatrefoils and a circle fill the double shields of the triforium, with a trefoil in the spandrel of the external arcade. The rich effect of such geometric decoration is yet further increased by making the mouldings of the apertures almost as complex as those of the archivolt (fig. 21). At Romsey Abbey a doubly moulded quatrefoil in the shield appears above two trefoil arches resting on a quadruple shaft, the whole set within a wide pointed arch, itself heavily moulded.[2] This common moulding brought the piercings into a new relation with the whole; they became the background for the pattern made by the solid parts (bar-tracery).[3]

The beauty of the geometric tracery of such early triforia as those of Ely, and of the rather later work at Lincoln, made them models to be followed in the designing of windows. At Lincoln, indeed (fig. 21), and elsewhere in England, an attempt was made to give to the window tracery the triforium's beauty of the play of light and shade against a recessed background, by making the tracery a projecting screen set clear of the lights of the window;[4] while at Christ Church, Dublin, and at Pershore about 1220 the whole upper window was merged in the triforium, with its lights set in the wall behind the tracery.[5] Usually, however, the tracery itself was enough to link the window with the design of the whole.

Since Gothic construction relied upon pier, arch, and vaulting ribs for its solidity, and not upon its walls, there was no structural reason against a great expansion of the window space;[6] and as the expansion of the actual panels of stained

---

[1] Cf. the Cathedral of Séez in Normandy, begun c.1270.

[2] Cf. the door of St. Cross, Winchester.

[3] In France the development of triforia was characteristically less rich and more architectural. At Séez, for example, each bay of the triforium is filled by three double lancet arches of equal height, the outer wide, the inner narrow, the lower parts being engaged in a balustrade, itself arcaded. At Amiens each bay has two arches filled by three lancet arches with elaborate imposts to their capitals, the 'shield' above being filled by a large trefoil aperture with leafy cusps.

[4] The scheme is also found in Champagne and in the clerestory of Leon Cathedral.

[5] A similar scheme is followed in the nave of Strasbourg Cathedral, finished in 1275.

[6] Kingsley Porter points out (Mediaeval Architecture, p. 108) that the development of stained glass is not a consequence of Gothic construction, but precedes it, being already perfected by about 1140. In England, too, the panels of glass are commonly smaller than technically they need be; architectural rather than pictorial effect is aimed at and achieved. The thirteenth-century interest in the art of glass-painting is evidenced in its

glass was naturally limited, this tracery offered an admirable solution by which great windows could be given solidity without loss of lightness or beauty. The two-light windows that had hitherto sufficed were superseded by such four-light windows with geometrical tracery as those of the Sainte Chapelle, with the two additional mullions and their tracery subordinated to the original single mullion and circle, making two planes of tracery.[1] As the width of the windows was gradually increased the tracery was further sub-divided. Sometimes a second sub-order springs out of the first, which rises as before out of the main order, while the great circle (as in the east windows at Ripon and Tintern) becomes filled with a system of tracery of its own.[2] In France the great windows usually retained the old system of an even number of lights, with a central mullion; in England the absence of an apse and the consequent development of a great window to close the east end favoured the use of a window with a central light.

The delicate tracery of the triforia was transferred not only to windows but also to wall decoration. The finest example of such usage is undoubtedly the west front of Salisbury (fig. 23), begun about 1239, with its great arcades with blind traceries repeating the forms and mouldings of the windows. Indeed its five stories of arcading, with a gradual rise and sudden cadence of scale, centred by the great triple lancet of the west window, and only varied by a row of quatrefoils with trefoils fitting into the angles, shows how splendid an effect could be gained by the decorative use of enriched arcading alone.[3]

In France such use was on a far smaller scale. At Saint Etienne, Sens, the tympanum, instead of being filled with figure sculptures in relief, is divided window fashion with a quatrefoil tracery in the top and four-light tracery below, all filled

influence on illuminations; alike in their colour—dark ruby red, blue, brown, and green—in their 'mosaic' backgrounds (e.g. in the Gospel book of the Sainte Chapelle) and in their schemes (e.g. in the Psalter called that of St. Louis, illuminated before 1223). Some English miniatures of about 1300 (e.g. Bodleian MS. Selden Supra 38) show a quite purposeless dimidiation of the background in blue and red, obviously derived from the alternate red and blue quarries of the windows. After the end of the thirteenth century architectural influence takes the place of the influence of stained glass on illuminations; but the quarry scheme survived in other minor arts. A fourteenth-century painted sacristy cupboard at Noyon, for instance, has alternate red and blue compartments, as have the great Apocalypse tapestries in the Musée de l'Évêché at Angers, on which the compartments are divided by stone mullions imitated in the tapestry.

[1] The earliest example of 'bar-tracery' in windows is probably in the apsidal chapels of Rheims, about 1230: that in Henry III's apsidal chapels at Westminster, begun in 1245, is probably inspired by the Rheims tracery. Fine examples are to be found in parts of Notre Dame de Paris that can be dated between 1235 and 1240, and in the clerestory of Amiens, about 1236, which shows trefoils with delicate leaf-cusping. The best-known English example is the cloister of Salisbury dating from about 1265; here the tracery and heads of the lights were alone glazed.

[2] Similarly in the east window of Merton Chapel the central circle of the tracery is treated as a rose, and little pediments with crockets and finials complete the heads of the lights below.

[3] Another fine example is the spire of St. Mary's at Stamford. A good example of the use of such tracery applied blind to an interior wall is the chapter-house of Furness Abbey, which has tracery of the triforium type with double lights and a pierced shield; the only modification is the omission of the central column. It is possible that the characteristically English development of such arcaded decoration is derived from the cognate Romanesque use in the English provinces of Western France, Poitou, Saintonge, and Angoumois.

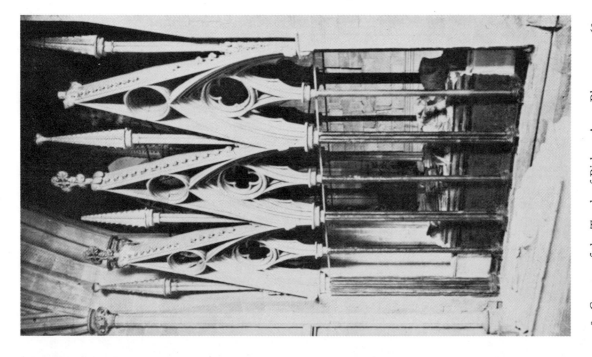

28. Canopy of the Tomb of Bishop Aqua Blanca, *c. 1268.*
Hereford Cathedral

27. Canopy of the Tomb of Bishop Bridport, *c. 1263.*
Salisbury Cathedral

30. Detail of the Westminster Abbey Retable; the wooden base is entirely covered with painted vellum, gilt gesso, and painted glass. *c.* 1260

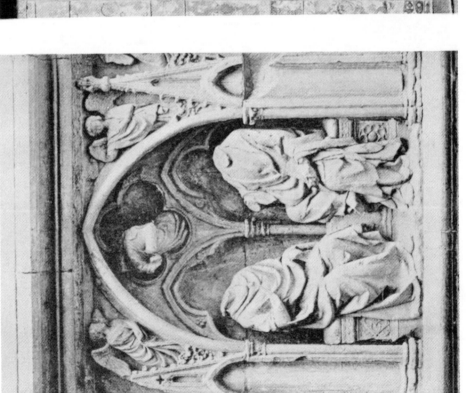

29. Detail of the West Front, Cathedral of Auxerre, *c.* 1250

in with bas-reliefs that are like the translation of stained glass into stone.[1] Fretted geometric tracery based on trefoil cusping adorns the arcade of the Upper Sainte Chapelle, finished in 1247, and the lower arcade of the tomb of Saint Etienne d'Aubazine, dating from the last decade of the century. Delicate blind geometric traceries are carved in low relief upon a background of stone inside the north transept at Meaux and on the north portal of Chartres and on the transept wall of Soissons; but nowhere is there a use of tracery comparable with the Salisbury façade.[2]

4

Meanwhile the arcade itself was receiving architectural elaboration. The use on Gothic façades of projecting porches with deeply recessed pointed arches and pinnacled shelters for statues above the intervening piers had made familiar the combination of an arcade and a gable-and-pinnacle scheme.[3] The decorative possibilities of the line were soon realized.[4] On the south portal of Chartres (fig. 24) the composition is still structural; on the west portal of Rheims it receives decorative emphasis of detail and exaggeration of line; at Peterborough it is the dominant feature of the whole façade. The combination of gable and cusped arch was developed on a smaller and more complex scale on the great west front of Wells[5] (fig. 22). Above the base runs a continuous gabled arcade, with quatrefoil piercings between the plain gables; within the arches is a subsidiary double arcade, with hoodlike projections formed of tri-lobed cusped arches below gables with finials. Some of these arches enshrine statues standing on pedestals raised above the base, while in some the subsidiary arcade is modified into tracery for windows. Relief is given to the whole composition by the projection of the buttresses, round which the arcade is continued. Above this arcade runs a loftier one, of narrow slender-shafted lancets, each crowned by a plain low-pitched gable, the whole surmounted by a subsidiary arcade of trefoil arches. The buttresses are

[1] Cf. the quatrefoil over the west door of Crowland Abbey, c. 1250, which is similarly filled with sculpture. For other examples see E. S. Prior and A. Gardner, *An Account of Medieval Figure Sculpture in England*, p. 277.

[2] The later use of such blind tracery on lesser objects is exemplified by such entries as 'une chaire à dossier couverte de veluyau, painte et ouvrée d'orbevoies' in the accounts of Etienne de la Fontaine, 1350. Havard, *Dictionnaire de l'ameublement*, s.v. Orbevoie.

[3] The construction is equally found in Norman work; see for example the tower gateway at Bury St. Edmunds, c. 1130, and the porch of St. Mary's, Glastonbury, c. 1186. On its origins see E. Lefèvre Pontalis, 'Les origines des gables', in *Bull. Mon.* lxxi, 1907, p. 92.

[4] The late formal type of town-canopy had sometimes (as at Notre Dame and on the Porte de la Vierge dorée at Amiens) been treated as a series of little tri-lobed gables, with the space between filled in with little symmetrical 'towns' with the most important of their towers coming over the lower angle at the junction of the little gables. Such canopies had even been transferred to gold work; a finial of the shrine of St. Eleuthère at Tournai (made in 1247; Dehaisnes, *Histoire de l'Art dans la Flandre*, Plate III) shows the saint sitting within a tri-lobed arch, with a 'town' canopy behind battlements above. Two rows of gables, the upper finished with a battlement and dome imitating masonry, decorate the wings of the reliquary tryptich from the Abbey of Floreffe in the Louvre. In Winchester Cathedral a cusped trefoil arcade of about 1260 has a little line of moulding set gable-fashion above it.

[5] See also the remains of St. Mary's Abbey, York.

similarly treated, but are emphasized through their division by two superimposed canopies, each holding the figure of a saint.[1] The central light of the whole composition is higher and a little wider than the rest, with its gable running up to break the line of the little arcade above.

Here the treatment, however minute in detail and decorative in intent, is on so grand a scale that it is definitely architectural in character. In France the tendency was to use canopied arcadings either architecturally, as a frame to windows with the buttresses between as pinnacles,[2] or else on a purely decorative scale.[3] The latter usage was especially common in northern Burgundy[4] (figs. 25–6).

From such architectural use the canopied arcading was soon transferred to tombs,[5] shrines, and other lesser monuments. The splendid canopy of the tomb of Bishop Bridport (d. 1263) at Salisbury (fig. 27) is a typical triforium arcade[6] enriched with leafage, crowned with low-pitched gables; between these, slender columns rise from a ground of figure sculptures to the cornice, above which they end in a double floriated finial. High pointed gables with a circle tracery and pinnacles on raised pedestals separate from the arch-column crown the slender arcading on the tomb of Bishop Aqua Blanca, d. 1268, in Hereford Cathedral (fig. 28). Naturally on such monuments as these, comparatively small in scale and comparatively independent of their architectural setting, a greater fantasy was possible than in more structural work. On the base of the shrine of St. Alban, built early in the fourteenth century, in his Abbey, the gables are filled with foliage, the pinnacles are shortened and flattened to act as pedestals to half-figures in low relief, and their place is to some extent taken by buttress-like pinnacles projecting far beyond the plane of the tomb. On the roof of the tomb of Saint Etienne d'Aubazine the line of the arcade is broken by sculptured figures seated leaning against the columns, while between the gables angels with censers, candles, cross, and books are shown rising from clouds. On the font at Harcourt, Eure, the arcade is cut just below the capital of the column, to form a decorative canopy without

[1] A similar treatment is used some forty years later for the buttresses of the Angel Choir at Lincoln.

[2] See R. de Lasteyrie, *op. cit.* i. 338. The usage first appears about the middle of the thirteenth century, one of the earliest instances being on the Sainte Chapelle.

[3] An exception rather in the English manner is the gabled and pinnacled arcade on the west front of Auxerre Cathedral. On the triforium at Amiens each arch is surmounted by a line of crocketed moulding set gable fashion.

[4] The elements of a gabled arcade frame the quatrefoil reliefs on the base of the central door at Auxerre (fig. 25); an arcading of such motives, arranged in pairs, with a trefoil tracery within the gable and a trefoil cusped triangle framing little figure in high relief instead of a pinnacle, decorates the base of the west portal of Sens. At Saint Père sous Vézelay, about 1240, a gabled arcade appears in higher relief, complete with pinnacles, finials, and crockets, and with little grotesque beasts as corbels to the pinnacles (fig. 26). On the base of the west door at Auxerre graceful standing figures take the place of the pinnacles; the same treatment, with the addition of a subsidiary canopy over the figures, occurs on the early fourteenth-century gallery above the great door of St. Jean des Vignes at Soissons.

[5] See F. H. Crossley, *English Church Monuments*, for photographs of many types of English medieval tombs decorated with canopied arcading.

[6] Cf. the double piscina in the Chapel of Merton College, Oxford, which has a triforium arcade within a gable, balanced and completed by pinnacles on either side.

31. Piscina in the Choir of Saint Urbain de Troyes, *c.* 1290

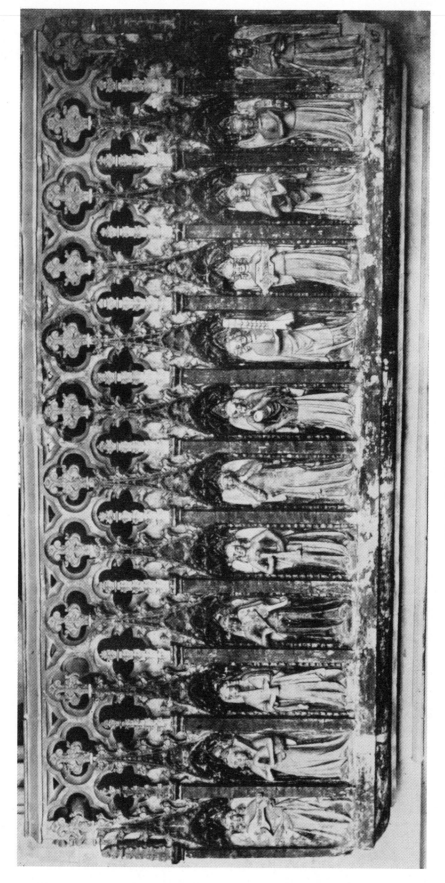

32. Minstrels' Gallery, Exeter Cathedral, 1340

supports.[1] Such fancies, however, became rarer as the decorative qualities of the new type of arcade were realized, and the tendency was rather towards the elaboration of its architectural features. Occasionally, as at Auxerre (fig. 29), the tracery within the arch was elaborated at the expense of the gable; occasionally, as on the Westminster Retable, it was given another rhythm by alternating the width of the arches and the gables that crowned them[2] (fig. 30). At Saint Urbain, Troyes, the piscina in the choir, dating from the end of the thirteenth century, has a most elaborate canopy (fig. 31). The arches, cusps, and gables are plain; but rich figure sculpture is arranged on either side of the pinnacles between, while above is an elaborate subsidiary canopy of the gabled type, topped with little battlements (from which archers are shooting)[3] in memory of the 'town' canopy from which it is ultimately derived. On the Minstrels' Gallery at Exeter, probably dating from about 1340 (fig. 32), a vaulted roof in false perspective is shown within the cuspings of the arches. Here, too, are signs of decadence in the architectural form; the columns are carried up to act as high pedestals for the pinnacles, while the rather over-heavy finials of the gables are framed in the upper row of two rows of quatrefoils pierced in the background. The whole effect is rich and decorative, but structural quality is lost.[4]

By the middle of the thirteenth century the motive was transferred from architectural decoration to all the minor arts. An early example of a trefoil canopy occurs in the illuminations of the Carrow Psalter (formerly in the Yates Thompson Collection) written between 1233 and 1250 in the neighbourhood of Bury St. Edmunds. The Psalter of St. Louis,[5] written between 1253-70, has every miniature set in a frame formed of two or four bays of a Gothic interior, with gables, rose or quatrefoil windows, and fretted arcading and pinnacles above. The setting is purely decorative and is applied even to such outdoor scenes as Noah's Ark and Samson tying torches to the foxes' tails. As the architectural canopies developed, the illuminated ones followed; the large illustrations of the Bodleian Manuscript of the Romance of Alexander[6] written in 1344, are framed in elaborate

---

[1] Cf. the treatment of the sedilia arcades in York Chapter House, c. 1300, with two pendants to one column, and the triple canopies with pendants in the fourteenth-century sedilia of Furness Abbey and Beverley Minster. The same scheme is represented in the arcade over the miniature of the Flight into Egypt in the St. Omer Book of Hours written not long after 1318; B.M. Add. MS. 36684, f. 56.

[2] A similar usage occurs in the illuminations of the French Manuscript of the *Somme le Roi*, c. 1300, B.M. Add. MS. 28162, f. 6 b.

[3] Cf. the chimney piece in the Hôtel de Jacques Cœur at Bourges, with a castle battlement from which soldiers are drawing bows and arbalests.

[4] A simpler version of this type, with a rather low-pitched arch, the gable above filled with conventional foliage, rather dumpy crockets, and the columns continued up into the pinnacles, appears on the side of the tomb of Robert the Wise in the Church of Santa Chiara at Naples, erected in 1343 by the Florentine brothers Giovanni and Pace for Jeanne d'Anjou. Cf. the tomb of Lope Fernandez de Luna, in the Cathedral of Saragossa; he died in 1382 but probably had the tomb erected in his lifetime. An early example of Italian canopy work, curiously different in spirit from the French examples it imitates, occurs in the Cappella della Spina at Pisa, built in 1323.

[5] Bibl. Nat. lat. 10535.   [6] MS. Bodl. 264.

canopies, with roofs and pinnacles and windvanes and musicians fiddling and trumpeting behind the parapet like the little bowmen of the Troyes piscina. Similar decoration was likewise applied to goldwork; flattened cusped arches in enamel appear between canopied figures of Saints in relief on the base of the silver-gilt statue of the Virgin, given to Saint Denis by Jeanne d'Évreux in 1339. Zones of canopy work of a simple kind decorate such fourteenth-century croziers as that in the Cathedral of Città di Castello, and the pastoral staff of San Galgano at Siena, and the fourteenth-century reliquaries of Italy, Spain (fig. 34), and Germany. Very rich traceries complete the elaborate canopies of such German wood-carving as the retable at Oberwesel (fig. 33).

Besides its architectural use as a continuous arcade, the arch, gable, and pinnacle motive was also employed as a single element of decoration. The type owes its development to the elaboration of the structural pinnacles of Gothic buttresses as shelters for statues with arched sides and pointed gables.[1] On Notre Dame de Paris, for instance, each side of the pinnacles is so treated, with blind tracery to fill the arch (fig. 35); on the south-west tower of Notre Dame de Senlis there are two tiers of very light empty 'tabernacles', while on the early fourteenth-century buttresses of Rheims and Bordeaux the arch is cusped and recessed to shelter the statue of a saint. This system of framing a single figure within a 'tabernacle' was soon used to enshrine little portable devotional images of our Lady and the Saints and (especially in Italy) to frame figures or doorways on a much larger scale.[2]

In France in the thirteenth century such tabernacles were often incised or carved in low relief to frame the recumbent effigy on tomb-slabs. The bas-relief tomb-slab of Evrard de Fouilloy, d. 1222, in Amiens Cathedral, has the figure framed in an elementary canopy without a gable; a tri-lobed arch is represented as supported on either side by a flying buttress and its terminal pinnacle. Between the figure and the columns of the canopy stand two censing angels.[3] A simple version of the ordinary gable-and-pinnacle canopy, with a plain gable, framed the figure of the eldest son of Saint Louis, who died in 1260, on his tomb at Saint Denis,[4] and such

---

[1] Such tabernacle pinnacles are more rarely found in England, where solid arcaded polygons with steepled roofs are more common.

[2] One appears in the great mosaic ciborium designed by Arnolfo di Cambio in S. Paolo fuori le mura at Rome, finished in 1285; another, likewise in the round, shelters the tomb of Mary of Hungary, carved by Tino da Camaino in 1325, in the Church of Santa Maria Donna Regina at Naples; and another, set against the wall, frames the almost contemporary tomb of Charles of Calabria in S. Chiara in the same city. The type was elaborated into such *tabernacoli* as that over the entrance to the Campo Santo of Pisa and the canopy of the tomb of Cansignorio in Santa Maria Antica at Verona; but there is a certain ornateness and irrelevance in these that show the decadence of the type.

[3] Variations of town-canopies were early used; on an incised slab of about 1230 in the Porte de Hal Museum at Brussels a pediment covers the arch, and is crowned with the louvres and chimneys of a house roof (W. F. Creeny, *Illustrations of Incised Slabs on the Continent of Europe*, p. 5); another in the same museum—that of Perone, wife of Gilles de Lerinnes, who died in 1247—has a similar pedimental canopy crowned by a building like the nave of a church (*ibid.*, p. 6).

[4] Formerly at Royaumont.

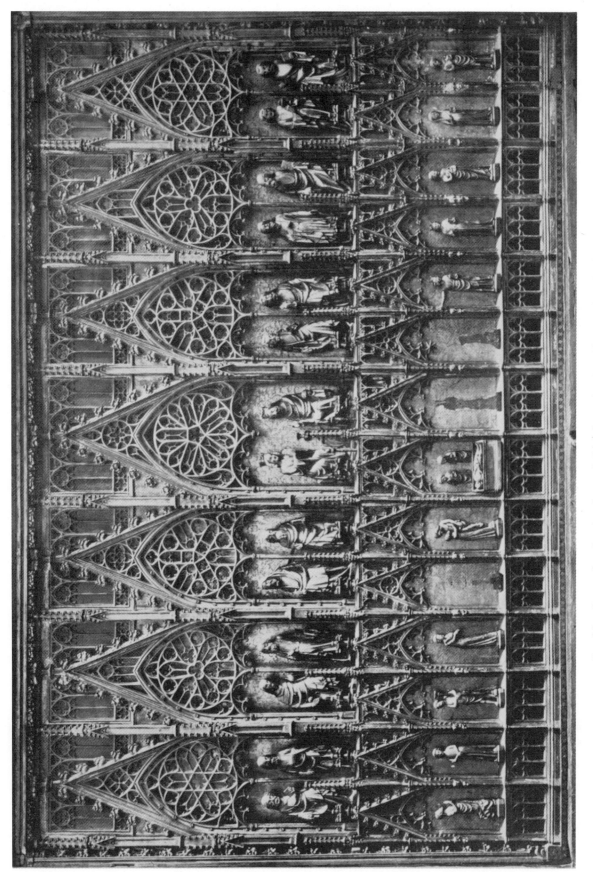

33. Retable of carved and painted wood, Liebfrauenkirche, Oberwesel. Rhenish, c. 1340

34. Reliquary, made at Barcelona, *c.* 1400

35. Detail of the Apse, Notre Dame de Paris, *c.* 1250

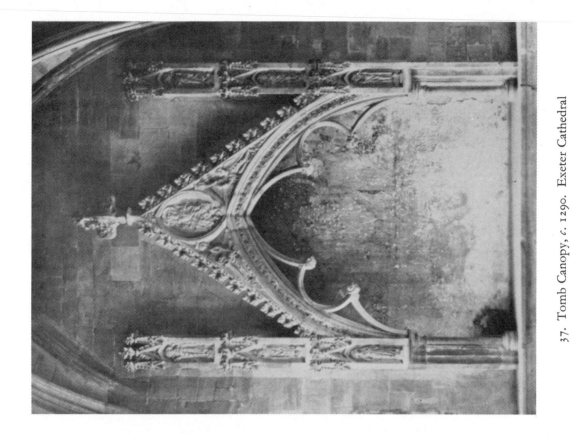

37. Tomb Canopy, *c.* 1290. Exeter Cathedral

36. Monument of Aveline, wife of Edmund Crouchback,
Earl of Lancaster. 1273. Westminster Abbey

canopies with slight variations remained in use until the middle of the fourteenth century.[1]

With the development of recumbent effigies in high relief, lying on altar-tombs, such canopies were translated into the round to crown and shelter them. Naturally, since the effigy was recumbent and seen in profile, the arch had to be widened to take the whole length of the figure, but the system remained unchanged. An early example, dating from about 1273, shelters the tomb of Aveline, wife of Edmund Crouchback, Earl of Lancaster, in Westminster Abbey (fig. 36); unfortunately it has lost its side pinnacles. A rather later canopy in the choir of the Cathedral of Bayonne is given a more monumental quality by the use of buttresses beyond the pinnacles. More usually the stronger counter-balance demanded by the wider arch was provided by widening and elaborating the pinnacles themselves; a fine canopy at Exeter (fig. 37), dating from the last decade of the thirteenth century, has each pinnacle widened to take three superimposed canopies each complete with arch, gable, and pinnacle, framing figures of Saints.[2] This scheme was carried over from sculpture in relief into other arts; the delightful Virgin and Child of the Psalter of Robert de Lisle,[3] illuminated in East Anglia before 1339, is so framed, with the side pinnacles elaborated to hold subsidiary canopies with figures of saints and angels; and the scheme appears with endless elaborations on engraved continental tomb-slabs of the early fourteenth century. Again, on the monument of Edmund Crouchback in Westminster Abbey, dating from 1296 (fig. 38), the side pinnacles are themselves elaborated into little empty tabernacles, with cusps and gables and pinnacles of their own.[4]

5

The second decade of the fourteenth century witnessed a change of temper in art as in life. Everywhere emphasis began to be laid on the human rather than on

[1] The chief variations lay in the disposal of the figures of censing and candle-bearing angels that were usually represented on either side of the effigy. On the incised slab of Pierre du Mesnil, d. 1266, in the Musée Archéologique of Rouen (Creeny, *op. cit.*, p. 15) the angels are in the spandrels, with their censers falling into the point of the arch; two more angels appear to be sitting on the capitals of the canopy-columns. Another slab of about 1280 in the same collection (*ibid.*, p. 22), commemorating Mehus du Chastelier, has the figures of the candle-bearing angels sticking out gargoyle-fashion from the capitals. Two slabs, one of 1302 and one of 1304, formerly in the Church of the Barnabites at Paris, had rounded canopies with the censing angels above, so that their censers fell behind the canopy (Bodleian 18350, Gaignières, pp. 1 and 20); another of 1312 in the Jacobins had similar angels with their censers falling into the spandrels of the canopy (*ibid.*, p. 21). In that of Jean Quarmelin in Sainte Geneviève the censers fell into the gable (*ibid.*, p. 43). The tomb of Gauthier Torigni, d. 1340, in the Jacobins, had the censing angels unusually small, throwing up their censers so that their line followed that of the gable of the canopy (*ibid.*, p. 23); while that of Pierre de Chanac, d. 1346, in the Chartreuse of Paris, had quite small angels above the canopy gable with their censers falling well below it (*ibid.*, p. 84). The tomb-slab of Ladislas of Poland, d. 1388, in Saint Benigne, Dijon, shows angels in little arches above his head, each censing with one hand and holding a shield in the other; while that of Druyes d'Aguyley, d. 1443, in the same church has a triple arcading above his head with censing angels in the two outer arches.

[2] Cf. the piers of the west front of Wells.   [3] B.M. Arundel MS. 83, f. 131 b.

[4] Cf. the combination of canopies and tabernacles in the painting above the choir stalls in Cologne Cathedral, dating from about 1350.

the divine; as a deep religious feeling was a dominant note of thirteenth-century
civilization, so a human 'courtoisie' set the pitch for the fourteenth. Men
strove less for an intellectual comprehension and more for a romantic expression.
The austerities of early monasticism were for the most part forgotten, and in
cathedral as in castle a more splendid pageantry added glamour to the day's ritual.
Such sentiment found a reflection alike in the literature and in the sculpture of
France, while in England the desire for richness and ornament found its special
expression in architectural decoration [1]—the creation of a new Curvilinear style.[2]
In it decoration became as important as construction; breadth of effect was sought
not in simplicity but in repetition. The stresses and balance of structural form
had become commonplace, and easy and flowing line given romantic emphasis
by graceful ornament had become the ideal.

In order to attain it all the elements of Gothic decoration were modified.[3] The
English triforium, that had played so large a part in the development of the earlier
Gothic style, was in some buildings abruptly superseded.[4] The simple arcaded
triforium found at Beverley about 1229 was at Exeter soon after 1280 treated
as a blind arcade with a balustrade of pierced quatrefoils above, while in the
nave of York about twenty years later it was treated as the lower story of the
great traceried window above it, keeping its canopied heads to crown its lights,
and divided from the main window by a transom pierced like the Exeter
balustrades. At Guisborough a few years later these canopies and transom are
further merged in the tracery of the window; in the choir of Selby about 1340 the
acceptance of the two-story scheme is complete, and all that remains of the triforium is a low pierced balustrade beneath the great windows. This amalgamation
lessened the former analogy between the window tracery and the architectural
tracery of the triforium, and made the many-mullioned windows the key of the
structure and its chief decoration.[5] A new freedom is soon evident in window
design. Instead of 'geometrical' tracery, in which circles and other figures are
complete, linked only where they touch tangentially, a new 'flowing' Curvilinear style
is achieved by omitting parts of the circle and merging the lines into ogival forms.

---

[1] English fourteenth-century sculptural decoration was simpler in its scheme than French; such work as
the chapter doorway at Rochester, c. 1340, with its figures of Church and Synagogue, and its seated Doctors
beneath canopies, is exceptional.

[2] Its popular name of 'Decorated' is descriptive enough, but 'Curvilinear' is more precise.

[3] At the same time it must be remembered that geometric ornament continued in use side by side with its
Curvilinear developments, and indeed eventually survived them.

[4] In the nave of Saint Denis, rebuilt between 1231 and 1281, the triforium had been backed with a series of
windows reproducing in their tracery the main lines of the triforium arcade, and the same scheme had been
followed at Amiens and Troyes, and a little later in the nave of Cologne Cathedral. Thence the transition had
been easy to the transformation of the triforium into a clerestory, which had been accomplished a few years
later. A little later, as in the Cathedrals of Evreux and Beauvais, the mullions of the windows were brought
down through the arcading or, as at Saint Urbain de Troyes, the clerestory was omitted altogether, and the wall
became as it were a part of the window filled in with stone. A parallel process was gone through in England.

[5] This is especially true of Yorkshire.

38. Monument of Edmund Crouchback, Earl of Lancaster, 1296.
Westminster Abbey

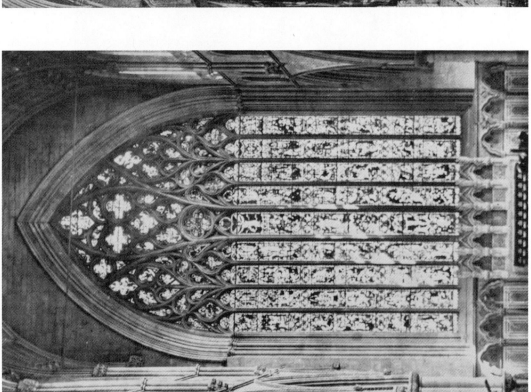

40. The West Window, York, c. 1400

39. The East Window, Carlisle, c. 1380

At the same time the area of the tracery was greatly increased, so that in many fourteenth-century windows its spread covers at least half of the field. The geometrical 'wheel' was merged into the curves of the sub-arches to create the great ogees that appear at Selby, Howden, and in Lincolnshire, and most beautifully of all in the great east window of Carlisle (fig. 39) and the west window of York (fig. 40). The central light, characteristic of the earlier English work, was commonly renounced; instead the tracery radiates from a central mullion like branches from a tree.[1]

In southern and western England the tendency was rather towards a reticulated type of ogival tracery, derived from the multiplication of the circles in the head, as in Tintern chapter-house, and the north transept of Hereford.[2] The comparatively simple lines of such tracery were commonly enriched with foiling.[3] The system of flowing tracery was also applied, with beautiful effect, to rose windows; one of the finest is the Southern Rose—'The Bishop's Eye'—at Lincoln (fig. 41). The architectural forms of arcaded triforia had ceased to govern the tracery of windows; indeed, the chief survival of architectural form is in the so-called 'arch' tracery with lancet lights running up into a simply decorated head; and this is more characteristic of village churches than of more splendid buildings. Instead, reticulated tracery, primarily designed as *cloisons* for glass, was applied to cloister arcades (notably at Westminster) and even to vaulting, for the additional liernes of such vaults as those of Tewkesbury are there chiefly to make a reticulated pattern with the main ribs.[4] The ogival line of the flowing tracery was also applied to nearly all the existing types of arcade. At Ely the bays of the choir built in 1338 to join the crossing to the fourteenth-century presbytery keep the triforium scheme of the earlier work, but altogether transform its style. The fanciful ogival tracery of the triforium shields, like that of the windows above, the recusped cuspings of the arches, the rosettes that stud the mouldings, and the additional tracery that leaves no quiet space on the greater spandrels, give them an ornate restlessness that is far removed from the sober dignity of the earlier work. A similar enrichment of geometric construction with ogival forms is evident in d'Estria's choir screen at Canterbury,[5] erected in 1304. The effect is happier and more congruous, however,

[1] In a well-known window at Dorchester, Oxon., *c.* 1310, it actually simulates the branches of a tree of Jesse, with sculptured figures in addition to those in the painted glass.

[2] The most typical examples of such reticulated tracery are the windows of Wells choir, dating from about 1330.

[3] As in the windows of Bishop Lucy's chapel at Oxford, *c.* 1320, the Hereford chapels, Malmesbury clerestory, and the chancel of Merton College.

[4] In the vaulting of the choir at Wells, *c.* 1350, the reticulated ornament is completely unstructural, and the whole recalls the style of wood rather than of stone.

[5] Such decorated canopies were likewise applied to the minor arts of decoration; but in them the architectural models were followed *longo intervallo*. The ornament of William of Wykeham's Crozier, probably made about 1370, is based on such canopied niches as those of Waltham Cross, erected between 1291 and 1293; the censer from Ramsey Abbey in the Victoria and Albert Museum owes something to the lantern of Ely Cathedral.

when the arch-form and its cuspings are themselves modified into ogival lines, a
change first found on the Eleanor Cross at Northampton, dating from between
1291 and 1294; or when the gable is thus curved, as on the graceful screen of the
transept of the Martyrdom at Canterbury (fig. 42) and the canopy of Bishop
Marcia's tomb at Wells. In the chapter-house at Howden the ogee arches are
delicately crocketed on both sides and filled in with a grille of quatrefoil tracery.[1]
In simpler work (as in the sedilia at Navenby, Lincs., dating from about 1310) arch
and gable are often merged into one heavily moulded ogival line.[2] Ogival canopies of this sort appear about 1340 on the choir screen at Southwell; [3] towards the
nave the side panels have ogival arches, towards the choir the rich arcading is
ogival, filled with flowing tracery and crowned with splendid crocketing. In the
later work in the stalls at Lancaster the rich tracery in the arch completely fills the
head, and the steep gables are filled with ornament, so that the old structural lines
are almost lost; while in the stall canopies of Norwich, carved about 1430, the ogee
line of the arches is clear, but the cusps have degenerated into a fret ending in
grotesque moon-shaped heads.

In the west of England there was a further elaboration of the lines of the
cusping.[4] On the tomb of Bishop Stapledon (d. 1317) at Exeter the low-pitched
segmental arch, the complex trefoil cusps, and the general richness and flow of line
mark a new epoch in sculptural decoration. On the choir screen at Exeter, dated
by the evidence of the Fabric-Rolls to 1324, the arches have a graceful and complex
foiling difficult to describe in words.[5] The same elegance and complexity is evident in the ogival foiling of the canopy arch over the tomb of Aymer de Valence,
Earl of Pembroke (fig. 43), erected in Westminster Abbey in the same year, in sharp
contrast with the severer lines of the arcade on the side of the tomb itself.[6]

Yet the new feeling for a flowing line could not find full expression when thus
conditioned by work applied to a single plane. It was essentially a three-dimensional feeling, an appreciation of the beauty of line curved in depth as well as in
height and breadth. One of the most notable effects of this appreciation was the
addition of depth to the planes of the arcade by transforming it into a series of

---

[1] Professor Prior (op. cit., pp. 387 et seq.) makes an interesting attempt to give a local classification to such
work, but has to admit that the various types were in general use.

[2] For a French instance see the lower windows of the Church of Saint Pierre, Caen.

[3] Professor Prior (op. cit., p. 392) notes that the fourteenth-century canopied wooden screens develop on
the borders of the great quarry districts that have a high tradition of sculpture in stone.

[4] The germ of this may be found in the cusping of the arcade in the interior of Salisbury chapter-house.

[5] Compare the base of the shrine of St. Etheldreda in Ely Cathedral, erected c. 1330.

[6] For a much simpler treatment of the same theme, slightly earlier in date, see Sir John de Stapledon's
tomb in Exeter Cathedral. Further north the scheme was a little simpler; on Bishop Gower's tomb at St.
Davids, probably erected before his death in 1347, the Gothic arch is cusped to give a cinqfoil opening, each
lobe of which describes a subsidiary cinqfoil. The design is further enriched by trefoil piercings within the
larger cusps, and by a rosette moulding and leafy crockets round the arch; but it is more primitive in type
than the Exeter work. Admirable later examples of the same type are the tombs in the south aisle at New
Winchelsea and the tomb of Sir Maurice Berkeley in St. Mark's, Bristol, c. 1470.

41. The Bishop's Eye, Lincoln, *c.* 1360

42. Transept of the Martyrdom, Canterbury Cathedral; the Screen, *c.* 1304

niched canopies.[1] The tendency had been made evident in the angular planes of the sedilia arcade of York chapter-house, built about 1300, and in the baying out of the gable of the arcades on the front of Wells. At Lichfield the arcade has become a series of recessed niches each with a base and canopy of its own; in the choir enclosure at Salisbury there is a projecting trefoil gabled canopy within the arch of the arcade. The same feeling found less graceful expression in the baying out and gabling of the upper lobe of the quatrefoil above the arcade of the north doorway at Christchurch Priory, to form a canopy for the figure within. Thence the transition was easy to the use of such a projecting canopy in the gable of an arcade;[2] but the ideal of a curving plane was not reached until this was merged in the line of the whole. One of the earliest and most successful instances of this fusion of line is the arcade that decorates the inside of the Lady Chapel at Ely (fig. 44), built between 1321 and 1349. The surface beneath the gable swells out to take the projecting ogival line of the arch, that is in its turn completed by swelling ogival cusps, themselves recusped. The whole surface is covered with delicate foliage, resembling seaweed in texture and form, while the spaces between the pinnacles and the gables are minutely carved with scenes from the life of the Virgin. The whole, in its subtlety, complexity, and accomplishment, represents the climax of English Curvilinear style.[3]

Such canopied niches form the basis of the greater part of English fourteenth-century decoration. They are used for the canopies of free-standing monuments, as for the tomb of Lady Percy at Beverley, with its decoration so rich that every compartment of the elaborate cusping has its little figure, and the very cusp-points are hovering angels; they are used for wall arcades, as at Wells (fig. 45), and for sedilia, as at Ely; for tomb recesses; in low relief on tomb chests, as on that of Edward III at Westminster; outlined in the flat as a decoration for Chertsey tiles, brasses, and tombstones; and ranged tier upon tier in stone, wood,[4] and glass. Bishop Brantyngham's great front at Exeter, begun in 1375, shows the scheme of Wells modulated into the new key, with tiers of statues under embowed canopies, elaborately cusped and crocketed; it was followed almost at once by the canopied reredos screens of Christchurch Priory and New College. For such work the canopy underwent fresh upward development; at Christchurch the finials of the two lower tiers of canopies broaden to form pedestals for the statues in those above, while all the pinnacles and columns that would normally appear at the sides of the canopies are merged into narrow piers running from top to bottom of the scheme, themselves divided into seven superimposed canopied niches on a lesser scale. The scheme is applied to glass in such windows as the east window of

---

[1] This responded to the increasing tendency of sculpture to be 'en ronde bosse'.

[2] As in a tomb canopy on the south side of Exeter Cathedral, and in the stall canopies of Gloucester, 1350, and the woodwork of All Saints', Hereford, 1380.

[3] See also the base of the shrine of St. Hugh's head (1350) in Lincoln Cathedral.

[4] For illustrations see F. Bond, *Wood-carvings in English Churches: Stalls and Tabernacle Work*. Oxford, 1910.

Gloucester (fig. 46), the windows of New College, Oxford, and hundreds of others. At Selby about 1340 even the corbels of the vaulting system are formed as finials to a canopy over a statue in the spandrel of the arch. Such canopied niches, again, were set back to back to decorate pinnacles (as at Boston) and cross-shafts,[1] while similar canopies crown the pages of such manuscripts as the Psalters of Humphrey de Bohun [2] and John of Gaunt.[3]

From them, too, a canopy of yet another type was evolved. With the Curvilinear style there was a great development of lanterns, such as the famous one at Ely begun in 1322 and finished twenty years later, and of spires, that everywhere 'prick'd with incredible pinnacles into heaven'. The influence of such spires is already evident in the design of the Eleanor Cross at Northampton, dating from about 1290. Consequently it seemed natural to elaborate the gable-finials and pinnacles of canopied niches into a lighter and more spire-like structure. The stone sedilia erected at Exeter by Bishop Stapledon (1308–25) show this tendency in pronounced fashion; the front-and-back finials and pinnacles are richly orna- mented, and from among them springs a second story of extremely slender arcad- ing surmounted by an airy pyramid of five tiers of pinnacles held together by buttress-like struts. On his great oak throne the system is the same but the scheme is even more elaborate; the ogival curves of the arcade are more strongly marked, yet another story is added, and the linking of the elements is more complex. A similar scheme appears in the stone canopy over Edward II's tomb at Gloucester about 1337 (fig. 48) with an added richness of detail, multiplicity of shafts, and rounded enrichment of forms.[4] This type of canopy was likewise used for many purposes: it appears in wood on the Norfolk and Suffolk font-covers (as at Ufford) and in the Winchester stalls; in glass, as in the west windows of Edington and Winchester, and the clerestory windows of Great Malvern (fig. 47); in sedilia, as at Dorchester, Oxon. (where it follows the local type of spire); and on many tomb slabs and brasses.[5]

Moreover, ogival line was applied with a new freedom to structural purposes; often, indeed, as in the strainer arches of Wells about 1338 and in the roughly contemporary strainers of Northamptonshire churches (for instance, Rushden), to give security to a structure planned with too little regard for solidity. A similar line appears in the sedilia canopies of Abbot Knowles's choir at Bristol (fig. 49),

[1] On Bishop Beckington's Chaingate of about 1465 at Wells they are even used as window mullions.
[2] At Exeter College, Oxford.
[3] Formerly in the Yates Thompson Collection.
[4] It is rather simplified in the famous canopy of three storeys over the tomb of Sir Hugh Despencer (d. 1349) at Tewkesbury, which served as a model for that of Sir Guy Brian (also at Tewkesbury) some twenty years later.
[5] A variant appears in the brass of a bishop, d. 1365, at Salisbury, which shows him set in the arch of a castle-like canopy, of diminishing height, flanked with turrets pierced with bow slits, with the warden of the gate below. The same rather unusual treatment is used in the tracery of a window given by Antoine de Balzac to the Church of Ambierle, Lot, made between 1470 and 1485.

43. Tomb of Aymer de Valence, Earl of Pembroke, 1324

44. Detail of the sedilia, Lady Chapel, Ely Cathedral, *c.* 1340

that have the gable shifted so that its point comes over the column of the arcade, forming an ogival lozenge of stone above the column.[1] The same originality and freedom are evident in the tomb niches of his presbytery, with a three-sided head to the arch, elegantly cusped, and five ogival gables, pierced, crocketed, and finialed, radiating from the sides and the head: a design that is graceful and rich, but in its lack of architectonic quality is better fitted to embroidery than to stone.[2] In its original home in the west of England the Curvilinear style had already worked out its destiny; and the most splendid of its further manifestations—culminating in the screen of York Minster—were to be in the north of England.

6

In the next generation western England developed a style that in its rigid angularity, its dryness and its severity, can hardly be conceived except as a reaction against the flowing line of English Curvilinear ornament. The Curvilinear style, it is true, had often emphasized its uprights, though it had consistently minimized horizontal line; but in the panelled system of the succeeding style, both received an equal emphasis. Yet, though a reaction of taste undoubtedly occurred, it reflected a change of social condition. The Black Death had modified economic conditions in England, alike for noble, ecclesiastic, burgess, farmer, and labourer; life was at once sterner and simpler.[3] The changing system of warfare was bringing romantic chivalry to an end, and in the subsequent Wars of the Roses was to change the dynasty. Even in thought the first timid seekers after experimental knowledge were beginning to challenge the medieval science of pure dialectic applied to traditional material. In its reasonable statement of spatial fact, in its regularity and lack of fancy, whether in design or in ornament, in its rejection of symbolic sculpture, the new style was a true reflection of its age; and in its proportion, mass, and order, it achieved a certain dignity of its own. There is little progress or variety in its ornamental detail, but much in its architectural plan and use. Just as its age was gradually renouncing the feudal order, so it was in some degree renouncing the Gothic tradition in its emphasis on wall rather than on vault, in its preference for the rectangle rather than the arch, and in the domestic and civic character of its style even when applied to ecclesiastical use. It had its true home, not, like Romanesque art, in the monastery, nor, like pure Gothic, in the cathedral, but in the college, the hall, and the parish church. It was, moreover, the Gothic style farthest removed from its French origins, and reflected the fact that England was at last conscious of her national integrity.

[1] The same characteristic also appears in much later work in the Rhineland: e.g. in the pulpit by Jean Hammer (1486) in Strasbourg Cathedral and in the canopy over a sculpture of the Annunciation (1483–8) in the Cathedral of Worms.

[2] A similar lack of constructional form is evident in the filigree arches of the roof, an imitation of woodwork in stone.

[3] The direct influence of the Black Death on the art of England has sometimes been exaggerated. See G. G. Coulton, *Art and the Reformation*, pp. 503 et seqq.

Naturally the change of style had been preluded in Curvilinear work. The new style was essentially west of England in origin. There is more than a suggestion of rectangular panelling in the choir of Wells, built about 1320 (fig. 45), in the canopies on either side of the windows, and the elongated canopied arcade below. The beginnings of Perpendicular tracery may be found in the introduction of a stone transom half-way up Abbot Knowles's windows at Bristol[1] about ten years later, necessitated by the transference to glass of the tiers of canopied niches evolved in stone for the decoration of screen and façade. Indeed, all Perpendicular panelling is a further development of such tiers of canopied niches, stiffened and simplified into a schematic form. If the horizontal line of the new tracery appears at Bristol, its vertical line makes its appearance in Abbot Wygmore's contemporary window in the south transept of Gloucester; the vertical bar of the second order cuts through the arched rib of the main order and runs up into the head.

It was at Gloucester—which seems to have suffered less from the Black Death than most English cities—that the elements of the Perpendicular style were worked out. Mature Perpendicular tracery first appears in the great east window, given to commemorate Crecy between 1347 and 1350; Perpendicular panelling was used as a veneer over the earlier walls soon after the middle of the century; and the characteristic fan-vaulting first appears in architectural form[2] in the lovely cloister (fig. 50), begun in 1351 and finished some thirty years later. This is structurally a negation of the Gothic vault; its designers 'shaped the vault conoid (or fan) as a decorative corbel on which the ceiling rested like a level [flagstone]'.[3] Its ribs perform no function, but like the panelling lines of wall decoration are merely a decorative tracery, of which the design could be varied at will. Yet the effect of the semicircular conoids meeting on a flat space at the crown, which like them is decorated with simply cusped and moulded tracery, is undoubtedly admirable; it gives the impression of inevitableness which is the true mark of great art. In the Gloucester cloisters its scale is comparatively small, and however great a creative effort its design may represent, its construction must have been relatively simple. But when the same system was applied a few years later to the vaulting of the north transepts of Gloucester and Tewkesbury, an engineering system of some ingenuity had to be evolved for the invisible reverse of the vault to give it security over a wider span. This achieved, the fan-vault could be applied to all the great buildings in Perpendicular style, and could give them that breadth of effect and sense of springing growth that they might otherwise have lacked.

The spread of the style was first evident in a general modification of the line of

---

[1] Later examples will be found at Ely; and more tentative attempts at Hull and Bridlington.

[2] The idea appears a little earlier on a smaller scale, in the miniature vaults of the Tewkesbury tomb canopies. A rudimentary fan-vault is *painted* on that of Sir Hugh Despencer, 1349, and another is carved on that of Sir Edward Despencer, *c.* 1370.

[3] E. S. Prior, *op. cit.*, p. 433.

Curvilinear ornament. After 1350 the canopies of tomb recesses, screens, stalls, sedilia, and the rest tend to have a level cornice above the canopy. At the same time the development of chantry building, and the consequent enlargement of the tomb canopy to form a screen to a tiny chapel, brought the canopies into a new relation with such pierced wall tracery as that which masks the Norman triforia at Gloucester. Two tiers of such pierced panelling, resting on a solid base similarly panelled, screen William Wykeham's chantry at Winchester; on the tomb of John Lord Tiptoft, Earl of Worcester, at Ely such tracery is used as a background to the ogival gables of the tomb-canopy; at Exeter Bishop Stafford's tomb, though it has the Curvilinear cusped arch and spandrel tracery, has the level cornice and panelled sides of the later style, while the Speke chantry shows the substitution of Perpendicular tracery for the cusped arch and a stronger emphasis on rectangular line.[1] Such a modification is soon evident in work on a larger scale; it is necessary only to compare the south-west porch of Canterbury Cathedral with the west front of Exeter to see how great the change was in effect, slight though it may be in fact.

The most characteristic development of the style is in the architecture of the fifteenth-century English parish churches, alike in the west—for instance at Curry Rivel and in the other Somerset churches—and in East Anglia, where the wool trade was also prosperous and the local confraternities had wealth with which to build such noble churches as those of Southwold, Boston, and Lavenham, and St. Nicholas, King's Lynn. But in these churches the style is one of pure architecture; plan, proportion, and regularity give beauty, the great windows give colour; and decoration as such is comparatively unimportant and remarkably uniform, consisting as it does of a reproduction of such Perpendicular tracery as adorns the windows on wall and screen, bench end and pulpit, altar, font, and tomb,[2] and even—as in the nave of Sherborne—as an arch-mould. In East Anglia, too, a stone that would carve easily and weather well for exterior work was scarce, and consequently Perpendicular panelling in outside work was commonly reproduced not in relief but in a mosaic of black flint and white chalkstone. Richness of effect was obtained —as for instance in the font and its steps at Walsingham—not by a great variety of ornament, but by its arrangement on a skilfully planned field. Where the decoration is more complex, as on the great western screens of the end of the fifteenth and beginning of the sixteenth century—such as the wooden screen at Minehead and the stone screen at Totnes, each based on an imitation of fan-vaulting—it yet has curiously little variety. The ribs and bosses of such vaulting, a battle-

[1] Cf. the screen of Fitz Hamon's chantry, 1397, at Tewkesbury, with a lighter cornice but similar tracery and panelling. A similar modification is evident in woodwork; for instance, the pulpit at Halburton, Devon, carved in 1420, has an upper tier of ogival canopies and a lower of panels of curvilinear tracery each set in recessed rectangular mouldings.

[2] Capitals become less and less important, and often, as at Bath Abbey, are no more than a moulded band round the column.

ment moulding, the usual Perpendicular tracery and panelling, and more or less elaborate vine leaf and foliate mouldings, in which there is a strong tendency to square leaf-forms, practically complete the repertory of the decorator. Even for the sumptuous decoration of King's College chapel, statuary and tabernacle work were bought by the foot.[1]

The amount of important cathedral construction was comparatively small.[2] Indeed, all Perpendicular ecclesiastical building on a more elaborate scale than the parish churches was done in the smaller field of chapel or chantry. Some of the most beautiful buildings in the style are college chapels, of which the finest is that of King's College, Cambridge, built about 1480. Similarly in civil architecture the best work is to be found in the Universities; in the Divinity School of Oxford, (fig. 51) about 1452, with window, arch, vault, and tracery all planned to the same almost triangular head, and in the great gate of King's College, Cambridge, in which the heraldic and architectural motives of the chapel are applied with no need of modification to another scheme.

Yet in decorative detail the richest Perpendicular work was not in such buildings designed for the use of the community, but rather in chantries planned to perpetuate the glory and profit the soul of the individual. The great monument of the style is Henry V's chantry in Westminster Abbey, erected about 1430,[3] that is marked by the large scale of the sculpture, the piercing of the turrets, and especially by its proud commemoration of the dead king—his descent from the Confessor, his coronations in England and in France, his prowess in the field—by the abundant use of heraldry, and the almost ostentatious spirit of the whole. But the finest examples of a truly English style in such work date from the beginning of the next century, when the Tudor magnificence of the Renaissance found expression in the last stages of the English Gothic style. The first such monument, Prince Arthur's chantry of 1502 (fig. 53), has a magnificent screen with a base of pierced Perpendicular panels, a middle story with an arcade of Perpendicular tracery enclosing the royal badges, and an upper of rich cusped tracery, window fashion, crowned with a battlement likewise pierced, the vertical lines of the whole emphasized by tall narrow niched piers ending in pinnacles. The final achievement of the Perpendicular style is Henry VII's chapel at Westminster (figs. 52, 55), dating from 1512; the greatest and most splendid of the chantries, it sums up, in fan-vault, window, screen, and wall, all that could be achieved with the comparatively simple elements of Perpendicular decoration in the creation of a whole of amazing richness and complexity.[4] Yet, vital though it seems, it is the last great monument

[1] Willis and Clark, *Architectural History of the University of Cambridge*, i, p. 482.
[2] Peterborough Cathedral has a fine fifteenth-century fan-vault to its retrochoir; Canterbury has the Bell Harry Tower, Perpendicular in plan but with many Curvilinear survivals alike in detail and general feeling; York has its enormous Perpendicular east window; Winchester its veneer of Perpendicular masonry over a Norman core; but there is no great ensemble.   [3] See *Archaeologia*, 1913–14, lxv. 153.
[4] Only in Oxford did Perpendicular linger on. The vault of the Cathedral (1511) is a year earlier than

45. Canopy work on the choir wall, Wells Cathedral, *c.* 1320

46. Light from the East Window, Gloucester Cathedral, c. 1350

47. Light from a window in the North Clerestory of the Choir, Great Malvern, c. 1460–70

of English Gothic art;[1] and indeed the last great monument to be produced in England for several centuries that should not owe anything to any foreign or anterior style.

7

In France, in the early fourteenth century, after the great harvest of the preceding age the fields of art lay fallow. France was passing through a time in which her new dynasty of Valois had to face troubles as unexpected as they were disastrous: defeat at English and Flemish hands, discontent among all the estates at home, the ravages of the Black Death, and a consequent upheaval of all her social, political, and economic foundations. In philosophy and learning France was losing her earlier primacy; the encyclopaedias of the English Bartholomew and the arguments of the English Occam and Alexander of Hales were beginning to supersede native learning in her universities.

Even before the Hundred Years War began, a certain decadence is visible in French building activity, especially in the building of churches. French structural Gothic was not capable of infinite development; the country that had created the Gothic style was ready to receive fresh inspiration.[2] This came from England, that had developed the Gothic style along other lines than France; and it was received when the successful invasion of France by Edward III brought much French territory into English occupation. The English Curvilinear style, just past its apogee in England, migrated to France.

In Brittany this influence was already active; Quimper, consecrated in 1289, and Tréguier, rebuilt in 1339, have long eastern limbs and broad windows like Exeter. With the progress of the century the analogies with the west of England became closer; the fourteenth-century choirs of Dol and Saint Pol de Leon have square eastern chapels[3] like Pershore and Ottery St. Mary, tomb niches and doorways like those at St. Davids, and details of triforium and window tracery that resemble Exeter and Bristol. When after the middle of the century the flowing Curvilinear style passed out of use in England itself, it continued to influence the architecture of Brittany; the choirs of Folgoët and Lamballe, built about 1370, have square ends and great traceried windows like Milton Abbey in Dorset or Dorchester in Oxfordshire; the spires of Folgoët and many other Breton churches are built on the English model.[4]

Henry VII's chapel; but the windows of Wadham chapel (1612) show reasonably correct Perpendicular tracery, and the last and perhaps the most famous fan-vault, the staircase at Christ Church, was not built until about 1630.

[1] For an account of its building see W. Lethaby, *Westminster Abbey re-examined*, 1925, pp. 155 et seqq.

[2] At Brive, for example, the nave of the Church of Saint Martin, begun in 1310, is a Gothic version of the great Romanesque church of Saint Savin sur Gartrempe.

[3] The English flat east end is of course found earlier, notably in Cistercian work. A thirteenth-century example that may owe something to English influence is the East End of Poitiers Cathedral.

[4] See E. S. Prior, *A History of Gothic Art in England*, p. 332.

Brittany has always been too poor to be a great creative centre; but soon the influence of the Curvilinear style was felt in isolated instances, even in the strongholds of French Gothic. English influence is evident as early as 1240 in the liernes of the Amiens vault, and reappears in the decorative details of the south porch of Saint Urbain de Troyes some twenty years later. The side of the throne of the statue of the Virgin presented to the Cathedral of Sens by one of its canons in 1334 is definitely English in style, even to the roses in the quatrefoils of the base;[1] while a rather heavy version of the type of tabernacle canopy used for Edward II's tomb at Gloucester decorates that of the Anti-pope John XXII (d. 1334) in the Cathedral of Avignon.[2] In the Cathedral of Narbonne there is a tomb of about 1350 decorated with arcading of the English transitional type, geometric in its line but with flowing traceries.

After Edward III's campaigns the English style was often in some sense imposed on districts that at the time were under English domination;[3] at Rouen Cathedral, of which the rebuilding was begun in 1370, John Wyllemer, an English mason in the employ of the Duke of Bedford, superintended the work, which, with its rows of statues under canopied arcades, and its markedly unstructural character, recalls the style of Wells, Salisbury, and Lichfield. The anglicisms of style that appear at Bordeaux, Le Mans, and Evreux under English rule may well be due to such English supervision.[4] Indeed some of the most typical Flamboyant work in northern France—for instance, Caudebec dating from 1426, and Saint Maclou at Rouen from 1437—was designed while Normandy was still English.

Naturally, however, the style even of the façade of Rouen is not the English Curvilinear but a derivative of it—the French Flamboyant.[5] All its characteristics were derived from England;[6] its vaulting-tracery of liernes and tiercerons, its breadth of arch, its use of segmental or flattened arches *en anse de panier*;[7] the decorative use of the ogival arch;[8] the use of flowing tracery in window, arch, and balustrade; the types of capital and base; the treatment of foliage as if it were sea-weed, and its use in crockets on gables and pinnacles and the upper edge of

[1] Cf. a type of screen tracery common in Suffolk.

[2] The tomb was made by Jean Lavenier of Paris. R. de Lasteyrie, *L'Architecture religieuse en France à l'époque gothique*, ii. 571.

[3] Normandy and Picardy had suffered almost more than any other provinces of France during the Hundred Years War, and an enormous amount of rebuilding was necessary. See R. de Lasteyrie, *op. cit.* i. 161.

[4] M. Enlart notes that three English sculptors—Thomas Colyn, Thomas Poppehove, and Thomas Hollewell—made the tomb of Duke John V of Brittany at Nantes in 1408. (*Manuel d'archéologie française, architecture religieuse*, 2nd ed., p. 643).

[5] The earliest example of pure Flamboyant style is probably the chapel of St. John the Baptist at Amiens, built by the Cardinal de la Grange between 1373 and 1376.

[6] See the admirable paper by M. Enlart in *Bull. Mon.*, 1906, lxx. 43. For a résumé of the question, see R. de Lasteyrie, *op. cit.* xiii.

[7] Such as appear in England on the tomb canopy of Bishop Hatfield at Durham, *c.* 1350, in the arches of the Bishop's Palace at St. David's, and on Bishop Edington's fronts at Winchester and Edington.

[8] The French 'arc en accolade', found in England *c.* 1290 and not used in France until the end of the fourteenth century.

48. Tomb of Edward II, *c.* 1337. Gloucester Cathedral

49. Sedilia of Abbot Knowles' Choir, *c.* 1320. Bristol Abbey

archivolts; the interpenetration of mouldings, and their merging in each other and in the main building—all these are English. English, too, was a fundamental difference from French Gothic in that the new style was based not upon structure but upon a decorative scheme of flowing ogival lines; yet the national spirit that informed it transmuted them into a new Flamboyant style. For one thing, when the elements were English they were differently used: the tracery of the hall of the Dukes of Aquitaine at Poitiers (fig. 54) is English in its branching growth and its flowing line, and even in the manner of its being set forward before the glass; but its use as a transparent screen above a great triple fireplace was entirely original.[1] Even in such ogival tracery as that of the balustrade of Saint Gilles, Caen (fig. 57), a French note was struck in the leafy crockets and in the interlaced arcade beneath. All the elements of the steepled funeral chapel at Avioth, Meuse, are English, but its form and effect are completely foreign. A curious and instructive comparison may be made between the Churches of St. Mary Redcliffe at Bristol and Saint Jacques at Liége. They are (except for the choirs) almost exactly alike in construction and proportion; yet a difference in the use of decorative elements masks the likeness to a surprising extent.

Again, the French lacked the sense of the beauty of line curving in three dimensions, that gives its especial charm of modelling to the later English Curvilinear work; their Flamboyant ornament was always based on simple vertical planes. The likeness with English work is therefore most marked in window traceries, that are of necessity limited to such a plane: the resemblance is close between the early fifteenth-century branching traceries of Saint Germain, Amiens, and the Chapelle des Jacobins, Saintes, and those of the Selby windows a century older. Such tracery was further elaborated in the Breton woodwork, for instance on the doors of Saint Pol de Leon and on such screens as that of Guern (fig. 58). There is a similar likeness between the reticulated traceries at Saint Etienne, Beauvais, and the West of England examples. The window of the Vendôme Chapel at Chartres, built in 1417, is a simplified version of half the great east window of Carlisle, dating from about 1350. Similarly there is a close analogy between the French and English brasses and incised tomb-slabs,[2] and the great painted tabernacles in the windows of Saint Maclou and the Cathedral of Rouen (fig. 59), in the Cathedrals of Evreux and Le Mans, in the Churches of Notre Dame at Saint Omer (fig. 60) and Saint Lô, and in those of the Sainte Chapelle of Bourges.[3] In other work, though the mouldings are extraordinarily rich, sharp, and deeply undercut, because of the vertical plane in

[1] Cf. the later development in the blind Flamboyant tracery imitating a window above the late fifteenth-century chimney-piece in the Salle des Gardes at Dijon.

[2] The continental examples are even more elaborate. Gaignières records (Bodley MS. 18349, pp. 128 and 136, and 18360, p. 21) two of 1349 and 1420 with twenty-one little figures in the architectural canopy, and one (the brass of a Bishop of Le Mans who died in 1399) with an extravagantly rich canopy with no less than forty-one little figures.

[3] Now in the crypt of the Cathedral. Farther east similar tabernacles appear in the great windows of the nave of Strasbourg Cathedral.

which the work is conceived and in spite of their elaboration and their interpene-
trations, the whole shares in the 'liny' quality of the contemporary Perpendicular
style rather than in the picturesque roundness of the three-dimensional Curvilinear.

The English proportion, again, was modified. In the porch of the Church of
Ablain Saint Nazaire in the Pas de Calais (fig. 61) the main arch (though divided by
a low-pitched arcade in the French manner) has the English breadth and proportion; in the side porch of Tours Cathedral the scheme is the same, but the height
of the arch has been increased by half as much again, and is filled for more than
half its width with tracery that is cut by a heavily moulded transom *en anse de
panier*. At Saint Germain, Argentan (fig. 62), the proportions are even loftier and
the scheme more original; there is no English parallel for the great double arches
set at an obtuse angle, nor for the horizontal cornice that cuts across the ogival
gable. France, indeed, soon tired of the relatively simple arch surmounted by an
ogival gable with leafy crocketings, such as appears on the west porch of Carpen-
tras; it lingered on for civil use, as for the turret door of the Bishop's Palace at
Evreux, built in 1484, and the almost contemporary door of the hall on the ground
floor of the old town hall at Bourges, but for more splendid work it was superseded by more elaborate compositions.

The Flamboyant style—like the later imported styles of the Renaissance—was
at first curiously uniform, showing little if any local differences;[1] but after the
middle of the fifteenth century a northern and southern style may be distinguished.
In the northern style, for instance in the west porch of Notre Dame, Alençon, and
in the façade of Saint Wulfran, Abbeville (fig. 63), begun under Cardinal Georges
d'Amboise in 1488,[2] the English arch and gable lines are kept; the traceries,
decorated in the head, rise from sharp close-set vertical mouldings, that recall the
vertical lines of the Gloucester Perpendicular; the foliate crockets are almost
square in shape; and there is everywhere evident a certain thinness and angularity
of line. A characteristic is the use of pierced turrets, such as had first appeared on
Henry V's chantry in 1430; a good example with ogival tracery screens the inside
door of the chapel of about 1490 in the Musée de Cluny, formerly the town house
of the Abbot of Cluny, and another, carved by Pierre Gringoire about 1500, was in
1521 adapted to form a staircase to the organ loft of Saint Maclou, Rouen (fig. 64).
Such pierced work, again, reappeared in the great Belgian buildings of the period,

---

[1] The difference lies rather in the date at which its various manifestations reached the different provinces,
which makes its chronological study extremely difficult. In this it differs from the English Curvilinear style, with
considerable local variation and a steady and fairly even chronological development. Mr. Enlart has characterized the want of development in the French style. 'Le style flamboyant ne pouvait évoluer, puisqu'il con-
sistait dans l'application à outrance de ses principes. . . . On ne saurait donc établir de chronologie dans les
variantes des formes. Une autre particularité est l'absence d'écoles ; d'une province de France à l'autre il n'y
a guère de différences dans ce style, qui est bien celui d'un peuple unifié.' 'Le style flamboyant', in Michel,
Histoire de l'art, iii. 6.

[2] M. Mâle has pointed out (*L'Art religieux en France au XVe siècle*, p. 236) how typical this façade is of
the decadence of the symbolism of Gothic iconography.

50. The Cloisters, Gloucester Cathedral. Finished in 1381

51. The Divinity School, Oxford, *c.* 1452

as in the balustrades of the Hotel de Ville at Arras, and in the Flemish wooden retables. Occasionally, especially in such later work as the south porch of Louviers (fig. 65), this style was much enriched with sculpture; but it is always, like much contemporary English Perpendicular work, a little soulless and mechanical.[1]

In the south, which probably received its knowledge of the English style not through Normandy but through Guienne and Gascony,[2] a different type of Flamboyant decoration was produced. The great alabaster ciborium of Saint Jean de Maurienne shows the niched piers of the English reredoses adapted to a new use; its style, though not English, is perhaps nearer to it than that of the north in its complexity of plan, its greater richness of modelling, and its more harmonious proportion. Obviously the side piers are versions of the same motive as that of the buttress piers of Saint Wulfran d'Abbeville; yet there is a less mechanical handling, a more human quality, indefinably expressed. This same richness, perhaps of spirit rather than of style, is equally evident in the porch[3] of filigree delicacy that juts out from the massive rose-red nave of Albi; all the elements of the northern style are there—the tabernacle-niches, the canopies filled with flowing tracery and crowned with ogival gables with leafy crockets and finials, the horizontal mouldings running across gabled compositions, the division of the main arch by transverse arches *en anse de panier*—yet an added freedom and an increased sculptural sense, fostered perhaps by the brilliant sunshine and strong shadow of the south, have modulated the whole into another key.

This change is even more marked in the magnificent choir screen within—a marvel with no English equivalent—that was erected under Louis d'Amboise about 1500 (fig. 66). Its great series of tabernacle canopies, more complex, more lofty, and more elegant than any in England, merge into the tracery of the background, behind which still run the ghosts of ogival gables; tabernacle and background alike are rich in leafy crockets and finials, and themselves have something of the curving vigour of natural growth; yet they retain the strength and significance of structural work in the contrast of pinnacle and ogee, of vertical

---

[1] The influence of the 'Northern' style is also found all up the Rhine from Cologne to Strasbourg; in the Rathhaus Tower (1407–14) and Gürzenich (1441–52) at Cologne, in the reticulated vaults of St. Castor's (1498) and the Liebfrauenkirche (*c.* 1500) at Coblentz; in the vaulting of the cloister of St. Stephanus Kirche, Mainz (1499), and in that of the Chapel of St. Lawrence (1495–1504) in Strasbourg Cathedral. In the same district, and elsewhere in Germany, elaborate pinnacled canopies of a type ultimately derived from Edward III's tomb at Gloucester crown altar pieces and ciboria of every kind. The English reticulated vault was translated into brick everywhere in the Netherlands; and thence made its way (once more in stone) into Spain, for instance in the Cathedrals of Palencia, Segovia, Salamanca, and Ciudad Rodrigo, in the Collegiate Church of Berlanga de Duero, and the Chapel of the Conception at Burgos. Such influences were spasmodically felt even in Italy; it is English reticulated tracery (suffering a sea-change) that inspires the famous windows of the Ca' d'Oro (1421–35) at Venice.

[2] The Chartreuse of Champmol, just outside Dijon, built by the Duke of Burgundy between 1383 and 1388, inaugurates the northern flamboyant style in the south-east of France.

[3] Begun 1473, finished 1502.

height and lace-like crocket, in strength of line and infinite delicacy of detail. The Flamboyant style may be derivative, it may mark the decadence of pure Gothic; but in the choir of Albi it achieves a masterpiece.

The styles of the north and south are united in the other great monument of Flamboyant art, the Church of Brou. Begun in 1480 by Marguerite de Bourbon, who died four years later, it was finished by Margaret of Austria, widow of Philibert le Beau of Savoy, who died in 1504.[1] The tomb of Marguerite de Bourbon is not far removed in style from such southern work as the Porch of Albi; but in that of Margaret of Austria (who as Governess of the Netherlands was closely connected with the north) and in the choir screen which she erected, a fresh strain of northern influence is apparent[2] (fig. 67). The tabernacles at the corners of the tomb have some kinship with those of the Albi Choir, but the balustrade, the firmly recessed arch, the tracery of the choir screen and its cusping, and the metallic finish of the whole are more in the northern spirit. The *anse de panier* arch is everywhere in use, often modified into a crown form; and indeed the disuse of the true Gothic arch is a marked feature of the decoration of Brou. There, almost for the first time, one is conscious that the Gothic style had indeed become decadent, after having served many more generations than that which created it.

Yet Brou, perhaps because it is nearer to Italy, perhaps because it is an individual creation, a glorified chantry for four people, seems more decadent than cognate work elsewhere,[3] notably at Troyes. The great Jubé of the Madeleine there (fig. 68), erected by Jean Gaide between 1508 and 1517, still keeps a clear memory of the Gothic canopied arcade; the columns are cut off at the capitals to form finials, the gables are reduced to fanciful four-sided panels, the pinnacles are enlarged into tabernacles over statues; but the structural line remains to justify the composition as a whole. Even the detail, with its able use of heraldic forms, is more satisfactory than the confused richness of Brou.

The style, however, could only give way before the rising tide of Renaissance decoration. For a time the two appeared side by side, as on the choir screen of Chartres or the stalls of Gaillon, carved in 1509,[4] where panels framed in Renaissance architectural motives are divided by little figures of apostles beneath towering tabernacles; for a time they were even merged, as in the Sacristy of the Church of Saint Jacques at Dieppe, with tabernacles set against classic piers, shell-headed tops to ogival arcades, and flamboyant tracery filling the space beneath a classic cornice.

---

[1] Its architects were successively Jehan Perréal and Van Boghem; its sculptors the Tourangeau Michel Coulombe and then the Swiss Conrad Meyt, who was chiefly responsible for the statues.

[2] A certain kinship is evident with such English work as the screen at Totnes (1459), Bishop Alcock's Chantry at Ely (c. 1500), and the canopy over the tomb of Bishop John Longland in Lincoln Cathedral. In the even ponderation and filigree quality of the foliage there is a likeness with such Scottish work as Roslyn Chapel, c. 1446.

[3] Work closely resembling that of Brou appears in the low countries: e.g., the Hotel de Ville at Ghent, 1518–35.

[4] Now in Saint Denis.

52. The Vault of Henry VII's Chapel, 1512. Westminster Abbey

53. Screen of Prince Arthur's Chantry, 1502. Worcester Cathedral

54. Chimney piece in the hall of the Palace of the Dukes of Aquitaine at Poitiers, 1393–1415

55. Bronze Grille to the Chantry of Henry VII, 1512. Westminster Abbey

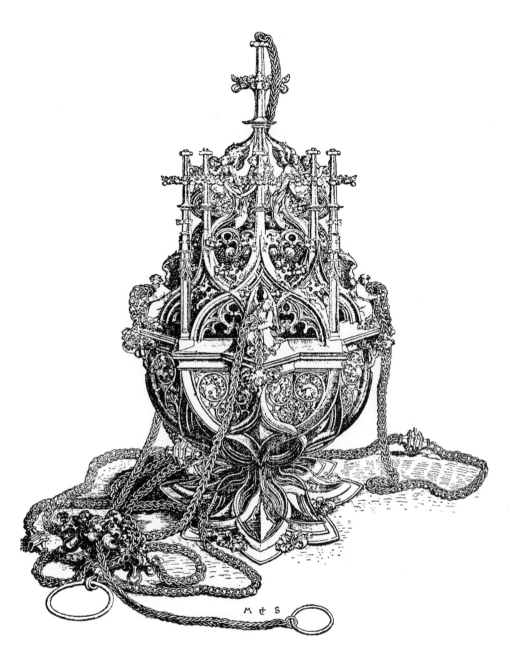

FIG. 56. Design for a Censer by Martin Schongauer, *c.* 1490.

The last stage came in the Jubé at Limoges, erected in 1533; all the detail is classic, but scaly scrolls mimic the lines of Gothic cusping, and the statues in the spandrels of the arches are sheltered by tabernacles formed of classical columns and domes.

Flamboyant decoration, however, lingered rather longer in the minor arts, that followed the lead of medieval architecture, but always at a little distance. The English, the northern and the southern varieties of the Flamboyant style, are each represented in surviving fifteenth-century goldwork. The magnificent enamelled gold reliquary from the Chapel of the Order of the Saint Esprit (fig. 70) was designed on the English tabernacle plan, and at the same time owed something to the English reredoses in its ranges of statues within canopies. The angular tracery of the northern Flamboyant style was easily adapted to metal work. It appears on the Processional Cross of the Grandes-Carmes of Paris (fig. 72); it makes an admirable foil to clustered leafage on the German goldwork of the middle of the century (fig. 71), and to the foliated outline of Spanish and Portuguese processional crosses; and in a simplified form influenced the contemporary Italian reliquaries and monstrances of architectural type. The southern Flamboyant style was even better suited to work in metal; all its characteristics are represented in miniature in such work as Martin Schongauer's design for a censer (fig. 56) and in some of the Portuguese goldwork in Manueline style. In Italy the school of Bartolomeo da Bologna emphasized its structural lines and endowed it with an architectural quality that was a prelude to the style of the Renaissance (fig. 73).

The spiny northern tracery, on the other hand, was especially suited to work in iron; it adorns the fifteenth-century iron door of the Treasury in Rouen Cathedral, and was applied to many lesser objects such as locks and coffers, while in Spain it inspired a series of magnificent grilles (fig. 74). The reticulated[1] and branching traceries were likewise adapted for the decoration of both iron and wood.

Flamboyant tracery was also applied to the decoration of oaken chests; a series of such chests clearly shows the development of a scheme based on an arcade, through a type inspired by window tracery, into the panelled system of the Renaissance (figs. 75-7). It was, indeed, the flamboyant ogee moulding that came to an ignominious and unrecognized end in the 'curved-rib' type of panelling fairly common in the north of France and the Low Countries.[2]

The most magnificent creations of the hybrid Flamboyant-Renaissance art were in Spain and Portugal, where Flemish craftsmen of remarkable technical skill worked to satisfy the taste of men who had inherited an oriental tradition of luxuriant decoration. In such circumstances the old scheme of ranged tiers of niches was elaborated out of all knowledge; such work as the exterior of the

---

[1] Such work has an English prototype in the magnificent iron gates given by Edward IV to the lower Chapel of St. George at Windsor.

[2] Found in England in such woodwork as that of Boughton Malherbe, dating from 1520.

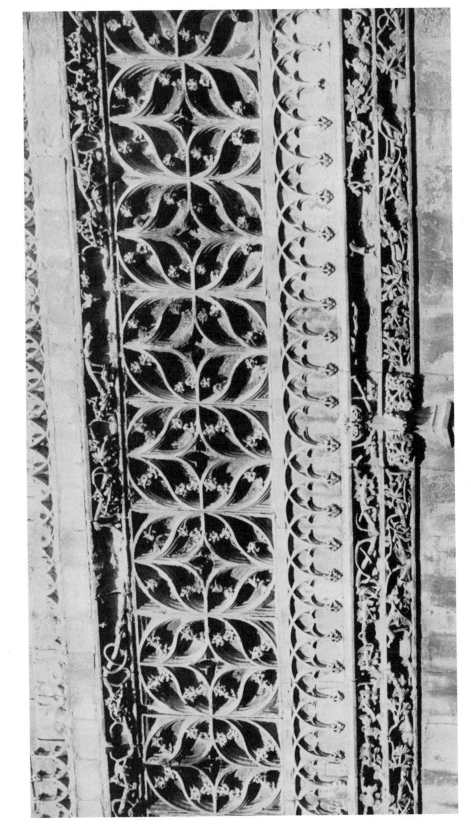

57. Detail of the Balustrade, Saint Gilles, Caen, *c.* 1485

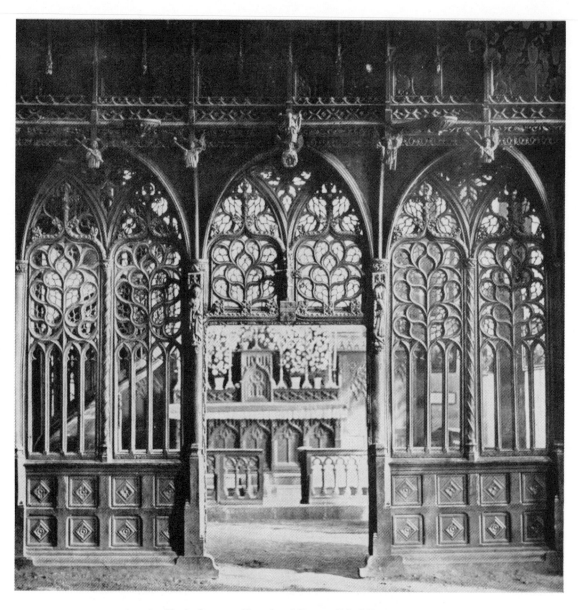

58. Choir Screen, Church of Guern, Morbihan, *c.* 1520

Presbytery at Toledo is not only far from the English models from which its arcades, its cuspings, its niches, its tracery, its pinnacles, and its angel musicians are ultimately derived, but even, though all its elements are Gothic, seems outside the whole Gothic tradition. When, as in Dancart's altarpiece in Seville Cathedral (fig. 78), such a scheme is yet further enriched, we are conscious that the end of the impulse that started in the lancets of Early Gothic has been reached; and when, as in the Cathedral Pulpit of Coimbra, Renaissance elements are added to the scheme, they seem a welcome simplification.

II

SPECULUM NATURAE

I

ONE of the greatest discoveries of the Middle Ages was that of the beauty of the natural world. Not since the Silver Age of Rome had the full loveliness of flower and leaf, bird and beast, been perceived: an ascetic view of nature, a life of warfare and danger, a civilization striving to keep a tradition it had ceased to understand, all worked together to blunt man's consciousness of natural beauty. But as the races of Europe recovered from the immense fatigue of the Dark Ages, this sense was reborn. Men had both leisure for contemplation, and the peace of mind that makes true contemplation possible.

The medieval saint found nothing ignoble or mean in the lowest creation of his Lord; in his conception the perfected beauty of the universe demanded inequality among the beings that composed it, in order that every degree of perfection might be reproduced and represented.[1] Every existing thing was a form of a revelation that was universal; greatness and smallness had no meaning before the infinity that included them in its divine plan. To contemplate nature in all its forms, and to apprehend its mystical meaning, was a divine faculty that raised man above the level of the beasts; 'Miserum esse videtur,' writes Honorius of Autun,[2] 'res propter nos factas quotidie spectare et cum iumentibus quid sint penitus ignorare.'

Such contemplation—and especially the beginnings of such contemplation, when the senses are as quick as the spirit—must lead to a new perception of reality. The cloistered Abelard experienced this: he writes 'the press of cities and suburban gardens, where the fields are pleasantly watered and the trees thick with foliage; where birds chirp and living pools mirror the sky, and the brook babbles on its way, and many other things entice man's ears and eyes'.[3] There is a new sense of the beauty and grandeur of trees and woods in the verse of Bernard Sylvester of Chartres, who died in 1167:

> Fronduit in plano platanus, convallibus alnus,
> Rupe rigens buxus, littore lenta salix.
> Monte cupressus olens, sacra vitis colle supino
> Inque laborata Palladis arbor humo,
> Populus albescens, lotus cognatior undis,
> Et viburna magis vimine lenta suo.
> In nodos et lata rigens venabula cornus,
> In validos arcus flexile robur, acer.

[1] Aquinas, *Summa Theol.* 1 a, q. 48, a 2, ad 3 c.   [2] Migne, *Pat. Lat.* clxxii. 119.
[3] Abelard, quoted G. G. Coulton, *Mediaeval Garner*, p. 89.

59. Detail of a window, Lady Chapel, Cathedral
of Rouen, c. 1400

60. Lights from a window formerly in
Notre Dame de Saint Omer, c. 1480

62. Porch of the Church of Saint Germain,
Argentan, c. 1500

61. South Porch, Church of Ablain Saint Nazaire,
Pas de Calais, c. 1530

Mobilibus tremulis et acutis frondibus ilex,
    Et mala Cecropias perdere taxus apes.
Quercus alumna, gigas abies, pygmaea myrica,
    Dumus et armato corpore spina nocens.
Rubus inhorrescens et eisdem rhamnus in armis
    Non nisi callosas extimuere manus.
Fagus amans hederas et coniuga vitibus ulmus,
    Quaeque parum cynus matre recedit humo
Concava sambucus frangique levis sycomorus
    Quique novae frondis gaudet honore frutex.[1]

The appreciation of natural beauty as a background to personal emotion colours all medieval lyric. Such appreciation seems first to have flowered in the south; but it was not long before the culture of the south—already too lyric, too individual, too much devoted to the 'gaie science' for endurance—received its death blow in the Albigensian Crusades. The lead in lyric creation passed to the north, but to a centre already established, and to a creation in many ways independent of the southern tradition. Champagne is more sensitive to the passing of the seasons than is Provence; its beauties are more mutable and more fleeting than those of the south; and it was there, at the end of the twelfth century and in the early years of the thirteenth century, that *reverdies* with the woods and meadows and gardens of spring and early summer as their natural setting, hymned the fairy freshness of May.

Ceinturet avoit de fueille
Qui verdist quant li tens mueille;
    D'or ert boutonade;
L'ausmoniere estoit d'amor
Li pendant furent de flor,
    Par Amors fu donade . . .
—'Bele, dont êtes vos née?'
—'De France sui la loée,
    Du plus haut parage;
Li rosseignols est mon pere
Qui chante sur la ramée
    El plus haut boschage . . .

Naturalism became more conscious and more romantic in its sentiment. The elements of tradition and of symbolism tended to disappear;[2] and as life became more urban and architecture more scientific there was a more sophisticated appreciation of the beauties of natural forms. Naturalism, that in its beginning had been a growth of monastic contemplation, became in its maturity the flower of a highly developed courtly civilization. The Cistercians of the thirteenth century, who sought a refuge from the world in the remote woodlands and valleys,

[1] Bernardi Sylvestri, *de mundi universitate*, ed. C. S. Barach and J. Wrobel, Innsbruck, 1876, p. 23.
[2] It is noteworthy that Guillaume Durand in 1284 could find only that flowers and fruiting trees were used in the decoration of churches to represent the fruits of good works; and his *Rationale* is extremely complete in its symbolism (Ed. Barthelemy, Bk. I, cap. xxi, vol. i, p. 51).

did not draw inspiration from their surroundings in their decorative arts but practised a style that is architectonic and formal; but the thirteenth-century cathedrals built in the centres of urban culture in the most civilized part of France had their decoration taken straight from nature. For natural beauty was to some extent shut outside the circuit of the city walls, and, for want of it, its spoils had to be brought into the garden and the market place. Alike in church and castle, flowers and fresh-cut leaves were spread beneath the feet and woven to crown the heads of those who came thither to rejoice. For garlands we now have to go to the distant east, for the *jonchée* of flowers upon the floor we must travel as far as Athens, where still the Church of St. Helena is spread ankle-deep in Persian roses for her festival. But through the sculptors of the end of the twelfth century and their successors, who found a beauty greater than the beauty of tradition in things of their own day, the memory of much that was fleeting still endures.

'Toutes les joies printanières du moyen âge, l'ivresse des Pâques fleuries, les chapeaux de fleurs, les bouquets attachés aux portes, les fraîches jonchées d'herbes dans les chapelles, les fleurs magiques de la Saint-Jean, toute la grâce éphémère des anciens printemps et des anciens étés, revivent à jamais.'[1] A certain austere and majestic consistency of style might be lost; but the loss is forgotten in the curiously touching charm of Gothic naturalism.

Urban culture, however, was not yet general, and correspondingly the naturalistic style of the thirteenth century, like its lyric poetry, was much less widely spread than is generally assumed. The royal domain, sophisticated by courtly influence, was its home and centre; and it was only exceptionally, and in a secondary form, that it spread beyond its borders.[2] About 1170, when stylization was still severe, it was on the capitals of the central door of Sens that bracken was used, on the gallery of the choir of Notre Dame de Paris that plantain leaves were carved, at Nointel and Saint Evrémond de Creil that arum fruit appeared within their hooding sheaths, at Saint Julien le Pauvre that arum and acanthus first came to life, at Saint Laumer de Blois and at Saint Quiriace de Provins that the formal foliage of Romanesque capitals gained the quality and texture of real leaves. At Chartres the column-pedestals of the north and south portals, that have no heavier burden than the statues they bear, have their twisted pillars growing into natural leaves ere the abacus is reached, while the substructure is set with oblong panels of foliage, half natural and half formal in its design.

Naturalistic decoration developed by a steady process of creative evolution. First, more or less naturalistic buds began to thrust forth from the close-set Romanesque foliage[3] (fig. 79); then gradually they blossomed into young and tender leafage, while

---

[1] E. Mâle, *L'Art religieux en France au XIIIe siècle*, p. 72.

[2] Naturalistic work in the Rheims manner appears spasmodically at Saint Pierre, Bordeaux, and even as far south as Caylus, Tarn-et-Garonne. For its use outside France, see p. 46.

[3] Such buds may find their prototypes in the palm-fruit that appears among palmettes of the Moissac type, as, for instance, in Saint Sernin, Toulouse.

63. Façade of Saint Wulfran, Abbeville; begun 1488

64. Staircase to Organ Loft, St. Maclou, Rouen.
By Pierre Gringoire, *c*. 1500

their stems sprang out with the vigour of early growth. At first, as at Semur (fig. 10), the old formal leaf and the freshly budded crocket that ends it were oddly matched; or, as at Saint Père-sous-Vézelay, natural leaves were timidly and awkwardly laid upon the bare architectural form; but with true accomplishment, as at Laon (fig. 80),[1] and on the Portail Saint Jean of Rouen Cathedral, springing life and true decorative modelling were simultaneously achieved.

Original and naturalistic though it might be, such ornament was stylized enough to form part of the architectural whole. On the capitals naturalistic foliage was given a decorative dignity by conventional colouring. The remains of painting on the capitals at Evreux, that date from about 1240, show the type of this colouring clearly enough. The shaft of the column remains its natural stone-colour; of the double wreath of leaves that forms its capital, the upper, of maple, has its leaves painted olive green, edged with black, with the back of the leaf dark purple; the lower, of ivy, has the leaves white, edged and ribbed with black, and again backed in purple; the astragal below is vermilion.[2]

Its forms, too, still respected the architectonic lines that Romanesque decoration had inherited as part of the classical tradition. The west door of Notre Dame, for instance, has a charming *rinceau*-frieze [3] of water-cress (fig. 81), while under the statues of the same porch appears an acanthus-like version of celandine leaves. The crockets are inspired by snapdragon flowers, the copings have their ornament based upon hepatica leaves. Everywhere architectonic principles were strongly felt; at first sight the decoration is accepted as conventional, but a careful analysis reveals its inspiration from the direct observation of nature.[4] Never have natural forms been more beautifully applied to work in metal than at this stage; and never more beautifully than by Frère Hugo d'Oignies (fig. 82). Sometimes more than one plant will be combined in a single spray; just as the philosophers of the time were occupied with the application of true methods of reasoning rather than with the search for detailed truth of fact, so the artists were concerned with the application of natural forms to decorative formulae rather than with botanical observation. 'Natura quidem non perfecit ea quae sunt artis, sed solum quaedum principia praeparat, et exemplar operandi quodam modo artificibus praebet. Ars vero inspicere quidem potest ea quae sunt naturae, et eis uti ad opus proprium perficiendum.' [5]

In the early stages of the style it was the leaves and flowers of the small plants

---

[1] Other excellent examples will be found in the Church at Baulne, Aisne.

[2] V. le Duc, *Dict. rais de l'arch.* ii. 533, s.v. Chapiteau. Cf. a contemporary capital by a Nuremberg sculptor now in the Cathedral Museum at Mainz, that shows hawthorn leaves painted pale green against a darker blue ground. For English examples of such coloured sculpture see W. Lethaby, *Westminster Abbey Re-examined*, 1925, pp. 79, 121, 205 et seqq.

[3] I am unable to find an English equivalent of *rinceau* and am therefore forced to use the French word.

[4] Other examples of this stage of naturalism are to be found at Moret-sur-Loing, Chennevières, Créteil, Bagneux, Jumièges, &c., &c.

[5] Thomas Aquinas, *In politic.* i, lect. i.

of medieval gardens that were used—columbines, primroses, ranunculus, cranes-bill, violet, aconite, pea, rue, broom, saffron, lily of the valley; a child picking flowers in an old-fashioned garden by the Aisne or the Oise might hit upon the whole artistic vocabulary of the sculptors of Laon and Noyon. Besides these a certain number of brook-side plants appear: bracken, plantains, wild arums, cresses, water-lilies, clover, and hart's-tongue ferns—plants that even the hot summers of France cannot wither;[1] but with the progress of the century all the spoils of the gardens of Champagne were represented—of such garden-orchards as Albertus Magnus describes.[2] 'In the middle is a grass-plot of fine grass carefully weeded and trampled under foot, a true carpet of green turf. At one end, on the south side, are trees: pears, apples, pomegranates, laurels, cypress, and others of the kind, with climbing vines, whose foliage to some extent protects the turf and furnishes a cool and delightful shade. Behind the grass-plot are planted aromatic and medicinal herbs in quantity; for example, rue, sage, and basil, and flowers such as the violet, columbine, lily, rose, iris, and others of the sort, which not only delight by their scent but refresh the eye with their beauty.' Familiar with the beauties of such a garden as this, they carved the capitals of Rheims with more than thirty kinds of plants—buttercups, wild and cultivated vines, roses, ivy, arum, rue, wild strawberries, pellitory, wallflowers, thistles, and the rest, beside branches of trees—olive, poplar, maple, elm, laurel, pear, chestnut, and oak.[3]

As the style progressed the architectonic tradition was obscured by a new power of seeing things as they are; a power that made Joinville, after fifty years, remem-ber the blue-patterned lining of the Sultan's tent, and the yellow stripes he saw on the coat of a boy in Syria. This new capacity for visualization, this new enjoyment of detail, is first to be seen in literature in a delight in telling of the hero's clothes—his embroideries and furs and chaplets of flowers—which appears in such early thirteenth-century romances as *Galéran*. Men had reached the point of being sure enough of tradition in thought to reason for themselves; and at the same time they were sure enough of tradition alike in literature and the visual arts to see for themselves.

Gradually a similar tendency becomes increasingly evident in foliage sculpture. The tradition of the Corinthian capital had survived to give a certain architectonic form to the earlier foliage capitals, but with the introduction of the great piers of grouped columns with a single frieze-like capital, the idea of the classic capital

[1] It will be noted that they are not the plants of the strictly traditional medieval herbals. Indeed, as medical books, the herbals were much less widely known than the cognate bestiaries, which were studied as works of edification.

[2] Albertus Magnus, *de vegetabilibus*, cap. 'de plantatione viridiarii' (Venice, 1517, lib. vii, fol. 122).

[3] See Lambin, *La Flore des grandes Cathédrales de la France*, 1897, and *La Flore gothique*, 1893. Burgundy had less taste for gardening, and its sculptors found scope enough for their skill in the deeply cut leaves of wild columbine and chrysanthemum, parsley, and scabious, all broadly treated on a large scale. Aristolochus, violet, sorrel, hepatica, strawberry, plantain, and ivy are also found; but roses, clover, mallow, bryony, celandine, potentilla, and cranesbill, all fairly common in sculpture in Champagne, are absent in Burgundy.

was gradually lost. At first, as in some of the capitals of the nave triforium at Rheims of about 1240 (fig. 83), though the leafage is naturalistic, symmetry is retained. The famous *Chapiteau des Vendanges* of a few years later shows an increasing naturalism; the Corinthian tradition remains only in the projection of the topmost leaves. Then, in some of the capitals of the nave (fig. 84) such reminiscences of symmetry are allowed to govern only the upper part of the capital, an architectural element which has its function to perform, while the lower part is more freely and naturalistically treated; and finally (fig. 86) the whole capital becomes a background for sprays of foliage that seem invisibly bound upon it. Similar stages are evident in the foliage sculpture of the other cathedrals. In the choir of Auxerre, dating from about 1250, the crockets of the capitals are almost lost in naturalistic foliage. At Laon the grouped capitals of the columns of the triforium, though adorned with perfectly natural leaves of fern and parsley, keep the classic shape; but the members that connect them are decorated with crossing leaves which contrast strongly with the forceful growing lines of the foliage of the capitals. On the north door at Noyon, however, such crossing forms are applied indiscriminately to the whole capital (fig. 85). The final stage of Rheims naturalism reaches a yet further development at Nevers: instead of tree-branches, set upright against the columns, that still keep a reminiscence, however faint, of the upward lines of the classic capital, water-lilies are so disposed, and all sense of architectonic form is lost (fig. 87).

A similar eclipse of architectonic form is evident in sculptured friezes and mouldings; the *rinceau* tradition has been forgotten, and instead simple leaves and trails of flowers are carved as if laid upon the stone. Pierre de Montereau decorated the jambs of his south door at Saint Denis with artichoke leaves and trails of roses [1] and blackberries (fig. 88) while rather similar mouldings of ivy and hemlock appear on the cloister door of Saint Quentin, Aisne.

With the next century the form of the capital was itself debased. The supporting column and its load became of the same size and shape, and the structural purpose of the capital was forgotten. The abacus became an applied member; the capital itself decreased in depth, and in the Flamboyant style sometimes disappeared altogether. Its decoration became a mere wreath of flowers and leaves; and naturalism itself was unnaturally intensified. The modelling of the deeply cut leaves of vine, oak, strawberry, or bryony was exaggerated; their forms were twisted and torn by the wind; a dramatic over-emphasis invaded the style (fig. 90). Only irregularly shaped leaves that offered opportunities for such over-emphasis were employed [2]— ivy, vine, hops, black hellebore, pomegranate, strawberry, mallow, fern, oak, maple,

[1] A rather similar rose-moulding appears at Selles-sur-Cher. The type of decoration was later applied to domestic decoration; in 1308 Mahaut, Comtesse d'Artois had a 'chambre aux roses' decorated with painted pewter roses in relief. J. M. Richard, *Mahaut, Comtesse d'Artois*, 1887, p. 334.

[2] e.g. in the Church of Rampillon, in La Chapelle-sous-Crécy, Seine-et-Marne, and in the Cathedral of Séez. A good English example is afforded by the triforium of the nave at St. Albans.

and passion flower—and the simple leaf forms of the early thirteenth century fell into disuse. By the end of the century the seaweed-like foliage of Limoges Cathedral indicates a definite decline, and by the beginning of the fourteenth century similar work in the Cathedral of Carcassonne shows a further decadence in its complete loss of architectonic form.

The spread of naturalistic ornament beyond France was strictly limited to those countries sophisticated enough to find in nature

> la fontaine
> Toujours courante et toujours pleine
> De qui toute beauté dérive.[1]

In England, the national 'stiff leaf' type of foliage arrived at about 1180 had established a strong tradition[2] (fig. 94), but French influences appear along the road to Canterbury. The naturalistic-classical style of Saint Leu d'Esserent appeared at Canterbury itself in 1181, and at Broadwater, Sussex, a little later.[3] The stylized naturalism of Laon is represented at New Shoreham, and the stiffer style of Rheims in the Saint's chapel at Canterbury. A second centre of such influences was provided by Lincoln Cathedral, whence it spread, for instance, to Southwell.

By the end of the thirteenth century the freer naturalistic style was fairly widespread. Some of the best English leaf-carving is that of the shrine of St. Frideswide at Oxford, carved in 1289, with ivy, maple, bryony, greater celandine, oak, sycamore, vine, fig, hawthorn, and columbine. Almost simultaneously a rosemoulding closely resembling that used by Pierre de Montereau at Saint Denis was carved on the church at Fyfield, Essex.

A predilection for leaves with a deeply cut outline was shown in the early fourteenth century in the use of vine, oak, and holly leaves by the East Anglian illuminators, and in such carving as the bryony sprays of the spandrels of the screen at Exeter, dating from 1320. Seaweed-like foliage of the Limoges type appeared in the Lady Chapel at Ely about 1340. In the contemporary foliage carving round the sepulchral niches in Bristol Abbey a further decline is evident. The type had become so conventional that the winged seeds of maple were set with hawthorn leaves, and maple leaves with may blossom; the journeyman must have worked from patterns and mixed them without regard to natural fact.[4] The style in England never, even in the earlier stages, achieved the same purity of line that was attained in France, and in the fourteenth century lost its way in a confusion of detail almost coralline in effect. Such Northern *bizarreries*

---

[1] Jean de Meung, *Roman de la Rose, c.* 1277.
[2] For examples of this and the other English styles, see S. Gardner, *English Gothic Foliage Sculpture.* A type of foliage much like the English stiff leaf occurs occasionally in the English provinces of France, e.g. at Saint Maixent, Deux Sèvres.
[3] Another and less easily explicable appearance of the type occurs at Oakham Castle, Rutland, before 1190.
[4] See Coulton, *Art and the Reformation,* p. 206.

65. Detail of the South Porch, Church of Louviers, Eure, 1496

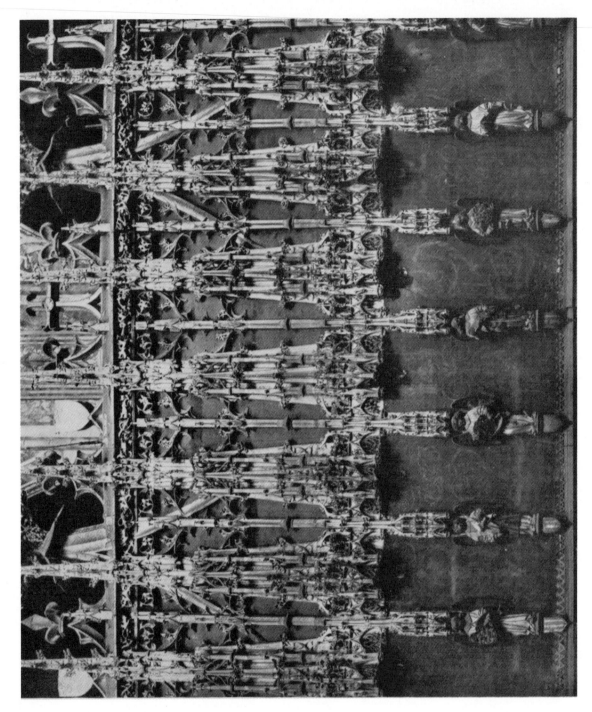

66. Detail of the Stone Canopy-work of the Choir, Cathedral of Albi, 1473–1502

as foliate masks came to add to the confusion (fig. 95).[1]   Indeed, the English craftsmen were far happier in their treatment of foliage as surface decoration in glass or embroidery (fig. 98) than in their plastic treatment of it.

East of France the stylized leafage of Laon appears at Magdeburg; the naturalism of Rheims, on the Cathedrals of Metz, Mainz, and Naumberg; and an example of bryony moulding of the Saint Denis type from a Rhenish church is in the Cathedral Museum at Mainz.   To the south-west the central door of Leon Cathedral, dating from the end of the thirteenth century, shows a frieze in the Rheims manner with sprays of chestnut, wild rose, parsley, oak, and fig; while rather simpler decoration in the same style appears on the Cathedral of Burgos.   But naturalism of this developed sort did not follow the Gothic vault in its dissemination through Christendom; in thirteenth-century Italy it hardly progressed beyond the primitive type represented in the capitals of the Cathedral of Todi (fig. 99), though foliage of the Rheims type unexpectedly appears to adorn the base of the angle-sculptures of the loggia of the Doge's Palace at Venice, carved about 1425.

The naturalistic style of the thirteenth century is, indeed, the mark of the creative centres of Gothic building architecture.   There men had ceased to use the static elements of Romanesque architecture, and by a great and continued effort of constructive thought had created the dynamic Gothic style.   It was more than a tradition of column and lintel and barrel vault which they destroyed; when they had created their shell of ogival vaulting, they were free of the old decorative tradition and could adorn it as they would.   And, since they were acutely conscious of the constructive necessity of the architectural forms they used, since they were more than ever before under the yoke of structural composition, in reaction they did not ornament their building only with severe and architectonic forms that should emphasize that structural quality that was already almost overwhelming in its severity and its greatness, but instead wreathed their capitals with the leaves and branches of natural vegetation, and adorned their walls with the growing plants of the garden and the orchard.

Naturalism in decoration and a pure constructional style in architecture were alike manifestations of the progress of enfranchised thought.   Just as men created a vernacular literature to express their life, so they created a naturalistic style of decoration to adorn it.   Both had their roots in the monastic tradition of classicism, but both passed beyond classicism and monasticism into fresh and true creation with a secular quality of its own.   The art of literature set the deathless tales of antiquity in surroundings at once modern and clearly visualized, and drew from the national epics and hagiography the material of stories with a new flavour of

[1] e.g. at Winchelsea, Ely, Beverley, Oxford, Dorchester (Oxon.), and St. Mary's, Minster, Thanet; and in the English domain in France, at Rouen Cathedral, on key-stones now in the Rouen Museum and on the stalls of Poitiers Cathedral. A whole moulding formed of a series of foliate masks occurs in the cloisters of Leon, and such masks are fairly common in Rhenish Germany, e.g. on the choir-stalls of Cologne Cathedral (c. 1350) and in the Chapel of the Teutonic Knights at Coblentz.

adventure and romance; sculpture gave new life to the calligraphic figures of the Romanesque style, while decoration transmuted the classic acanthus and the stylized foliage of early Romanesque art by seeing them afresh in the light of natural beauty.

The sequence is clear, the development logical; yet it results in an achievement that has an element of surprise as well as of inevitableness. No great art has so paradoxical a beauty as the Gothic cathedral, for nowhere else have pure architecture and pure naturalism been so perfectly allied. All its beauty is of antithesis; the vastness of scale and the smallness of detail; the purity of line and the confused glow of colour; the sense of transcendent greatness and the extraordinary minuteness of symbolism; the inclusion of all that is simple and human in a whole that is religious and divine. Unity was the aim of the Middle Ages; and in their religious art they achieved a synthesis that remains unequalled.

2

In fourteenth-century France that stage of civilization was once more reached in which art is at the service of individual fancy. Creative thought and action were centred not in the service of an idea, but in the service of man. The cathedral is the architectural type of the thirteenth century; the castle of the fourteenth. The castle was no longer a mere refuge from hostile attack, but had become a centre of courtly life, where with greater urbanity there grew up a more sophisticated appreciation of nature. Castles and cities were alike built in precincts of tilled and planted land set in a wide chase where their lords might hunt at will. Consequently forest and orchard scenery became one of the great types of beauty for the laymen of the fourteenth century. In 1323, Jean de Jandun wrote a long Latin eulogy of the forests near Senlis: [1]

'To be at Senlis is to live in the midst of a circle of forests of which the tall and leafy trees do not grow so close one to the other that they leave no passage for him who would walk through them. Yet they are not so widely spaced that they cannot refresh the traveller by their shade as they cut off the burning rays of the sun with their leafy tops. . . . There are not only great trees, but likewise small, and others of middling size. Among the smallest will you see growing, according to the season, sweet-scented abundance of strawberries, hazelnuts, pears, and apples. On the trees of middling height (yet a fairer sight) flocks of nightingales and other birds, both great and small, disport themselves, and tell their joy in the musical notes of their songs, rejoicing all those that hear them. Another kind of being that is the glory of Senlis is this: to be in gardens watered by running streams, in flowery orchards and fertile herb gardens; to be in the wide meadows, where the pleasant green of the springing grass and the fair diversity of brilliant flowers make a smiling picture for the eyes of men; and to be likewise on the banks of the clearest springs which rise on the hillsides, so pure and so clear that, however deep they are, their bed may still be seen.'

Such were the delights of an age in which men were civilized and cultured

[1] Le Roux de Lincy and L. M. Tisserand, *Paris et ses historiens*, Paris, 1867, p. 74.

67. Monument of Margaret of Austria, Church of Brou, *c.* 1510

68. Detail of the Jubé, Église de la Madeleine, Troyes, 1508

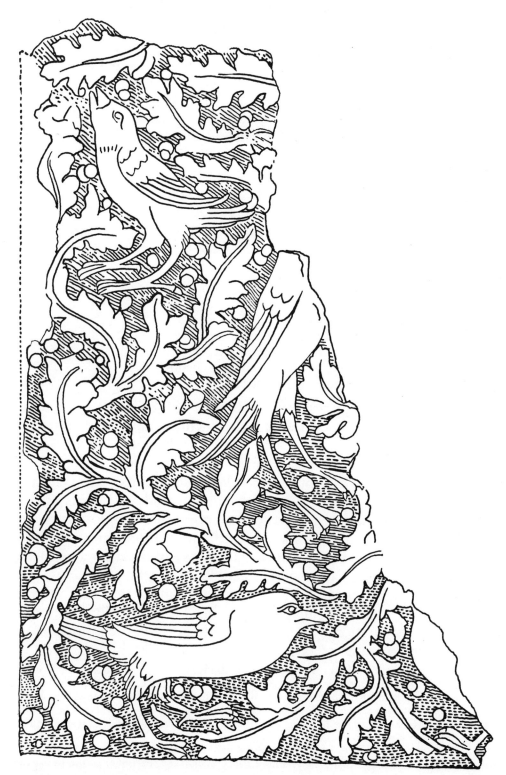

FIG. 69. Gesso decoration from the Coronation Chair of the Kings of England. By the King's painter, Master Walter, 1300–1. Westminster Abbey. From a drawing by Sir T. G. Jackson.

enough to appreciate nature; and the decorators strove to bring the illusion of such delights even within doors.[1] Everywhere naturalistic decoration was practised on a larger scale, and from the leaf and the spray progressed to the tree and the forest. By a *tour de force* of the sculptor's art, such orchard and forest scenes were represented in stone. Three trees, an oak, a pear, and a cherry, exquisitely simplified and adapted to the decorative scheme, appear on the gable of the tomb of Saint Etienne d'Aubazine, set up about 1280; while a capital in the cloister of the Jacobins at Toulouse and another from Saint Urbain de Troyes[2] are adorned with similar trees and birds. An exquisite relief of a youth standing in a tree to pick fruit while two monsters gnaw at its roots decorates a tomb, probably that of Adelaïs of Champagne, in the Church of Saint Jean de Joigny (fig. 100): a decorative theme turned into an allegory of Time that gnaws at the roots of life.[3]

Everywhere art was portraying

> Beaux oisillons en verts buissons . . .
> Et toutes les bestes sauvages
> Qui pasturent par ces bocages;
> Toutes herbes, toutes florettes
> Que valetons et pucellettes
> Vont en printemps en bois cueillir
> Que fleurir voient et feuillir . . .

An early fourteenth-century orphrey of English embroidery[4] has a naturalistic tree of Jesse, with birds nesting in the branches, while a delightful pattern of birds alighting on branches of oak adorns the gesso work of the coronation chair at Westminster, made by the King's painter in 1300–1 (fig. 69).

Such decoration, too, was obviously suitable for secular use; the 1317 inventory of the King of France[5] includes a surcoat embroidered with trees and finches. So, just as the plants of the cloister garden had crept into religious ornament, the plants of the forests and the thickets where the Court hunted came to found a new style of civil decoration. It is the plants that appear in donations of the right of wood-gathering:[6] 'l'espine, l'aubespin, le genest, le pourfust, le garais, la bruère, la fogière, le genievre, la bourdeine, le houx et le frasgun,' that adorn the enamels of the time. Forest trees—oak, maple, lime, blackthorn, holly, ash, beech, and pine—all came into decoration;[7] as did knopped and pollarded branches, faggots of lesser boughs and wreaths of knopped twigs. Great branching boughs adorn

[1] It must be remembered that the illuminators had already founded a tradition of how trees should be represented. The manuscript of the Apocalypse, written for Edward I as Prince, or for his wife, between 1254 and 1272 (Bodleian MS. Douce 180), shows in its miniatures charming verdure grounds and trees that are absolutely conventional, but yet recognizable as oak, chestnut, and vine.   [2] Now in the Louvre.

[3] The theme is derived from *Barlaam & Josaphat*. See Mlle. Pillion in *Revue de l'art ancien et moderne*, 1910, p. 321.

[4] *Catalogue of the Spitzer Collection*, Etoffes, Plate III.

[5] Bouquet, *Recueil des historiens des Gaules et de la France*, xxii. 771.

[6] See, for example, the donation made by Jeanne d'Alençon, in 1288, of rights in the forest of Ruissy Laborde, *Les Ducs de Bourgogne*, iii. 2.

[7] e.g. *Inventaire de Louis d'Anjou, 1379–80*, ed. Moranvillé, p. lvii.

72. Processional cross of the Grands-Carmes of Paris, *c.* 1500

71. Silver gilt pax, by Hans Tuog of Nuremberg, 1453

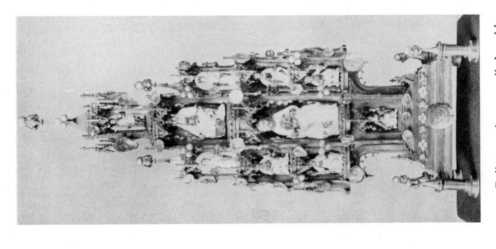

70. Reliquary in enamelled gold. Franco-Flemish, *c.*1400. From the Chapel of the Order of the Holy Ghost

73. Reliquary of silver gilt by Pietro da Parma and
Bartolommeo da Bologna, *c.* 1435. Treasury of the
Basilica of St. Antony, Padua

the staircase of Jean sans Peur in the Hôtel de Bourgogne at Paris (fig. 101).
Several silver cups survive that are made 'fagot-fashion';[1] and the chapel at
Amboise, dedicated to the huntsman, St. Hubert, has the colonnettes of its façade
formed as trees with spreading roots and lopped branches.[2] A whole architecture
of such branches adorns a silver reliquary in the Church of San Giovanni in Monte
at Bologna (fig. 102)[3] and they form a common canopy to German sculptures of the
late fifteenth century.[4] Lesser branches of holly,[5] oak, maple,[6] and other forest
trees occur many times among the decorative motives recorded in the inventories;
surviving instances of their use in metal-work are the cup of Diethers I, Archbishop of Mainz from 1434 to 1453, which is formed of two red jasper bowls
mounted in silver gilt rims splendidly decorated with knopped branches incised
and in relief,[7] and the badges of the minstrels of the Ghent Corporation, that have
similar rims of cut logs.[8] The illuminators occasionally made use of the style; a
Milanese Book of Hours, written for the use of a member of the Humiliate Order,[9]
has its borders each formed of a bare and twisted tree that has known the woods-
man's axe. A border of lopped branches, combined with banderoles of mottoes,
not uncommonly frames heraldic tapestries of the early sixteenth century,[10] and
such a frieze appears in sculpture on Limoges Cathedral. The adoption of 'bastons
noylleux' as a badge by the house of Burgundy[11] served to perpetuate the style.

Forest and orchard in their summer glories provided even more admirable subjects for the craftsman. Louis of Anjou, in 1379–80, had a covered cup of gold of
which the foot was finely enamelled 'd'un terraige ou pré vert, de où naissent petis
arbrisseaux de diverses manieres, et connins de plusieurs couleurs et contenances
parmi; et d'iceulx partent plus grans arbres, tenans par le lonc l'esmail du gobelet,

---

[1] A fine example of 1493 belongs to New College, Oxford. Cf. Palgrave, *Kalendars and Inventories of Henry VIII*, ii. 289.

[2] The architectural use of lopped tree forms was fairly common in Spain and Portugal at the end of the fifteenth century; the door of San Gregorio at Valladolid has every pillar so shaped, while the door of the sacristy at Alcobaça in Portugal is framed by two sculptured trees with lopped branches. They outline a horse-shoe arch in the convent of the Canons Regular of Évora, *c.* 1491, and crown an arch of twisted columns in the Church of the Carmo in the same city.

[3] A design in similar style was rather later engraved by the German master WA.

[4] e.g. cloister sculptures of the Resurrection and the Tree of Jesse of 1488 now in the Cathedral of Worms. An altar-piece of carved wood dating from 1518 in the Church of St. Cornelius at Babenhausen, nr. Darm-stadt, has a most elaborate canopy all of naturalistic boughs; columns, capitals, tracery, and pinnacle forms are all retained, but are all transformed into branches. An exceptional English use is the stem of the font of All Saints', Norwich. [5] Laborde, *Les Ducs de Bourgogne*, ii. 36.

[6] Moranvillé, *op. cit.*, p. 362. [7] Now in the Gräfliche Gesamthaus, Erbach.

[8] By Corneille de Bonde; now in the Musée Archéologique of Ghent.

[9] Burlington Fine Arts Club Exhibition, 1908, No. 261.

[10] e.g. Bodley Gaignières 18361, p. 14. Tapestry made for Françoise de Luxembourg, Comtesse d'Egmont, between 1528 and 1537.

[11] Cf. Douët d'Arcq. *Nouveau recueil des comptes de l'argenterie des rois de France*, p. 193. 1387: 'Pour la broderie . . . sus deux longues houppelandes de satin vermeil . . . en chascune desquelles a batons doubles appellés *copeis*, faiz au travers d'icelles houppelandes tout du lonc et au travers des manches, entre lesquels bastons sont faictes de broderies, ceintures et lettres qui dient ESPERANCE, et plumes aux bouz avecques annelès . . . et fleurettes de mais semés parmy.'

entre lesquels a dains de diverses contenances, gisans, paissans, estans et d'autres
manieres, fais sur le vif.'[1] New College, Oxford, still possesses a coco-nut cup of
the fourteenth century, with its stem formed as the trunk of a tree, from which
spring branches alternately lopped and leafy to hold the nut. The tree rises from
a foot chiselled to represent a meadow[2] surrounded by a palisade (fig. 103). In
1416, the Duc de Berry had a set of hangings for a room, the twelve woollen hangings for the walls and the red satin hangings of the bed embroidered with tall
pine trees with bears and lions beneath on a groundwork of pine branches and
cones,[3] and another set of bed-hangings and wall-hangings embroidered with the
figure of a man against a background of orange trees, oaks, pines, and chestnuts,
with three herons in the branches.[4]

The theme of knights and ladies going to seek their pleasure in the woods and
valleys became as familiar in the decoration of the late fourteenth century as in its
verse. In 1422 the English sold a set of red hangings belonging to Charles VI
'semez de plusieurs rainceaulx, ouvrez d'or et de soye, et y a quatre personnages,
c'est assavoir: ung chevalier et une dame à pié qui s'en vont au boys jouer, et deux
varlez, dont l'un tient les cheveaulx, et y a une volerie d'oyseaulx de rivière.'[5]
Just such a scene appears on a cup, which, in the seventeenth century, belonged to
M. de Caumartin, of which a drawing has been preserved in the Gaignières
Collection at Oxford[6] (fig. 105). Little was needed to change such a forest scene
into a hunting scene. The forest, indeed, if it formed a necessary part of the
courtly life of the castle, did so in virtue of the sport it provided. Hunting was
one of the three knightly interests: 'tout mon temps', says Gaston Phoebus, 'me
suis délité par espécial en trois choses: l'une est, en armes; l'autre est, en amours;
et l'autre si est en chasse'. Women hunted as well as men; and a charming fourteenth-century aquamanile[7] shows a lady riding to the chase, wearing a little round

[1] H. de Moranvillé, *Inventaire de Louis d'Anjou*, p. 85. He also owned a golden hanap 'tout ciselé a menus
grains et embouti à VI arbres dont les trois sont de vignete et les autres trois à feuilles de trèfles' (*ibid.*, p. 75),
while Philippe le Bon in 1420 had an egg-cup of gold 'ouvré à arbreceaulx et feuillages de fresiers'. L. de
Laborde, *Les Ducs de Bourgogne*, ii. 257.
[2] Holes in this probably once held the sockets of figures of rabbits or sheep.
[3] Guiffrey, *Les Inventaires de Jean, duc de Berry*, ii. 214.
[4] *Ibid.* ii. 215. Chaucer withers and devastates such decoration to be a setting, in his *Knight's Tale*, for his
allegory of the ills wrought under Mars: (l. 1975 et seqq)
>First on the wal was peynted a foreste,
>In which ther dwelleth neither man ne beste,
>With knotty knarry bareyn treës olde
>Of stubbes sharpe and hidous to biholde;
>In which ther ran a rumbel and a swough,
>As though a storm sholde bresten every bough.
[5] Bibliothèque de l'École des Chartes, vol. 48, 1887, p. 106.
[6] Bodleian MS. 1861, p. 63. Cf. Philippe le Bon's inventory of 1420: a set of eleven tapestries 'de volerie de
plouviers et perdrix, esquels sont les personnages de feu Monseigneur le duc Jean et Madame la Duchesse sa
femme, tant à pié comme à cheval.' Laborde, *Les Ducs de Bourgogne*, ii. 267.
[7] Lent by Madame Chabrières-Arlès to an Exhibition in Paris in 1913. S. de Ricci, *Exposition d'objets
d'art ... à l'ancien Hôtel de Sagan, mai-juin* 1913, No. XIII.

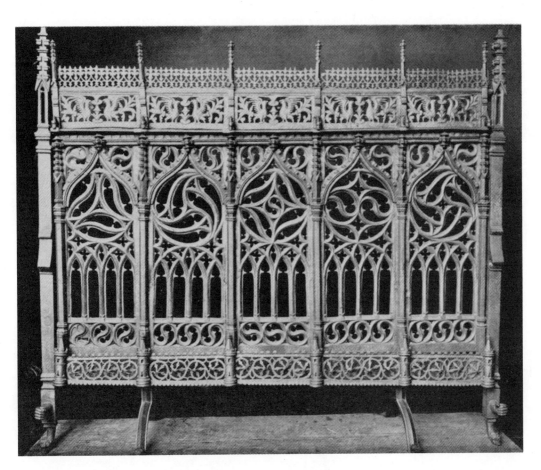

74. Wrought iron grille. Spanish, *c.* 1520

75. Carved oak chest. French, *c.* 1480

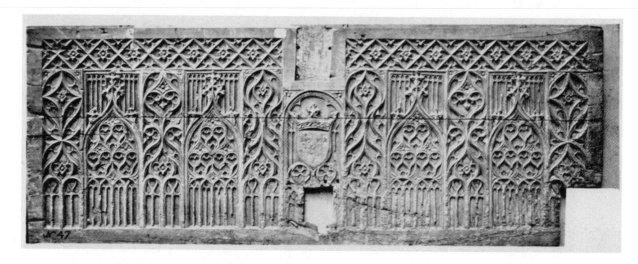

76. Carved oak chest. French, *c.* 1490

77. Carved oak chest. French, *c.* 1510

78. Detail of the retable of the Capilla Mayor, Seville Cathedral, by the Fleming Dancart.
Begun in 1482

80. Capital of a column of the Triforium, Cathedral of Laon, *c.* 1230

79. Capital from the Church of Saint Pierre, Lisieux, *c.* 1200

riding hat, and with hawk on wrist. Charles V had two tapestries with ladies hunting and hawking.[1] The Duc de Berry, besides the forest hangings already mentioned, had another set of white taffetas that differs only by the addition of huntsmen and hounds, and Philippe le Bon had a set of hangings of crimson silk worked with a queen and her ladies carrying sparrow-hawks, against a forest background.[2] The 'Chevauchée' of knights and ladies appears on many fourteenth-century ivory mirror cases; the lover and his lady ride together through the forest, sometimes bearing falcons and sometimes followed by hounds.[3] Similar scenes adorn many fourteenth-century Italian marriage coffers, while the famous cup at King's Lynn, dating from the time of Edward III, has each of the five panels of its bowl enamelled with the figures of a man and a woman hunting, with dogs chasing hares on the five corresponding panels of the foot.[4] The element of love and romance was not lacking, and the hunting tower in the wood was often the favourite sojourn of king or courtier[5] and became in a sense the symbol of his pleasures; when Isabeau de Bavière entered Paris in 1389 she was greeted not only with pageants of angels and the Trinity but also with the representation of a tower set in a wood full of hares, rabbits, and birds. The tapestries of Charles V's boat in 1369 were worked with a tower, with does and fawns about it, and in 1380 Charles V had a golden ewer and goblet enamelled with his 'Tour du Boys' at Vincennes[6] with does on the knop.

There was already a tradition of the artistic representation of the chase. Hunting scenes had appeared in Romanesque sculpture, both to illustrate the legend of St. Eustace, as on a capital at Vézelay, and as pure decoration, as on the Cathedral of Angoulême. In the thirteenth century the chase was celebrated alike in verse[7] and in decoration. The fragments of the Jubé of Chartres show, on one of the spandrels, a charming scene of a rider blowing his horn in a wind-swept forest, and beasts innumerable flying before him. The St. Eustace window at Chartres has delightful scenes of the chase; and about 1226 Frère Hugo d'Oignies used such scenes to adorn a binding of the Gospels.[8] Models for every art were provided by the illuminations of learned treatises on the sport;[9] for instance accurate and naturalistic scenes of birds and falconers appear in the Vatican manuscript,[10] written

[1] J. Guiffrey, *La Tapisserie*, p. 50.   [2] Laborde, *Les Ducs de Bourgogne*, ii. 267.
[3] See R. Koechlin, *Les Ivoires gothiques français*, i. 383.
[4] See Jewitt and Hope, *Corporation Plate*, ii. 201; Jackson, *English Plate*, i. 112.
[5] In 1414 the Duke of Burgundy had the idea of passing part of the summer in tents in the middle of a forest, that he might hunt the more easily (Havard, *Dictionnaire de l'ameublement*, s.v. Chambre); and some thirty years later game began definitely to be preserved in parks. See Antoine Astesan's description of the Bois de Vincennes in 1451, Leroux de Lincy and Tisserand, *Paris et ses historiens*, p. 547.
[6] Laborde, *Glossaire des émaux*, 332, s.v. gobelet.
[7] *La Chasse au Cerf*. Jusserand, *Les Sports dans l'ancienne France*, p. 199.
[8] Now belonging to the Sœurs de Notre Dame de Namur. A man hawking is a frequent subject on thirteenth-century Limoges gemellions.
[9] For a bibliography of these see H. Werk, *Altfranzösische Jagdlehrbücher*, Halle, 1889.
[10] Cod. pal. lat. 1071.

in Sicily or South Italy about 1260, of Frederick II's *De arte venandi cum avibus*; while the fine illuminated manuscripts of the *Livre de Chasse* of Gaston Phoebus, Comte de Foix, dating from the early fifteenth century,[1] show delightful hunting scenes, in which stags and rabbits play a subsidiary part, artistically speaking, in relation to the background of forest, thicket, and field. The miniatures are shaped, designed, and framed like tapestries, and could serve as cartoons for the weaver; there can be little doubt that there is a close relation between them and wall hangings such as those of the Duc de Berry. Another and rather later type of hunting book, such as *The boke of hunting that is cleped maystere of game*,[2] provided little pictures of huntable beasts apart from their natural background.

The illuminators were quick to transfer such scenes from technical treatises to other manuscripts. A copy of the Apocalypse[3] written in France between 1254 and 1272 for Edward I as Prince, or for his wife Eleanor, has on the front page a spirited scene of dogs chasing a rabbit; the Peterborough Psalter has a lively stag-hunt (fig. 106) and a rabbit hunt, and among the multitudinous grotesques of the Ormesby and Gorleston Psalters are many of dogs chasing rabbits. Similar grotesques appear on Spanish manuscripts of the late thirteenth century.[4]

Hunting scenes continued to adorn French manuscripts all through the fourteenth and fifteenth centuries. In the first half of the fourteenth century they were but one of the multitudinous grotesques that came in from Flanders, but of all these grotesques they were those that had the strongest appeal to French taste. A French Book of Hours, for instance, written in the first half of the fifteenth century,[5] has hunting scenes of several kinds : some naturalistic, some mythological and some frankly grotesque. Gradually the naturalistic type came to predominate, as in the manuscript of Bressuire's translation of the Decades of Livy, written for the Library of Charles V. By the middle of the fifteenth century, as in a manuscript of *Le Mireur du Monde* written for Louis d'Estouteville about 1460,[6] scenes of coursing and stag hunting have almost ousted other marginal decorations; all the stages of stag hunting are portrayed—the picnic under the trees before starting, the finding of the stag, the hunt (on one page the hounds hunt him from the bottom of the page all up the margin to the top), the stag taking to the water, the kill, and the curée.

Such ornament early spread from manuscript illuminations into other fields of decoration. All the types of the illuminations were represented; the naturalistic type, the type combined with grotesques, and the type that showed hunting dogs and beasts alone. Clémence of Hungary in 1328 had eight tapestries 'à ymages et

---

[1] Notably Bibl. Nat. MS. français, 616. Such influence is evident in certain carvings of the period, e.g. on a panel from an oak coffer said to have come from Rufford Abbey (V. and A. M. 82, 1893) with scenes from the legend of St. George and the Dragon against a pictorial forest background.

[2] e.g. Bodleian MS. Douce 335, English, first half of fifteenth century.

[3] Bodleian MS. Douce 180.   [4] e.g. Mr. Dyson Perrins's *Fueros de Aragon*.

[5] Bodleian MS. Douce 135.   [6] Bodleian MS. Douce 336.

81. Frieze from the West Door, Notre Dame de Paris, *c.* 1220

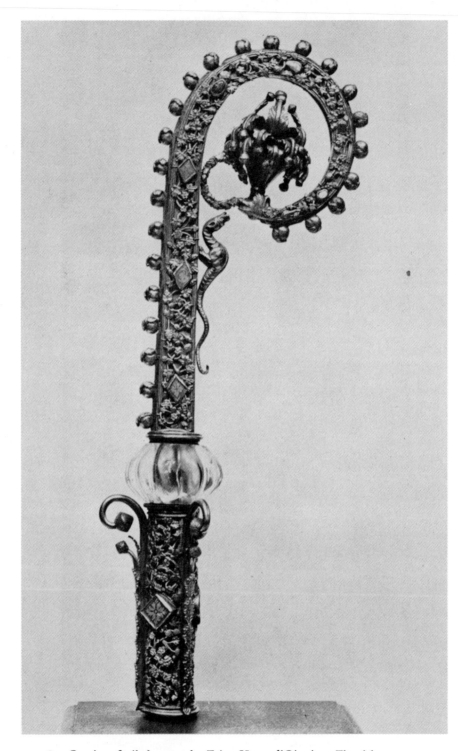

82. Crozier of gilt bronze, by Frère Hugo d'Oignies. Flemish, c. 1220

à arbres, à la devise d'une chasse',[1] and Charles V had a litter painted with oak trees and does 'faits d'apres le vif', on a ground of leaves and green bracken, with hounds hunting hinds on the ends,[2] and had his hall in the Louvre painted in 1366 with birds and beasts 'qui se jouaient dans de grandes campagnes et accompagnées de figures de cerfs.'[3]   A room in the Palace of the Popes at Avignon (fig. 107) has splendidly decorative paintings of hunting, hawking, fowling, and fishing dating from the middle of the fourteenth century.[4]   Scenes of hunting, like woodland scenes, were also used to adorn the plate which represented so large a part of the huntsmen's treasures: Louis of Anjou, in 1379–80, had a cup of silver gilt, 'esmaillié d'asur a gens qui chacent a diverses bestes, et y a arbrisseaus vers',[5] and the Duke of Guienne a crystal flask with hounds and stags.[6]   On some plate recorded in Louis of Anjou's inventory of 1379–80 hunting scenes took their place beside fantastic and grotesque animal scenes.[7]   Occasionally, too, hounds and their prey were used separately in decoration; Louis of Anjou likewise had gold and silver vessels either shaped as or decorated with bears, stags, rabbits, hares, long-eared stag-hounds, spaniels, and white, yellow, and red dogs.[8]

With the progress of the fifteenth century the various types of hunting were more definitely characterized in art;[9] a magnificent set of Flemish tapestries of about 1460 from Hardwick Hall[10] represents scenes of bear, boar, otter and stag hunting, and of hawking. Wolsey's inventories include tapestries of hawking and hunting, of a dog carrying a bolt out of the water, of a wild boar with two arrows

---

[1] Michel, *Histoire de l'art*, iii. 348.

[2] *Ibid.*, iii. 113.

[3] Sauval, *Histoire et antiquités de la ville de Paris*, quoted Michel, *op. cit.* iii. 113.

[4] Such work is important in the general history of art in that it provided the inspiration for the wooded backgrounds of later painters, notably of the Danubian school. See, for instance, the landscape with St. George and the Dragon in the Pinakothek at Munich, by Albrecht Altdorfer, d. 1538.

[5] Moranvillé, *op. cit.*, p. 310.

[6] Pannier, 'Les joyaux du Duc de Guyenne', in *Revue archéologique*, 1873, xxvi. 316. Such decoration continued in use until the end of the fifteenth century. Enamels of dogs and rabbits decorate a fine fifteenth-century Italian monstrance in the V. and A. M. (287, 1864), and hounds, hares, and stags appear among conventional foliage on Bishop Foxe's silver-gilt salt cover made between 1487 and 1492 and now at Corpus Christi College, Oxford.   Hunting scenes continued in fashion for a long time; as late as 1600 the Galerie des Chevreuils at Fontainebleau was painted with the King and his Court going to the Chase.

[7] 'XI hennaps d'une façon, dorez et sizelez dedenz à feuillages et a laceis, et a chascun un grant esmail ou fons, et ou premier esmail a une fontaine ou boivent bestes et oisiaux. Et ou secont esmail a une biche en couchant, et devant elle a un levrier en séant qui a la crouppe d'azur. Ou tiers esmail a un renart et un singe qui se sient et baillent la foy l'une à l'autre. Ou quart email a II arbres et connilz par manière d'une garenne. Ou quinte esmail a un ours qui prant une lièvre par les oreilles. Ou sisieme esmail a un lou qui prant un porc épi. Ou VIIe esmail a un levrier qui queurt après un lièvre et desuz le lévrier a un petit heriçon. Ou huitieme esmail a un levrier qui tient un lièvre vert, et derrière le leuvrier à un dain. Ou neuvieme esmail a un demi lyon saillant contre un demi serf, et au dessouz a connilz par manière de garenne. Ou dizieme esmail a un arbre lacié et III connilz au dessouz par manière de garenne. Et en l'onzième esmail a un levrier qui chasse au connilz' (Laborde, *Glossaire des émaux*, ii. 88).

[8] Moranvillé, *op. cit.*, p. liv.

[9] A bear hunt is included among Philippe le Bon's tapestries in 1428; Pinchart, *Histoire de la tapisserie dans les Flandres*, p. 25.

[10] At present lent by the Duke of Devonshire to the V. and A. M.

in him, and of a dog and a hawk taking a heron;[1] while whole sets were woven at
Florence with scenes of hunting seventeen different kinds of beasts.[2]

3

Meanwhile a time had come when to a generation of courtiers hunting itself had
begun to seem sophisticated, and as they rode to the chase they looked with
romantic envy at the shepherds and woodcutters of the meadows and the woodlands. Eustache Deschamps wrote a Chanson Royal of the joys of a woodman's
life:

> Dieux nous a bien en ce monde ordonné
> Car l'air des champs nous est habandonné;
> A bois couper quant je vueil m'esvertue;
> De mes bras vif; je ne robe ne tue . . .
> Par moy à Dieu doit grace estre rendue;
> J'ay Franc Vouloir, le seigneur de ce monde.[3]

Those who were cut off from the pleasures of manual work had figures of workmen to adorn the accessories of a more sophisticated life. In 1380 the Duke of
Anjou had a silver-gilt flask enamelled with men 'qui font pluseurs contenances,
comme couper arbres et autres besoignes',[4] while Philippe le Bon in 1420[5] had a
set of hangings woven with peasants and woodcutters. Life, indeed, was beginning
to be urban enough for men to be sensitive to pastoral charm. Already Philippe
de Vitri, the friend of Petrarch, was singing the praises of country life in his *Dit
de Franc Gonthier*; true delight lay

> Soubz feuille vert, sur herbe delitable,
> Lez ru bruiant et prez clere fontaine,

far from the carved colonnades and painted halls of places. *Bergeries* gradually
crept from literature into the visual arts. Rural scenes of French peasant life adorn
not only illuminated calendars,[6] but such fourteenth-century manuscripts as the
Lyons copy of Virgil's eclogues. The manuscript of Guillaume de Machaut's
poems, illuminated by the 'Maître aux Boqueteaux',[7] has delightful village and
country backgrounds to its miniatures of the author's allegory; Amour, for

---

[1] Brewer, *Letters and Papers of Henry VIII*, iv, pt. 3, 3045.

[2] 1567: doe, chamois, ibex, boar, lion; 1568: stag, bear; 1574: wolf; 1575: hare, rabbit; 1577: badger, otter,
wild-cat; 1578: unicorn, wild goose, swan, wild duck. Müntz, *Histoire de la tapisserie en Italie*, p. 66. Cf. the
sixteenth-century north Italian chimney-piece ascribed to Tullio Lombardi with a frieze of hunts of boar,
lion, wild goat, bear, stag and bull. (V. and A. M. 655, 1865).

[3] *Œuvres*, ed. Marquis de Queux de Saint-Hilaire and G. Raymond, iii, no. cccxv.

[4] Moranvillé, *op. cit.*, p. 451.

[5] Laborde, *Les Ducs de Bourgogne*, ii. 267. The then Duke had another set in 1461 (Guiffrey, *La Tapisserie*,
p. 88) and in 1466 gave another to his niece. A good fifteenth-century tapestry of this type is now in the Musée
des Arts décoratifs at Paris.

[6] And such scenes as the Angel appearing to the Shepherds. This is represented in a remarkably naturalistic setting as early as the Jubé of Chartres.

[7] Bib. Nat. français, 1584.

83. Capital from the Triforium of the Nave, Cathedral of Rheims, *c.* 1240

84. Capital of a pier in the Nave, Cathedral of Rheims, *c.* 1250

85. Grouped capitals of the North Door, Cathedral of Noyon, *c.* 1230

instance, presents Doux Penser, Plaisance, and Espérance to the author against a background of a cottage, mill, oven, village cross, duck pond and wood, all drawn naturalistically, but in strictly decorative perspective. Soon the pastoral appears in decoration. As early as 1352 the *Comptes royaux* mention a red velvet cap embroidered with oaks, with children knocking down pearl acorns for the pigs that feed beneath.[1] Louis d'Anjou, in 1379–80, has a crystal goblet set on a foot of silver gilt 'esmaillié de vert à flouretes jaunes, et semé de brebis de pluseurs couleurs; et y a VI brebis paissans sur leurs piés et trois bergieres jouans de la cornemuse, emmantelées de petis manteaus à fretes d'or et d'asur semées de serpentelles; et sont enchapelées de trois chapeaux differens en façon et chascune tient son chien à une corde de fil d'argent . . .'[2] He has also a table fountain standing on an enamelled base, formed as a green meadow, with rabbits going in and out of their holes, while two shepherds play on the flute and the horn, and a woman spins, as they guard their little flock of nine sheep and three dogs.[3] Seven years later, the Duke of Burgundy has six green tapestry cushions with white sheep under a golden hawthorn, for the Duchess's chariot.[4] Such decoration was even applied to clothes; in 1389, the Duke of Burgundy wore, for the Queen's state entry into Paris, a pourpoint of green velvet, embroidered with an oak-tree before and behind, and on the sleeves two hawthorns of gold and pearls, with a flock of sheep embroidered in pearls and gold beneath the trees.[5] It was chiefly in tapestry and embroidery that such *bergeries* were represented, whether as illustrations of the rustic loves of Gombaut and Macée[6] or as *genre* scenes.[7] *Bergeries* passed even into sculpture:[8] an amusing pattern of sheep in quatrefoils with a shepherd and shepherdess in the middle to support the arms of the province appears on a mantelpiece of the old Town Hall of Bourges (fig. 108).

[1] Laborde, *Glossaire des émaux*, ii. 206, s.v. Chapel.

[2] Moranvillé, *op. cit.*, p. 35.

[3] *Ibid.*, p. 222. Two ewers with figures of shepherds are recorded in the 1408 inventory of Valentine de Milan. F. M. Graves, *Deux inventaires de la maison d'Orléans*, p. 134.

[4] Guiffrey, *Histoire de la tapisserie en France*, p. 20.

[5] L. Farcy, *La Broderie*, p. 94.

[6] See Guiffrey, *Histoire de la tapisserie*, p. 68.

[7] In 1393, Jean Cosset wove a tapestry of shepherds (Guiffrey, *op. cit.*, p. 42); in 1403, Louis d'Orléans had a set of green hangings with shepherds and shepherdesses eating nuts and cherries (Laborde, *Les Ducs de Bourgogne*, iii. 206); in 1404, Philippe le Hardi had 'un tapis de la danse des Bergers' (Guiffrey, *La Tapisserie*, p. 53); in 1420, the Duke of Burgundy bought a set of red velvet hangings with shepherds and shepherdesses (Havard, *Dictionnaire de l'ameublement*, s.v. Broderie); and in 1432, the Prioress of the Hotel Dieu had a similar set (*ibid.*, s.v. Bergerie). Margaret of Flanders had green tapestries with a shepherd and a shepherdess weaving garlands beside their flock (Dehaisnes, *Histoire de l'art dans la Flandre*, p. 343). The references to plate similarly decorated are less frequent: in 1416 the Duke of Guienne had a salt-cellar with a shepherdess in a meadow (*Rev. Arch.* 1873, xxvi. 310), and the 1561–2 inventory of the Château de Pau (ed. Molinier, pp. 73 and 76) includes three enamelled figures of shepherdesses sitting or standing in meadows with their sheep, that probably date from the fifteenth century. The influence of *bergeries* may have had a certain influence on the popularity for tapestry of the scene of the Angel appearing to the Shepherds.

[8] See also J. Schlosser, 'Armeleutekunst alter Zeit', in *Jahrbuch für Kunstsammler*, i, 1921, p. 47.

Soon, too, it was not enough to watch the shepherd and envy his pleasures; but princes had to play at being shepherds that they might share the pastoral joys.

> J'ay un roy de Cecile
> Veu devenir bergier,
> Et sa femme gentille
> De ce propre mestier
> Portant la pannetière
> La houlette et chapeau,
> Logeant sur la bruyère
> Auprès de leur troupeau.

As early as 1404, Philippe le Hardi had 'un grand tappis de haute lice, à moutons, où sont pourtraiz Madame d'Artois et Monseigneur de Flandre.'[1] A tapestry of about 1500 in the Victoria and Albert Museum shows a lady in a court dress of gold brocade with tasselled sleeves, bearing a crook and wearing a great red garden hat, seated among shepherds and woodcutters, and graciously pretending to be of their band. Such pastoral impulses were gradually transmuted into other forms by the revival of the classical pastoral inaugurated by Politian's *Orfeo* in 1471. Louise de Savoie ordered a set of ninety-two scenes to be embroidered, 'de bergerye, prinses sur les buquoliques de Virgille.'[2]

4

The medieval ideal of beauty and safety was always something shut off; at first the cloister, shut off from the world; then the castle and the walled town, shut off from the menace of attack and the fear of enemies; and then, in the fifteenth century, the almost continuous wars and civil strife, the treachery and intrigue, the dangers and disillusionment of the outside world gave a new charm to the enclosed garden, shut off alike from strife, meanness, and danger. It is after the horrors of Agincourt that Alain Chartier finds a garden in spring more lovely than ever before.

Just as, in the early years of the Middle Ages, the cloister had been the home of beauty, peace, fine thinking, and fine feeling, so now, as the epoch drew to its close, the walled garden became the centre of all that was fair and peaceful in love, in life, and in religion. France, in the fourteenth century, had recreated the art of living nobly and gracefully, in luxury beautiful enough for restraint, with manners refined enough for freedom. *Courtoisie* may seem to a modern mind artificial and insincere; but in its own day it had its roots in truth and represented the flower of a great civilization. And the home of *courtoisie* was the castle garden, with its wattled fences to keep out the wind, its flowery banks to rest upon, its

---

[1] Guiffrey, *La Tapisserie*, p. 53.   [2] Havard, *Dictionnaire de l'ameublement*, s.v. Broderie.

86. Capital of a pier in the Nave, Cathedral of Rheims, *c.* 1250

87. Water-lily capital of a pier in the Nave, Cathedral of Nevers, *c.* 1260

88. Mouldings from the South Door of the Abbey of
Saint Denis. By Pierre de Montereau, *c.* 1235

89. Panel of sculptured stone from an interior wall, Cathedral of Rheims, *c.* 1280

rose-trellises for the eyes' delight, and its plots of sweet herbs for a pleasant smell.

> En mai fut fete, un matinet
> En un verger flori, verdet,
> Au point du jour,
> On chantoient cil oiselet
> Par grand baudor,
> Et j'alai fere un chapelet
> En la verdor.[1]

The enclosed garden was the scene of romance and of allegory; and it became the one fitting shrine in which to represent Our Lady. Van Eyck set his *Adoration of the Lamb* in a 'flowery mead', and even the stable of Bethlehem was graced with growing flowers.[2]

In the middle of the century, René of Anjou was content to leave his more sumptuous palaces to live in the pavilion surrounded by gardens, from which he could date his letters 'en nostre jardin d'Aix'. Even within the palace walls, the custom of the *jonchée* brought the garden within doors: Froissart[3] describes the Count of Foix entering his room and finding it 'toute jonchée de verdure fraîche et nouvelle, et les parois d'environ toutes couvertes de verds rameaux pour y faire plus frais et plus odorant.'[4] Such adornments were fleeting and seasonal, and were soon imitated in more permanent form. At the Tournai fêtes in 1455, the hall was decorated with 'ung praiel portatif, duquel les verdures, arbrisseaulx et fleurs estoient de chire, jentement et ingénieusement ouvrées.'[5] The gallery of the Queen's apartments in the Hotel St. Pol was, about 1360, painted with a great wood of trees and shrubs—apples, pears, cherries, plums, and other orchard trees, covered with fruit, rising from a garden gay with lilies, roses, and other flowers, with children picking the flowers and eating the fruit. The painted trees soared up into the vaulting, which was blue and white to imitate the sky.[6] Such scenes, on a smaller scale, were later reproduced in tapestry (fig. 109); hangings with children picking flowers or eating cherries are to be found in many fifteenth-century inventories,[7] and appear under the name of 'Infantilages' in the inventories of Wolsey.[8]

[1] J. Bedier, *Les Chansons de Colin Muset*, 1912, p. 14.

[2] e.g. in Hugo van der Goes, *Adoration of the Shepherds* of 1465 in the Uffizi, which has pots with iris, tiger lily, and columbine in the foreground. [3] *Chroniques*, t. xii, p. 369.

[4] The late M. Enlart drew my attention to items in the accounts of the Collegiate Church of Notre Dame de Saint Omer for 1395, 1456, 1462, 1482, and 1483, which show that at Whitsuntide the church was adorned with branches of trees, painted clouds were hung from the roof, and grass was spread about the choir. L. Deschamps de Pas, *Les cérémonies religieuses dans la Collégiale de Saint-Omer au XIIIe siècle*, Saint-Omer, 1886, pp. 33, 34 and notes.

[5] Havard, *Dictionnaire de l'ameublement*, s.v. Prael.

[6] Sauval, *Histoire et antiquités de la ville de Paris*, quoted Michel, *Histoire de l'art*, iii. 112.

[7] e.g. the Duke of Burgundy's in 1404 (Pinchart, *Histoire de la tapisserie dans les Flandres*, p. 15), and among the tapestries of Charles VI sold by the English in 1422 (*Bib. de l'École des Chartes*, xlviii, 1887, p. 77). Fifteenth-century paintings of rose-gathering and other garden subjects still survive at Schloss Lichtenberg in the Tyrol.

[8] Brewer, *Letters and Papers*, iv, pt. 3, pp. 2764 and 2767. As late as 1556–61 Karcher was weaving at

It was especially as the scene of courtly amusement and romance that the garden
was celebrated in decorative art; the scenes of combat of the earlier middle ages
were succeeded by scenes of hunting and love-making to represent the chief pur-
suits of chivalry. A fourteenth-century ivory cup[1] is typical; it is carved with
scenes of a man and woman embracing; a lover teaching his lady the ABC; a man
and woman picnicking together; a knight crowning his lady, and a couple playing
lutes, each scene divided from the next by a tree bearing flowers or fruit. Lovers
together in an orchard are one of the commonest types of secular ivory carvings
in the late thirteenth and early fourteenth century; sometimes he gathers flowers
for her to weave into a garland, sometimes they caress or embrace each other,
sometimes they converse together, sometimes he comes back from hunting and
shows her his hawk or his hound, sometimes he kneels to declare his love.[2] Such
scenes were commonly represented in tapestry; a fountain or pool was often set in
the middle of the garden to provide a centre for the composition. Isabeau de
Bavière, in 1398, had such a tapestry, 'd'esbatemens, et y a dames et hommes qui
peschent à la ligne et font plusieurs autres esbatemens.'[3] Margaret of Flanders had
a tapestry 'devisé d'un chevalier et d'une dame seant en un vergier delez une fontaine,'[4] and Charles VI in 1420 owned a set 'à personnages d'enfans et oiselez, et au
milieu a une fontaine et une dame qui remue l'eau à ung bastonnet.'[5] Sometimes
the fountain is missing, and a rose trellis takes its place in the decorative scheme, as
in Margaret of Flanders's tapestry 'd'un chevalier et une dame en un parc de rosiers,
ou le chevalier present à ladicte dame une rose.'[6] The poet's *Verger de Jeunesse* was
illustrated in tapestry,[7] and the garden appeared, alike in literature and in decoration, as the setting of allegory.

It was as a background to such scenes that the 'verdure' decoration of the earlier
forest schemes was developed in the 'mille-fleurs' style to represent the grassy
banks studded with flowers that were the garden's chief adornment. Such tapestries as the 'Dame à la Licorne' (fig. 165) in the Musée de Cluny, and the 'Concert de
Rohan' in the Musée de l'Évêché at Angers, have the whole ground powdered

Ferrara small tapestries with children dancing against trellises of roses, campanulas, and jasmine. (Müntz,
Histoire de la tapisserie en Italie, p. 58). About the same time the Villa Sanvitale at Fontanellato was painted
with the story of Diana and Actaeon against a background of vine trellis with children playing among its
leafage. (Michel, *Histoire de l'art*, v. 585).

  [1] Now in the Church of Vannes.
  [2] See R. Koechlin, *Les Ivoires gothiques français*, 1924, i. 375 and 381. Similar scenes likewise adorned
plate: see, for instance, Moranvillé, *op. cit.*, p. lxii.
  [3] Guiffrey, *Histoire de la tapisserie en France*, p. 18.
  [4] Dehaisnes, *Histoire de l'art dans la Flandre*, p. 344.
  [5] Guiffrey, *La Tapisserie*, p. 67.
  [6] Dehaisnes, *Histoire de l'art dans la Flandre*, p. 343. With the Renaissance such scenes were transferred to
an indoor background, for instance in the frescoed frieze of about 1550 with men and ladies playing cards and
making music in the Palazzo Poggi at Bologna and in the gallery painted by Veronese with women playing all
kinds of musical instruments in the Barbarò Villa at Maser near Treviso. Michel, *Histoire de l'art*, v. 540.
  [7] e.g. tapestry of Charles VI, sold by the English in 1422, 'ung tappis de salle, de tappisserie d'Arras, à or
sur leyne, du Verger de Jeunesse.' *Bibliothèque de l'École des Chartes*, xlviii, 1887, p. 97.

with garden flowers—primroses, anemones, periwinkles, pinks, pansies, and columbines,[1]

> With daisies pied and violets blue,
> And lady-smocks all silver white
> And cuckoo-buds of yellow hue . . .

Even the garden's wattled fence became an element of decoration.[2] The trees of the earlier orchard-garden went out of fashion; but the herbs of the enclosed garden were worthy to adorn the tapestry and plate of kings. In 1388 there is mention in Charles VI's accounts of green tapestries with borage leaves;[3] in the next year Valentine of Milan had a dress embroidered with pearls in a pattern of borage flowers,[4] and in 1417 the Duc de Berry had six hanaps of silver gilt enamelled at the bottom with borage flowers.[5] Louis of Anjou in 1380 had plate decorated with pumpkins, parsley, and leeks;[6] Philippe le Hardi in 1404 had a room of green tapestry 'à pos de margolaine',[7] and a year later his wife owned another with a fountain and 'une Damoiselle qui plante j pot de margolaine.'[8] In 1471, a room in the Château de Chanzé was painted with gooseberry bushes, 'dont les groyselles sont rouges.'[9]

The flowers of the fifteenth-century garden were not very numerous; some—ragged robin, broom, mallow, blackberry, clover, scabious, daffodils, lavender, cranesbill, bachelor's buttons—were almost hedgerow flowers; but they and the garden flowers proper—iris, hollyhocks, columbines, lilies, periwinkles, roses, violets, and clove-pinks[10]—were honoured in every art. Froissart sings:

> Sus toutes flours tient on la rose à belle,
> Et, en après, je croi, la violette.
> La flour de lys est belle, et la perselle;
> La flour de glay est plaisans et parfette;
> Et li pluisour aiment moult l'anquelie;
> Le pyonnier, le muget, la soussie,
> Cascune flour a par li sa merite';

[1] Such ornament was soon employed as a background to heraldic decoration (e.g. in tapestry with the arms of Charles the Bold in the Berne Museum), and also, by analogy with the garden backgrounds, to symbolic pictures of Our Lady, for such religious tapestries as those of Angers.

[2] It occurs as late as the windows of Brou.

[3] Guiffrey, *Histoire de la tapisserie en France*, p. 22.

[4] F. M. Graves, *Deux inventaires de la maison d'Orléans*, p. 72.

[5] Guiffrey, *Inventaires de Jean, Duc de Berry*, i. 185. It may be these same cups that reappear in the 1467 inventory of Charles the Bold. Laborde, *Les Ducs de Bourgogne*, ii. 60. Others enamelled on the covers with borage and violets are mentioned in the Lettre d'attestation.

[6] Moranvillé, *op. cit.*, p. lvii.   [7] Farcy, *La Broderie*, p. 94. Cf. Laborde, *op. cit.* i. 154.

[8] Pinchart, *Histoire de la tapisserie dans les Flandres*, p. 16.

[9] Havard, *Dictionnaire de l'ameublement*, s.v. Peintre. A room in the Donjon of Vincennes was painted with bunches of cherries, and another at La Menitré with gooseberries. C. Enlart, *Manuel d'archéologie française*, Pt. II, 2nd ed., 1929, p. 69, note 2.

[10] These are those enumerated in Jon Gardener's *Feate of Gardening*. Of these, the thirteenth-century garden only included the rose, violet, lily, iris, peony, and columbine; the gilly-flower and lavender became garden flowers in the fourteenth century and the carnation in the fifteenth. C. Joret, *La Rose dans l'Antiquité et au Moyen Âge*, Paris, 1892, p. 288.

and patterns of roses, lilies, columbines, violets, daisies, poppies, iris, marigolds, cornflowers, and periwinkles are recorded in the inventories of Louis d'Anjou.[1]

The fifteenth century was a time of pre-eminently visual inspiration, in which painting forged ahead of literature; and in representations of gardens and garden flowers we have a truer measure of its artistic sensibility than is afforded by almost any other art. Some French illuminations of about 1420, of which the best example is a Book of Hours of the use of Chalons-sur-Marne in the collection of Mr. Dyson Perrins,[2] have their miniatures set in delicate borders, each formed of natural flowers of a single sort drawn on the page with no framing or coloured background (fig. 110). The style could only be achieved by a true artist, and does not found a school; but it is noticeable that, early in the fifteenth century, there was a tendency to use only a single kind of flower even in important decorative schemes; Louis d'Orleans, for example, had in 1403 a set of tapestry hangings woven with wild marsh iris on a white ground;[3] Philippe le Bon another set 'au bout d'en hault faiz de trailles de rosiers sur champ vermeil.'[4] Even in architectural decoration there was a tendency to use a single flower, and that the rose.[5] Often, however, alike in illumination and in other forms of decoration, flowers of several sorts were used together, conventionally disposed and naturalistically treated. As early as 1379–80 Louis of Anjou had a gold cup engraved within and without with a loosely twined chaplet of lilies, roses, and holly, with a rose in the middle,[6] and in 1409 the Count of Hainault had in his Hotel du Porc-épic at Paris a set of green tapestries with rose trees and columbines.[7] The portable altar given by the English to Chartres Cathedral in 1420 has its rim decorated with alternating shells and naturalistic field-daisies; the foundress's cup at Christ's College, Cambridge, dating from about 1440, has its diagonal bands filled with oak, vine, and rose sprays in relief. Charles the Bold, in 1467, had a golden goblet enamelled with roses, two with rose-branches, several with daisies, and two silver bottles enamelled with columbines.

[1] Moranvillé, *op. cit.*, p. lvii. Such decoration made its way into Italy a little later. The frame of Gentile da Fabriano's Adoration of the Magi (now in the Royal Gallery at Florence) has charming naturalistic panels with cornflowers, convolvulus, autumn crocuses, and other flowers. Venturi, *Storia dell' Arte italiana*, vol. vii, pt. 1, p. 196.

[2] Burlington Fine Arts Club Exhibition, 1908, no. 205. Another example of the same type, probably by the same hand, is a Book of Hours of the use of Paris, in the collection of Mr. Hamilton E. Field; *ibid.*, no 204.

[3] Laborde, *Les Ducs de Bourgogne*, iii. 208. A fine French fifteenth-century tapestry all of naturalistic thistles was exhibited in Paris in 1913 by M. Demotte. S. de Ricci, *Exposition d'objets d'art . . . à l'ancien hôtel de Sagan, mai–juin*, 1913, No. lxxii.

[4] Laborde, *Les Ducs de Bourgogne*, ii. 268. A similar type of decoration appears on plate, for instance on a cup 'semée de violettes' that belonged to the Duke of Guyenne in 1416. (L. Pannier, 'Les joyaux du Duc de Guyenne,' in *Rev. arch.* 1873, xxvi. 310), and in the rose-frieze of the Reliquary of San Bernardino in the Convento dell' Osservanza of Siena (1460). Bunt, *Goldsmiths of Italy*, 1926, p. 56.

[5] e.g. on a fourteenth-century capital in the Church of Saint Maurice, Vienne, and on the fifteenth-century piscina in the chapel of the Castle of Vincennes. A charming Franco-Flemish tapestry of about 1490 in the Metropolitan Museum, New York, has three figures set against a striped background covered with rose-sprays.   [6] Moranvillé, *op. cit.*, p. 73.   [7] Pinchart, *Histoire de la tapisserie dans les Flandres*, p. 21.

91. Console from the Puits de Moise, Chartreuse de Champmol, Dijon. School of Claus Sluter, 1399

93. Detail of the Cornice, Cathedral of Nevers, c. 1460

90. Capital of a pier in the Nave, Church of Saint Gengoult, Toul, c. 1300

92. Capital. French. c. 1510

94. Capital in the Nave, Wells Cathedral, *c.* 1240

95. Capitals in the Lady Chapel, Ely Cathedral, *c.* 1340

Flowers, moreover, were not always used only for their beauty's sake; some additional significance was often found for them. Often it was heraldic,[1] sometimes symbolical. The obituary roll of John Islip, Abbot of Westminster between 1500–32, is adorned with drawings of flowers each of which symbolizes a virtue or a spiritual gift.[2] For Jean Regnier the periwinkle was the emblem of loyalty,[3] while the columbine, through an analogy between *ancolie* and *melancolie*, was the flower of sadness. It was therefore appropriate enough for Louis d'Anjou to have a cup formed as a columbine and held up by three bats;[4] and his own melancholy was made poetically evident when he wore a tunic of red velvet embroidered with five hundred and sixteen columbines.[5] It was often with this sense that columbines were used in illuminations; in the Très Riches Heures of Jean de Berry, written before 1416, the office for the Fourth Sunday in Lent is bordered with snails of Resurrection and the columbines of sadness;[6] while for the *Vigiles des Morts* of the 'Heures de Boussu'[7] columbines are used with the pansies of thought and the forget-me-nots of remembrance.[8] The flower borders of this manuscript, indeed, are all touched with symbolism.[9] The scene of the Annunciation is bordered with the fresh primroses of spring.[10] The pages opposite the miniatures of the Passion have each a border spotted with blood and sweat, with a single pansy.[11] Only opposite the scourging a palm of victory is added, and opposite the crowning a branch of flowering rose. The Crucifixion has its pansy, though not upon a golden border like the rest, but on one of dark and stormy violet, lit only by a faint dawn beneath; while the garden of the Sepulchre is symbolized by a trellis covered with pansies,

---

[1] See Vol. i, p. 95.

[2] The gilly-flower is labelled *constancia*, the daisy *temperancia*, the borage *justicia*, the pansy *spes*, the marigold *prudencia*, the pink *fides*, the pimpernel *caritas*, the honeysuckle *fortitudo*, the violet *consilium*, the lily of the valley *intellectus*, the corncockle *sapiencia*, the lily *pietas*, the iris *sciencia*, and the columbine *timor Domini*. Cf. a 'Canon d'autel' made at Fontevrault in the first half of the sixteenth century, on which a lily is labelled *puritas*, a carnation *obedientia*, a thistle *patientia*, a daisy *spes*, a violet *fides*, and a columbine *humilitas*. See F. Walston, La 'Carta Gloria' du Musée de Naples, in *Gazette des Beaux Arts*, 1929, p. 142.

[3] P. Champion, *Histoire poétique du XVᵉ siècle*, i. 246.

[4] Moranvillé, *op. cit.*, p. 345. He also had one of the same shape 'à VI feuilles, ou bout desquels par dehors a testes de mandegloire.' Laborde, *op. cit.* ii. 23.

[5] Moranvillé, *op. cit.*, pp. 599 et seqq.

[6] Snails similarly appeared on a jewel in the oratory of Charles V in the Louvre, 'où sont plusiers lymaçons yssans de grosses perles, et au dessus nostre Seigneur en yssant du sépulcre' (Labarte, *Inventaire de Charles V*, p. 249).

[7] Bib. de l'Arsenal, MS. 1185.

[8] Cf. Molinier, *Inventaire des meubles du Château de Pau*, 1561–2, p. 40: 'Ung boucquet d'or où il y a une encolye, une pensée et ung soucy esmaillé au naturel.'

[9] See H. Martin, 'Les "Heures de Boussu" et leurs bordures symboliques', in *Gazette des Beaux Arts*, 1910, 4th series, t. iii, p. 115. The manuscript was written soon after 1490 in French Flanders or Hainault.

[10] A similar border adorns a page of the Hours of Marie de Bourgogne (Berlin MS. 78, B. 12) showing the owner praying before her patron saint.

[11] Cf. two garters and two collars 'esmaillées à larmes et à pensées,' in the 1455–6 Inventories of the Duke of Orleans. Laborde, *Les Ducs de Bourgogne*, iii. 332 and 377. In Portugal such ornament was widely used; the tomb of São Francisco do Porto (1479) is entirely covered with tears in relief. It appears again on a flask and a key and a brooch shaped like a book in the inventory of the Château de Pau in 1561–2 (ed. Molinier, pp. 45 and 49).

columbines, and forget-me-nots. Even birds and butterflies are made to play a symbolic part: the Heures du Saint Esprit have twenty-three pages bordered with winged creatures: cocks, cranes, storks, swans, sparrow-hawks, and all sorts of birds, flies, ladybirds, butterflies, and dragonflies.[1]

Illumination, however, was in the fifteenth century becoming more and more industrialized, and few Books of Hours show so delicate a symbolism as this. For the most part their painters, between 1475 and 1520, were content to sprinkle their borders with detached sprays of iris, clover, strawberry, pansy, pimpernel, violet, stock, rose, pink, daisy, and daffodil, with little regard to anything but their decorative beauty and the natural truth of their presentment (fig. 111).[2] Sometimes, indeed, naturalism is stronger than the traditions of decorative art, and the flowers are painted to cast shadows on their parchment background. Such work, however, demanded much skill and patience for its satisfactory execution, and for the general market the naturalistic style was modified in other directions. The use of quartered and lozenged grounds in heraldry and livery had brought in a fashion for backgrounds of different colours, arranged in panes, stripes, lozenges, or fantastic shapes. The traditional rather characterless foliage of the industrial illuminator was set against such a particoloured background, and to its more or less conventional leaves were added the bright-hued flowers of the naturalistic style. The style was originated just before 1450, and for some seventy years remained the standard product of the industrial illuminator.[3]

5

In cloister, forest, and garden men had learnt to see Nature as she is; and they saw not only grass and plants and trees but also the birds and beasts that lived among them, and seeing them, set them in sculpture, painting, enamel, and embroidery. Birds and beasts played their part in orchard and forest scenes; in 1296 a cloth of Arras was given to St. Paul's for the repose of the soul of Hugh de Vienne, 'cuius campus est aureus, et avibus rubeis super ramunculos arborum',[4] while a later inventory of the Collegiate Church of the Holy Trinity at Arundel[5] includes two blue altarcloths 'wrought with squyrelles, birddes and braunches'. The hangings of blue satin embroidered with orange and lemon trees made for the

[1] A border of doves symbolizing the gifts of the Spirit occupies the same place in a Dutch Book of Hours of the late fifteenth century in the collection of Mr. Dyson Perrins.

[2] It is almost unnecessary to quote examples of a style represented in every great collection; perhaps the most famous is the Grimani Breviary of the early sixteenth century in the Biblioteca Marciana at Venice.

[3] Good examples in the Bodleian are MS. Douce 364, mid fifteenth-century, with a complicated patchwork background; MS. Douce 383, earlier than 1504, with some borders striped diagonally in bright green, crimson, grey, scarlet, and blue; MS. Rawl. liturg. E 34, late fifteenth century, with paned, lozenged, striped, and medallion borders; and MS. Rawl. liturg. E 36, early sixteenth century, with the ground a patchwork of fantastic shapes.

[4] Dugdale, *History of St. Paul's Cathedral*, 1818, ed. p. 329.

[5] *Archaeologia*, 1908, lxi, pt. 1, p. 89.

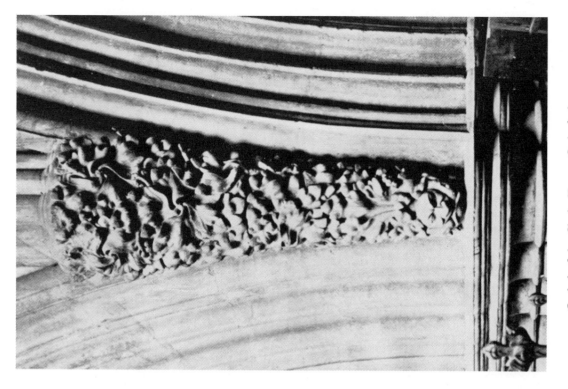

97. Corbel of the Choir, Exeter Cathedral, c. 1300

96. Corbel of an eastern bay of the Nave, Ely Cathedral, c. 1240

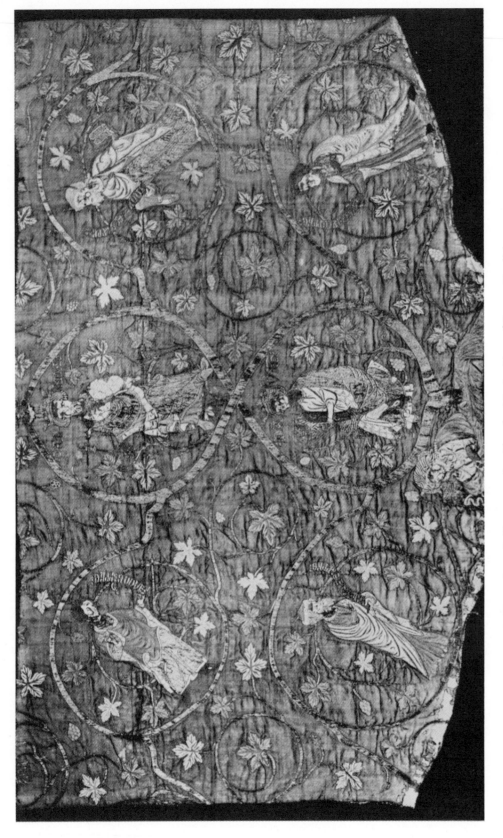

98. Part of a red silk cope embroidered with the Tree of Jesse. English, c. 1300

King's visit to Dijon in 1390 were powdered with doves.[1] Birds and beasts, too, were represented apart from any forest or garden background. Villard de Honnecourt drew snails, swans, grasshoppers, two parrots and a cat, not to mention a lion with the note 'Et bien saciés que cil lion fut contrefais al vif.'[2] On Lyons Cathedral the medallions of the lower part of the portal show two fowls scratching themselves; a squirrel in a nut tree; a crow perched on a dead rabbit; a water bird catching an eel; a snail on a leaf; and a pig searching for acorns. In the great English psalters naturalistically treated animals appear side by side with grotesque and more formal decoration. A page of the Ormesby Psalter, for instance, has a great D enclosing figures of the Trinity in Majesty, ornamented with two seraphs, and two even larger greenfinches; in the margin there are a monkey on a hound pursuing an owl on a rabbit; a border of flies and ladybirds;[3] a man on a bear fighting another on a lion; a peasant resting; a trumpeter; and many dragons. Another page (fol. 38), besides a fine interlaced border and a miniature of God anointing David, has a man-headed beast slinging stones at a snail; a butterfly, that looks as if it had just alighted on the page; a winged dragon chasing a centaur (in a neat green coat with white spots) who is shooting at the butterfly; a robin looking at a goldfinch, and a magpie looking at an owl; a hawk eating meat, and a man-bodied bird brandishing a sword against a squirrel who is eating a nut.

Cybo of Hyères set spiders, bees, grasshoppers, flies, caterpillars, and stag-beetles in the margins of his work (fig. 112); Richard II had a dress for a Christmas dance embroidered with leeches in a rocky stream, and sewn with fifteen whelks and fifteen mussels of silver-gilt, as well as fifteen cockles of white silver.[4] A crowd of little birds mobbing an owl are carved on misericords at Gloucester, Norwich, and Beverley, while at All Saints, Hereford, the carver has represented rats, mice, weevils, and woodlice.

Men soon ceased to think of birds as described in *volucraires* or depicted on eastern stuffs, and knew and observed them afresh; in the calm and leafy solitudes of wood and garden they came to appreciate with more sensibility than ever before their bright colours, their jewelled quickness, their swift flight and their sweet song.

> Li oisillons de mon païs
> Ai oïs en Bretaigne,
> A lor chant m'est-il bien avis
> Qu'en la douce Champaigne
> Les oï jadis.

Even in the towns men still had birds to see and hear. The French early had the custom of keeping birds in cages. In *L'Escoufle*, written about 1200, Aelis and her

---

[1] Farcy, *La Broderie*, p. 94. [2] See Mâle, *L'art religieux en France au XIIIe siècle*, p. 74.

[3] The *volucraires* of the Middle Ages (e.g. Bartholomaeus Anglicus *de proprietatibus rerum*, Bk. XII), gave lists of all the flying creatures mentioned in the Bible, and included gnats, flies, grasshoppers, &c., as well as birds.

[4] *Archaeologia*, lxii, pt. 2, 1911, p. 503.

companion, installed as embroideresses at Montpellier, have seven or eight cages
of birds in their windows. In the reign of Charles VI, the birdsellers of Paris were
allowed to hang their cages in front of the shops of the goldsmiths and money-
changers on the Pont au Change, on condition that at festivals, such as the entries
of kings and queens into Paris, they should release at least four hundred birds.[1]
Even in their palaces kings kept an aviary for their pleasure. The Duc de Berry
kept starlings, goldfinches, quails, nightingales, and doves.[2] Charles VI in 1380
kept doves and white finches, and 'nos rossignols de nostre Chastel du Louvre,'[3]
and Louis XI a hundred years later had canaries, finches, greenfinches, and
chaffinches.[4] It is not surprising that the 'Beau Bréviaire' of Charles V, mentioned
in the inventory of 1380, should have the conventional vine and ivy branches of
its borders made gay with birds: swans, pheasants, cocks, eagles, owls, barn-owls,
magpies, woodpeckers, hoopoes, parrots, wrens, bullfinches, siskins, tomtits,
greenfinches, yellowhammers, and most charming goldfinches.[5]

Such decoration was soon transferred to other arts. The English embroideries
of the early fourteenth century[6] are rich in birds and beasts. On the cope
at Saint Bertrand de Comminges, for instance, medallions of birds alternate
with medallions of scenes from the life of Christ, while at the junction of the
medallions are little figures of animals—dogs of many kinds, foxes, lions, sheep,
rabbits, and squirrels. The cope of St. Silvester has twenty-eight little medallions
of birds; the orphreys of the Pienza cope similar medallions of pelican, cock,
peacock, falcon, hawk, heron, partridge, pheasant, thrush, finches, magpies, and
a pair of swallows. The cope of Cardinal Carrillo de Albernoz in the Cathedral of
Toledo has three rows of gabled arcading with birds above—peacocks, herons,
finches, hawks, and others, all represented about one-third the size of the human

---

[1] Havard, *Dictionnaire de l'ameublement*, s.v. Volière. At the coronations of the kings of France, birds were
released in Notre Dame de Paris. Abbé Lebeuf, *Histoire de la diocèse de Paris*, i. 17.

[2] Guiffrey, *Inventaire du Duc de Berry*, 1, cxxx.

[3] Laborde, *Glossaire des émaux*, ii. 408.

[4] Havard, *Dictionnaire de l'ameublement*, s.v. Volière. René of Anjou had a large aviary in his room at Aix:
A. Lecoy de la Marche, *Extraits des comptes et mémoriaux du Roi René*, 1873, p. 128.

[5] H. Martin, *La Miniature française*, p. 63. The fashion spread from France to England and the Low
Countries; a Book of Hours of about 1390, showing strong Dutch influence [Bodleian MS. Lat. liturg. f. 3]
has many and admirable birds; while a perfectly delightful aviary perches among the conventional foliage of
a manuscript, probably painted by Jacques Coene about 1400, in the National Library of Belgium [MS. 10767].
The style was perpetuated into the fifteenth century. [See especially the MS. of *Les Histoires Romaines* of Jean
Mansel, illustrated by Loyset Lyedet in 1454 for Philippe le Bon, Bib. de l'Arsenal MS. 5087–8; and Book of
Hours written in the last quarter of the century in the Netherlands: Bodleian MS. Douce 219–20.] From the
Low Countries the style invaded Spain; a delightful aviary adorns the Book of Hours written for Don Juan
Rodriguez de Fonseca, Bishop of Palencia, in 1505. [E. Bertaux, *L'Exposition retrospective de Saragosse*, 1908,
Saragossa and Paris, 1910, p. 122.] In England, such paintings appear early in the fourteenth century
[e.g. Magdalene College, Cambridge, no. 1916, and the Peterborough Psalter of about 1305; Bib. royale de
Belgique, 9961–2] as they do in Germany in the fifteenth [e.g. a Latin bible, illuminated at Mainz, and finished
in 1453, with plovers, partridges, pheasants, bullfinches, &c., in its borders, as well as many sorts of beasts.
It is now in the Ducal Library at Gotha].

[6] Such as the Butler Bowden, Pienza, Lateran, and Toledo copes.

99. Capital in the Nave, Cathedral of Todi, *c.* 1260

100. Relief from the end of a tomb, probably that of Adelaïs of Champagne, Countess of Joigny, in the Church of Saint Jean de Joigny, *c.* 1290

figures within the arcading. Decoration of the sort was also used for hangings—
Louis d'Anjou bought in 1416 a set of hangings of white satin, embroidered with
falcons and other flying birds[1]—and was also freely applied to work in metal.[2] The
King of France in 1363 had 'une pie, estant en son ny, assis sur un hault pié
d'argent doré et esmaillé,'[3] and the Duke of Anjou in 1380 had plate decorated
with woodcock, peacocks, finches, swans, white and brown pigeons, thrushes,
and owls.[4] Little enamelled medallions of birds were applied to all kinds of metal-
work; a good surviving example is the fourteenth-century staff of Archbishop
Wilhelm von Gennep in the Treasury of Cologne Cathedral. Sometimes, too,
caged birds were represented; in 1408 Valentine de Milan had a little cage of
silver-gilt containing a silver finch,[5] and the inventory of tapestries in the castle of
Middelbourg in 1477 records a set of hangings of white damask embroidered with
branches and parrots, with a lady in the middle and parrots in a cage.[6] Even in the
sixteenth century Leo X ordered tapestries, probably designed by Giovanni
d'Udine, that represent the perfect classicalization of the medieval type, with children playing with peacocks, parrots, pheasants, and swans.[7]

6

Naturalism, moreover, did more than modify the treatment of plants and animals
in decoration; it brought back to ornament those scenes of contemporary life that
had hardly played an important part in the minor arts since the days of the Attic
vase-painters. A new sense of the importance of present happenings is evident in
the increase of chronicles, and such history-writing was not confined to literature.
The same spirit is evident even in so small a thing as the orpheys of the cope given
by Richard of Windsor to St. Paul's about 1192 'in quorum uno breudatur castrum
de Windlesor' in alio Ricardus legens evangelium super aquilam ante episcopum'.[8]
The Chertsey tiles of the chapter-house at Westminster, dating from about 1255,
have seated figures of Henry III, his Queen, and the then Abbot. Sometimes
an historic ceremonial was commemorated; the Coronation was represented

[1] Lecoy de la Marche, Le roi René, ii. 110.
[2] There was a fashion for feather-pattern grounds: e.g. Charles V, 1380, 'un hanap d'or couvert plumeté';
Duc de Berry, 1416, 'un grant hanap de jaspre vermeil, garny d'argent doré, ouvré en manière de plumes';
Laborde, Glossaire des émaux, ii. 454.
[3] Laborde, Glossaire des Émaux, ii. 503.
[4] Moranvillé, op. cit., p. lv.
[5] F. M. Graves, Deux Inventaires de la Maison d'Orléans, p. 138. Professor Borenius tells me that the
Eucharistic dove was sometimes so represented at an earlier date.
[6] Pinchart, Histoire de la Tapisserie dans les Flandres, p. 71.
[7] Müntz, Histoire de la Tapisserie en Italie, p. 26. The MS. style was further developed in Italy in the fifteenth
century with gold-outlined floriated scrolls as a background to brilliantly coloured birds: e.g. Bodleian MS.
Canonici Liturg. 114. Such a style is reduced to the limitations of engraving in some of the patterns of Martin
Schongauer.
[8] Inventory of St. Paul's, 1245, in Archaeologia, l. 476.

in the painted Chamber at Westminster soon after 1262.[1] Jane, abbess of the Convent of Lothen in Westphalia, with three of her sisters embroidered carpets with scenes of the foundation of her convent in 1265.[2] Sometimes, too, an historic series was represented; in 1244 the wainscot of the King's lower chamber at Clarendon was painted with a border of the heads of kings and queens,[3] and in the reign of Edward II John Thokey, Abbot of Gloucester, had the wainscot of his great parlour embellished with the portraits of all the monarchs up to his day.[4]

From such historic scenes and portraits the transition was easy to the representation of people and events of a more ordinary kind. Little naturalistic heads of the most varied sort decorate the spandrels of the late thirteenth-century church of Rampillon, Seine et Marne (fig. 114); and similar series of heads in quatrefoils appear alike on the north door at Rouen (fig. 115), on the base of the tomb of St. Frideswide at Oxford,[5] and on English embroideries of the early thirteenth century. About 1300 they were used in the round on corbel stones, at York, Wells, Lichfield, Bristol, Exeter, and Ely, and as far south as Saint Nazaire, Carcassonne; and a few years later they were used to adorn the margins of the Gorleston Psalter.

Meanwhile literature was finding in everyday life an increasingly worthy theme: at first in the fuller descriptions of detail in the romances, and then in the last third of the thirteenth century in the various 'Dits'—des Forgerons, des Boulangers, des Rues de Paris, des Cris de Paris and so on. A similar development took place in decoration. Hunting scenes had already become a commonplace of thirteenth-century decoration; and all the other scenes of everyday life crept into the minor arts in the fourteenth century. The throng of the Paris streets, the life of the Grand Pont, with cake-sellers, smiths, the miller's men, beggars, couriers, goldsmiths, watchmen, friars, lords going hawking, coaches, and the water-mills and boats beneath the bridge, all appear in a manuscript of the life of St. Denis, presented by the Abbot to Philippe V in 1317 (fig. 116);[6] while, on other manuscripts of the

[1] Walpole, *Anecdotes of Painting*, ed. Dalloway, i. 40, note. Bishop Langton had his hall in the Palace of Lichfield painted with the ceremony of the coronation in 1272. Such decoration founded the tradition that was later carried on in such paintings as Mantegna's frescoes of about 1460 in the Palace of Mantua of the meeting of the Marchese Ludovico Gonzaga and his son, and Melozzo da Forli's decoration of the Vatican Library between 1477 and 1480 with the scene of Pope Sixtus IV receiving Platina as his Librarian.

[2] Müntz, *Histoire de la tapisserie en Allemagne*, p. 3. They were inscribed 'Quis quis me calcat, bona me facientibus optat'.

[3] J. C. Wall, *Mediaeval Wall Paintings*, p. 75. In 1300 the chamber of the Comte d'Artois was ornamented all round 'd'une rengiée de têtes de rois, moulées en plâtre a l'image des rois de France.' J. M. Richard, *Mahaut Comtesse d'Artois*, p. 331. Jean de Berry had the great gallery at Bicêtre painted with a series of the Kings of France and another of the Emperors of East and West. C. Enlart, *Manuel d'archéologie française*, Part II, 2nd ed., 1929, p. 173.

[4] Walpole, *op. cit.* i. 30, note. See B. M. Cotton MS. Domitian viii, f. 128. Cf. the medallions of heads of Kings, Bishops, &c. in the initials of English MS. of the first half of the fourteenth century [e.g. the Exeter Psalter, Bodleian MS. 738], and the series of Popes' heads in the trefoils of the fourteenth-century windows in the Lady Chapel at Wells.

[5] Cf. the six naturalistic heads carved on the plinth of the tomb of Bishop William de Marchia, d. 1302, at Wells. Another series are painted under the battlemented cornice of the adjacent curtain wall.

[6] Bibl. Nat. MS. français 2090-2.

101. Staircase of the Tower of Jean sans Peur, Hotel de Bourgogne, Paris, *c.* 1400

102. Silver reliquary. Italian, *c.* 1460.
Church of San Giovanni in Monte, Bologna

103. Coco-nut cup with tree mount. English, *c.* 1380.
New College, Oxford

104. Silver gilt plate. French, *c.* 1340

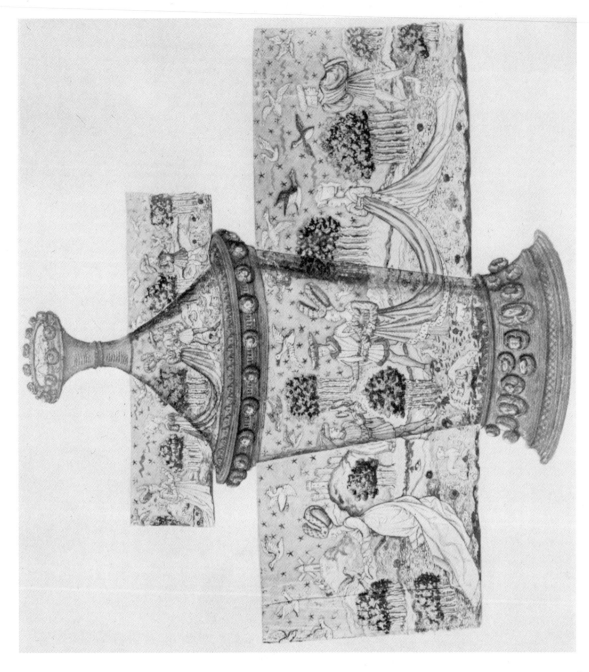

105. Painting of an enamelled cup, belonging in the seventeenth century to M. de Caumartin. The cup French, c. 1400

time, little irrelevant scenes of ordinary life are added to the earlier animal grotesques, or even take their place. The psalter executed for Joffroy d'Aspremont at
the end of the thirteenth century,[1] besides many monsters and animals, has a little
marginal scene of the owner going into battle while his wife prays for him, and
another which shows him feeding a squirrel and restraining his dog from
attacking it. A Book of Hours of the Maestricht School, written about 1300,[2] has
marginal drawings of wrestlers, knights tilting, tumblers, musicians, and an abbess
spinning, with her white cat bringing her a new spindle in its mouth. The famous
Ormesby Psalter has only a few such scenes,[3] but the Gorleston Psalter,[4] dating
from the early years of the fourteenth century, has marginal pictures of a black-
smith's forge, a man ploughing, the arrest of a cutpurse, a duck carried off by a
fox, saying 'queck', and other such scenes; while the Louterell Psalter[5] has scenes
of cooking and a delightful picture of ladies travelling in a coach.[6] It was, however, the French illuminators who made the greatest use of the style. The marginal
drawings of the manuscript of the Alexander romances,[7] finished by the illuminator, Jehans de Grise, in April 1344, would serve to illustrate a complete account
of French fourteenth-century life. There is a woman churning, a man ploughing,
reapers with scythe and sickle wearing great shady hats, men digging, a smith
shoeing a horse, men working a grindstone, bird-catchers with their nets, men
warming their hands at the fire and tasting the new beer; windmills; children on
stilts and swinging, and others being led by a jester to dance before the King;
pick-a-back boxers, games of hand-slapping and blindman's buff; *caroles*[8] and
dances of men wearing stag's horns and beast-masks; two Punch-and-Judy shows,
dancing bears, jugglers, musicians of many kinds, beggars walking on stumps and
crutches, boating scenes, a preacher, mourners, tents and houses, and knights
tilting, with a lady waiting to give a crown to the victor (fig. 117). It is not surprising to find similar scenes alike in carving and in metal work. Some charming
late thirteenth-century reliefs on the right of the transept door of the Notre Dame
de Paris show students of the University attending a lecture, arguing, being
examined, and paying their dues. A misericord from St. Nicholas', King's Lynn,[9] is
decorated with a scene in a carver's workshop, with the master and his three
apprentices working; while a capital of about 1320 in the north transept of
Winchester shows a monk playing draughts. Equally varied scenes appear in
goldwork; Louis of Anjou, for instance, had a cup enamelled with trees and a
green meadow, with himself, his wife, and his son sitting under the trees, while

---

[1] Bodleian MS. Douce 118.   [2] B.M. MS. Stowe 17.
[3] Notably a farmer's wife chasing a fox, who has carried off her cock.
[4] In Mr. Dyson Perrins's collection.
[5] Made for Sir Geoffrey Louterell about 1340; as this book goes to press, there are hopes that it may be
acquired for the British Museum.
[6] For another such scene, see Bodleian MS. Douce 131, fol. 43.   [7] Bodleian MS. Bodl. 264.
[8] Cf. the very lively *carole* on a fifteenth-century capital in the church of Arceuil, Seine.
[9] Now in the Architectural Museum, Tufton Street.

his chamberlain served them with sweatmeats on bended knee,[1] and a goblet enamelled with a knight giving his hand to a lady up some steps to a terrace, on which was a beggar with his dog holding a basin, and the inscription 'Donnez au povre qui ne voit.'[2] A great *nef* of his was enamelled with all the figures of the *Dit des crieries de Paris*, 'qui vont criant leurs denrées, ainsi comme l'en fait par Paris; et sur chascun personnage a escript en un roolle ce qu'il porte.'[3] He also had plate decorated with games of chess, dicing, hand-clapping, 'poirier' and knuckle-bones, with dances and with scenes of ladies arming their knights; while the great silver crémaillère of his kitchen bore figures of the master cook, in a long dress and a high cap, holding chitterlings; the turnspit, in a short coat, holding a spit with a goose on it; a third cook with two partridges, and the cook's boy, bare-legged and capless, carrying the carcass of a sheep.[4]

Later such scenes passed into wall decoration, there to found a tradition of *genre* painting for later ages. About 1480 the lower arcade of the Chateau d'Issogne in the Val d'Aosta was painted with a series of lively and amusing shop-scenes—the chemist's, the cheesemonger's, the draper's, the greengrocer's, and the armourer's, which last seems to have served the purposes of a club.

There was, too, a topographical naturalism. The illuminations of the Très Riches Heures of the Duc de Berry show his castles as their background; the calendar scene for March has the fortress of Lusignan, the betrothal scene of April takes place just outside the walls of Dourdan, the May-day hunting party rides through the woods of Riom; and the Devil tempts Christ with the Duke's favourite castle of Mehun sur Yèvre, where his treasures were kept. The inventory of the Castle of Angers in 1471 mentions a hanging painted with all the towns between Provence and Genoa.[5] A similar naturalism is evident in the castellated decoration of the Oldenburg Horn[6] and in a cup of about 1500 in the Victoria and Albert Museum[7] (fig. 118) with a whole town upon its cover—walls and gates, a winding street of steep-roofed houses, and the church steeple to crown the whole.[8]

7

It is from the French naturalism of the Middle Ages, and not from any fresh source whether of antiquity or of their own time, that the artists of the Renaissance derived their scenes of courtly and peasant life. Alberti, when he gives as

[1] Moranvillé, *op. cit.*, p. 85.　　　　　　[2] *Ibid.*, p. 347.　　　　　　[3] *Ibid.*, p. 252.

[4] *Ibid.*, p. lix. Cf. the decoration of fifteenth-century Italian pots, 'scudelle da donne di parto' with birth and nursery scenes; and wedding presents—coppa amatoria—with the head of a woman and ribbons with amatory inscriptions.

[5] Havard, *Dictionnaire de l'ameublement*, s.v. Peinture.

[6] In the Rosenborg Slott at Copenhagen.　　　　　　　　　　　　　[7] 245. 1894.

[8] Such topographical naturalism in decoration survived into the seventeenth century. The 'Chambre de repos du Roi' at Saint Germain, decorated before 1669, had the country houses of the King—Saint Germain, Versailles, Fontainbleau—painted on the spandrels of the vault. (H. Jouin, *Le Brun*, p. 262.) A similar scheme was used for the Gobelins tapestries of the *Maisons de Plaisance*, designed by Le Brun. His cartoons are preserved in the Musée des Arts décoratifs at Paris.

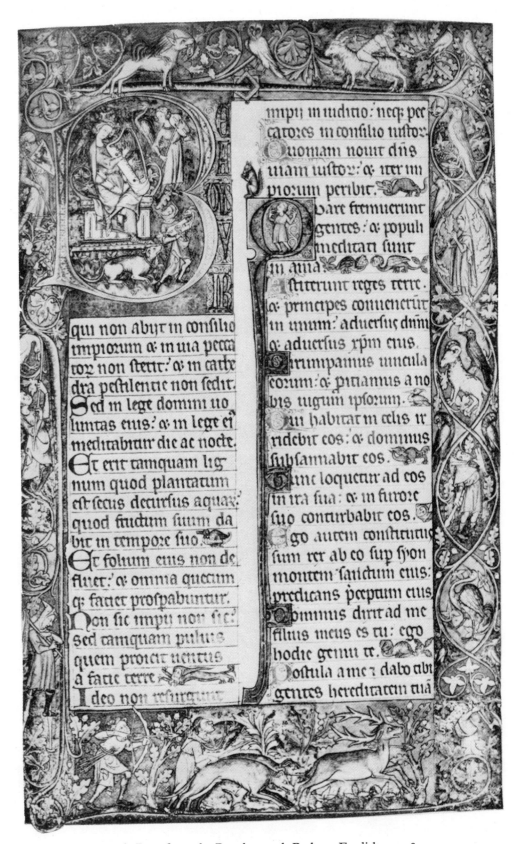

qui non abijt in consilio
impiorum et in uia pecca
tor non stetit: et in cathe
dra pestilentie non sedit.
Sed in lege domini uo
luntas eius: et in lege ei
meditabitur die ac nocte.
Et erit tanquam lig
num quod plantatum
est secus decursus aquar:
quod fructum suum da
bit in tempore suo.
Et folium eius non de
fluet: et omnia quecum
q; faciet prospabuntur.
Non sic impij non sic:
sed tanquam puluis
quem proicit uentus
a facie terre.
Ideo non resurgunt

impij in iudicio: neq; pec
catores in consilio iustor.
Quoniam nouit dns
uiam iustor: et iter im
piorum peribit.
Quare fremuerunt
gentes: et populi
meditati sunt
in uana.
Astiterunt reges terre.
et principes conuenerut
in unum: aduersus dnm
et aduersus xpm eius.
Dirumpamus uincula
eorum: et piciamus a no
bis iugum ipsorum.
Qui habitat in celis ir
ridebit eos: et dominus
subsannabit eos.
Tunc loquetur ad eos
in ira sua: et in furore
suo conturbabit eos.
Ego autem constitutus
sum rex ab eo sup syon
montem sanctum eius:
predicans preceptum eius.
Dominus dixit ad me
filius meus es tu: ego
hodie genui te.
Postula a me et dabo tibi
gentes hereditatem tuam

106. Page from the Peterborough Psalter. English, *c.* 1280

107. Fresco of hawking, in the Wardrobe Tower, Palace of the Popes, Avignon, *c.* 1350

subjects of painting and poetry 'the memorable actions of great men . . . the manners of private persons . . . and the life of rusticks, pictures of pleasant land-skips, of havens, of fishing, hunting, country sports, of flowery fields and thick groves'[1] is laying down no new doctrine, but is handing on the tradition of medieval France. Lorenzo Ghiberti's borders to the north door of the Baptistery at Florence (fig. 119) are transcribed, with slight variations, from French sculpture of an earlier date: there are the same plantains, the same primroses, the same violets and roses, the same daisies and dandelions; only the classic bronze makes possible a purer outline and a more precise treatment of detail than the stone of Champagne. Even his squirrels, partridges, quails, owls, finches and other birds are derived from an earlier style of decoration in France.[2] Ghiberti's design, however, is less natural; those tied bunches of roses, that awkward superposition of clumps and clusters of flowers, belong rather to some minor art of tapestry or illumination than to architectural decoration. Indeed, Italy had a different and less vital interest in Nature than France. It was Aeneas Silvius, who had learned the northern point of view during his long sojourn in Germany, who really appreciated, as a northerner, the yellow gorse on the hillside and the blue fields of flax waving in the wind; it was the French-bred Petrarch who described the rustic labours of the fields of Capronica and the view over the Lombard plain from St. Columban's hill.

Italy is a country that depends upon marble and bronze, cypress and ilex, space and flowing water, rather than on flowers, for the beauty of her gardens. Lorenzo might hymn the 'Belle fresche e purpuree viole', but naturalism remained, to a great extent, one of the alien medieval styles that Italy suffered for a time without making truly her own.[3] Just as Politian takes his scenes of rustic life and his touches of natural description from Hesiod or Lucretius, so do the Italian decorators borrow their acanthus, their oak, and their olive from classic reliefs and not from the gardens of Fiesole.[4] The Frenchmen of the fifteenth century strove to make their houses like gardens; the Italians of the Renaissance to make their gardens a part of architecture. The changeable nature of medieval room decoration, based as it was upon hangings that could be altered at will, was founded upon a northern sympathy with the changing seasons and an admiration for the mutable face of nature; whereas the whole scheme of Renaissance decoration had its source and reason in the worship of the unchanging beauties of classic art.

It was not long before Lorenzo and Vittorio Ghiberti set Greek acanthus and Roman heads within the wreathing leaves of their medieval rose and columbines

---

[1] *De re Aedificatoria*, trans. Leoni, p. 192.

[2] Cf. the miniatures of duck and plover on the typically Renaissance MS. *De Sanguine Christi*, by Francesco della Rovere. Vatican, Urbino MS. 251.

[3] A picture in the Vatican shows that Fra Angelico (d. 1455) painted a complete naturalistic landscape background, and then had to block it out with conventional gold.

[4] Cf. such Italian pattern books as that of J. B. Mutiano, *Il primo Libro, di fogliami antiqui, con la regola delle foglie maestre per imparar a spicigar detti fogliami,*' 1571.

(fig. 120). It was not until naturalistic decoration had been stylized into classically regular sheaves of leaves and fruit, bound with fluttering ribbons (figs. 121, 122),[1] that it was acclimatized in Italy. Then its treatment was less vital than that of classic acanthus and anthemion. Even in fine work in stone, such as the jambs of the great door of S. Maria Novella, designed by Alberti about 1456, and in the pilasters of Verocchio's monument to Giovanni and Pietro de Medici of 1472, there is a certain heaviness of form and lack of subtlety in execution. They do not look as if their creation had given their sculptors any keen pleasure. Only the Della Robbias, in their more fictile medium, could achieve naturalistic decoration in relief that, in its *genre*, is really good.[2]

The artists of the sixteenth century knew that naturalistic decoration had its classic justification, so the painters of the schools of Squarcione and Crivelli could frame their subjects in hanging garlands. Giovanni da Udine was free to design dropping strings with clumps of fruit to hang between some of the windows of the Loggie of the Vatican. None the less it is false to suppose that the 'observation of reality' which is commonly accepted as a mark of the Renaissance is in fact characteristic of it; it is rather an inheritance from the Gothic Age. The simple representation of nature had indeed little charm for the Italian artists of the mature Renaissance; Michel Angelo spoke with disdain of the Flemish School who were content to paint 'hovels, and very green fields shaded by trees, rivers and bridges, that they call landscapes . . . in which there is neither thought nor art; no proportion, no symmetry, no care in selection, no grandeur.'[3]

Only as *imprese*, cut and twisted to crown the glory of the individual, did flowers enter the Renaissance scheme. Lorenzo and his friends go to the joust dressed in shot silk embroidered with rose sprays :

> E parte rose fresche in su uno ramo
> E parte son rimasi sol gli stecchi,
> E son le foglie giù cascate al rezzo.[4]

It is only because the *cerquate* were the badge of the della Rovere that so much Castel Durante ware is decorated with yellow oak leaves on a blue ground. Almost the only engraved designs for ornament are such devices as Alciatus' Emblems of 1522, which include fourteen trees—cypress, oak, willow, fir, pine, quince, ivy, ilex, apple, box, mulberry, almond, laurel, and white poplar. Each is

[1] In this instance such foliage is also combined with the Medici *impresa* of a diamond ring.
[2] e.g. in the decoration of the ceiling over the great door of the Cathedral of Pistoia, 1505. The fig-tree in Andrea della Robbia's 'Adam and Eve' should be compared with the tree on the gable of the tomb of St. Etienne d'Aubazine some two centuries earlier.
[3] E. Michel, *Nouvelles études sur l'histoire de l'art*, p. 175. Vasari in 1547 says that 'German landscapes (i.e. engravings) are to be found in the house of every cobbler', but until the end of the century few Italian painters of any distinction occupied themselves with such themes.
[4] Luigi Pulci, *Giostra* (1468), quoted Monnier, *Le Quattrocento*, ii. 47.

108. Mantelpiece of the Hall, Old Hôtel de Ville, Bourges (now Petit Collège), *c.* 1485

109. Verdure tapestry with children and birds. Franco-Flemish, *c.* 1480

111. Initial from a page of an Antiphonal. Flemish, *c.* 1490

110. Page from a Book of Hours of the use of Châlons sur Marne. French, *c.* 1420

endowed with some symbolic meaning, expressed in Latin verse; for the ilex the legend is

> Duritie nimia quod sese rumperet ilex
> Symbola civilis seditionis habet.[1]

Plants, indeed, play a curiously small part in the Italian decoration of the mature Renaissance. The Italians of the sixteenth century, haunted by a fear of death that they were afraid to acknowledge, were apt to find in the beauty of flowers a tragic *memento mori*. It was only in the northern countries, where hedonism can never hide the facts of life, that men still had the courage to surround themselves with flowers.

There, too, the Renaissance style was not only slowly felt in art, but was introduced in its most naturalistic form: in England the tomb of Henry VII was carved by Torrigiano in 1516 with circular wreaths of fruit, oak and roses, with spandrels filled with natural roses, and classical arabesques only on the dividing pilasters. Tudor England was content to perpetuate the patterns of the fifteenth century: Wolsey had hundreds of verdure tapestries, several of hawking and shooting, and one of woodcutting, while his hangings, paned in the white and green of the Tudor livery and embroidered with branches of red and white roses, might be the borders of the illuminators translated into terms of silk.[2] It was naturally the Tudor Rose that dominated English decoration;[3] but the rose was treated naturalistically as often as heraldically, while the strawberries, columbines, and pansies of the fifteenth-century illuminators are also mentioned in the inventories of Tudor jewels and plate.[4] Similar decoration appears on the splendid Luttrell carpet formerly at Cotehele,[5] with cherries, lilies, honeysuckles, and daisies, wreathing three great shields of arms (fig. 123).

Hall's *Chronicle* records many feasts and pageants with dresses and settings as naturalistic as any in fifteenth-century France. At Henry VIII's coronation feast eight knights with trappings of green satin embroidered with golden brambles appeared in 'a Pagente made like a Parke, paled with pales of white and green, wherein were certain Fallowe Dere, and in the same Parke curious Trees made by

[1] Cf. the device of Charles Cardinal Archbishop of Lyons in Beauvais Cathedral—two olive trees with scrolls inscribed *Folium ejus non defluet* and between them a tablet with the verses

> Semper oliva viret foliis et splendida palma
> Et virides ramos delphica laurus habet.
> Sic vera celebris princeps virtute vigebat
> Flaccescet nullo tempore nobilitas.

[2] Inventory of 1522, Law, *History of Hampton Court*, i. 61. Cf. the hanging behind the King in the picture of Henry VIII at Hampton Court.

[3] e.g. Wolsey's table carpets, Law, *op. cit*. i. 69; Henry VIII's cups with roses, fleurs-de-lis and pomegranates (the badges of Katherine of Aragon), Palgrave, *Kalendars and Inventories*, ii. 277; collars and girdles, *ibid*. ii. 263 and 264.

[4] 'A salte of golde wrought wt. branches of strawburyes wt. a tufte of strawburyes or hawse upon the cover,' *ibid*. ii. 291; 'a horne of golde enamyled wt. redde and white colombynes,' ii. 264; 'a coller of golde wt. paunsis and roosis,' ii. 263.

[5] H. C. Maxwell Lyte, *A History of Dunster*, ii. 547. It was made between 1514 and 1538, and is mentioned in Dame Margaret Luttrell's will in 1580.

crafte, with Busshes, Fernes, and other thynges in like wise wroughte, goodly to
beholde.'¹ Eight years later, at a tournament in honour of the King's sister the
Queen of Scotland, he and three of his courtiers appeared with dresses and horse-
trappings of black velvet, embroidered all over in gold with branches of honeysuckle, the leaves all loose and stirring as they moved.²

The 'esbattements' of the garden tapestries of the fifteenth century survived in
both French and English Renaissance tapestries³ and hangings of petit-point;
while another medieval type is represented by such entries as 'a covering for a
cushion of black silk wrought, fashioned like a Park, with men, women and
beasts', in an inventory of 1547.⁴ The garden scheme with a central pool survived
in English stump-work until late in the seventeenth century. Indeed all the
naturalism of Elizabethan decoration, when it is not influenced by the foreign
emblem designers, continued to be of the traditional type. Elizabeth's barge had
a canopy with branches of wild rose on a ground of green sarcenet powdered with
golden daisies; while her inventories record many flower-strewn garments, like
a mantle of white lawn, 'enbrodered alover with workes of silver, like pome-
granetts, roses, honiesocles, and acorns', a 'forepart' of white satin embroidered
with 'daffadillies of Venice golde', and dresses embroidered 'like wilde fearne-
brakes',⁵ and like a dead tree. The insects of the fifteenth-century illuminated
borders were perpetuated in dresses 'embroidered all over with wormes of silke of
sondrie colours', 'with spiders, flies, and roundels, with cobwebs', 'with bees and
sondrie wormes', and with 'workes of snailes, wormes, flies and spiders'.⁶ Trees
of the medieval sort form the background of the plaster frieze in the Presence
Chamber of Hardwick Hall; and the final decadence of medieval forest-decoration is
to be found in Elizabeth's hall at Theobalds, decorated with painted trees, complete
with both fruit and birds' nests,⁷ and in her Banqueting House at Whitehall, as described by Holinshed in 1581: 'The top of this house was wrought most cunninglie
upon canvas, works of ivie and hollie, with pendents made of wicker rods, and
garnished with baie, rue, and all maner of strange flowers garnished with spangles
of gold, as also beautified with hanging toseans made of hollie and ivie, with all
maner of strange fruits, as pomegranats, orenges, pompions, cucumbers, grapes,
carrets, with such other like, spangled with gold, and most richly hanged.'⁸
Elizabethan England, indeed, was more interested in vegetables than in flowers.

¹ Hall, *Chronicle*, 1809 edition, p. 512.   ² *Ibid.* 584.
³ e.g. Inventory of Wolsey's goods in 1530: a tapestry of a gentlewoman playing on 'chavicymballes' and
men playing on other instruments. (Brewer, *Letters and Papers of Henry VIII*, iv, pt. 3, p. 2764.)
⁴ 'Apparel of the Duchess of Norfolk', G. F. Nott, *Works of Henry Howard*, vol. i, Appendix, p. cix.
⁵ Inventory of the Queen's Wardrobe, 1600; Nichols, *Progresses of Elizabeth*, iii. 503.
⁶ Nichols, *op. cit.* iii. 506.
⁷ W. B. Rye, *England as seen by Foreigners in the days of Elizabeth and James I*, p. 44.
⁸ Cf. a temporary banqueting house erected in Greenwich Park in 1559: 'made with fir poles and decked
with birch-branches and all manner of flowers, both of the field and garden, as roses, july flowers, lavender,
marygolds, and all manner of strewing herbs and rushes.' Nichols, *Progresses of Elizabeth*, i. 73.

112. Page illuminated by Cybo of Hyères, c. 1390

113. Misericords, *c.* 1300. Wells Cathedral

Tusser's *Points of Husbandry*, written in 1573, for the benefit of mistresses of manor houses and farm houses, has very little on flowers as such, and only includes marigolds and primroses for strewing the floor, and violets 'for sallets' besides a very few common flowers 'for windowes and pots'. Therefore it is hardly surprising that the Elizabethan additions to the medieval vocabulary of decorative flowers should be plants of the kitchen-garden variety. Swags of vegetables adorn the plaster work of Montacute, finished soon after 1580, and the carpets described in the will of Dame Anne Shirley, d. 1622–3,[1] were decorated with gillyflowers, woodbines, cucumbers, cabbages, hawthorn, thistles, and apples. The best Elizabethan flower patterns were derived, not direct from the garden, but from printers' devices; and few of these are so elegant and so truly decorative as the plaster ceiling panels at Speke Hall [2] (fig. 126), each adorned with scrolling sprays of the traditional rose, vine, and columbine.

In France, too, the tradition of the fifteenth century still lingered on, though the Flamboyant technique limited foliage sculpture to plants such as holly, thistle, thorns, seaweed, endive, and parsley, that afforded the utmost scope for intensity of movement and emphasis of modelling. The choir-stalls at Amiens, finished in 1522, show blackberry, nightshade, passion-flower, thistle, clematis, and vine, carved with the maximum of twisted motion. Gradually such technique was modified and adapted to the representation of classic acanthus. On many manuscripts of the late fifteenth and early sixteenth centuries silvery scrolling acanthus foliage appears among the pinks and thistles, the strawberries and sweet peas of the naturalistic borders;[3] though even acanthus leaves were sometimes incongruously brightened with blue and pink flowers, it was they and not the garden flowers which had the strongest appeal for the generations of the Renaissance. The naturalistic style survived for a time as part of the stock-in-trade of the second-rate illuminators,[4] and of the minor printers who specialized in Books of Hours; but the artists of the courts of Italy soon transmuted it into Trajanic *rinceaux*.[5] Similarly in

[1] Shirley, *Stemmata Shirleiana*; a surviving carpet of the type, dated 1614, with pumpkins, fruit, vines, foxgloves, roses, pomegranates, lilies, and honeysuckle, is at present lent by Sir Hamilton Hulse, Bart., to the V. and A. M. A similar variety of fruit and vegetables is to be found in the patterns published by Paul Flindt at Nuremberg in 1611.

[2] M. Jourdain, *English Furniture and Decoration in the Early Renaissance*, p. 104. Cf. the plaster work of the Oak Room, Burton Agnes, 1601–10.

[3] e.g. Bibl. Nat. Néerlandais 1, a translation of Boethius, written in 1491–2, for Louis de Bruges, seigneur de la Gruthuyse; Bibl. de l'arsenal, 5083, Josephus, written for Philippe de Bourgogne, seigneur de la Beure; Bodleian MS. Douce 383, a copy of the Romance of *Gyron le Courtois*, illuminated for Engelbrecht of Nassau, d. 1504; Douce 223, *Hours*, written for some one connected with the Benedictine Abbey of St. Peter's at Blandin near Ghent; and innumerable other examples.

[4] It survived in Spain in the illumination of such documents as Rules and Constitutions of Confraternities (e.g. that of St. Peter at Madrid, 1558, Bodleian MS. Douce 130).

[5] e.g. in the Hours, written *c.* 1527, probably in Milan, for Bona Sforza, wife of Sigismund I of Poland. Bodleian MS. Douce 40. Cf. the 'Gothic leaf' type of decoration found on albarelli from Florence and Faenza *c.* 1475–80 and the rather contorted scrolling foliage, at once medieval and Renaissance, engraved by Israhel van Meckenen, who died in 1503.

woodwork the transition stage between medieval and Renaissance foliage was comparatively short.[1]   Forest and pastoral scenes were still represented [2] in architectural sculpture, though the Gothic foliage mouldings were compressed into such little garlands of fruit and flowers, classically banded with ribbons, as appear upon the choir-screen of Chartres Cathedral, begun in 1514.   But Court life still had as its background the 'pays du satin', 'duquel les arbres ne herbes iamais ne perdoyent ne fleur ne feuilles, et estoyent de damas et velours figuré; ou les bestes et oyseaulx estoyent de tapisserye'.[3]   In tapestry the verdure type was developed into a new *genre*, which in Wolsey's inventory of 1530[4] is called a 'wilderness', representing a thicket of brambles and undergrowth, with a tangle of ragged robin and bachelor's buttons, and birds and rabbits and a hind or doe half hidden among the leaves (fig. 127).   Hunting and 'esbattements', too, were brought up to date, as in the eight hangings of brown velvet each with an oval medallion of the 'plaisirs du feu Roy Henry' set among arabesques recorded in Gabrielle d'Estrées' inventory of 1599.[5]

8

Meanwhile the weakening of the trammels of the scholastic tradition was bringing about a revival of the study of botany. In two illuminated manuscripts, a Book of Hours of the use of Paris, of about 1510,[6] and the Hours of Anne of Brittany, written between 1508 and 1510,[7] naturalism becomes scientific. Each page is decorated with most delicate drawings of a single plant, of which flower, leaves, bud, fruit, stalks, and roots are shown, with its Latin name written above and its French below. Over three hundred plants are represented,[8] each at its most characteristic moment: raspberries half ripe, forget-me-nots just opening in the morning sun. The miniatures are by Jean Bourdichon; and he may well have designed, if he did not execute, such unusual borders. A similar scientific naturalism is evident in certain tapestries of the period (fig. 129). The scientific study of botany was further established by the publication in 1356 of Jean Ruel's *de Natura stirpium*, chiefly compiled from Greek and Latin writers; while the pastoral tra-

---

[1] e.g. in the Palace at Grenoble and on the desk ends of Christchurch Priory, Hants.

[2] e.g. the forest background to the Golden Fleece panel over the chapel door of the Hotel Lallement, Bourges, *c*. 1520, and the pastoral scenes of the Good Shepherd panels of the ceiling of the Grosse Horloge of Rouen, 1517.

[3] Rabelais, *Pantagruel*, Bk. V, Ch. 30.

[4] Brewer, *Letters and Papers*, iv, pt. 3, p. 3045. Such tapestries are commonly attributed to Enghien.

[5] Deville, *Dictionnaire du mobilier*, p. 303. The medallions represented a bull-fight, a tournament, a bear-fight, tilting, a stag hunt, the 'Jeu du ballon', a boar hunt, archery, and a feast. Cf. the Brussels tapestry of the later sixteenth century of 'Les Fêtes de Henri III Roi de France', of which some are in the Galleria degli Arazzi at Florence, and the Paris tapestries of *c*. 1620 of the 'Chasses du roi Francois Ier', of which some are in the Bavarian State Collection.

[6] Formerly in the collection of Sir George Holford.

[7] Bib. Nat. MS. Latin 9474.

[8] For a complete study of the manuscript, see Leopold Delisle, *Les grandes Heures de la Reine Anne de Bretagne et l'Atelier de Jean Bourdichon*, Paris, 1913.

dition was carried on in such work as Noël du Faïl's *Propos rustiques* of 1547 and *Baliverneries* of 1548—rustic stories, simple, witty, good-humoured, with charming natural descriptions.[1] France, indeed, was still interested in nature, and expressed its interest in works as diverse as treatises on agriculture by dwellers in the country and pastorals in the manner of Theocritus by inhabitants of the towns.[2] Even Etienne de Laune was content to perpetuate the medieval tradition in the calendar-scenes of peasant life he published in 1575; even the Roman-trained de l'Orme proposed to modify the classic order in harmony with the naturalism of the French Gothic tradition. He wreathed his capitals in oak and vine, laurel and olive,[3] and wrote:

'Au lieu de la frise je voudrois emploier quelque façon de lierre, qui seroit conduit en manière de frise, avec une fort bonne grâce. Quant à la corniche, couronnes, denticules, gueulle, cymace, cymacion, astragales, filet quarré et austres, ie voudrois disposer tout cela par liaisons, comme si c'estoient branches d'arbres qui sortissent par le dehors, les unes de travers, les autres de pointe. . . .'[4]

In the Hotel de Mauroy at Troyes, built in 1560, the pillars of the courtyard have Corinthian acanthus foliage at their base, from which trails of naturalistic ivy climb up the shaft of the column. Bernard Palissy, himself a man of science and not an artist, since he had not the artistic capacity to stylize his subjects, brought for a time a ruthless naturalism into one province of decorative art. Lizards and snakes and frogs and shells in decorative form had already found a place in decoration;[5] but Palissy, since he could not model them, actually cast from life all manner of natural things—snakes, adders, slow worms, tortoises, salamanders, lizards, frogs, eels, mullet, tench, roach, gudgeon, rays, cockchafers, butterflies, centipedes, crayfish, crabs, lobsters, sea-snails, cockles, whelks, watersnails, limpets, scollops and many other sorts of shells; oak leaves, acorns, laurel, vine, strawberry, ivy, rose, bramble, olive, mulberry, fern, hart's tongue, and rue; and applied the models of them to his faïence plates and dishes (fig. 128). Such naturalism is France's equivalent for the worst extravagances of Elizabethan medievalism; but

[1] Cf. F. de Belleforest's *Pastorale amoureuse, contenants plusieurs discours non moins plaisants que recreatifs avec plusieurs descriptions de paysages*, 1569.

[2] 1544, Sannazaro's *Arcadia* in French; 1555, Vauquelin de la Fresnaie's *Foresteries*; 1557, Hesiod's *Works and Days* in French; 1558, Du Bellay's *Divers jeux rustiques*; 1559, *Daphnis et Chloe* in French; 1565, Ronsard, *Bergerie*; Remy Belleau, *Bergerie*.

[3] Cf. the fluted pillars of the Scuola di San Rocco at Venice, begun in 1517. One is girdled with vine, one with laurel, and one with oak.

[4] *Premier livre de l'architecture*; quoted Havard, *Histoire et philosophie des styles*, p. 191.

[5] e.g. in bronzes by Andrea Riccio, *c.* 1500, who is said to have cast snakes from nature. Wenzel Jamnitzer's work in metal (examples in the Treasury of Ragusa Cathedral, the Galerie d'Apollon of the Louvre, and the Kunsthistorisches Museum of Vienna) are a little later than Palissy's early work. On them see E. Kris, *Der Stil 'Rustique'*, in *Jahrbuch der Kunsthistorischen Sammlungen in Wien, neue Folge*, Band I, 1926, p. 137. Other instances of the use of lizards, snakes, &c., in decoration are a design for a covered cup by the 'Master of 1551' (V. and A. M., E. 030, 2742, 1910), the famous silver bell in Horace Walpole's collection of about the same date, and a design by Virgil Solis (d. 1562) for a jug. (V. and A. M., E. 042, 2874, 1910).

as soon as Palissy came to the court he had to use more sophisticated models provided by François Briot and other silversmiths of the day.

The classical doors of the screen of the Palais de Justice at Dijon, probably
carved by Hugues Sambin about 1585, have charming panels of rose-sprays as
traditional in their feeling as the Elizabethan plaster work at Speke Hall, and the
contemporary wooden doors of the north transept of Saint Maclou at Rouen have
their columns covered with naturalistic trails of ivy. Under Henri II, the decoration was limited to bay, myrtle, olive, oak, acanthus, and palm, and in the worst
years of the wars of Religion, men turned from pastoral to foreign epic;[1] but once
a measure of peace was restored, the scientific study of nature resuscitated the old
tradition.[2] Artists learned to examine the beauties of flowers with renewed curiosity.
The fashion for emblematic needlework had caused the embroiderers to study their
models with fresh attention. An intelligent French gardener, Jean Robin, set himself to meet the demand by opening a garden with hothouses, where rare plants
could be cultivated to serve as models. His scheme met with great success; in a
few years Henri IV bought the establishment, and as the Jardin du Roi (later the
Jardin des Plantes), it continued to be a focus of interest in rare and beautiful
blossoms.[3] Two other developments of French social life had also a marked
influence upon the taste for flowers—first, the building of country houses surrounded by spacious gardens;[4] and second, the re-establishment of trade with the
Levant, which led to the importation of many plants from the East. The crown
imperial and fritillary, then called the guineahen flower, or chequered daffodil,
were introduced into Europe in the sixteenth century; and Gesner saw the first
tulip in flower in Councillor John Henry Herwart's garden at Augsburg in 1559,
and published the first picture of it in 1561. It is not till 1611 that the first tulips are
recorded to have flowered in France, in the garden of Fabri de Peiresc, conseiller
du Parlement de Provence.[5] By 1634 the mania for cultivating tulips had reached
such a height that at Haarlem merchants gave up their businesses to devote their
whole time to them, and were willing to exchange lands and treasures for a
new bulb.

Meanwhile the pattern-engravers were beginning to avail themselves of the botan-
ists' treasures. As early as 1560, Hans Lenckner was publishing panels of mixed
flowers and fruit in naturalistic style.[6] With the turn of the century, such patterns

[1] Tasso's *Gierusalemme* in French, 1595; Dante's *Commedia* in French, 1596.
[2] At the same time the literature of nature revived. Du Bartas, *La Semaine*, 1578; Gauchet, *Plaisir des champs*, 1583; Jean de Lingende, *Pastorales*, 1605; Sidney's *Arcadia* in French, 1624; Racan's *Bergeries*, 1625; *Sylvie*, 1627.
[3] See de Jussieu's speech before the *Académie des Sciences: Année 1727*, p. 131.
[4] Parkinson, in 1629, is the first English writer to give the place of honour to the flower garden and to set the kitchen gardens away at the side of the house.
[5] His agents sent him plants from Paris, Brittany, Holland, Italy, Portugal, Africa, and even from Japan, China, and the Cape of Good Hope. Michel, *Nouvelles études*, pp. 261 et seqq.
[6] V. and A. M. Dept. of Engraving, E. 029, 4254-6, 1910.

114. Details from the Façade of the Church of Rampillon,
Seine et Marne, *c.* 1290

115. Detail of the Door of the North Transept, Cathedral of
Rouen, *c.* 1315

116. The Grand Pont of Paris, from the MS. of the Life of Saint Denis
presented by the Abbot of Saint Denis to Philippe V in 1317

were multiplied: in 1593 Paul Flindt published engravings of detached sprays of natural flowers,[1] and in 1604 Theodor de Bry issued a set of engravings of vases of flowers—periwinkles, tulips, lilies, pansies, daisies, poppies, roses, campanulas, iris, nasturtium, larkspur, calceolaria, fritillary, foxglove, crown imperial, and columbine—from drawings by Jacob Kempener. In 1608 P. Vallet published engravings of the flowers in the *Jardin du Roi*, and these were followed in 1612 by de Bry's *Florilegium novum* and by Michael Snyder's plates of vases of flowers, of which another series was published in 1614. Gradually more formal styles took a second place; after the second edition of Vallet's book appeared in 1623, the tide turned, and flower patterns began to dominate the minor arts. In 1625 Le Clerc published a volume of designs of bouquets which was followed in 1630 by similar designs by N. G. La Fleur. After the 'tulipomania' of 1634, the stream of such publications increased: N. Cochin's *Livre nouveau de fleurs* appeared in 1635 and 1645, M. Robert's botanical engraving in 1638, Le Febvre's *Livre de fleurs* in 1639, Moncornet's in 1645, and Langlois's engravings of tulips, hyacinths, narcissus and iris in 1648. All the flowers of *Lycidas* found their place in decoration:

> The rathe primrose that forsaken dies,
> The tufted crow-toe, and pale jessamine,
> The white pink, and the pansy streaked with jet,
> The glowing violet,
> The musk rose, and the well-attired woodbine,
> With cowslips wan that hang the pensive head.

Emblem designers were content to leave more elaborate conceits and to concentrate their declining influence upon flowers: at Cheverny the panels of the Salles des Gardes were, in 1634, entirely painted with such emblems.[2]

The designs that, at first, had been bouquets and vases of flowers ready for adaptation, began to be printed ready planned for some especial craft or purpose. The embroiderers had prior claims; in 1647 Anne of Austria paid a special visit to the Duchesse de Chaulnes in order to admire a complete set of furniture and hangings embroidered with all kinds of flowers on a gold ground, that had occupied her and her ladies for eight years.[3] Embroidery became more and more naturalistic; 'cette riche bigarrure,' says Etienne Binet,[4] 'qui contrefait un printemps de soye est fort difficile, à cause qu'il faut tellement naïver les fleurs, qu'il faut qu'on

---

[1] V. and A. M. Dept. of Engraving, E. 017, E. 4233, 1910.

[2] Iris with the motto *Calidissima nascor in undis*; tulips with *Nil nisi flore placet*; pinks with *Perii non marte sed arte*; daffodils with *Mei me perdidit ardor*; tiger-lilies with *Vocat in certamina martis*; sunflower (with the arms of Hurault) *Arma gero comitis*; gentian, *Parva coelorum gesto colores*; lilies, *Amas lilia Gallus eris*; columbines, *Nil metuas armata cucullis*; crocus, *Calcatus laetior exit*; and Campanula, *Et signum campana dabis*. Cf. the Carrousel des Fleurs held at the Court of Savoy in 1620, when each knight bore a flower as his badge with an appropriate motto. Menestrier, *Traité des tournois, joustes, carrousels et autres spectacles publics*, Lyons, 1669, p. 226.

[3] Havard, *Histoire et philosophie des styles*, p. 319. A typical embroidery pattern-book is the *Livre de fleurs*, published by Guillaume Toulouze, Maistre brodeur de Montpellier in 1656.

[4] *Essai des merveilles de nature*, p. 358.

croye que ce sont les vrayes fleurs, collées là dessus, et non pas des figures mortes'. The enamellers found in flower patterns the ornament best suited to the new technique of Toutin and Bouquet,[1] and produced endless watchcases, lockets, and other jewels so adorned. Such decoration was even applied on a larger scale; the brothers de Villiers, visiting the Louvre in 1657, admired in the cabinet of Anne of Austria a set of furniture of which the table, guéridons and chair frames were of fine blue enamel painted with a quantity of tiny flowers in many colours.[2] Lace-makers, tapestry-weavers,[3] goldsmiths, wood-carvers, painters, and printers, all found the subjects they needed in flower decoration. Not even the predominant classical style could at first do more than arrange the flowers more formally: Moncornet's *Livre nouveau* of 1665 and Vauquer's *Livre des. fleurs* of 1680 were both welcome and successful, and the King's apartments at Versailles could fitly be graced with silver 'pots à bouquets' chased and fretted with strawberries and strawberry blossom.[4] Bernini might protest at Paris,[5] 'Qu'il ne faut point de fleurs aux bordures de tapisseries . . .' but Monnoyer, the flower painter, could add discreet garlands even to the academic Galerie d'Apollon.

In England, though the Italianate Wotton relegated paintings of '*Landskips* and *Boscage* and such *wilde* works' to open terraces and summer houses,[6] the pattern makers justified their garlands as being 'in the Italian taste'.[7] In England, too, the virtuosity of Grinling Gibbons perpetuated flower-garlands into the eighteenth century,[8] and as late as 1694 Sir Christopher Wren designed the decoration of a room at Hampton Court with long narrow panels of flower decoration on a dark ground.[9] In Germany and in garden-loving Holland the style had even longer life,[10] and there botany was associated with kindred scientific interests by the inclusion of shells, coral, seaweed, and shellfish.[11] The Dutch, too, saw no reason for excluding the kitchen garden from their decorative schemes, and designs for swags at the Town Hall of Amsterdam, made by Artus Quellin about 1645,[12] show both

[1] An early pattern book of flower designs for enamellers was published by Johann Paul Hauer in 1650.

[2] Hautecœur, *Le Louvre et les Tuileries de Louis XIV*, p. 27.

[3] Notably in the 'Pergola tapestries' woven at Brussels in the second half of the seventeenth century, of which fine examples are in the Spanish Royal Collection at Madrid.

[4] Guiffrey, *Inventaire général du mobilier de la Couronne*, i. 58 (1673).

[5] In 1665. Charles Perrault, *Mémoires*, ed. Bonnefon, p. 77.

[6] Elements of Architecture. *Reliquiae Wottonianae*, 1651, p. 287.

[7] e.g. *A New Book of Festoons after the Italian Taste*, by Henry Roberts, London, c. 1670.

[8] e.g. at Petworth. Grinling Gibbons did not die till 1720. Carvings at Ribston Hall, Yorks., show his tradition carried on into the time of James II or even Anne. H. A. Tipping, *Grinling Gibbons*, p. 220. Cf. also English plaster work of the same period, such as that of Acklam Hall, Yorks., c. 1683, and Melton Constable, 1687. See M. Jourdain, *English Decorative Plasterwork of the Renaissance*, figs. 93, 95, and 118.

[9] In the Wren Portfolio of the Soane Museum. Lenygon, *Decoration in England, 1660–1770*, p. 4. In 1699 Verrio painted the King's dressing-room at Hampton Court with a border of orange trees in pots standing between jasmines, with parrots and other birds. Law, *History of Hampton Court*, iii. 68.

[10] Cf. the *Neues Blumen und Laube Büchlein* of c. 1660, the Amsterdam edition of F. Le Febvre's flowers of 1679, and Johann Conrad Reuttiman's Augsburg pattern book of 1691.

[11] Crabs first appear among the birds, beasts, fruit, and flowers in the *Sonige Eenvoldige Vruchten en Spitzen Voor D'Ancomen Kunst Liefhebbende Leucht* of 1611.   [12] Engravings published as *Hangende Festonnen.*

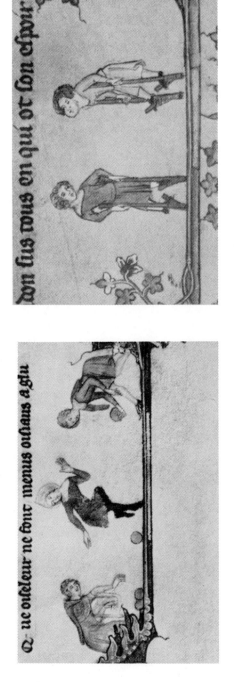

117. Marginal figures from the Romance of Alexander

118. Goblet and cover of gilt metal partly painted.
German, *c.* 1500

shells and lobsters and vegetables such as peas, beans, carrots, and turnips, as well as vine and roses, pine and oak. The Dutchman, Grinling Gibbons, brought the style to England, and some of his carving shows equally varied elements (fig. 133).[1]

Before this, however, the style had died in France. Pastoral pageantry was falling out of fashion when la Fontaine wrote his *Vers pour des bergers et des bergères* in 1678; des Yveteaux no longer dressed at home 'en berger, un chapeau de paille doublé de satin rose sur la tête',[2] and though La Grande Mademoiselle wished 'qu'on allât garder les moutons dans nos belles prairies, qu'on eût des houlettes et des capelines . . . qu'on imitât ce qu'on avait lu dans l'Astrée',[3] the time for such disguises had not yet come round again in the cycle of history. Nature figured in art only in the work of the classical landscape painters;[4] and it was they who inspired the design of the seventeenth-century verdure tapestries of Beauvais and Audenarde. Interest was turning from the flower beds of the Botanic garden to the avenues of Le Notre, and the court agreed with Madame de Rambouillet that 'Les esprits doux et amateur de belles choses ne trouvent jamais leur compte à la campagne.'

[1] At the same time, seaweed inspired the design of Dutch and English marquetry and of Flemish lace.

[2] Arnoud, *Racan*, p. 204.

[3] In 1643 ten panels of Aubusson tapestry had been woven to illustrate the *Astrée*. Perathon, *Essai de catalogue descriptif des anciennes tapisseries d'Aubusson et de Felletin*, p. 62.

[4] See P. E. Crump, *Nature in the Age of Louis XIV*, 1928.

III

THE MARK OF THE INDIVIDUAL

I

IN circumstances in which the personality and leadership of an individual have an urgent significance for his fellows, there is need for a mark by which they may easily recognize him. To distinguish a leader in battle and to differentiate friend from foe in fighting at close quarters, some mark on shield or helm has been used at least since the Early Iron Age; the Attic vase painter portrayed the heroes of the Trojan Wars with devices on their targes; and when northern Europe reached its own epic age, its heroes likewise commonly bore some mark upon their shields. Moreover, to rally their hosts in battle, this charge was repeated upon the standards of the leaders. William of Poitiers, writing towards the end of the eleventh century, describes Harold's banner of golden stuff, charged with the figure of an armed man; and before William of Normandy made his descent on England the Pope gave him a banner, represented on the Bayeux hanging as charged with a cross within a bordure. Such devices were individual and arbitrary; they might be changed as often as their bearer willed,[1] and had no more permanent significance than his casual nickname.

During the age in which feudal administration was beginning to develop beyond the personal work of the lord, great men had to adopt personal devices to use upon their seals, and these tended to approximate to those used on shield and banner.[2] As early as 1037 Robert le Frison, Count of Flanders, sealed with a lion, and in 1088 Raymond de Saint Gilles, Count of Toulouse, sealed with his armorial device of a cross 'vidée, clichée et pommettée'. Some time between 1138 and 1146 Gilbert of Clare, Earl of Hereford, used a seal with the three chevrons that later appear on the Clare coat,[3] and in 1164 Philip of Alsace had on his seal a shield with the rampant lion that was to become the bearing of his house. By the time of Stephen seals were coming into greater use in England, and in the reign of Henry III they were general among the knightly class, and were for the most part armorial in design.

About 1180 three facts combined to give a new importance to the shield-device; the use of the closed helm in battle made some token of identity upon the shield a necessity, the development of tournaments[4] led to the decorative elaboration of

---

[1] Even on the Bayeux hanging the same warriors bear different charges on their shields in different episodes.

[2] For a good general account of the early development of heraldry see J. Woodward, *A Treatise on Heraldry*, i. 50.

[3] *Encyclopaedia Britannica*, 11th ed., *s.v.* Heraldry.

[4] The first tournament in France is said to have been held in 1066.

119. Detail of the jamb of the bronze North Door
of the Baptistery, Florence. By Lorenzo Ghiberti,
1403–24

120. Detail of the jamb of the bronze South
Door of the Baptistery, Florence. By Lorenzo
and Vittorio Ghiberti, 1452–62

121. Detail of the jamb of the Great Door, S. Maria Novella, Florence. Executed by Giovanni Bertini from the designs of Leon Battista Alberti, 1456–70

122. Detail from the Monument of Giovanni and Pietro de Medici in the Old Sacristy of San Lorenzo, Florence. By Verocchio, 1472

such devices for use when they figured in a mimic warfare less grim than real battle, and the inheritance of surnames tended to cause such devices to descend together with the name from father to son.[1] The first great seal of Richard I, cut about 1189, is the first on which a King of England is represented with closed helm, and also (and to some extent as a consequence) the first which displays an armorial bearing—a lion rampant—on the half of the shield that is shown. At his meeting with the Emperor of Cyprus in 1191 King Richard is recorded to have had his saddle-cloth ornamented with 'a pair of golden lioncels facing one another open jawed, one forepaw of each extended towards the other beast as though to rend it'.[2] In France, too, the royal coat was gradually coming into being: a single fleur-de-lis appears as the device of the counter-seal of Philip Augustus in 1180.[3] The origins of such charges remain obscure. Affronted rampant lions are a common type of decoration on twelfth-century eastern textiles, of which many were imported into Western Europe, while fleur-de-lis appear on the tower of Babal Hadid at Damascus; but though the elements of European heraldry may be Eastern—the Arab emirs used heraldic bearings in the eleventh century[4]—and its development may owe something to contact with the East in the crusades,[5] its use in one form or another is universal at a given degree of civilization, and the course of its medieval development is conditioned not by Eastern usages but by the organizing influences of feudal society. It is significant that the textile type of Richard's lions are on his second seal, cut in 1198, modified into the three passant gardant lioncels that still mark the royal shield of England; while in 1225 Louis VIII multiplied Philip Augustus's fleur-de-lis into the blason of 'France ancient'. In warfare only the great lords who led a host into battle needed a distinguishing device, which served for their followers' use as well. When Richard Cœur-de-Lion marched from Ascalon in 1192 his army's shields were decorated, apparently without other distinctions, with 'fiery red prowling lions or golden flying dragons',[6] while a few years later John Garland records that 'the shield makers of Paris serve the towns throughout France and England, and sell to knights shields . . . on which are painted lions and fleurs de lis'. For a time, indeed, all the king's 'mesnie' used his arms; the tomb-effigy of the King of France's grocer, who died in 1247, was set against a background of fleurs-de-lis.[7] But when

[1] Barnard, *Mediaeval England*, ed. Davis, p. 196.
[2] Barnard, *op. cit.*, p. 208.
[3] Woodward, *Heraldry*, i. 346.
[4] Such bearings were used alike on shields, pennons, and standards. See Y. Artin Pasha, *Contribution à l'étude du blason en Orient*, London, 1902, p. 11.
[5] The imperial eagle which the Hohenstaufens adopted in 1345 appears to be of Eastern origin. It is a common type of ornament on Bagdad or Sicilian brocades of the twelfth century (e.g. examples at Siegburg, in the Schloss Museum of Berlin, and on the Alb and Maniple of Bernulphus at Utrecht) and was used by the Ortokid family in the eleventh century.
[6] Barnard, *op. cit.*, p. 197.
[7] Once in the church of the Jacobins, Paris. Bodleian MS. 18350, Gaignières, p. 29.

tournaments, from being mimic mellays, became a series of single combats, each knight naturally needed his own distinguishing mark.

> Chascun de soy armer se peine
> D'armeures neufves et fresches.
> Li un y porte unes bretesches
> En son escu reluisant cler,
> Cil un lyon, cil un cengler,
> Cil un liepart, cil un poisson.
> Cil porte son heaulme en son
> Beste ou oisel ou flour aucune.
> Cil porte une baniere brune
> Cil blanche, cil ynde, cil vert,
> L'autre y poez veoir couvert
> D'armes vermeilles foillollées.[1]

The artist was soon able to vary and beautify the scenes of combat he painted on castle walls[2] with all the devices of blasonry.

> Peigne, teigne, forge et entaille
> Chevaliers armés en bataille,
> Sur beaux destriers trestous couverts
> D'armes indes, jaunes ou verts,
> Ou d'autres couleurs piolés
> Se plus piolés les voulez.[3]

Even churches were sometimes thus decorated; that of Saint Jacques-les-Guerets has a frieze of armed and mounted knights bearing lances with pennons along the south wall of the nave; while the 1295 inventory of St. Paul's includes two copes embroidered with figures of knights fighting.[4]

The use of such armorial bearings gradually became systematized[5] into the art of heraldry. In the course of the thirteenth century this system became fixed and codified, and by the fourteenth century the hereditary system of armorial bearings was fully established.

Gradually, too, heraldry crept into decorative art. Soon after 1200 improvement in coat armour brought a smaller shield into use, and it became the fashion to

---

[1] *Galéran*, thirteenth century.

[2] e.g. At the Château de Saint Florest, Puy de Dôme, in the 'casetta dei soldati' of the castle of Avio, in the 'loggia dei Cavalieri' at Treviso and in the castle of Angera. The Painted Chamber at Westminster was painted with 'all the warlike pictures of the whole Bible'. (W. R. Lethaby, 'The Painted Chamber', in *Burlington Magazine*, July 1905, vii. 263.)

[3] *Roman de la Rose*, before 1318, v. 1705.

[4] Dugdale, *History of St. Paul's*, 1818 ed., p. 317.

[5] This appears to have been done first in France, the original home of tournaments. It is noteworthy that Spain until the end of the fourteenth century followed the Oriental rather than the European use. Pedro the Cruel on the Alcazar of Seville followed Moorish custom and set a long inscription in his own honour over the great door, with quatrefoils, with shields and devices of castles and lions above. Nine great shields of arms of more European type decorated the façade of the convent of San Pablo in Valladolid, built between 1442 and 1463.

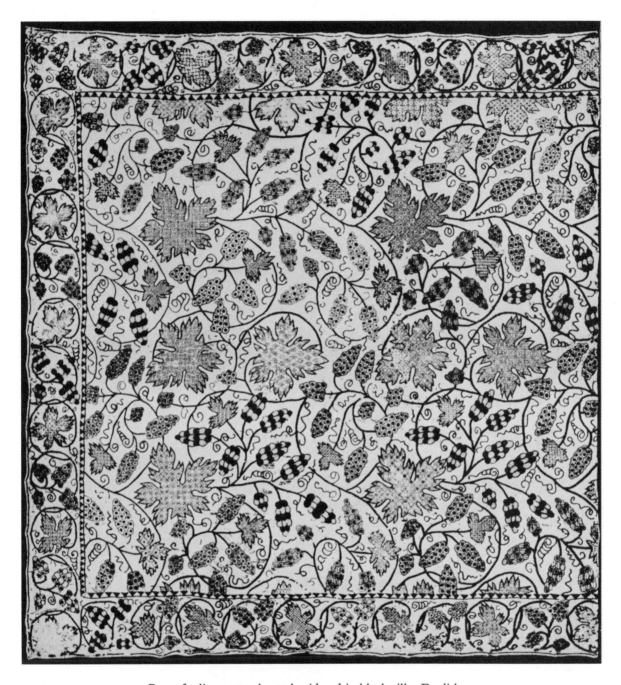

123. Part of a linen coverlet embroidered in black silk. English, *c.* 1570

124. Details of a table carpet formerly at Cotehele, made between 1514 and 1538

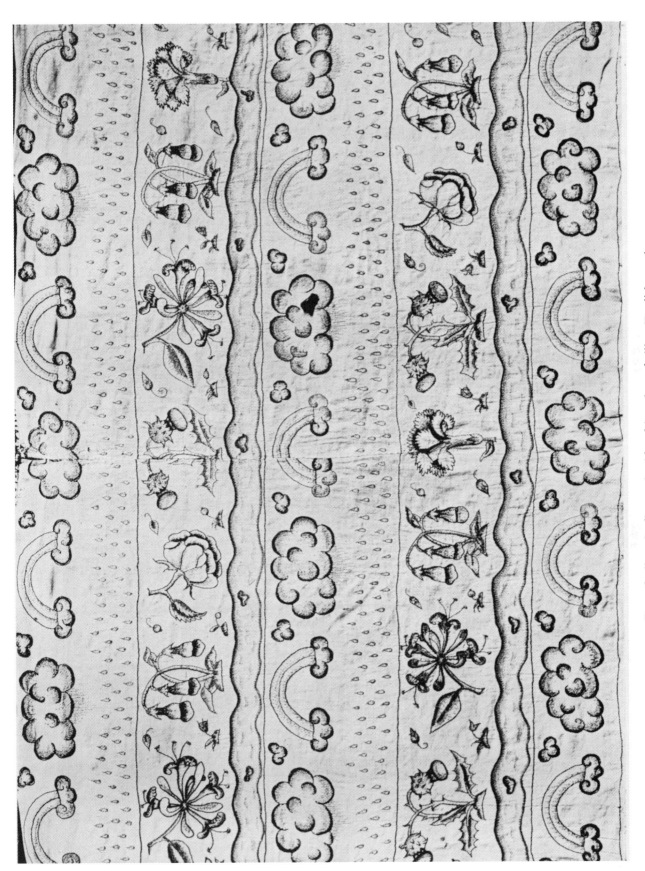

125. Part of a linen bodice, embroidered in coloured silks. English, c. 1600

126. Plaster ceiling of the drawing room, Speke Hall, Lancashire, 1605

embroider the arms upon the surcoat. *Gaydon*, written at this time, describes [1] a

> Cote à armer d'un cendal de Melant:
> Plus est vermeille que rose qui resplent,
> A. iii. lyons batus d'or richement.

A Close Roll of 36 Hen. III [2] describes 'unam robam de meliori sametto violaceo, quam invenire poterunt, cum tribus parvis leopardis in parte anteriori, et aliis tribus parte posteriori.' [3] Clothes embroidered with armorial bearings continued in use during the fourteenth century. [4] Women, too, are frequently represented wearing robes embroidered with their arms. In the fifteenth century they are often shown wearing a kirtle of the arms of their own family, covered with a mantle of their husband's coat. [5]

From such garments the use of heraldic embroideries spread to many other fields. The devices of blazonry were in some sort the symbol of the Church's great attempt to order and to Christianize war, and there was no incongruity in applying them to ecclesiastical use. The 1295 inventory of St. Paul's includes 'unum pulvinar consutum de serico scutelato de dono Wilhelm de Monteforti Decani.' [6] The Syon cope, dating from about 1300, has some sixty coats of arms on its border, forty-six on the stole and eighteen on the maniple. [7]

Similarly coats of arms began to appear in the decoration of illuminated manuscripts; the Ormesby Psalter has shields of arms set sideways as line-endings, or arranged to fill a long oblong panel; and the same decorative use of coats is to be seen in the almost contemporary Gorleston Psalter, which has its miniature of the Crucifixion bordered with oblong panels of the arms of France and England.

---

[1] v. 6403.   [2] Walpole, *Anecdotes of Painting*, ed. Dallaway, i. 24.

[3] Such a coat, embroidered in England a hundred years later, was at some time cut down to form a chasuble, and is now in the Musée de Cluny (fig. 134). It was formerly at Schloss Braunfels.

[4] Count Raoul of Flanders in 1302 had 'une courte-pointe . . . brodée de vert escuchons de diverses armes et la bordure toute semée de chevaliers et d'escuchons' (Dehaisnes, *Histoire de l'art dans la Flandre*, p. 391). Girart de Soucelle, who died in 1339, was represented on his tomb (at Chaloché, Bodley MS. 18359, Gaignières, p. 30) wearing a surcoat charged with six shields of arms, while Walter de Machecol a little later had one powdered with more than twenty shields of his own arms (at Villeneuve, *ibid.*, p. 232), and the accounts for the funeral of Geoffroi de Valennes in 1352 include 'Une bote de cendaux de plusieurs couleurs, laquelle fut semée de XXX petits escuçons des armes dudit chevalier.' (Havard, *Dictionnaire de l'ameublement*, s.v. semé).

[5] e.g. Margaret Peyton, born Barnard, in a window of about 1485 at Long Melford. Anne, Countess of Stafford, born a Neville, was formerly represented in the north window of Lichfield Cathedral, dating from 1480, with a mantle of her own arms lined with her husband's.

[6] Dugdale, *History of St. Paul's*, 1818 ed., p. 316.

[7] Warwick, Castille and Leon, Ferrars, Geneville, Everard, Knights Templars, Clifford, Spencer, Lindsey, Butler, Sheldon, Monteney of Essex, Champernown, England, Tyddeswall, Grandison, Fitzalan, Hampden, Percy, Chambowe, Ribbesford, Bygod, Mortimer, Grove, de Bassingburn, and others. The 1315 inventory of Christchurch, Canterbury, includes a white cope with the arms of the King of Scotland, three copes with the arms of bishops, and five with the arms of other persons (W. St. John Hope, *Heraldry for Craftsmen and Designers*, p. 321), while the 1388 inventory of Westminster Abbey includes six murrey coloured carpets woven with the arms of Edward III and Philippa of Hainault, and many others with arms of English nobles, as well as an altar frontal used at the burial of Edward III with the arms of England and France woven in gold on red and blue velvet. (*Ibid.*, p. 322.)

Shields of arms, again, were often combined with some more or less naturalistic foliage as a border to stained glass windows (fig. 135) and formed one of the commonest types of decoration for the enamelled copper gemellions made at Limoges.[1] Rather similar decoration in painting was freely used for castle halls; between 1295 and 1298, the castle of Hesdin in Flanders had a room painted with a powdering of shields of its owner's arms,[2] and in 1307 the hall of the castle of Lens was painted with 'une renghée d'escus armoiés.'[3] Nearly fifteen hundred shields of the nobility of Forez decorate the vault of the fourteenth-century Salle de la Diana at Montbrison. Floor tiles were similarly ornamented (fig. 136); the paving of the chapel of Saint Pérégrin at Saint Denis has fleurs-de-lis crowned by a trilobed arcading. A more complicated form of such patterning decorated the dormitory floor tiles of the monastery of Saint Etienne at Caen,[4] which had a rose-window pattern filled in with nineteen coats of arms on a ground of formal foliage. Heraldic devices became one of the commonest forms of decoration for the hangings that made the bare walls of castles beautiful. In 1352 King John of France had his embroiderers working night and day to finish hangings of blue velvet embroidered with 8,544 fleurs-de-lis,[5] and between 1350 and 1364 he ordered 239 pieces of tapestry, either woven with his coat or with a powdering of fleur-de-lis. So usual did such hangings become that it is not at all uncommon in manuscripts of the late fourteenth or early fifteenth century to see Solomon, Our Lady, and God the Father all enthroned under baldequins of the arms of France.[6] Naturally such decoration was also applied to funeral monuments. The enamelled copper tomb-slab at Saint Denis, of Jean de France, the son of Saint Louis who died in 1247, had a border of alternate shields of arms and roundels with angels,[7] while that of Alix de Bretagne (d. 1221) and her husband Pierre de Dreux (d. 1250) in Saint Yved de Braine had an elaborate border of ninety-three shields, as well as a background of heraldic diapers.[8] With the development of the altar tomb such heraldic decoration took on a new importance; round that of Marie de Dreux[9] (d. 1274) there were thirty-six little figures, each representing a mourner of her family, with their shields of arms

[1] A fine example in the Treasury of Conques has the shield of France in the centre and six others round it. Similarly the 'cassette de Saint Louis', given by Philippe le Bel with the hair-cloths of St. Louis to the Abbey of Notre Dame du Lys, near Melun, is decorated with shields of arms of France ancient, Castille, Burgundy ancient, Montfort, Courtenay, Dreux, Brittany, Flanders, Navarre and Champagne, Graville, Dammartin, Toulouse, Coucy, Beaumont, Roye, Jerusalem, Bar, Montmorency, Normandy and Harcourt. It is now in the Church of Dammarie; Viollet le Duc, *Dictionnaire du Mobilier*, i. 81.

[2] Dehaisnes, *Histoire de l'art dans la Flandre*, p. 417.

[3] *Ibid.*, p. 413. The courtyard of the castle of Issogne, belonging to the family of Challant, is decorated with a great series of shields of arms of the great men of the family with the inscription: 'Miroir pour les enfants de Challant.' E. Bérard, 'Antiquités romaines et du Moyen Âge dans la vallée d'Aoste' in *Atti della Società di Archeologia e belle arti per la provincia di Torino*, iii. 124.

[4] Bodley MS. 18361, Gaignières, p. 2.

[5] Deville, *Dictionnaire du Tapissier*, p. 264.

[6] e.g. Bodley MS. Rawl. liturg. e. 14.

[8] Bodley MS. 18346, Gaignières, p. 99.

[7] Bodley MS. 18347, Gaignières, p. 26.

[9] *Ibid.*, pp. 78–80; Saint Yved de Braine.

127. Wilderness tapestry. Flemish (Enghien), *c.* 1510

128. Plate by Bernard Palissy, *c.* 1565

129. Tapestry. French, *c.* 1510

above, while on that of Jeanne de Chastillon[1] (d. 1290) a row of mourning monks appeared beneath a simple arcading, with a shield of arms hanging between each arch. This scheme was soon varied. A tomb chest of the late thirteenth century at Chichester has quatrefoils alternately filled with figures of weepers and with shields. Often, too, the mourners were omitted; a row of shields hangs beneath a simple tri-lobed arcading on the tomb of Sir John Pitchford, of about 1285, in Pitchford Church, Salop; similar shields hang in a more elaborate gabled arcade on the lower story of the Eleanor Cross at Northampton, while on the tomb in Westminster Abbey of William Earl of Pembroke, who died in 1296, the shields are hung from pegs by short straps on the upper edge. Such decoration translated into architecture adorns the spandrels of the wall arcade of the aisles of the Abbey, which date from about 1260: the first four bays have shields of arms hung by side straps from two projecting heads (fig. 137), while twenty-four more shields were painted in the spandrels of the remaining bays. Ten triangular shields fill the spandrels of the gabled arcading on the gateway of Kirkham Priory in Yorkshire, built between 1289 and 1296.[2]

The decorative use of shields of arms was soon developed into a diaper; the chasuble on the tomb of Raoul de Beaumont, buried at Angers in 1197, has circles with fleurs-de-lis, leopards, and fantastic birds, with large fleurs-de-lis between,[3] while Jean de France, who died in 1247, appeared on his tomb wearing a robe lozenged[4] with castles and fleurs-de-lis.[5] The upper cushion represented under the head of the effigy of Aveline Countess of Lancaster in Westminster Abbey, dating from about 1275, is covered with a lozenged diaper of her husband's arms, while the lower cushion has a similar pattern of her father's arms.[6] Such lozenged diapers were also used for hangings; for instance in 1297 Angers Cathedral had a set so patterned with the arms of France and England,[7] and in 1380 Charles V had a set lozenged in blue and white satin, with the blue panes embroidered with the arms of France. From embroidery they were transferred into other arts; lozenged diapers of France and Castille, for instance, decorate the north rose window of Chartres, made while Blanche of Castille was Regent of France, and appear again

---

[1] Bodley MS. 18347, Gaignières, p. 27.

[2] A fourteenth-century development of this decoration appears on the Percy tomb of about 1340 in Beverley Minster, the spandrels of which are filled with little figures of Lady Eleanor Percy and her husband each holding shields of their own arms. In the early fifteenth century splendid use was made of shields as vaulting bosses, for instance in the Chichele porch at Canterbury, 1422–3.

[3] Farcy, *La Broderie*, p. 41. A thirteenth-century coverlet in the Hotel-Dieu of Rheims is lozenged with fleurs-de-lis and with a variety of lions, fishes, birds, and grotesques.

[4] It is probably from such lozenged diapers that the lozenge was adapted as a form especially for the arms of women. It first appears in 1306, according to Sir William St. John Hope.

[5] Bodley MS. 18347, Gaignières, p. 26. On her tomb in Westminster Abbey Eleanor of Castille wears a dress diapered with the charges of her paternal arms.

[6] Christ Church, Canterbury, in 1315 possessed an alb with lozenges of the arms of the King and of Leybourne, and another with those of Northwode and Ponyngg in squares. W. St. John Hope, *Heraldry for Craftsmen and Designers*, p. 120.   [7] L. Farcy, *La Broderie*, p. 90.

in the windows of Amiens and the Sainte Chapelle; the engraved pavement of the steps of the altar of the Virgin in Saint Denis has a similar pattern, with lobed outlines to the lozenges; and the altar itself is of stone entirely covered in front with lozenges of glass, behind which towers of Castille appear on a red ground, fleurs-de-lis on blue, and roses and eaglets on purple. The famous Valence casket, made at Limoges between 1290 and 1296, is enamelled with a lozenged diaper of Valence, England, Dreux, Angoulême, Brabant, and Lacy, connexions of William de Valence, Earl of Pembroke (fig. 141). The tomb of Charles d'Évreux, who died in 1336, in the Church of the Cordeliers at Paris, had the columns of its canopy painted with lozenges of his arms alternating with formal leaf patterns;[1] and similar decoration in carved stone, with quatrefoil rosettes alternating with the lilies of France and the Castles of Castille, appears as a dado on the Church of Saint Omer. A lozenged diaper of fleurs-de-lis appears alike on some of the colonnettes of Saint Denis and on the reliquary cross of Montreuil-sur-mer (fig. 138). Occasionally lozenges were taken from such diapers and used as a powdering in a less formal scheme; the reliquary of Charroux (fig. 139) has little lozenges of single fleurs-de-lis and heraldic castles scattered on a ground of scrolling filigree.

In the middle of the fourteenth century this type of diaper was modified into a 'compas', or circle divided into radiating panels. Many of Charles V's heraldic tapestries were planned on this scheme,[2] which was also transferred to plate. Louis d'Anjou had innumerable pieces of gold work with enamels 'assemblés en fourme de compas',[3] and a 'compas' of this sort adorns the enamelled lid of a lost nautilus cup, which since the fifteenth century has been among the treasures of All Souls College, Oxford[4] (fig. 140).

Another development of the use of heraldic robes was the use of armorial mantles in the representation of heraldic and other beasts, birds, and butterflies. The fourteenth-century seal of Calais shows a boar with a cloak tied round its neck, flying up to display the arms of the town upon it;[5] while the half florin of Edward III has a sejant crowned leopard wearing a cloak of the royal arms.[6] In 1316 a set of hangings was made for Jeanne de Bourgogne with 1,321 parrots

[1] Bodley MS. 18346 Gaignières, p. 16. A later English example of such a usage is the paintings of about 1350 in Hailes Church, Glos. with the arms of Richard Earl of Cornwall, the imperial eagle, Castille and other coats.

[2] For instance 'un chambre de drap d'argent, à cinq compas brodez aux armes de France et aux daulphins.' Farcy, La Broderie, p. 92.

[3] e.g. Laborde, Notice des Émaux, ii. 1.

[4] See Joan Evans, in Proc. Soc. Ant., 2nd series, xxx, 1918, 92; and C. Enlart, L'émaillerie cloisonnée à Paris sous Philippe le Bel et le maître Guillaume Julien, in Monuments Piot, XXIX (1927–8), p. 1 et seqq. Cf. Moranvillé, Inventaire de Louis duc d'Anjou, p. li: 'VIII esmaux de plitre qui sont sur tour de compas à IIII pointes; et en IIII d'iceulx sont en escus les armes de France esmailliées, et es autre les armes de Navarre.'

[5] Cf. a panel of the vault of Henry V's chantry at Westminster, that shows his antelope lying upon the ground, cloaked with a drapery that flies up to display the arms of France and England quarterly.

[6] W. St. John Hope, Heraldry for Craftsmen and Designers, p. 215. The goblet owned by Charles V in 1381 with 'ung lyon ou convescle emmantellé des armes de France et d'Angleterre' may well have been a gift from Edward III (Labarte, Inventaire du mobilier de Charles V, p. 72)

130. Panel of Flemish tapestry, c. 1620

131. Commode of marquetry in flower designs. French, *c.* 1675

'amantelés des armes nostre sire le Roy',[1] 661 butterflies with the arms of Burgundy on their wings, and 7,000 trefoils to powder the ground. A year later she had 'j escrinet paint à oyselés vestus de mantelès de plusieurs armes'.[2] Charles V had two tapestries with stags (his badge), 'emmantellez aux armes de France',[3] and the 1418 inventory of the Château de Vincennes includes a candlestick arising from a lily, supported by two birds in mantles of France and Navarre.[4] Occasionally such decoration was adapted to a lozenged diaper; in 1379 the Church of Saint Sepulchre in Paris had a tapestry 'losengé à lyons et à lycornes emmantellés de manteaux armoiez des armes de Castile et d'Alençon.'[5] A variation on such a scheme is used on an interesting late fourteenth-century tapestry now in the Rijksmuseum at Amsterdam (fig. 142), which shows unicorns, stags, and elephants wearing cloaks of the arms of Comminges impaling Beaufort and Turenne,[6] seated within battlemented castles. Above these fly angels holding crowns, with herons flying behind them. The castles are set lozenge-wise; between each is a rose with the same arms charged upon its heart.[7]

Not only were beasts cloaked in heraldic mantles, but sometimes they held the arms,[8] and sometimes they themselves were the field for heraldic decoration. Charles V owned eleven tapestries with lions charged with the arms of France and Bohemia, as well as four embroideries decorated with butterflies 'qui ont des elles de France'.[9] Sometimes birds and arms were combined in powderings; Charles V had a set of white satin vestments embroidered for Notre Dame de Paris to celebrate the birth of the Dauphin in 1369, with the orphreys 'brodez par quartiers aux armes de Frances et oyseaulx d'or, tenant en leur bec roles escripts de *Ave Maria*'[10] and a set of hangings 'aux armes de France et de Navarre, lozengée de papegaux.'[11]

In the course of the fourteenth century the shield ceased in fact as well as in art

[1] Douet d'Arcq, *Comptes de l'argenterie des Rois de France*, 1874, p. 74.
[2] Douet d'Arcq, *Nouveau recueil des comptes de l'argenterie*, p. 17.
[3] Labarte, *Inventaire du mobilier de Charles V*, p. 380. He also had two cushions of blue velvet 'brodé a bestes sauvaiges emmantellées des armes Monseigneur le Dauphin'. *Ibid.*, p. 373.
[4] Havard, *Dictionnaire de l'ameublement*, s.v. Chandelier.
[5] Guiffrey, *Histoire de la tapisserie en France*, p. 26.
[6] My thanks are due to Mr. A. van de Put for his kindness in identifying these arms. The coats are quarterly, 1 and 4, argent a bend azure and six roses gules in orb (Roger de Beaufort) 2 and 3, or three bends gules (for coticed or and gules) (Turenne), and the same dimidiated with gules four otelles argent (originally a cross patty throughout) (Comminges). Guillaume III de Beaufort acquired Turenne in 1350. In 1349 he married Eleanor de Comminges. (Morère, *Grand Dictionnaire*, 1759, ix. 1296.) The tapestry must have been woven between 1350 and his death in 1394.
[7] Cf. p. 108.
[8] In 1405 Margaret of Flanders had a set of hangings of green cendal embroidered with owls bearing the arms of Burgundy; Dehaisnes, *Histoire de l'art dans la Flandre*, ii. 909. The Franks Bequest in the British Museum includes the fifteenth-century Mazer of Count Louis of Flanders decorated with silver gilt lozenges enamelled with parrots having shields of Flanders hanging from their beaks.
[9] Labarte, *Inventaire du mobilier de Charles V*, p. 380, and Nos. 2618, 1064 *bis*, 2752, and 3050. Such butterflies, with the arms of Brittany and Anjou on their wings, appear on some of the tapestries of the apocalypse made for Louis I of Anjou and Marie de Bretagne, now in the Musée de l'Évêché at Angers.
[10] Farcy, *La Broderie*, p. 91.
[11] Labarte, *Inventaire du mobilier de Charles V*, p. 367.

to be the most important field of heraldry; improvements in armour had greatly reduced its value as a defence and consequently its significance in the field.[1] Meanwhile the development of feudal law was giving a new importance to the square banner. The *Coustume de Poitou* shows that its use was the right of a man, whether count, viscount, or baron, who had the 'droit de chastel'—the high, middle, and low justice: while the mere 'Chastelain' who had not such rights could only show his arms on a shield.[2] Such banners were not employed in decoration before the middle of the fourteenth century; an early example of their use is the eight square banners of arms that filled the sides of the canopy on the tomb slab of Alix of Brittany, who died in 1344.[3] About 1420 banners began to appear on English seals; that of Walter Lord Hungerford shows his shield flanked by the banners of his lordships of Heytesbury and Hussey. Such usage, however, was soon superseded by the great development of the decorative side of heraldry consequent upon the increasing importance and elaboration of tournaments.

2

The men of the fourteenth century were peculiarly sensitive to the picturesqueness of the pageantry of war. Froissart shows little enthusiasm for pure beauty, but never fails to express his delight in vessels on the sea with their banners and pennants and blazoned shields shining in the sun; and in the glint of sunlight on helmets and armour and the lances of a company of soldiers on the march. But as war became grimmer and more mercenary, the tournament came into the inheritance of martial glamour and beauty; and as the use of heraldry tended to take a less important place in battle, its development during the fourteenth century was increasingly conditioned by the usages of the joust. Men no longer went into battle vowed to God and the saints, but entered the lists vowed to the service of their lady; her token might become their badge, and their mottoes might more or less clearly indicate their devotion. The usages of romantic chivalry brought these new elements into decorative art; *courtoisie* was as important an element of life within the castle as within the lists, and its devices might fitly adorn the hangings and furniture, which were helping more and more to turn the castle from a place of defence into a place of ease and beauty. A casket of the time of Philippe le Bel (fig. 143), enamelled with shields of France and England and a shield 'd'or à la croix d'azur vairée d'or' in quatrefoils shows the influence of such sentimental

---

[1] The Aldeburgh brass of 1360, at Aldborough in Yorkshire, is probably the last English effigy on which the shield appears as part of the martial equipment, while the Wantone brass of 1347, at Wimbush, Essex, is the first on which the effigy bears no shield.

[2] P. C. F. Menestrier, *Le véritable Art du Blason*, Lyon, 1671, p. 18. In England an 'écu en bannière' was used by knights, bannerets, and ladies. See Woodward, *Treatise on Heraldry*, i. 62.

[3] Formerly in the Church of the Mathurins in Paris; Bodley MS. 18350, Gaignières, p. 15.

132. Gold casket, formerly belonging to Anne of Austria. French, *c.* 1660

133. Mirror frame in carved limewood, ascribed to Grinling Gibbons, *c.* 1690

chivalry alike in the two pairs of lovers that decorate the cover and in its inscription:

> Dosse Dame ie vous aym léalmant,
> Por dié vos prie que ne m'obblie mie.
> Vet si mon cors a vos comandemens
> Sans mauvesté et sans nulle folie.

Louis d'Anjou had a 'drageoir' and two goblets enamelled with scenes of a lady helming her knight for the lists, while his squire held his horse in the background.[1] Jousting scenes were a favourite scheme for the painting of a castle hall: as early as the twelfth century Philippe Mouskes in his rhymed chronicle[2] describes such a decoration. It continued in fashion throughout the Middle Ages; in 1307 the countess Mahaut d'Artois had the Castle of Lens painted with 'ès pignons de la sale Chevaliers joustans'.[3] Such scenes were also represented on furniture[4] (fig. 142) and plate.[5] Often the knights represented were made identifiable by the charges represented on their shields.[6] Viollet le Duc describes[7] a pricket candlestick enamelled on a background of fleurs-de-lis with the figures of four mounted knights, each bearing a shield and stretching out his hand ready to take his banner from two men on foot and to enter the lists. The charges on their shields, housings, and banners show that the knights are Charles of Anjou, King of Sicily, the lords of Dammartin and Dreux-Bretagne, and the Duke of Burgundy. The knight could be represented riding in the lists even on his tomb, as is Aymer de Valence on the gable of his tomb-canopy in Westminster Abbey.

Every usage of the lists was reflected in decorative art. The irregularly shaped jousting shield, with its deep notch for the spear on the dexter side, appeared on seals in place of the plain shield of war.[8] The two forms of shield were carved one above the other on the long cusped panels of a stone window of the late

---

[1] Moranvillé, *Inventaire de Louis II duc d'Anjou*, pp. 350, 473, and 494. The Church of St. Mary Magdalen at Bermondsey still possesses a fine late fifteenth-century silver-gilt plate with a medallion of such a scene.

[2] i. 377.

[3] Dehaisnes, *Histoire de l'art dans la Flandre*, p. 413. Similar paintings still survive in the hall of the Château de Cindré, Allier.

[4] Another good chest panel with a knight charging his adversary is in the Saffron Walden Museum.

[5] Edward I had a cup chased with knights on horseback (Havard, *Dictionnaire de l'ameublement*, s.v. Pade), and in 1347 the Dauphin had a great basin enamelled with a Knight Hospitaller jousting with another knight (Laborde, *Glossaire des Émaux*, ii. 151 s.v. bacins à laver). In 1408 Valentine de Milan had a covered cup of gold with men jousting on the cover (F. M. Graves, *Deux inventaires de la maison d'Orléans*, p. 136). The inventory adds 'Porter à Paris pour vendre.'

[6] Cf. the contract for painting the gallery at Conflans, 1320, 'et sera l'image du conte d'Artois, en tous lieuz là où il sera, armoiez des armes dudit conte; et les autres ymages des chevaliers, nuez de plusieurs couleurs, et leurs escus, en lieu où ils apperront, seront armoiez de leurs armes, et enquerra l'en queles armes ils portoient ou temps qu'ils vivoient'. J. M. Richard, *Mahaut Comtesse d'Artois*, p. 356.

[7] *Dictionnaire raisonné du mobilier français*, ii. 56, s.v. Chandelier. The famous Joûtes de Saint Denis, held to celebrate the admission of Charles VI to the order of knighthood, were commemorated in a set of tapestries woven between 1397 and 1400. Michel, *Histoire de l'Art*, iii. 350.

[8] e.g. on the seals of John Tiptoft, Earl of Worcester, in 1449, and William Herbert, Earl of Huntingdon, 1479.

fifteenth-century house at Petherton, Somerset, known as King Ina's palace; and tilting shields alone appear on the armorial panels of the George Inn at Glaston-bury. The jousting helm with large crest and heavy mantling was everywhere used to crown the shield.[1] The whole was usually completed by supporters: a usage, possibly decorative in origin,[2] influenced and changed by the custom of dis-guising 'tenants' to hold the knight's shields and banners before the tourney. Such supporters were in the fourteenth century as varied as the disguises of the 'tenants'. Louis d'Anjou, for instance, had plate and hangings on which his arms were shown supported by angels, lions, and eagles with outstretched wings hold-ing the shield in their beaks.[3] All kinds of schemes were adopted for the display of shield and banner with supporters; the seal used by William Lord FitzHugh of Marmion has the shield and helm topped crest-fashion by a lion's head, with the rest of the lion appearing behind the shield with paws thrust out on each side to hold banners of his arms.[4] The seal used by Margaret Lady Hungerford and Botreaux in 1462 has a rather different scheme; it shows her half-kneeling in her widow's dress to read a book with a great banner on either side of her; on one side that of Hunger-ford and Botreaux, upheld by a lion, and on the other that of her parental Botreaux and Beaumont, upheld by a griffin.[5] In Germany the knight's lady was sometimes shown holding his shield; a relief of about 1430 in the Altertumsmuseum of Mainz shows a fashionable lady in a flowing robe holding two tilting shields, while the windows of the north aisle of Cologne Cathedral, presented in 1508-9, have their lower quarries filled with ladies holding shields.

The plan of showing the banner supported by the heraldic beast of the family became the recognized scheme in the fifteenth century; it was probably stereo-typed by the devices set at the top of the pavilions of the joust. Queen Jeanne d'Évreux had a *nef* with two banners of her arms each set in little castles and sup-ported by two wild men.[6] A tapestry belonging to Charles V in 1381, powdered with large fleurs-de-lis diapered with smaller ones, with a lion in the middle, had four beasts in the corners holding banners.[7]

[1] An example without supporters is the gable end of the shrine of St. Simeon at Zara, *c.* 1380, with the arms of Lewis the Great of Hungary. On the tomb of Count Gottfried of Arnsberg (d. 1371) in Cologne Cathedral are quatrefoils enclosing his shield and others with his crested helm. In 1389 Valentine de Milan had a set of hangings of blue velvet powdered with golden fleurs-de-lis, 'à heaumes de plusieurs seigneurs, desquelles les armes de l'Empereur et du Roy de France sont ou millieu'. F. M. Graves, *Deux inventaires de la maison d'Orléans*, p. 71.

[2] See Woodward, *Treatise on Heraldry*, ii. 27. Stephen Longespee, who died in 1260, used the long swords of his nickname as supporters to his arms on his seal. A typical instance of the use of supporters and crest is provided by the lesser seal used by William Montagu, Earl of Salisbury, between 1337 and 1344.

[3] Moranvillé, *op. cit.*, p. xix. The eagle similarly displayed used by Ferdinand and Isabella of Spain was adopted out of devotion to St. John.

[4] Hope, *Heraldry for Craftsmen and Designers*, p. 216.   [5] *Ibid.*, p. 217.

[6] Leber, *Collection des meilleures dissertations*, 1838, xix. 142. Cf. a silver gilt fountain owned by Louis d'Anjou in 1380, with two wild men holding banners of his arms on the plinth, with a castle in the middle surmounted by a ship with banners of his arms at either end. Moranvillé, *op. cit.*, p. 223.

[7] Labarte, *Inventaire du mobilier de Charles V*, p. 379.

In England their use is characteristic of the fifteenth century and is commonly sculptural. The tomb of Lewis Robsart, Lord Bourchier, the standard bearer of Agincourt, erected in Westminster Abbey in 1431, has a lion on one side and an eagle on the other each holding banners of his arms carved in high relief. In architectural decoration they played an important part. The house of Nevill Holt, in Leicestershire, built by Thomas Palmer not long before his death in 1476, has its buttresses shaped as shafted columns, of which the capitals serve as pedestals for sejant lions and antelopes of York and Lancaster, that once held banner-vanes. At Hampton Court Henry VIII's heraldic beasts appeared on pinnacles and copings, gables and battlements, bridges and gates; lions, dragons, leopards, hinds, harts, greyhounds, and antelopes, each bearing a gilded banner vane with the crown, rose, fleurs-de-lis, or portcullis. Such figures were even used on plate and furniture; Henry VIII had table-ornaments shaped as 'a white greyhound and a dragon standing upon mounts'[1] and 'four cappes with vanes of silver and gilte, engraven with the Kinges armes and rooses for the postes of a beddstede'.[2] With the Renaissance shields were substituted for banners, but heraldic beasts survived as a characteristic Tudor decoration of the newel-posts of staircases.[3]

Supporters, however, were but one of many usages of the tournament that made their way into decoration. While the knights were awaiting their challengers their shields were commonly hung from a tree beside the lists,[4] and this fashion of displaying the shield passed into decorative art at the end of the thirteenth century.[5] On the arcading on the tomb of Eleanor of Castille (d. 1290) in Westminster Abbey shields of Castille, Leon, Ponthieu, and England hang by their guiges from tree stocks, of which the foliage rises above the shields to fill the heads of the arches. The seal of Roger de Leybourne, who died in 1284, shows his shield of seven lions rampant hung upon a tree, with his banner charged with a single lion behind, and his helm with a lion crest at the side. The type seems to have gone out of fashion for a while, and to have been revived in the second half of the fourteenth century. Edmund Mortimer, Earl of March, used in 1372 a seal showing a large shield of Mortimer hanging from a tree and supported by two sejant lions whose heads are covered with helms crested with panaches of feathers,[6] while the seal of

---

[1] Brewer, *Letters and Papers of Henry VIII*, iv, pt. 2, p. 224.   [2] *Retrospective Review*, 2nd series, i, 1827, p. 133.

[3] e.g. at Crewe Hall, Knole, and Charlton House, Kent. Foreign instances of the use, perhaps due to English influence, occur on a sixteenth-century staircase in the Kunstgewerbemuseum at Cologne and on the staircase of the Palacio de San Boal, *c.* 1540, at Salamanca.

[4] Jean le Maingre describes the great elm before the tents of the knights; 'à trois branches de cest arbre avoit pendu à chacune deux escus, l'un de paix, l'autre de guerre'. *Mémoires de Jean le Maingre, dit Boucicaut, Maréchal de France*; quoted Havard, *Dictionnaire de l'ameublement*, s.v. Pavillon.

[5] It was perhaps by an analogy with the Tree of Life that the shield of Jean Chauvin, d. 1339, was shown hanging from a simple floriated cross on his tomb slab in the Church of the Barnabites at Paris. Bodley MS. 18350, Gaignières, p. 5.

[6] Burlington Fine Arts Club, *Catalogue of Exhibition of British Heraldic Art to the end of the Tudor Period*, 1916, p. 82. Cf. 1369 Inventory of Charles V: 'Deux petiz orilliers brodez à bestes sauvaiges qui ont testes de hommes armez.' Labarte, *Inventaire du mobilier de Charles V*, p. 317.

Thomas Lord Despencer, in use before 1397, has his shield in the middle, and on either side a tree from which hangs a lozenge of arms: on one Clare, for his lordship of Glamorgan, and on the other a lion for his barony of Burghersh.[1]

The pavilions of the lists were commonly decorated with the arms and devices of the knights. Henry V, for his interview with the King of France, had 'a large tent of blewe velvet and grene richly embroidered with two devises, the one was an Antlop drawing in an horse mill, the other was an Antlop sittyng in an high stage with a braunche of Olife in his mouthe; and the tente was replenished and decked with his poysie "After busie labour cometh victorious rest" and on the top . . . was set a greate Egle of golde.'[2]

Heraldic beasts were from time to time represented beneath such pavilions; Charles V in 1369 had a set of hangings of red cendal embroidered with a lion seated in a pavilion with the arms of France.[3] Clerambault gives a painting of a tapestry that once belonged to the Cathedral of Lyons, to which it was given or bequeathed by Cardinal Charles de Bourbon, Archbishop of the see between 1437 and 1488: the ground was striped vertically and powdered with the cipher Ch.B. in gothic letters; in the middle was a blue pavilion powdered with the Cardinal's fleur-de-lis and charged with his bend sinister, flying a banner with the badge of a hand and a scimitar and bearing the motto 'N'espoir ne peur'. Within the pavilion was a lion, holding the Cardinal's shield. The cords of the pavilion were held by two griffins and two bears all holding banners of the badge and motto.[4]

To decorate the 'shields of peace',[5] the trappings of the horses, the robes of the

[1] Margaret, daughter of Richard Beauchamp, Earl of Warwick, about 1435 has the shields of her father and her husband and herself on her seal hanging from the Beauchamp ragged staff. Other examples of shields hung from trees occur on the seals of Thomas de Holand, 1353, Sir Robert de Marne, 1366, Ivo Fitz Warin, 1398, and John la Warre, 1390. W. St. John Hope, *Heraldry for Craftsmen and Designers*, pp. 129 and 198. A curious survival of the practice occurs in the group of the risen Christ and the Magdalene at Autun, who have between them an oak tree with two shields of the donor's arms hanging from its branches, while up its stem winds a banderole with the legend 'Noli me tangere'. The fashion was perpetuated in the pageants of Tudor days. In the tenth year of Henry VIII there was a pageant for the French ambassadors with five trees: 'ye first an Oliue tree, on which hanged a shield of ye armes of the Church of Rome; the ij a Pyneapple tree wt. the armes of the Emperour; the iij a Rosyer wt. the armes of England; the iiij a braunche of Lylies, bearing ye armes of Fraunce, and the v a Pomegranet tree bearing ye armes of Spayn'. Hall, *Chronicle*, 1809 ed., p. 595. Similarly two 'trees of much honour', 34 ft. high, with leaves of cloth of gold and flowers and fruit of silver and gold, a hawthorn for the English king, and a mulberry for the French, were set up at the Field of the Cloth of Gold to hang the royal shields on before the jousts. *Ibid.*, p. 6.

[2] Hall, *Chronicle*, 1809 ed., p. 90. Olivier de la Marche describes the tent of Messire Jehan de Bonniface when he held the field against Jacques de Lalain, 'de soye blanche et verde, et par-dessus avoit un blason des armes du chevalier, timbré d'une dame tenant un dard en sa main, et par dessus avoit en escrit "Qui a belle dame garde le bien" ', Havard, *Dictionnaire de l'ameublement*, s.v. Pavillon. The inventory of Valentine de Milan and her husband, drawn up in 1408, includes a pavilion and its hangings of white embroidered with the spines of hedgehogs, and another worked with horseshoes. F. M. Graves, *Deux inventaires de la maison d'Orléans*, p. 163.

[3] Labarte, *Inventaire du mobilier de Charles V*, p. 376.

[4] P. Gelis Didot and H. Laffillée, *La peinture décorative en France du XIᵉ au XVIᵉ siècle*. The monument of Marchese Spinetta Malaspina, d. 1352, erected at Verona in 1536 and now in the V. and A. M., shows him mounted beneath a pavilion of which the curtains are held back by Roman warriors.

[5] The will of Prince John of Eltham, drawn up in 1334, directs that two men are to follow the bier bearing

134. Chasuble of red velvet embroidered in gold, cut down from a surcoat or hanging of the arms of England. English, *c.* 1440

136. Heraldic tiles, *c.* 1260. Chapter House, Westminster

137. Shield of the Earl of Cornwall, from a spandrel of Westminster Abbey, *c.* 1260

135. Detail of border of window, Church of Saint Sié, Vosges, *c.* 1300

knights, and the pavilions of the lists, the use of personal badges was developed and elaborated. The use of such badges was as early as the use of armorial bearings. A sprig of broom—a badge said to have been adopted by Geoffrey of Anjou as an emblem of humility—appears on either side the throne on the great seal of Richard Cœur-de-Lion; and the foundation of the Ordre de la Cosse de Genest some fifty years later[1] and its subsequent development brought the broom-plant into decorative use. In the collar of the order it was treated formally. The same scheme was applied to the brocading of the chasuble of the Cardinal de Bourbon, Archbishop of Lyons between 1437 and 1488,[2] which is horizontally striped in the royal colours, with lines of the collar of broom pods and garters inscribed with the motto 'Esperance'. On dresses and plate it was more often treated naturalistically. In 1387 the King of France had two hunting cloaks and some thirty dresses embroidered with broom sprays, two aulnes long, going all round the dress over the shoulders,[3] while a few years later Valentine de Milan owned a covered cup of gold enamelled with flowering and seeded broom.[4] Occasionally it was used as a background to figures; Louis d'Orléans had a tapestry 'à genestres flories et à grans personnages'.

The broom was often combined with some other plant used as a personal device. In 1399 Queen Ysabeau had tapestries 'à bordure de moron et de geneste en bende'.[5] In 1401–3 Charles VI had more than fifty decorated with the leaves of pimpernel and broom, and with the arms of France and Dauphiné.[6] Eight years later the Duc de Guyenne had a cloak embroidered round the left armhole with golden eyelets worked like peacock feathers,[7] with twenty-four branches of may and eight of broom running down the sleeves and spreading over the back. The heraldic significance was emphasized by little leaves and pods among the may and broom of gold sewn with silks in the king's colours; white, green, red, and black.[8] Similarly Charles VI had at the Hotel St. Pol a *drageoir* of silver gilt chased all over with broom, with a roundel of France ancient on the lid set in a wreath of broom and may,[9] and a tapestry with great golden fleurs-de-lis powdered with branches of broom, and his motto 'Jamais' between.[10]

his helmets and shields, 'lun pur la guerre de nos armez enters quartillez et lautre pur la paix de nos bages des plumes d'ostruce' (G. W. Eve, *Decorative Heraldry*, p. 120).

[1] It is said to have been instituted on the occasion of the marriage of Saint Louis in 1234.

[2] Now in the Musée des tissus historiques at Lyons.

[3] Douet d'Arcq, *Nouveau recueil des comptes de l'Argenterie des rois de France*, p. 194.

[4] F. M. Graves, *Deux inventaires de la maison d'Orléans*, p. 137.

[5] Guiffrey, *Histoire de la tapisserie en France*, p. 16.   [6] *Ibid.*, p. 24.

[7] On one of his manuscripts Charles VI is represented with peacock feathers embroidered on his dress within a border of peacocks gorged with a crown, and scrolls with 'James' (Geneva MS. fr. 165; H. Martin, *La miniature française* f. cxvii). Peacock's feathers were later adopted as a badge by the house of Austria, and appear on their manuscripts, e.g. Bodley Douce 219, *c.* 1477–82, written for Maximilian of Austria or Engelbrecht of Nassau.

[8] L. Pannier, 'Les Joyaux du Duc de Guyenne' in *Revue Archéologique*, 1887, xxvi. 219.

[9] Havard, *Dictionnaire de l'ameublement*, s.v. Drageoir.

[10] *Bibliothèque de l'École des Chartes*, xlviii, 1887, p. 74. Guiffrey, *Inventaire des tapisseries du roi Charles VI*

Other plants were also in early use as badges; in the twelfth century Enguerrand de Candavène set sheaves of oats—in punning allusion to his name—upon his seal. Edward I is said to have inherited his device of a golden rose on a green stem from his Mother, Eleanor of Provence. Such use was greatly multiplied soon after 1400. Philippe le Hardi, preparing his expedition against England, had his motto— *Moult me tarde*—embroidered within a wreath of his wife's marguerites on the sails of his ships,[1] and Margaret, wife of Jean sans Peur, wears on her tomb at Dijon a dress embroidered with her marguerites.[2] In 1411 Charles d'Orléans had 3,900 pennons painted with the device of the nettle for the army he sent against the Duke of Burgundy, and two years later his inventories include forty-one robes embroidered 'à la devise de l'ortie'.[3]

Badges, however, were as varied in kind as the charges of the shield. Froissart says[4] that Charles VI took his device of a flying stag with a golden collar and the motto *Caesar hoc mihi donavit* from a vision seen in a dream. The Duke of Orleans in 1426 had a set of blue velvet hangings embroidered with gold fleurs-de-lis, his arms and his device of little wolves, with the punning motto *Il est lou il est*.[5] The Duke of Berry fell in love with a girl named Ursine, so took as his device the bear and the swan, *ours-cygne*.[6] The manuscript of his *Grandes Heures*,[7] illuminated by Jacquemart de Hesdin before 1413, has several pages bordered with swans and bears in quatrefoils (fig. 150), with his arms and monogram with scrolls between of his motto *le temps venra*. Similar decoration appeared on several pieces of his plate.[8] In 1416 he had a set of bed-hangings of black, em-

---

vendues par les Anglais en 1422. A miniature of Charles VI and Pierre Salmon painted in 1409 shows the king wearing a dress embroidered with sprays of roses with his motto 'Jamais' on the hem, standing against a bed similarly embroidered, with 'Jamais' on the tester, while a courtier standing by has his sleeves embroidered with fig sprays. (Bibl. Nat. MS. franc. 23279, fol. 19; H. Martin, *La Miniature française*, Pl. CXV.) The design even of jewels was adapted to the scheme; Charles d'Orléans had a collar set with fourteen rubies and sixty-two large pearls 'environné de fleurs de geneste esmaillées de blanc et de noir'.

[1] Palliser, *Historical Devices, Badges, and War Cries*, p. 54.

[2] The Duke of Guyenne about 1415 adopted the forget-me-not and his wife the marguerite, and the two plants appeared on a set of hangings of white embroidered silk. L. Pannier, 'Les Joyaux du Duc de Guyenne' in *Rev. Arch.*, 1873, xxvi, p. 214.

[3] Laborde, *Les Ducs de Bourgogne*, iii. 206. Cf. the 1408 inventory of Valentine de Milan: 'une chambre de sarge vers à feuilles d'orties'. F. M. Graves, *op. cit.*, p. 164.

[4] *Chronicles*, Bk. II, chap. 104. It was also used by Charles VII, Louis XI, and Charles VIII. Palliser, *Historical Devices, Badges, and War Cries*, p. 111.

[5] Laborde, *Les Ducs de Bourgogne*, iii. 302. See *Œuvres complètes du Roi René*, ed. Quatrebarbes, iii (1846), p. 117.

[6] M. Guiffrey suggested that these may not represent the name Ursine, but the fief of Lourcine. *Les Inventaires de Jean duc de Berry*, 1894, i. cxxix. It has also been suggested that they represent Ursin, St. Ursin being one of the patrons of Berry.

[7] Bibl. Nat. Lat. 919.

[8] In 1401 he had a flask of silver gilt, enamelled in the middle with his arms, with four white swans, each holding a scroll with the motto *le temps venra* (Guiffrey, *Les Inventaires de Jean duc de Berry*, ii. 18), and in 1406 he was given a salt-cellar with a white swan holding a similar scroll on the lid, sitting on a golden bear (*ibid.*, i. 179.) A little later he had a salt-cellar called the 'Sallière du pavillon', shaped like a ship, with castellated poop and prow, on one of which was a white swan with a shield of the Duke's arms round his neck, and on the other a bear wearing a helm likewise enamelled with the Duke's arms.

138. Reliquary cross. French, *c.* 1250. Church of
Montreuil sur Mer, Pas de Calais

139. Reliquary of filigree and enamel. French,
c. 1260. Church of Charroux, Vienne

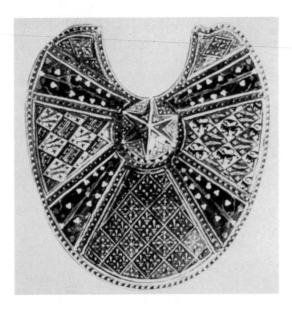

140. Lid of a nautilus cup, enamelled with a diaper
of the arms of France and Navarre, Hainault and
Clermont-Nesle, Champagne and Nesle. French,
c. 1300. All Souls College, Oxford

141. Casket of copper, gilt and enamelled, with a diaper of the arms of England, Angoulême,
Valence, Dreux, and Brabant. Probably made for William de Valence, *c.* 1290–6

broidered with branches of an orange tree (another of his badges), crowns, bears, and swans; and another of red with orange branches, scrolls with *le temps venra* and interlaced initials.[1] Such amatory devices were even used in battle; in 1414 the Dauphin was in love with a girl called la Cassinelle, and went to war against Burgundy with a standard bearing a K, a swan (*cygne*), and an L to represent her name.[2]

Such rebus badges were, however, much less common in France than devices of a more symbolic sort. Jean sans Peur in later life adopted the device of the briquet and flames, with the motto *Ante ferit quam flammam micat*, which was inherited by his son Philippe le Bon. The various inventories of the Dukes of Burgundy show its use not only on robes and standards but also on chariots and plate.[3] With its adoption by the Order of the Golden Fleece, founded in 1429, its use was multiplied among the knights of the order. The personal mottoes used in France were commonly amatory in type. Nicholas Rolin adopted the motto *Seule* on his marriage and it appears as a powdering on the tapestry given by him and his wife to the hospital they founded at Beaune about 1440, with their initials and the impaled arms of Rolin and Salins. After the assassination of the Duke of Orleans in the rue Barbette his widow, Valentine of Milan, took as her device a runnel or 'Chantepleure',[4] with the letter S, for 'Seule, souvent, se soucioit et souspiroit', and the motto *Rien ne m'est plus, plus ne m'est rien.'*[5] Sometimes the allusion was religious. Pierre de Rohan had for his badge a pouch powdered with staves and shells, surrounded by a rosary, with the motto *Dieu gard de mal le pèlerin*;[6] while Anne of Brittany had the Franciscan girdle as her device.[7]

Sometimes the badge was changed to correspond with the changed fortune of its bearer. René of Anjou on his marriage adopted the device of a brazier in flames[8] (fig. 151) with the mottoes *D'ardent desir*; *Devot lui suis*, for his wife; when he was widowed he used a broken bow, with the motto *Arco per lentare,*

---

[1] Guiffrey, *Les Inventaires de Jean duc de Berry*, ii. 217.

[2] *Juvenal des Ursins*, ed. Michaud and Poujoulat, ii. 496.

[3] Laborde, *Les Ducs de Bourgogne*, ii. 34 et seqq.; *Glossaire des Émaux*, ii. 320 s.v. Foisil. For knives enamelled with the device see *Exposition de 1878. L'Art ancien*, p. 275. The copy of René of Anjou's *Mortifiement de Vaine Plaisance* made for him and his third wife Isabel of Portugal shows the briquet, flint, and flames, with the Duke's motto *Aultre n'aray* and the Duchess's *Tant que je vive*. Brussels, Bibliothèque royale, 10308; P. Durrieu, *La Miniature flamande*, Pl. XXXVIII.

[4] In 1455 she gave her brother a golden chantepleure 'pour porter une plume sur son chappeau.' Laborde, *Glossaire des Émaux*, ii. 204.

[5] Brantôme, *Dames illustres*, Discours 2.

[6] See for example Bibliothèque Nationale, Estampes, Gaignières, Pc. 18, fol. 33.

[7] It appears all over the walls of her oratory at Loches; and decorated a pair of flagons and three bowls of gold, 'wt. frers girdells aboute the feete and cover and also aboute the knoppe of the cover a doble Romayne A and within the armys of Fraunce and a crowne above', that passed into the possession of Henry VIII (Palgrave, *Kalendars and Inventories*, ii. 283). The Franciscan cord was used for vaulting ribs and door mouldings all over Portugal *c.* 1490–1515; it appears in Spain all round the Palace of the Mendoza—'la casa del cordón'—at Burgos and on the façade of the University of Alcà.

[8] It appeared fifteen times on his tomb at Angers. See Bodley MS. 18346, Gaignières, p. 5.

piaga non sana; and when his children and grandchildren were dead and the old prince was left solitary he took the device of a single sprig rising from a golden mound, with the motto *Vert meurt*.[1]

The motto itself became an important element in decoration. The inventory of Louis d'Anjou includes a surprising number of objects inscribed with the mottoes of the joust: *Prenez en gré; A mon pooir; A jamais; A ma vie; Loiauté passe tout;*[2] *Je ne puis mieulx; Pour mieux valoir*, and so on, over twenty in all.[3] The use long remained in fashion: Charles the Bold in 1467 had cups inscribed *La plus du Monde*, *Tant plus y pense*, and *J'ay obey*, as well as with Charles VII's *Espérance* and the philosophic *Moien*.[4]

The political factions of fifteenth-century England made the use of badges in that country more serious and more strictly heraldic than in France. The idea of badges as distinguishing all the members of a man's household and following was far stronger than the French idea of the device as a thing even more personal than the coat of arms. By 1389 this political abuse of badges had become so strong in England that it had to be ordered that no one should wear the badge of any nobleman unless he was retained by him for life, in peace as in war, under sealed indentures; while no valet or archer was to wear them unless he were a menial servant engaged by the year.[5] A certain number of badges, indeed, were used as collars as the mark of informal orders of chivalry, bound together in allegiance to a party or person. A collar of Edward IV's Suns and Roses, linked by the Fitz-Alan oak leaves, appears on the effigy of Joan, Countess of Arundel, at Arundel; while the more famous Lancastrian collar of SS[6] is still in official use. Such collars passed for a time into the repertory of decoration. The collar of SS appears as part of the pattern on a silver gilt cup and cover, probably made for Prince Edward the son of Henry VI, which has a powdering of EEs and slipped lilies and trefoils between the collars, and crowns on the lobes[7] (fig. 152). The

---

[1] Lecoy de la Marche, *Le Roi René*, Paris 1875, ii. 78. Comte P. Durrieu, *Comptes Rendus de l'Académie des Inscriptions et Belles-Lettres*, 1908, p. 102. L. Germain, in *Bull. Mon.* lxi, 1896, p. 5. For examples see Bibliothèque Nationale, Estampes, Gaignières, Pc. 18, fols. 10 and 11.

[2] Cf. a belt with the same inscription owned by Louis de Valois, duc de Touraine, in 1389. F. M. Graves, *Deux inventaires de la maison d'Orléans*, p. 61. It was used as a motto by Pope Innocent VIII.

[3] H. Moranvillé, *Inventaire de Louis I duc d'Anjou*, p. xxix.

[4] Laborde, *Les Ducs de Bourgogne*, ii. 34. Philippe le Bon's inventory of 1420 includes a spectacle case and a dog collar with *Y me tarde*, a bed tester embroidered with *Autre n'auray* (*ibid.*, ii. 265, 266, 268). Such detached mottoes were less used in England, but Henry V had his *une sans plus* 'flourished upon leech damask' for his French Queen's Coronation. Palliser, *Historical Devices, Badges, and War Cries*, p. 368. Often the motto was set on a scroll and combined with the badges of the owner; Valentine de Milan, for instance, in 1389 had a set of satin hangings embroidered with suns and stags, with a dove in the middle holding a scroll inscribed *à bon droit* and a brooch with a doe enamelled white, with a scroll inscribed *plus haut* (F. M. Graves, *op. cit.*, pp. 71 and 72).   [5] *Retrospective Review*, 1827, p. 302.

[6] Much speculation has been devoted to its meaning; the SS most probably stands for the *Souverain* motto of Henry IV, such as appears round his ostrich feathers on the seal of 1399 (*Archaeologia*, xxi, 1846, p. 365). Pierre de Lusignan's Order of the Sword also had a collar of SS, here signifying *Silence*. J. Huizinga, *The Waning of the Middle Ages*, 1924, p. 76.

[7] It is now at Oriel College, Oxford, which bought it in 1493. Dr. M. Rosenberg suggests (*Der Goldschmiede*

142. Tapestry with beasts wearing cloaks of the arms of Roger de Beaufort, Turenne, and Comminges. Flemish, woven for Guillaume III de Beaufort between 1350 and 1394

143. Casket of copper gilt, enamelled with shields of France and England. French, c. 1300

144. Carved oak coffer. English, *c.* 1350

145. Fragment of embroidery. English, *c.* 1300

1402 inventory of St. Paul's includes two copes with orphreys of the collars of SS of John of Gaunt, with his stag lying in the middle of each.[1]

English badges were often taken from the charges of the shield itself, as were the de la Pole's leopards' heads and wings, the Bourchiers' water-budgets, and the Veres' silver mullets; sometimes they were identical with the crest, like the Courtenay dolphin, the Vere boar, and the Hungerford sickle.[2] When they were not thus heraldic, English badges were usually less romantic and naturalistic than the French;[3] the ostrich feathers used by the sons of Edward II,[4] the Percy crescent and swivel, the Lovel hanging-lock, the Zouch eagle and crooked billet are all more formal and heraldic than the French devices;[5] and even the Bohun swan was not treated as freely as the swan of the Duke of Berry. The animal badges, too, were more formally used; it is rather exceptional to find Henry IV's antelope treated as on the stalls at King's Lynn, where it appears both naturalistically and heraldically represented. Henry V, however, thanks probably to his French connexions, had badges more fantastically and more naturalistically treated, such as appear in the decoration of his chantry in Westminster Abbey.[6] But usually even the roses of York and Lancaster were stereotyped into severely heraldic flowers, and the Wars of the Roses gave them such political significance that they were rarely treated with naturalistic freedom. By the time of Henry VII a Tudor rose could even be represented with supporters like a coat of arms.[7] Badges were most commonly used as powderings; Humphrey de Bohun in 1322 left seventeen carpets and bankers of green powdered with his badge of the swan;[8] the Black Prince in 1376 left to Canterbury Cathedral a set of black tapestries powdered with ostrich feathers, and to his son worsted hangings powdered with mermaids, swans with women's heads, and ostrich feathers in embroidery; and Edward Earl

---

Merkzeichen, Ausland und Byzanz, p. 249) that the hall-mark may be Burgundian. Mr. Cripps had earlier suggested (*Old French Plate*, p. 37), that the mark was that of Paris for 1462–3; but M. Carré (*Les poinçons de l'orfèvrerie française*, p. 127) negatives this.

[1] *Archaeologia*, l. 502.

[2] W. St. John Hope, *Heraldry for Craftsmen and Designers*, p. 181. Cf. the Low Country usage; for instance the cope, now in the Halle aux Draps of Tournai, given by Guillaume Fillastre, Bishop of Tournai, 1460–73, embroidered with stags' heads with his initial between the horns and martlets between the heads.

[3] Naturally there were exceptions even in France; for instance, Louis I, Duke of Anjou, used the devices of a double cross, the crescent of his Order of the Crescent, and the eagle and lion of his adopted mother, Joan of Sicily (H. Moranvillé, *Inventaires de Louis I, duc d'Anjou*, p. xx) with the motto, *Je le doy*.

[4] And by the sons of all the Kings of England until Arthur Tudor constituted them the badge of the Prince of Wales. See also Sir Harris Nicolas, 'Observations on the Origin and History of the Badge and Mottoes of Edward Prince of Wales', in *Archaeologia*, xxi, 1846, p. 350.

[5] An exception that proves the rule is John, Duke of Bedford, who, thanks to a Burgundian wife, had badges and mottoes in the French style. His Book of Hours (B. M. Add. MS. 18850), painted in Paris between 1423 and 1430, gives his badge as a golden root and his motto as *à vous entier*; his wife's as *j'en suis contente* and a spray of juniper. Branches of this are shown wreathed with scrolls of his livery colours with the motto.

[6] For a discussion of these badges see W. St. John Hope, 'The Funeral, Monument, and Chantry Chapel of Henry V,' in *Archaeologia*, lxv, 1913–14, p. 129.

[7] Catherine of Aragon's pomegranate was a little more freely treated; e.g. 'a cuppe of golde wt. a cover and theron an image of Seynt Kateryne enamyled white wt. a wreth of pomegarnette about it'. Palgrave, *Kalendar and Inventories*, ii. 282.   [8] *Archaeologia*, xxi, 1846, p. 349.

of March in 1380 bequeathed a bed of black satin powdered with white lions and gold roses. The tomb of Richard II in Westminster Abbey shows him wearing a robe powdered with the badges of his house; his mother's white hart, his grandfather's sunburst, the Anjou broomplant, and his own ostrich feathers.[1]

Even at the end of the fifteenth century the English use of badges remained formal; the Leigh Cup, for instance, given by Sir Thomas Leigh to the Mercer's Company in 1499 or 1500, is covered with a lozenged tracery of cabled moulding, each lozenge enclosing a badge of a flagon or a maiden's head.[2] Similarly on the chimney piece in the Bishop's palace at Exeter, set up by Peter Courtenay soon after 1485, his own dolphins and his king's portcullises are reduced to the little bosses of a formal moulding, though the bold treatment of the arms below redeems the effect of the whole.

Such naturalistic flower badges as were used in England were commonly of a canting sort.[3] The seal of Thomas Lord Roos of Hamlake, 1431–61, shows his peacock crest flanked by two large flowering plants of hemlock;[4] while the chimneypiece of a room in Tattershall Castle, built about 1433, shows the shields of the family alliances of Cromwell alternating with panels carved with his Treasurer's purse wreathed in natural gromwell (fig. 153).[5] In the time of Richard II Thomas Mowbray, Duke of Norfolk, appeared in the lists 'his horse being barbed with crimson velvet embrodered richly with Lions of silver and mulberry trees'[6] in canting allusion to his name; while some sixteenth-century glass at Lullingstone, Kent, shows a wreath of peach-boughs round the arms of Sir John Pechey.

In England canting mottoes and badges usually referred to the name or device of their bearer and not to his lady.[7] Such canting devices, indeed, were commonly used in England by ecclesiastics who did not bear arms. The tomb of Bishop John Harewell, d. 1386, in Wells Cathedral has two charming hares at its foot; John of Whethamsted, d. 1465, has his wheatears on his tomb at St. Albans;

[1] His rose, sun, and feathers appear again on a gold covered cup described in the 1380 inventory of Louis of Anjou, enamelled inside 'de blanc et de rouge cler en maniere d'une double rose; et ou milieu d'icelle a un solail d'or; et tout le dehors dudit hennap est très nettement taillié à plumes.' Moranvillé, *Inventaire de Louis duc d'Anjou*, p. 76; cf. the 1528 inventory of Henry VIII: 'A pomander with ostrich feathers and red roses.' Brewer, *Letter and Papers*, iv, pt. 2, p. 2244.

[2] The Foundress's beaker at Christ's College, Cambridge, made for Margaret, Countess of Richmond, in 1507, has a reticulated pattern with the daisies of her name at the intersections, and the lozenges filled in with roses, fleurs de lis, and portcullis-shaped letters MM. The knop is of portcullises surmounted by four daisies and a Tudor Rose.

[3] Canting *charges* had early been used on English coats: e.g. Roses for Rosoy, 1201, Falcons for Falconer and Corbies for Corbet, 1170, and Conies for Connesburgh. See Woodward, *Treatise on Heraldry*, i. 52.

[4] W. St. John Hope, *Heraldry for Craftsmen and Designers*, p. 200.

[5] See G. MacN. Rushforth, *Antiquaries' Journal*, vi. 163.

[6] Hall, *Chronicle*, 1809, ed. p. 4.

[7] The same is true of the Low Countries: cf. the tomb slab of Martin de Visch, Seigneur de la Chapelle, d. 1452, in the Cathedral of Bruges. Its background is powdered with his motto *moy* and a dog, while the border is of bridles, in Flemish 'mooi'. An exceptional French use is the device of Agnes Sorel on her Chateau de Beauté, a sallow tree (surelle) and the rebus $\frac{A}{L}$, A sur L. Palliser, *Historical Devices, Badges, and War Cries*, p. 240.

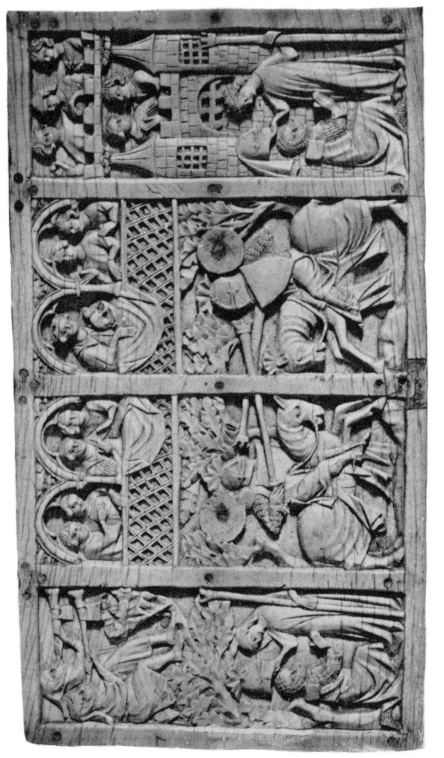

146. Top of an ivory casket carved with a tournament scene. French, c. 1280

147. Misericord in the Church of l'Isle Adam, *c.* 1450

148. Carving over the door of the Maison aux Licornes, Montferrand, *c.* 1500

149. Title-page of the inventory of the jewels of Charles V of France. French, *c.* 1410

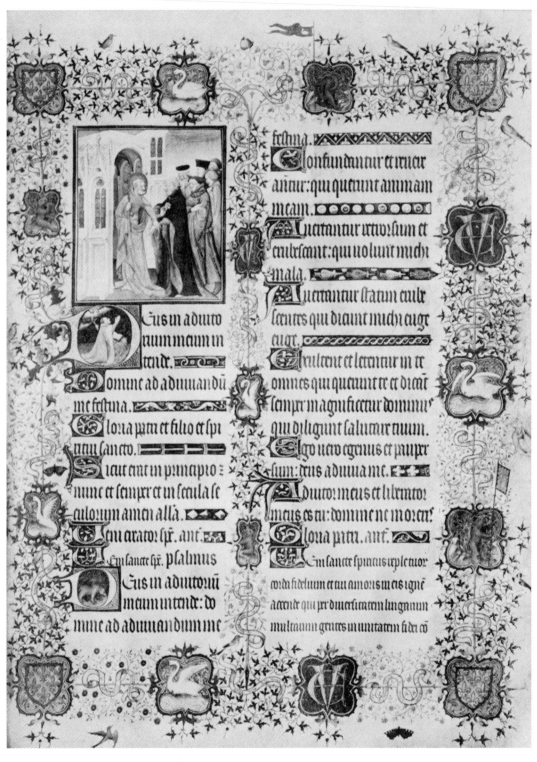

150. Page of the *Grandes Heures* of the Duc de Berry, painted by Jacquemart de Hesdin and his school before 1413

Bishop Alcock's cock and globe appear in the carvings of his chantry at Ely (fig. 154); Bishop Goldwell set gold wells on the vaulting bosses of the presbytery at Norwich. Thomas Ramrygge, Abbot of St. Albans between 1492 and about 1520, has his shield supported by rams with collars inscribed *rygge* on his chantry; Bishop Hugh Oldham has owls with scrolls inscribed *dom* on the roof of his chantry at Exeter (fig. 155), built in 1509; and Abbot Islip's rebus of an eye and a slipped tree adorns the cornice of his chantry chapel of about 1530 at Westminster.

In the fifteenth century personal badges were the commonest feature of English decoration in church as well as in castle. The individual himself dominated both the spiritual and the material church; the most important church buildings of the fifteenth century were chantries set up as a memorial to the honour of an individual and endowed as a chapel whence God might ever receive the prayers of the priests for his soul. Naturally such chantries were freely decorated with all the heraldic devices of the individuals they commemorated.[1]

The walls and windows of the Chapel of King's College, Cambridge (fig. 158), are alike decorated with every conceivable form of the arms and badges of its founder: in the windows alone there are 94 Lancaster roses, 13 Tudor roses, 12 York *roses-en-soleil*, 70 hawthorns, 52 portcullises, 50 fleurs-de-lis, and 23 initials He. R.[2] A long series of Tudor and Yorkist badges—portcullis, rose, falcon and fetterlock, rose and sun, gartered rose, and so on—appears on the screen of Prince Arthur's chantry at Worcester; while Henry VII's Chapel at Westminster is adorned with every kind of heraldic decoration, even the exterior walls being divided into stone panels each centred with one of the royal badges.[3] The vestments were likewise adorned with badges; Henry VII had a set of copes woven in Florence with three great crowned portcullises linked by sprays of red and white roses, and bequeathed them to Westminster.[4]

Such devices were used not only on chantries, but on whole churches that owed much to a noble founder or rebuilder. The boars and mullets of John de Vere, Earl of Oxford, appear on the porch of Lavenham Church, and the piers and arches of Wingfield Church, Suffolk, are studded with the leopard's heads, wings, and Stafford knots of Michael de la Pole, Earl of Suffolk (d. 1415) and his wife Catherine Stafford.[5]

[1] The usage was a little less common on the Continent, but important examples still survive. The Chapel of the Bourbons in Lyons Cathedral has its balustrade carved with the winged stag of Charles VII and his motto, *Espérance*; the mouldings of the Church of Brou are studded with the knotted P and M of Philibert of Savoy and Margaret of Austria, her marguerite daisy and his palm, and the crossed branches and briquets of Burgundy; while on the holy water stoup and elsewhere appears her motto: *Fortune infortune forte une*. The unfinished Royal Mausoleum of Batalha in Portugal has for its chief decoration the last two words of the device *Leau te starey tão y zerey*—I will be loyal to you even though I be in the tomb—repeated more than two hundred times.

[2] Willis and Clark, *Architectural History of the University of Cambridge*, 1886, i. 581.

[3] Rather similar panelling appears at St. Osyth's, Essex.

[4] Nicholas, *Vetusta Testamenta*, i. 33. One is now preserved at Stonyhurst.

[5] Cf. Yelvertoft Church, *c.* 1500, which has on the exterior a fourfold dado, the lowest frieze of circular

Mottoes were in England didactic or political or modelled on a war cry, and were rarely amatory like those used in France.[1] Henry III was one of the earliest of the English kings to use a motto; a Close Roll of the twentieth year of his reign orders that his great chamber at Westminster is to be painted with a good green colour like curtains, and near the great window the motto *Ke ne dune ke ne tine, ne prent ke desire*: 'he who gives not what he has, receives not what he wishes for,'[2] and the same motto in its Latin form, *qui non dat quod habet, non accipit ille quod optat*, was in 1248 painted in the hall of his manor at Woodstock.[3] Edward III had as his motto the fatalistic *It is as it is*, and had it embroidered on a white linen doublet worked at sleeve and hem with devices of clouds and vines.[4] Again, the *Hola* warcry of Lord Wenlock appears on the fifteenth-century glass in the Wenlock Chapel at Luton.[5]

Italy followed the French fashion for more fanciful devices. Alfonso V of Aragon and I of Naples in 1446 ordered Manises tiles with his badge, the arms of Aragon-Sicily and Aragon-Naples, his motto *Diu dominus mihi adjutor et ego dispiciam inimicos meos*, and his devices of a book, a millet plant, and the 'sege perillous'—the burning chair of the Morte d'Arthur.[6] Canting flower badges were also fairly common;[7] the degli Agli of Florence had their arms surrounded by a wreath of garlic,[8] and Doge Cristoforo Moro, d. 1417, has a mulberry frieze on his tomb in San Giobbe, Venice;[9] the Rovere used oak branches as a device.

The banner played an important part in war, pageant, and funeral in fifteenth-century England and France. It was long and narrow; next the staff came the arms of the country, fleurs-de-lis or cross of St. George, while the rest was usually

medallions with whorled tracery, the two middle friezes of shields in quatrefoils, and the uppermost of lozenged tracery. In France the fleur-de-lis becomes an important element in the decoration of the late fifteenth century and early sixteenth century, treated not as an heraldic charge, but as a motive of architectural ornament. It is outlined in late flamboyant window tracery, for instance in the Cathedrals of Troyes and Auch and in the Church of Saint Florentin, Yonne. It appears again as a cresting, set in roundels, on the balustrade of the Cathedral of Senlis, crowned on the Jubé of the Madeleine of Troyes (1508–17), and combined with crosses and shields on the magnificent stonework of the Choir of Albi, about 1500. Filled with flamboyant tracery and finished with flamboyant crockets it appears again on many French carved panels of about 1500.

[1] Instances of amatory mottoes are the motto of Henry VI, 'Une sanz pluis', which appeared enamelled on eight crowns recorded in the 1430 inventory (Palgrave, *Kalendars and Inventories*, ii. 143) and the motto on the Windsor stall plate of John Lord Scrope, 1461: 'autre que elle.'

[2] Walpole, *Anecdotes of Painting*, ed. Dallaway, p. 6.   [3] *Ibid.*, p. 15.

[4] W. St. John Hope, *Heraldry for Craftsmen and Designers*, p. 325. The motto painted on his shield was the cry: *Hay, hay, the wythe swan; by Godes soule I am thy man*.

[5] P. Nelson, *Ancient Painted Glass in England*, p. 52. French parallels are rare, but Gaignières has recorded a wall-painting done for Jean de Montaigu about 1410, with pumpkin leaves and the motto ILPADELT, the abbreviation of the war-cry of the Montaigus: *Je l'ay promis à Dieu et l'ay tenu*. Bodley MS. 18361, Gaignières, p. 72.   [6] Lady Evans, *Lustre Pottery*, p. 113.

[7] The Sforzas' quinces, that appear for instance on Andrea della Robbia's relief of the Baptism of Christ at S. Fiora, Pieve (Marquand, *Robbia Heraldry*, p. 87), are borne in allusion to Cotignola, where the family came from. (Quince: pomo cotogno.)

[8] On a lustre dish in the Victoria and Albert Museum.

[9] The Church of the Impruneta at Florence—a name corrupted from S. Maria in Pineta—has two tabernacles by Luca della Robbia, *c.* 1450–60, with a decoration of natural pine cones, *ibid.*, p. 8.

151. *Stemma* of King René of Anjou, by Luca della Robbia, between 1466 and 1478

152. Beaker with collars of SS and EE. Probably made for Edward, son of
Henry VI. Oriel College, Oxford

diagonally striped in the livery colours, with the chief charges of the coat (or the heraldic beast) next the national arms, and the rest powdered with badges and scrolls of the motto. In 1437 his tailor sent the Earl of Warwick a bill for such banners for his ship: four hundred 'pencels' with the ragged staff, and 'a grete stremour for the ship of XL yerdis length, and VIII yerdes in brede, with a grete bere and gryfon holding a ragidd staffe, poudrid full of raggid staves, and for a grete cross of St. George';[1] and his manuscript biography[2] shows the ship with the Warwick Arms emblazoned on the great sail and the tailor's long banner flying at the masthead.

The banner type of decoration passed into several fields of art. Its diagonal stripes of the livery colours first appeared as a background to such purely heraldic panels as the Windsor stall plates,[3] and thence were transferred to heraldic stained glass. The windows which Sir John Norreys put into his manor-house of Ockwells, in the reign of Henry VI, have their backgrounds diagonally paned with quarries of the Norreys badge—three distaffs—and lines of the motto *Feythfully serve*, and in the middle tilting shields, helms, and crests of Norreys and his friends and relations.[4] One window has the King's arms, with scrolls of his *Dieu et mon droit*; and one Margaret of Anjou's, with her *Humble et Loiall*. Towards the end of the century decoration of this type appeared in tapestry. Gaignières has recorded[5] a tapestry made for René II, Duke of Lorraine, before his death in 1507, striped in red, white, grey, and blue, with ciphers of RE and the arms of his wife and himself in the middle. The border is of his device, a hand issuing from clouds and holding a sword, with banderoles round the blade bearing the mottoes *Toutes pour une* and *Une pour toutes*. The outer border is of seventy-two shields of arms. Another, made for Hughes de Melun, Prince d'Espinoy, who died in 1553, was striped in red and white, the red powdered with HH and white marguerites, and the white with HH and flames. In the middle was a tree, from which hung a shield of his arms, surmounted by his helm and surrounded by the chain of the Golden Fleece. At the foot of the tree lay a lion. On either side were scrolls with the motto of the Golden Fleece, *Ante ferit quam flammam micat*, and his personal motto, *Quam forti pectore in armis*, with shields of his fiefs in the corners.[6] Tudor inventories are rich in hangings and furnishings striped and paned in the Tudor green and white, often charged with roses and portcullises. Wolsey had a tapestry, woven abroad and designed in the French style, with his

---

[1] Dugdale, *Warwickshire*, 1730 ed., p. 408.   [2] B. M. Cott. MS. Julius E. iv.
[3] e.g. the stall plate of Sir John Beaufort, Earl of Kendall and Earl and Duke of Somerset, c. 1440.
[4] See E. Green, 'The identification of the Eighteen Worthies commemorated in the Heraldic Glass in the Hall windows of Ockwells Manor House in the parish of Bray in Berkshire,' in *Archaeologia*, lvi, pt. 2, 1899, p. 323.
[5] Bodley MS. 18361, Gaignières, p. 4. Banners are little used in Spanish decoration before the sixteenth century, when a number were often arranged 'en soleil' round the shield, as on a tapestry with the arms of the Duke of Cardona. Bodley MS. 18361, Gaignières, p. 10.
[6] Bodley MS. 18361, Gaignières, p. 7.

arms and hat supported by Angels in red vestments standing on clouds, the whole on a paned ground. The border was likewise paned in squares, each bearing a single charge from his arms—his lion rampant gules, his cross engrailed or, his bird, his leopard's face azure, and his Tudor rose [1]—with shields of his own arms and of his Province in the corners.

A rather similar heraldic scheme was used for a more symbolic tapestry, belonging to Winchester College, probably woven to commemorate the birth of Prince Arthur at Winchester. It is paned in red and blue, damasked in a formal flower pattern in a darker shade, on which ground appear large sprays of red and white roses and the motto IHS. In the middle are the arms—azure three crowns or in pale—ascribed to King Arthur (fig. 156).[2]

3

The ornamental use of heraldry was naturally influenced by the general currents of decoration. Shields early played a part in architectural decoration (for instance at Westminster) and soon, instead of being mere incidents in an architectural whole, were themselves framed in an architectural setting. Such usage, however, seems to occur earlier in the lesser than in the greater arts: on the golden denier of Saint Louis, struck between 1266 and 1270, the shield appears within a cusped border; and similarly some fourteenth-century seals show their owner's shield against an architectural background.[3]

On fourteenth-century plate, too, armorial bearings were often set in an architectural scheme, as on a goblet of Louis d'Anjou's with 'arches en maniere de fenestrages rons' on the foot, enamelled with his Order of the Cross, with roundels of his arms above.[4]

In the fourteenth century such usage was commonly transferred to stone. Panels with shields set in carved or pierced quatrefoils appear on many tomb-chests (fig. 157).[5] The scheme consorted well with Perpendicular systems of panelling and adorns many fifteenth-century English fonts, chantries, and tombs.[6] On a larger scale it inspired the design of King's College Chapel (fig. 158). In France

[1] Bodley MS. 18361, Gaignières, p. 34. A similar detached use of his charges appears in the decoration of his plate; e.g. in 1530 six bowls with a gilt cover, with leopards' heads, lions, birds, and roses, and the motto *Juges le Melior*, and four bowls with great martlets, and on the cover a leopard's head with a ring in his mouth. Brewer, *Letters and Papers of Henry VIII*, iv, pt. 4, pp. 2769 and 2770.

[2] A. Kendrick, in *Walpole Society*, xiv, 1925–6, p. 31.

[3] The seal of Edmund of Woodstock, who was beheaded in 1330, shows a shield impaling his own and his wife's arms set in an architectural panel with cusped tracery of a circle enclosed in a double triangle surrounded by smaller circles enclosing lions rampant and roses.

[4] Moranvillé, *op cit.*, p. 84.

[5] Such as that of Archbishop Reynard von Dasser, made in 1362, in Cologne Cathedral, and that of Cardinal Simon Langham, d. 1376, in Westminster Abbey. Burlington Fine Arts Club, *Catalogue of Exhibition of British Heraldic Art*, 1916, p. 85.

[6] e.g. the tomb of Bishop Edward Stafford, d. 1419, in Exeter Cathedral.

153. Detail of a carved stone chimney-piece with the arms of Ralph Lord Cromwell and his device of the Treasurer's purse wreathed in gromwell. Tattershall Castle, c. 1433

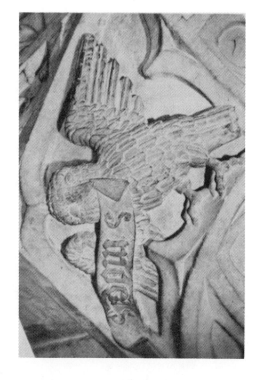

155. Rebus of Bishop Oldham, from his Chantry in Exeter Cathedral, 1509

154. Rebus of Bishop Alcock, from the frieze of his Chantry in Ely Cathedral, c. 1500

156. Detail of a tapestry with the arms of King Arthur. Flemish, probably woven
to commemorate the birth of Prince Arthur, 1487. Winchester College

shields of arms were similarly made a part of Flamboyant architectural decoration, alike in architecture and wood-carving. Indeed heraldry played an increasingly important part in the final stages of Gothic architectural decoration: the ordered symbolism of the church was beginning to break up, and the symbol of the individual helped to fill the gaps in the scheme. Louis II de Bourbon in the time of Charles VI built the chapel of the 'Petit Bourbon' at Paris, with fleurs-de-lis and the arms of Bourbon ensigned with the collars of his orders on the bosses of the vault. On the left of the altar he set up an oratory screened by a tracery of carved wood, with four shields as its chief decoration within—the King's, the dauphin's, his wife's, and his own.[1]

In Spain the choir of San Juan de los Reyes at Toledo (fig. 159), built about 1486, is a magnificent example of such decoration. The panels are carved with great eagles bearing crowned escutcheons of the Royal arms, and immensely long inscriptions wind round the outside and inside in honour of God and the Kings, conceived altogether in the oriental tradition.

The Angels that figured in the architectural decoration of the thirteenth and fourteenth centuries[2] came to be used as supporters for heraldic bearings. Charles V had the passage to his oratory in the Hôtel St. Pol painted with a number of angels[3] holding a curtain of his livery colours, while on the blue vault was a heavenly host singing and playing on musical instruments.[4] The contemporary paintings in St. Stephen's Chapel, Westminster, dating from between 1350 and 1360, showed a similar array of Angels, just under life size, holding great semicircular mantles of rich brocade to form a draped dado, above which appeared the glory of their peacock wings framed by a painted canopy (fig. 160), crowned by a long line of shields of arms of contemporary lords and knights. From such schemes the transition was easy to one in which the angels held not mantles, but shields; and Sauval records that on the chimneypiece of Charles V's room at the Louvre, built in 1365, his arms appeared 'soutenues par deux anges et couvertes d'une couronne.'[5] Such a use seems soon to have become fairly common.[6] The post-mortem inventory of Queen Jeanne d'Évreux, made in 1372, includes a *drageoir* surrounded by enamelled shields of her arms held by little angels,[7] while

---

[1] Sauval, *Histoire et antiquités de la ville de Paris*, iii. 25.   [2] See p. 13.

[3] The scheme (apart from the curtains of livery) is found slightly earlier; in 1315 the walls of a room in the Castle of Hesdin were painted with the 'légion des anges.' Enlart, *Manuel d'Archéologie française*, ii. 164.

[4] Sauval, *op. cit.*, quoted Michel, *Histoire de l'Art*, iii. 112.

[5] Sauval, *op. cit.*, ii. 279. Cf. also four cushions of red velvet with the arms of France and Bohemia supported by angels and armed men; Labarte, *Inventaire du mobilier de Charles V*, p. 375. Charles VII sometimes used angels as supporters, as did several of his successors from time to time. Louis XIV finally made them the official supporters of the arms of France. An unusual variant is the six-winged seraphs that supported shields on the late fourteenth-century chimney of the Grande Salle of the Palais des Comtes at Poitiers.

[6] It is possible that it was especially in use among members of the Order of St. Michael: the door of the Château de Fougères sur Bièvre, built by Pierre de Refuge, Knight of the Order, in 1470, has five charming angels bearing shields.   [7] Leber, *Collection des meilleures dissertations*, 1838, xix. 141.

the great golden tabernacle described in Louis d'Anjou's inventory of 1380[1] was adorned with the double cross of his Order of the Cross held by two kneeling angels.[2]

Such angel-supporters occasionally appear on seals,[3] but in the fifteenth century their use was almost confined to the decoration of tombs and ecclesiastical buildings, for which they seemed more appropriate than the fantastic 'tenants' of the joust. They are especially common when it was desired to introduce the arms of the donor below the figure of a saint: a charming instance of such a use is given by the angels holding shields below the carving of the Assumption at La Ferté Milon (fig. 161). They were much used on the great wooden roofs that are one of the glories of English fifteenth-century architecture.[4] They are carved on a stone boss of about 1390 in the cloister of Worcester Cathedral; they adorn the capitals of the chapel of the Hôtel de Cluny[5] and the consoles at the Abbey of Saint Wandrille, and the early fifteenth-century windows of the Sainte Chapelle of Bourges, now in the crypt of the Cathedral, have delightful angels holding roundels enclosing shields of arms. Angels carry shields on the soffits of the canopy of Richard II's tomb, on Henry IV's tomb at Canterbury, and on the spandrels of Henry V's chantry at Westminster, and in various architectural settings they appear on many English tombs between 1420 and 1490. The most beautiful of these is perhaps that of the Duchess of Suffolk in the church at Ewelme (fig. 162); the complex curves of the canopy, the exquisite colour and surface of the tinted alabaster, and the dignified figures of the angels, each holding a shield of arms, that stand keeping solemn watch round the tomb, make a decorative whole that well shows how noble fifteenth-century art could be. Most frequently used on the tombs of women and ecclesiastics, who could have no strictly heraldic supporters, angels appear fairly commonly on men's tombs as well.[6] The shield of arms was the symbol of the individual; and on a tomb its custody by an angel symbolized the

---

[1] Moranvillé, *op. cit.*, p. 26.

[2] A dial or 'cadran' described in the same inventory shows angels yet more freely used as supporters: 'ou milieu a un heaume et un escu des armes de France plaines et la couronne dessus, et au plus haut est le timbre d'une fleur-de-lys double, et deux angles sur un terrace vert, à genous, qui sont emmantelez, tiennent a l'une de leurs mains l'escu et à l'autre le heaume; et deux autres partans de deux nues faites au vif, a manteaux gestez entour leurs reins, tiennent à l'une de leurs mains la couronne et à l'autre l'un des fleurons de ladite fleur de lys.' *Ibid.*, p. 391.

[3] The shield on that of Oliver Rouillon, 1376, is borne by an angel standing behind it and by two demi lions couchant at its base, while on that of Richard Nevill, Earl of Salisbury, 1429, the shield is supported by two angels, one holding the Nevill shield and the other that of Longespée (Woodward, *Treatise of Heraldry*, ii. 279).

[4] Great angels holding shields of arms end the hammer beams of the roof of Westminster Hall, constructed between 1394 and 1398; and they appear again on the padpieces of the roofs at Knapton, Wymondham, Mildenhall, Outwell, Falkenham and other East Anglian churches.

[5] And of Alphington Church, Devon.

[6] e. g. the tomb of Sir John Cassey, d. 1444, at Dodford, Northants; and the tomb of Thomas Cokayne, d. 1488, at Youlgrave, Derbyshire. They were sometimes used side by side with other supporters: on the tomb of Rudolf von Scherenberg, Prince Bishop of Würzburg, made by Tilman Riemenschneider between 1496 and 1498, are six tilting shields, two without supporters, two held by lions, and two by angels; while on

157. Tomb of Cardinal Simon Langham, Archbishop of Canterbury, d. 1376. Westminster Abbey

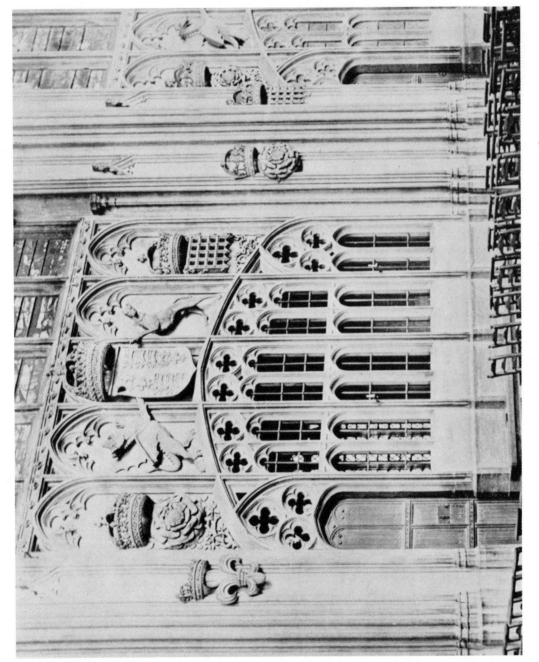

158. The Chapel of King's College, Cambridge, decorated between 1508 and 1515

angelic guardianship of the soul of the deceased; and indeed apart from any memorial idea, the conception of the patron saint and guardian angel had come to play so important a part in relation to the individual that it was fitting to express it in his personal device. Confraternities used the figure of their patron saint to support their shield,[1] and sometimes enthroned the saint and set angels on either side bearing shields, as on a Flemish morse with the figure of St. Bavon in the Louvre. By an interesting analogy the instruments of the Passion, that had often been represented in Doom-scenes as held by angels, were charged upon shields borne by angel supporters. The console supporting the late fifteenth-century statue of Christ, seated bound and crowned with thorns and awaiting Crucifixion, in the Church of Sormery, is adorned with his shield hanging by three nails from the cross, with angels holding other instruments of the Passion as supporters. Such shields of the 'arma Christi' held by angels were also represented on tombs; that of Sir Richard Choke, d. 1483, at Long Ashton, Somerset,[2] has his own achievement of arms borne by angels, and the canopy rising from consoles carved with Passion-shields held by angels, whose beautiful wings sweep up to take the place of pinnacles between the gables of the canopy.[3]

Other decorative influences also modified heraldic usage. Heraldry was admitted to play a part in such decorative schemes as those of the Neuf Preux and the Neuf Preuses;[4] and in such allegory as that of a great golden nef symbolizing the Ship of State that belonged to the Duke of Berry in 1402.[5] The twelve Peers of France were represented standing below shields of their arms upon its foot. On the body of the vessel were scenes from the life of Saint Louis; at the prow were two angels blowing trumpets, and in the stern a crowned figure of Saint Louis himself. The mast, with a sail powdered with fleurs-de-lis, was upheld by two angels, while another was at the helm; and in the crow's-nest were two more angels bearing a cross and a banner with the arms of the Duke, ensigned with his coronet and mantled with the fleurs-de-lis.

The chief influence upon heraldic usage, outside the tournament itself, was, however, the naturalistic style in decoration. As early as the thirteenth century the fleur-de-lis was treated as if it were a flower; on the south portal of Saint Denis is a moulding formed of a naturalistic lily-stem from which spring purely heraldic fleurs-de-lis. Sometimes heraldic fleurs-de-lis had their ground filled in with more naturalistic foliage; the Breviary of Philippe le Bel, illuminated before 1297, has some of its backgrounds diapered with counterchanged lilies, filled in with delicate

the chantry chapel of Sir John Speke in Exeter Cathedral (1517) his arms appear supported alternately by angels and by hedgehogs.

[1] e. g. St. Michael on the seal of the Echevins of the City of Roulers, St. Aubert on the seal of the Bakers' Guild of Brussels.

[2] See *Archaeologia*, lxxiv, 1923–4, Pl. XII.

[3] In the chantry chapel of Sir John Speke (1517), angels hold the Arma Christi as well as his own shield.

[4] Guiffrey, *Les Inventaires de Jean Duc de Berry*, ii. 103.　　　　　[5] Cf. p. 148.

leafage.[1] In the fourteenth century fleurs-de-lis and natural lilies were often combined, especially on plate;[2] and fleurs-de-lis were often set against a more or less
naturalistic background. Charles V in 1369 had a set of hangings 'ouvrée par
manière d'eschiqueture de feuillages et petiz treilliz, et sur chascun quartier de
l'eschiqueture a une fleur-de-lis',[3] one with a wavy pattern in red and white and
rinceaux of fig-leaves centred with lions' heads, and charged with fleur-de-lis,[4] and
another of blue satin, embroidered with five wreaths of roses with a great rose in
the middle with three fleurs-de-lis in its heart.[5] Similarly the royal badges of
broom, pimpernel, and may were often treated with great decorative freedom.[6]

The usages of the tournament were somewhat modified in the second half of the
fifteenth century. It tended to become more of a pageant, with a larger element of
masquerade. The joust at the marriage of Charles the Bold and Margaret of York
in 1474 had as its *motif* the story of a giant prisoner, led by a dwarf. The Poursui-
vant was named 'Arbre d'or'; golden trees were painted on the doors of the tilt-
yard, were worn on the sleeves of the Bastard of Burgundy's livery, and appeared
everywhere on banners. A real pine tree, with gilt trunk and branches, was set up
opposite the ladies' gallery.[7] Such pageantry made a new link between heraldry
and the general trend of art, and the various types of naturalistic decoration were
in turn adapted to heraldic use. The surroundings of the tree from which shields
were often represented as hanging were more clearly indicated; the seal used by
Thomas Lord Holand and Wake about 1353 shows it growing in a rabbit warren,[8]
while that used about 1385 by Thomas of Woodstock, the son of Edward III,
shows his shield and two of his wife's shields of Hereford hanging from a tree set
within a paling[9] surrounded by water, on which float two chained Bohun swans,

---

[1] B. N., MS. lat. 1023; H. Martin, *La miniature française*, fig. xxii.

[2] In 1351 the King of France ordered a golden spoon with the handle chequered 'de fleurs de lys d'armoierie
et de fleurs de lys après le vif'. Laborde, *Glossaire des Émaux*, ii. 319. A few years later Louis d'Anjou had
more than twenty-five pieces of plate chased with fleurs-de-lis and natural leaves; *Ibid.*, p. 68. The 1380
inventory of Charles V includes, 'Ung hanap d'or aux armes de Mons. d'Estampes . . . enlevé de lys et
de fleurs de lys' and 'Ung autre hanap, semé de fleurs de lys et de lys de taille.' Labarte, *op. cit.*, pp. 69
and 70.

[3] Labarte, *op. cit.*, p. 368. A rather more naturalistic treatment seems to be indicated in a set of red satin
hangings 'lozengee de filz d'or, et dedans les lozenges semée de liz blans', belonging to Valentine de Milan
in 1389. F. M. Graves, *Deux Inventaires de la Maison d'Orléans*, p. 71.

[4] *Bibliothèque de l'École des Chartes*, vol. xlviii, 1887, p. 79. J. Guiffrey, Inventaire des tapisseries du roi
Charles VI vendues par les anglais en 1422.

[5] Labarte, no. 3589; Farcy, *La Broderie*, p. 92. Cf. the set of vestments given to the Cathedral of Angers
in 1391 by Pierre d'Avoir, seigneur de Chateau Fremond, embroidered with roses each with his arms in the
middle. Farcy, *La Broderie*, p. 41. Louis d'Anjou in 1380 had a cup 'ou milieu duquel a un esmail roont fait
en manière de rose, et les grans fueilles sont des armes d'Anjou et les petites des armes de Bretagne'. (Moranvillé, *op. cit.*, p. 74).

[6] See p. 95.

[7] Olivier de la Marche, *Mémoires*, Bk. II, chap. iv.

[8] W. St. John Hope, *Heraldry for Craftsmen and Designers*, p. 211.

[9] In the illuminations of René d'Anjou's copy of the *Mortifiement de Vaine plaisance* (Brussels Bib. roy. MS.
10308), the Duchess's arms appear within a paling. The crowned ermine of Brittany is similarly shown on
the Hotel Lallemant at Bourges.

the badges of his wife Eleanor de Bohun.[1] The frescoes of the Palazzo Davanzati at Florence, painted by a pupil of Orcagna about 1395, show shields of arms hanging from naturalistic trees rising from a flowery mead. With the beginning of the fifteenth century such designs appeared on French tapestries. In 1416 Jean de Berry had five tapestries of Paris make with shields of arms hanging from his device of the orange tree;[2] and six more powdered with orange trees with a large tree in the middle from which hung his shield, with bears and swans bearing his arms on either side.[3] Four years later Philippe le Bon had two panels of green Arras with a tree in the middle from which hung the arms of the Duchess Margaret, with a flock of sheep at its feet.[4]

Armorial devices were added to the powderings of leaves and flowers; in 1393 the King of France had five red tapestries powdered with poppies, with his arms and those of the Dauphin,[5] while in 1432 the Duke of Bedford had the gallery in the Palace of the Tournelles painted with green gourds, with the banners of himself and his wife.[6] The fine panel of the arms and badges of Lady Margaret Beaufort on the gatehouse of St. John's College, Cambridge, shows them set against a background of her daisies and other flowers. The mille-fleurs tapestries, too, made an admirable background to badges and coats of arms: the tapestries of Charles the Bold, captured by the Swiss at the battle of Granson in 1476,[7] show his device of the briquet and flint against a background delicately powdered with foxgloves, pinks, ragged robin, flags, violets, daisies, stocks, and other flowers; and a fine tapestry with the Tudor arms five times repeated in a quincunx against a mille-fleurs ground is at Belvoir Castle (fig. 163).[8] Another of about 1540 in the Austrian State Collection shows the black imperial eagle and arms of the Emperor Charles V against a 'wilderness' verdure of columbines, primroses, narcissus, hollyhocks, brambles, roses, mulleins and other flowers, remarkable for its beauty of design and execution.[9] Verdure grounds were also used as backgrounds to more elaborate and more naturalistic heraldic ornamentation. Charles VII had as

[1] W. St. John Hope, *Heraldry for Craftsmen and Designers*, p. 213.

[2] Guiffrey, *Les Inventaires de Jean de Berry*, ii. 279. [3] *Ibid.*, ii. 24.

[4] Laborde, *Les Ducs de Bourgogne*, ii. 272. Menestrier attributes the origin of the Order of the Golden Fleece to a pastoral pageant acted at her marriage to Charles of Burgundy. *Le Véritable Art du Blason*, Lyon 1671, p. 246. Cf. for an earlier combination of sheep and heraldry the candlestick in the form of 'Ung mouton blanc sur ung entablement d'argent doré, semé des armes de France, et de la Royne Jehanne', described in the 1372 inventory of Jeanne d'Évreux. Havard, *Dictionnaire de l'Ameublement*, s.v. Chandelier.

[5] Guiffrey, *Histoire de la tapisserie en France*, p. 22.

[6] Havard, *Dictionnaire de l'Ameublement*, s.v. Galerie.

[7] Now in the Museum of Berne.

[8] A certain number of Rhenish tapestries of the last third of the fifteenth century show the achievement with supporters and crest set against a verdure background. A good example from Friedberg is in the Hessisches Landesmuseum at Darmstadt.

[9] A tapestry at Drayton House shows the arms of Robert Dudley, Earl of Leicester, complete with helm and mantling, supporters and motto, also set against 'wilderness' verdure background, with a cock and hen pheasant and chicks below. It has been ascribed to Sheldon, but seems Flemish in type. See J. Humphreys, 'Elizabethan Sheldon Tapestries,' in *Archaeologia*, lxxiv, 1923–4, p. 181.

his 'heraldic beast' a winged stag gorged with a crown; and in at least one tapestry [1] (fig. 164) such stags appear in a 'park' scheme of decoration. This tapestry has a verdure ground with a wattled enclosure. Outside the fence are two lions, with a tilting shield with the arms of France between them. Within the enclosure are three winged stags, each gorged with a royal crown from which hangs a shield of France with three fleurs-de-lis. The middle one holds the Royal banner. A banderole above the stag to the left is inscribed:

> Armes porte très glorieuses
> Et sur toutes victorieuses,

while a similar banderole to the right bears the couplet:

> Si nobles na dessoubz les cieux
> Je ne pourraye porte mieulx.

Over the standard is another banderole, with the inscription:

> Cest estendart est une enseigne
> Qui a loial françois enseigne
> De jamais ne labandonner
> S'il ne veut son honneur donner. [2]

The 'fountain' scheme of decoration was represented among the hangings of Jean de Berry in 1416 by a set with a fountain in the middle with his swans and bears round it, [3] and the type with people amusing themselves in a garden was given heraldic significance in two tapestries made for Margaret de la Rochefoucauld-Barbezieux about 1490. [4] The first showed a garden planted with orange trees (the badge of the La Rochefoucaulds) entwined with banderoles of their motto, *C'est mon plaisir.* Above was a colonnade, with shields of La Rochefoucauld and its alliances hanging in the arches. In the garden was the lady, working on a tiny loom, with four of her ladies spinning, embroidering, knotting, and sewing. Three men, one of them old and walking with a stick, appeared in the background. The second tapestry had similar orange trees and mottoes, with the same lady and

---

[1] Now preserved in the Musée des Antiquités de la Seine Inférieure at Rouen. A later version of such a scheme translated into stone is carved over a chimney-piece in the Château de Chitré, Vienne. It is dated 1557.

[2] A drawing in the Gaignières Collection (B. N., Estampes Gaignières, p.c. 18, fol. 1) shows a tapestry of the same sort with the arms of Charles VII held by winged stags standing in a meadow of white lilies. On a scroll is the inscription:

> Si sont les Armes de haut pris et de grant excellence
> Du tres hault roy de France Charles septiesme de ce nom.

Another drawing (*ibid.*, f. 2) shows the arms of Louis XII as they appeared over the door of the Chambre des Comptes in his palace at Paris. The supporters are winged stags gorged with crowns and wearing little mantles powdered with fleurs-de-lis.

[3] Guiffrey, *Les Inventaires de Jean Duc de Berry*, ii. 211. Another tapestry at Drayton House shows the arms of Robert Dudley, Earl of Leicester, on either side of a medallion of a fountain surmounted by his badge of a bear and a ragged staff, set in a formal garden. *Archaeologia*, lxxiv, 1923–4, p. 196.

[4] Bodley MS. 18361, Gaignières, pp. 58 and 59.

159. Detail of the Choir of San Juan de los Reyes, Toledo, c. 1486

160. Drawing of paintings in St. Stephen's Chapel, Westminster, painted between 1350 and 1360

Leonard Barnard, del.

other personages playing with birds. Similarly five of the tapestries of the 'Dame à la Licorne' show garden scenes with 'esbattements' modified to symbolize the five Senses; in one a lady plays a small portable organ, in another a maid offers her flowers to smell, in another she tastes a sweatmeat; and on all she has on either side of her heraldic beasts—a lion holding a pennon and a unicorn a banner of the arms of Le Viste.[1] In two of the tapestries the beasts even play a certain part. In that of Sight, the lion has the banner, and the unicorn kneels with his fore feet in the lady's lap to look at himself in the mirror she holds,[2] while in that of Touch the lady herself holds the banner and caresses the unicorn's horn, and both the beasts wear tilting shields of the arms of Le Viste. The sixth (fig. 165) shows the lady beneath a pavilion of blue damask powdered with tears, with the motto *Mon seul desir* at the top, its curtains held back by a lion and a unicorn, the one holding a pennant and the other a banner of the arms of Le Viste.

Such beasts holding banners as part of a naturalistic scheme appear again on one of the Flemish tapestries of about 1509, given to Rheims Cathedral by Robert de Lenoncourt in 1530. Its subject is the Perfections of our Lady; the loom at which she works is framed by pillars which serve as bases to banners of his arms, supported by unicorns. The unicorns may here figure as emblems of virginity, but by analogy with other beasts they play a heraldic part. Lions holding banners of the Papal arms appear again on Pieter van Aelst's allegorical tapestry of Faith, Love, and Justice, in the Galleria degli Arazzi of the Vatican.

The Italian weavers followed the French in introducing heraldic elements into naturalistic schemes; in 1470 Gherardo da Vicenza made a cartoon for the Ferrara looms of 'paesi con animali e l' arma ducale'.[3] The type is perpetuated in England as late as 1585, when the Great Chamber at Gilling had each of its panels painted with a formal tree growing in a deer park and hung with the shields of the 'armigers' of each Wapentake of Yorkshire.[4]

4

The Renaissance was an age of individualism in life and art; the development of personality became the end of man. The portrait came into its own as a *genre* in literature and painting. Montaigne brought the mind of a philosopher to the study of his personality; the autobiographies of such men as Cellini and Palissy spare us

[1] See H. Martin, 'La dame à la licorne', in *Mémoires de la société nationale des antiquaires de France*, 8th series, vol. vii, 1924–7, p. 137, and A. Kendrick, 'Les tapisseries dites de la dame à la licorne' in *Actes du Congrès international de l'Histoire de l'Art*, 1924, ii (Paris, 1926), p. 662.

[2] Cf. a rather earlier tapestry illustrated in the Gaignières Collection (B. N., Estampes, Gaignières, p.c. 18, fol. 15) with a lady in a high hennin seated in a fenced garden and a unicorn in her lap. In the background are three scrolls inscribed *Venena pello* and the arms of Bourbon and eight garters inscribed *Espérance* appear in the border.

[3] Müntz, *Histoire de la tapisserie en Italie*, p. 55.

[4] M. Jourdain, *English Decoration and Furniture of the Early Renaissance*, p. 90. Cf. the green gallery at Theobalds, 'Excellent well painted round with all the shires of England and the armes of noblemen and gentlemen in the same.' M. F. S. Hervey, *The Life of Thomas Howard, Earl of Arundel*, p. 34.

no episode of their careers; and de l'Orme, writing his *Premier Tome de l' Architecture* in 1567, used 'Je' so often that the printer of the 1648 edition ran out of capital J's and had to alter the opening paragraphs of nearly all the chapters.[1] This point of view made every symbol of the individual worthy of representation; and the chief of these were naturally his arms and badges.

Heraldry was still an art living enough to modulate itself into the new classic mode. In Italy the outline of the shield was curved into new freedom; the della Robbias used battle-shields, tilting-shields, heater and kite-shaped shields, and fanciful 'Tuscan' forms. Such shields were freely used in architectural decoration; Bramante set Tuscan shields in roundels round the base of the exterior of S. Maria delle Grazie at Milan, Mantegna made magnificent use of the arms and badges of the Marquis Ludovico Gonzaga in the decorations of the *Camera degli Sposi* in the Castle of Mantua. The Tempio Malatestiano at Rimini shows a remarkably free use of heraldic decoration: little tilting shields hang from the swags of the middle cornice; larger shields, set in wreaths, fill the spandrels of the arches; and shields of many shapes, each more graceful than the last, emerge from the rinceaux and rose sprays of the pilasters and frieze of the façade. On the Palazzo Venier at Recanati, Giuliano da Maiano even set shields of arms on classic capitals.[2] The tapestries of the months, woven by Vigevano for Marshal Trivulzio between 1499 and 1518, have borders of forty coats of arms set in simple frames. The shield was displayed in new ways; Giuliano da Sangallo filled his pediment at Poggio a Caiano with a shield with ribbons waving on either side, and similar ribbons, most Roman in their flutterings, bring the seven-sided shields of the screen of S. Petronio at Bologna into harmony with their classical surroundings. The angels of fifteenth-century Gothic heraldry were gradually transformed into the *putti* of the Renaissance. A chubby child angel stands behind the shield and holds up a della Robbia *stemma* of the Ginori family,[3] and two winged *putti* support the shield of Conte Guerra in a medallion of about 1495 in the Collegiate Church of Montevarchi.[4] The flowery garlands of the earlier style were woven into heavy wreaths, like the 'grand chappeau de triomphe' that surrounded the arms of Charles IX on the triumphal arch erected for his entry into Lyons in 1570.[5] Helm and crest were conveniently omitted, and the fantasies of tilt-yard and battle-field given a classic twist.

The men of the Renaissance were still 'gente de ferro e di valor armata', and in the many Italian wars of the fifteenth century the use of badges increased, while with the passing of shields and surcoats heraldic coat armour fell into disuse.[6] As an aristocratic oligarchy superseded a trading democracy in the government of the states, the decorative use of such badges became more important, especially in

[1] H. Clouzot, *Philibert de l'Orme*, p. 94.   [2] Venturi, *Storia dell' Arte Italiana*, viii, pt. i, p. 396.
[3] A. Marquand, *Robbia Heraldry*, p. 45; the medallion is in the collection of Mr. F. J. Ryan of New York.
[4] *Ibid.*, p. 107.   [5] Laborde, *Glossaire des Émaux*, p. 207.
[6] The leaders in the Neapolitan war of 1460 definitely adopted the use of badges in place of coats.

161. Detail of a panel of the Assumption of the Virgin. Church of La Ferté Milon, *c.* 1500

162. Alabaster tomb of Alice, Duchess of Suffolk. Ewelme Church, Oxon., 1477

163. Detail of a tapestry with the royal arms of England. Brussels or Tournai, *c.* 1510

Florence. In 1448 Piero di Cosimo de' Medici was permitted to add his own arms and devices to the tabernacle he had given to the Church of S. Miniato: a frieze with the three Medici feathers, white, green, and red—for Faith, Hope and Charity—enclosed within the Medici ring, with the motto *Semper*; a medallion with his own personal device of a falcon holding the ring, with the same motto; and little lateral finials enclosing medallions with the heraldic *palle*.[1] At the beginning of the sixteenth century such decorative use of badges was adapted alike to the medallions of della Robbia ware that decorated villa walls,[2] to the decoration of ceramic pavements[3] (fig. 169) and of maiolica ware,[4] to the borders of illuminated manuscripts,[5] and to ecclesiastical[6] and domestic embroideries.[7]

Such devices, moreover, were applied even to the architectural decoration of buildings in severely classical style. Alberti's Palazzo Rucellai at Florence has a lower frieze of the Medici rings and feathers, and an upper frieze of yards and sails; the Palazzo Bartolini is similarly decorated with a frieze of the Medici rings and the Bartolini-Salimbeni poppy heads, and the Palazzo Spinelli with a frieze of roses set in wreaths of feathers. In 1485 Innocent VIII decorated the saloon ceiling of his classic Belvedere with his arms and his device—a peacock and the motto *Léauté passe tout*—and Sixtus V, the Peretti pope between 1585 and 1590,[8] had lions and pears—two of the charges of his coat—set on the friezes of two façades of the palace of the Lateran.

In France, where the reign of Francis I inaugurated a St. Martin's summer of chivalry,[9] even more was done to adapt the decorative use of heraldry to the new style.[10] Diapers of fleurs-de-lis[11] and ermines were used as surface decoration for

[1] A. Marquand, *Robbia Heraldry*, p. 3.

[2] e. g. A medallion by Giovanni della Robbia, *c.* 1515, combining the Medici badge of ring and feathers with the motto 'Semper' and the Bartolini-Salimbeni poppies, with the motto 'Per non dormire': see Marquand, *op. cit.*, p. 219.

[3] e. g. the Medici badges on the tiles of the Sala Borgia of the Vatican made by Luca di Andrea della Robbia *c.* 1518, and on the tiles of San Silvestro al Quirinale, *ibid.*, p. 233.

[4] e. g. Castel Durante plates in the Salting Bequest (734 and 800) with the arms of the Gonzaga and their music-stave device below.

[5] e. g. the Psalter (Bodleian MS. Montagu e. 9) with the badges of the Medici Pope—the family rings, feathers, and 'Semper', and his personal devices of the yoke with the motto 'Suave', and the flaming ragged staves.

[6] Beatrice d'Este, wife of Ludovico il Moro, gave altar hangings embroidered with her device, a sieve held by a hand on either side, with the motto 'Ti a mi, e mi a ti'. Palliser, *Historical Devices, Badges and War Cries*, p. 194.

[7] e. g. the cover of embroidered net in the Victoria and Albert Museum (263, 1880) with squares worked with the badge of Louis II of Mantua d. 1478—a bird perched on a fuse with the motto 'Vrai amour ne se change', and that of his wife Barbara of Brandenburg, d. 1481, a white doe gazing at the sun with the motto 'Bidir Graft'.   [8] Müntz, 'Les arts à la cour des papes,' in *Mon. Piot*, 1898, p. 83.

[9] The *Vie de Bayard* by the Loyal Serviteur was published in 1527; and *Amadis de Gaule* was translated from the Spanish between 1540 and 1556.

[10] Even the medieval scenes of combat were brought up to date; the Château d'Assier, Lot, is adorned with a scene of bombardment with canons of about 1530, while a house at Viviers, Ardèche, has a frieze of mounted knights in combat of about 1560.

[11] Such diapers form part of the ornate and curiously miscellaneous decoration of the court of the College of St. Gregory at Valladolid, *c.* 1495.

columns, in the arcade of Gaillon, at the Hôtel Lallemant and on the west façade of the Cathedral at Bourges, and on the Maison des Piliers at Beauvais. These last are finished with a row of shields, and have a floriated crown for capital. The shield itself was adapted as a part of various schemes of Renaissance decoration. At the Hôtel d'Écoville at Caen are elaborate hanging trophies with helmets and shields of arms. On a mantelpiece at Blois the arms of Francis I and Claude de Lorraine appear divided by candelabra pilasters beneath a frieze of shells and swags held by *putti*; while Francis's arms and devices appear in an equally classic setting on the ruined Porte Montre-Écu at Amiens, dated 1531.[1] Sometimes the satyr or *putti* finials of a classical rinceau were adapted to become the supporters of the shield. On the tomb of the Easter Sepulchre in the Church of St. Jean at Joigny, four angels of the classic Renaissance type uphold three wreaths with fluttering ribbons; the wreaths at the sides frame medallions of the donor and his wife, while the central one holds a shield of the 'arma Christi'. This medieval motive is again treated with classic freedom on the retable of the Church of Arques, where angels holding the lance and sponge and the Pillar of Scourging support a shield with the pierced heart set before a trophy of the other emblems of the Passion. The most perfect example of the mingling of heraldic ornament with the classical figure sculpture of the French Renaissance style is the panel over the west door of the Church of Nantouillet, with four most graceful figures in the style of Jean Goujon, upholding three shields, above a sundial[2] (fig. 171.) Badges, too, were adapted to adorn buildings and monuments in the new style. Charles VIII's Renaissance tomb in Saint Denis had his emblem of wreathed swords set between medallions of mourning women.[3] A frieze of Charles de Chaumont's punning badge of a flaming mountain goes round the façade of Chaumont;[4] the lower door of the Hôtel de Cluny has a powdering of the shells of St. James and the pilgrims' staves that were the badges of Jacques d'Amboise.[5] Even in the severe classicism of the middle of the century, badges could still find a place; the porch of the Chapel of Champigny-sur-Veude, finished about 1543, has a frieze of crowned L's, garters inscribed *Espérance*, crowned wings, and pilgrims' staves, wallets, and shells, with an inner frieze of broken lances, on a flaming ground. The widowed Catherine de Medici used devices of broken fans, mirrors, plumes, and necklaces, and flames drowned in tears, with the motto *Ardorem exstincta testantur vivere flamma*, and sculptured trophies of such broken trinkets adorn

[1] Such decoration was transferred to the minor arts; Bourges Cathedral in 1537 owned 'un parement de velours noir, semé de huict escussons de la feue Reine, liés de fleurons d'antiquité'. (Farcy, *La Broderie*, p. 99.)

[2] The only awkwardness in the composition is the mantled helmet over the shield on the left. The figures should be compared with the supporters of the arms of Diane de Poitiers on the north front of Écouen.

[3] Bodley MS. 1834, Gaignières, p. 48.

[4] It also appears on Charles de Chaumont's Castle of Meillant.

[5] Cf. the beribboned shell and harp badges on the frieze of the archbishop's palace at Sens, begun *c.* 1521. Naturally such usage was even commoner on furniture: see the bed of Antoine, duc de Lorraine, in the Musée Lorrain at Nancy. (See Léon Germain in *Bulletin monumental*, li, 6th series, i, 1885.)

164. Tapestry with the Heraldic Beasts of Charles VII of France, *c.* 1450

165. One of the set of tapestries of the 'Dame à la Licorne'. Made for a member of the family of Le Viste of Lyons, probably Claude Le Viste. French, c. 1510

her classic façade of the Louvre. More often, however, with so severely classic a style only the motto was used; the frieze of triglyphs and bucrania on the Chancellerie of Loches, dating from 1551, is completed with the motto *Justicia regno prudentia nutrisco*.

In Spain the medieval tradition of heraldry was modified into Renaissance forms. The portal of the Hospital of Santa Cruz at Toledo, built between 1504 and 1514, has graceful Renaissance pilasters with Tuscan shields of the arms of the founder and crosses of the Order hanging from a garland of fruit. Heraldry plays a noble part on the entrance to the University of Salamanca, where it helps to give significance to a scheme of plateresque decoration in which every ornate fancy seems to find a place. Badges were freely used;[1] Ferdinand's bow and Isabella's sheaf of arrows appear on either side of the royal arms in place of supporters on the choir screen of Palencia Cathedral, and adorn the metope-like panels of the frieze of the Colegio de San Gregorio at Valladolid. The double columns and crossed clubs of Charles V appear on the façade of the Ayuntamiento of Seville, and with his shields adorn his fountain in the Alameda de la Alhambra at Granada, designed by Pedro Machuca in 1545. The beams of his apartments in the Alhambra itself are inscribed all over with his motto *Plus Oultre*, while the frieze bears a legend in his honour that perpetuates the Moorish tradition of laudatory inscriptions.

Germany and the Low Countries were far less accomplished in their Renaissance use of heraldry. Only occasionally was such decoration fused into the architectural whole; for instance the Hall of the Grand Conseil at Malines has capitals with the arms of Malines, the cross and Briquet of Burgundy, the columns of Hercules and motto *Plus oultre* of Charles V, and the saltire of knotty boughs and motto *Fortune infortune forte une* of Margaret of Austria. Similarly on a chimney-piece of the Hôtel de Ville at Douai the arms and badge of the Emperor Charles V appear soberly framed in classical frieze and pilasters. Far more often, however, shields of arms were simply hung upon a more or less classic background, with no thought of relevance or congruity; a flagrant example of such use is the great chimney-piece of the Salle des Séances of the Châtellenie of Bruges, carved by Lancelot Blondeel in 1529–34 in honour of Charles V[2] (fig. 172). Rhenish wall-monuments of the late sixteenth century perpetuate the scheme. In work on a smaller scale the German engravers such as Hans Sebald Beham achieved considerable success in heraldic designs consisting of shield, helmet, crests, mantling, and motto, which followed the medieval tradition; but when they attempted a classic frame to the shield they were far less happy. Theodore de Bry could find no more fitting a frame for his 'arma Mortis' than classical grotesques with monkeys playing fiddles among coiling snakes.

[1] They came into use much later in Spain than in France or England.

[2] Cf. such tombs as that of Ernest, Duke of Saxony and Archbishop of Magdeburg, in Magdeburg Cathedral, made by Peter Vischer in 1497; the tomb of Jean, Comte de Mérode, d. 1550, in the Church of St. Dymphna at Ghent; and the monument of Bishop Theodor Bettendorf, d. 1580, in Worms Cathedral.

The Italian workmen employed by Henry VIII introduced into England the scrolling shield, the triumphal wreath and *putti* supporters, and gradually the style became acclimatized. The triple bay at Hengrave Hall, dating from about 1530, shows *putti* holding shields, and the panelling of the hall at Wear Giffard has a Renaissance frieze of dolphins, *putti* and scrolls framing tilting shields of Italian shape.[1] Badges, too, were more freely treated; the standing cup and cover given by Henry VIII to the Barbers' Company in 1523 has his rose, fleur-de-lis, and portcullis wreathed in delightful classical foliage; while an almost contemporary carved wooden ceiling shows the rose and lily, and the pomegranate of Catherine of Aragon, even more naturalistically treated.[2]

With the Elizabethan glorification of the individual such heraldry came into its own. In 1594 Lord Cobham set his arms in almost arrogant magnificence over the south porch of Cobham Hall, and again five years later over the chimney-piece in the Picture gallery. Such arms over chimney-pieces became indeed a regular feature of English country houses, especially in the Cotswolds and the West Country, from about 1560 for about a century.[3] Books such as the *Mirror of Maiestie or the Badges of Honour conceitedly emblazoned* published in 1618[4] provided the country craftsmen with models. In England, too, men were unconscious of the unsuitability of heraldic decoration to a strictly classic style. At Lumley Castle the classical metopes of the Hall screen, dating from 1590, are carved with the birds and roses of the Lumley coat,[5] while the classic façade of the Exeter Guildhall has a frieze of a series of little shields in strap-work cartouches. An English tapestry shows the shield of the Earl of Pembroke set in the middle of an arabesque scheme completed with classical *imagini*.

In every country heraldic decoration was modified that it might more clearly show its owner's noble descent. Not only was quartering piled on quartering, but

---

[1] The Gothic tradition died hard; the tomb of Anthony Harvey, d. 1565, in Exeter Cathedral, has Gothic quatrefoils filled in with his crest and shield alternating with Gothic foliate masks and Caesar's heads of Renaissance type, surmounted by his coat in a Renaissance frame set against a background of perpendicular tracery.

[2] V. and M. 116. 1908. Department of Woodwork. Cf. the naturalistic rose and pomegranate trees used in the Court festivals. See e.g. Hall, *Chronicle*, 1809 edition, p. 585, for the Twelfth Night pageant of 8 Hen. VIII. Perrin, *Description of the Kingdom of England and Scotland*, 1558, states: 'The English make a great use of Tapestries, and of painted linens which are well done, and on which are magnificent roses, embellished with fleurs de lys. . . .' Quoted, *Archaeologia*, lxxiv, 1923–4, p. 181.

[3] They tend gradually to increase in size, from small ones that are part of a complex scheme of decoration, as at Castle Ashby, to such large ones as those at Boughton and Barlborough Hall, 1584. See J. Alfred Gotch, 'Heraldry of the Renaissance in England,' in *R. I. B. A. Journal*, 3rd series, vol. iv, 1897, p. 265.

[4] Reprint ed. H. Green and J. Croston, Holbein Society, 1870. The influence of such repertories is evident in such work as the ceiling of 1620 of Earlshall, Fife, with shields of several Scottish families, and of the kings of 'Araby, Saba, Tharse, Castile, Neapolis, Lydea, Friesland', &c., and of Julius Caesar, Alexander, Joshua, David, and Hector. See *R. I. B. A. Journal*, 3rd series, iv, 1897, p. 271.

[5] Even in the eighteenth century English classicists permitted themselves the use of such decoration; the frieze of the entablature of the Pavilion at Mereworth Castle, built in 1736, has the Nevill bull and the Cavendish knot on the metopes; while the frieze of Robert Adam's gateway to Syon House, c. 1773, has the Percy crest on the lion heads and in the centre of the paterae.

166. Singing gallery from S. Maria Novella, Florence. By Baccio d'Agnolo, c. 1500

167. *Stemma* of F. dal Legname of Padua. Italian, 1497

168. Frieze from a tomb, with portrait head and badges, by Matteo Cividale, *c.* 1480

169. Tiles from the Cortile of Isabella d'Este's apartments in the Castello Vecchio of Mantua, with her devices and those of the Gonzaga family. Italian, *c.* 1500

170. Detail of the tomb of the Poncher family, by Guillaume Regnault and
Guillaume Chaleveau, 1523

whole pedigrees were turned to decorative use. The pedigree of Charles the Bold, on his father's and his mother's side, decorates the sides of his tomb at Bruges, with each ancestor represented by their crowned or coronetted shield, and with little classical figures to link the shields of man and wife together (fig. 173). Margaret of Austria in 1524 had 'Quatre pièces de belles et exquises tapisseries ... armoyées des armes de la généalogie et descente de ma dicte dame'[1]; and tapestries of about 1540 made for the German market show such heraldic genealogical trees, with personages one above the other after the manner of a tree of Jesse, each with shield, device, and a scroll of his name and title.[2] On the Château des Piastes at Brieg a Milanese sculptor in 1552 carved statues of Duke Frederick II and his wife over the arch, with busts of his ancestors to form a double frieze on the story above; while in England the Lord Lumley of Elizabeth's time decorated his inner gate-house at Lumley Castle with eighteen shields to show his descent from a Norman of the Conquest.

5

As jousting became more and more a matter of pageantry that came to be increasingly literary in its symbolism, badges and devices tended to develop into *imprese*, that had as much in common with the 'emblems' of the poets[3] as with the devices of the tiltyard. The *impresa* that was designed primarily for decorative use is one of the most characteristic creations of the Renaissance; intended for the glorification of the individual by means of the arts, literary in its symbolism, usually classical in its allusion, and stereotyped and perpetuated by the methods of printing and engraving, it sums up in a small compass many of the characteristic tendencies of the new age. The *impresa* was less fixed than the heraldic badge, but its design and its motto were more closely linked. René of Anjou was one of the first to give such a literary turn to badges: his *Livre du cuer d'Amours épris* gives verses explanatory of his own and other *imprese*. Such conceits, however, were at the beginning of the sixteenth century more characteristic of Italy than of France; Baldassare Castiglione describes the devising of such *imprese* as one of the pleasures of the court of Urbino about 1504.[4] Such badges were introduced to the French by the campaign in Italy. Brantôme describes[5] the Countess of Escaldasor appearing at a festival held while Gaston de Foix was master of Pisa in a dress of sky blue satin, 'toute couverte et semée autant plein que vuide de flambeaux et papillons volletans à l'entour et s'y bruslans', in token that 'j'advertis les honnêtes hommes qui me

[1] Havard, *Dictionnaire de l'Ameublement*, s.v. Armoiries.
[2] Müntz, *Histoire de la Tapisserie en Allemagne*, p. 9. One of the finest examples is a Brussels tapestry in the Bavarian National Museum at Munich with the pedigree of Ott-Heinrich, with each personage holding his shield. Bibliothèque Nationale Estampes Gaignières, Pc 18, includes drawings of several tapestries made with the arms of their owner's ancestors, that are disconcertingly at variance with their date.
[3] See p. 152.
[4] J. Cartwright, *Baldassare Castiglione, the Perfect Courtier*, i. 102.
[5] *Vie des dames galantes*, Paris, 1838, Discours I, tome ii, p. 254.

font ce bien de m'aymer et admirer ma beauté, de n'en approcher trop près.' The French were quick to imitate such devices, and when Louis XII set out for Alessandria to attack Genoa in 1507, he wore a dress embroidered with bees swarming out of a hive with the motto *Non utitur aculeo rex*. [1] From the beginning of the sixteenth century until the end of the Grand Siècle every King and Queen of France had an *impresa*; [2] and their court followed their example. Such *imprese*, too, were freely used in decorative art; the salamander used by Francis I with the motto *Nutrisco et extinguo* appears on the glass of the chapel of Vincennes, richly framed in the coffering, and on the frieze and even on the columns of the castle of Villers Cotterets; while on the denuded walls of Chambord it still appears more than eight hundred times. The screen at Saint Bertrand de Comminges has panels with the broken wheel and feathers, with the motto *Fortunat solus nostros Deus ipse labores*, of its giver, Jean de Mauleon; and everywhere at Écouen, even on the glazed tiles of the floor, are the triple crescents and the motto *Donec totum impleat orbem* of Henri II. The user of the most elaborate *imprese*, however, was undoubtedly Diane de Poitiers. Her identification of herself with the divine Diana made possible a whole mythological scheme for her castle of Anet. [3] The triple crescents that she shared with her royal lover appear on chimney-pieces, the cresting of the roof, windows, doors, and indeed on every possible field, just as they do on her plate (fig. 178), and even on the frame of her sunshade. [4] The very clock over the entrance had a bronze stag to strike the hours with its foot, and the motto

> Phoebo sacrata est almae domus Dianae,
> Verum accepta cui cuncta Diana refert.

A tapestry made for her, bordered with crescents, D's, deltas, bows, arrows, with the motto *Consequitur quodcumque petit*, and a tomb with *Sola vivit in illo*, has an allusion to Diane's refuge from the Queen's anger at Anet in its device of the

---

[1] See Pliny, *Hist. Nat.*, Bk. xi, chap. 17. For a picture of the dress see Bibliothèque Nationale fonds français, 5091, fol. 15 verso. The device reappears with other *imprese* on the ceiling of the Chapel of the Hôtel Lallemant at Bourges, built between 1512 and 1526.

[2] Charles VIII's device—wreathed swords and the motto *Si deus pro nobis, quis contra nos*—was hardly an *impresa*; but in Anne of Brittany's, an ermine with *Malo mori quam foedari*, and later a friar's girdle with *J'ai le corps delié*, device and motto were more closely linked. Louis XII had a porcupine, with the motto *Cominus et eminus*; Francis I a Salamander and flames, with the motto *Nutrisco et extinguo*; Claude de Navarre, his first wife, a swan transfixed with an arrow, and a full moon, with the motto *Candidi candidis*; and Eleanor of Austria, his second, a Phoenix, or a tree growing up to the sun, with *His suffulta*. Henri II used a crescent or three crescents, with *Donec totum impleat orbem*; Catherine de' Medici, as his wife, a crowned comet, with *Fato prudentia major*, and as his widow, broken fans and necklaces and flames drowned in tears, with *Ardorem extincta testantur vivere flamma*. Francis II had a burning column and two globes, with *Lumen rectis, unus non sufficit orbis*; Charles IX two intertwined columns, with the legend *Pietate et justicia*. Henri III had three crowns, one for France and one for Poland, with the motto *Manet ultima coelo*, and Louise de Vaudemont a sundial, with *Aspicio ut aspiciar*. Henri IV used the *main de justice* and the sword, with the motto *Duo proteget unus*, and Marguerite de Valois a Pentacle with the word *Salus*. Louis XIII had the clubs of Hercules and the motto *Erit haec quoque cognita monstris*, and Louis XIV the sun and motto *Nec pluribus impar*.

[3] Begun about 1547 and finished soon after 1552.   [4] See *Gazette des Beaux Arts*, xix, 1879, p. 169.

171. West Door, Church of Nantouillet, Seine et Marne, *c.* 1550

172. Chimney-piece of the Salle des Séances of the Châtellenie of Bruges. By Lancelot Blondeel, 1529–34

island of Delos, chained to a rock, with the motto *Sic immota manet*. The decorative use of such quasi-heraldic emblems was fostered by the publications of such books as *Le Imprese Illustri* of Ruscelli, published at Venice in 1566, Luca Contile's *Ragionamento . . . sopra la Proprietà delle Imprese*, published at Pavia in 1574, and the *imprese* of Camilli published at Venice twelve years later.[1] The most important of such works is Paradin's *Devises Héroiques* published at Lyons in 1557, with cuts of all the best known *imprese* of the Renaissance—Salamander, crescents, portcullis and the rest—and a few less familiar, each accompanied by a short motto and a brief explanation in prose.

In England elaborate *imprese* first appeared at the jousts held in honour of the Emperor's ambassadors in 1522, and French influence is clearly evident in the devices.[2] Six years later, at the jousts held for the French ambassadors on the occasion of the Duke of Orleans' marriage, the challengers were, 'appareled in bases and bardes all of one suite, the right side was ryche tyssue embroidered with a compasse or roundell of blacke veluet and in the compasse a right hand holding a sworde, and about the sword were pennes and peces of money of diuerse coyones, all embrawdered, under the hand was embraudered Loialte, and on that side of the bard was written in embraudery, Bi pen, pain nor Treasure, truth shall not be violated.'[3] Such devices were not common in decorative art in England until the end of the century. French influence was stronger at the Scottish court. In the Oxburgh bed-hangings,[4] embroidered by Mary Queen of Scots, the *imprese* of her friends and relations are decoratively combined. They have medallions embroidered with Mary's own *impresa*, a hand issuing from a cloud, holding a sickle and pruning a vine, with the motto *Virescit vulnere virtus*; a sun with sunflowers and *Non inferiora secutus*, the *impresa* of Margaret of Navarre; and an armillary sphere in a cloud of feathers, above the sea, with the punning motto *Las pennas passan y queda la Speranza*,[5] in a border with more *imprese* and the arms of France,

---

[1] Some of the engraved emblems approximate to the *impresa* type, as those of Bartolommeo da Brescia published in 1568, with emblems surrounded by short Latin, Greek, or Italian mottoes framed in elaborate cartouches with labels 'del offuscato', 'del desioso', &c., and a small shield of arms below. Even the printers had their *imprese*, such as the dolphin and anchor with the motto *Festina lente* of Aldus Manutius, and the hand and pair of compasses with the motto *Labore et constantia* used by Plantin about 1560.

[2] Hall, *Chronicle*, 1809 ed., p. 630. Henry VIII had a dress 'embroidered with L. L. L. of golde, and under the letters a harte of manne wounded, and great rolles of golde with blacke letters, in whiche was written, mon nauera, put together, it is, Ell Mon ceur a nauera, she hath wounded my harte. . . . Then followed Sir Nicholas Carewe, his base and barde was white Damaske, on whiche was embroidered with clothe of gold: a prison and a man lokyng out at a grate, and over the prison came from the prisoner a rolle, in whiche was written in Frenche, in prison I am at libertie, and at libertie I am in prison, and all his apparell was garded with shakells of silver.' Nine other knights had *imprese* of hearts, spheres, and feathers, with mottoes such as 'My harte is betwene ioye and pein', 'my harte is bounde', 'my harte is broken', and 'sance remedye.' Four years later rather similar devices were used at the Shrove Tuesday jousts at Greenwich: a heart in a press with flames about it, and the motto *Declare je n'ose* and burning hearts watered by watering cans held by ladies' hands. *Ibid.*, p. 707.

[3] *Ibid.*, p. 22.   [4] See p. 122 and p. 157.

[5] An armillary sphere was the emblem of Manuel of Portugal, with the punning mottoes *Spes mea in Deo meo. Spera in Deo et fac bonitatem.* Cf. Rabelais, *Gargantua*, chap. ix (ed. Burgaud, des Marets and Rabery,

Spain, Scotland, and England. Yet more such *imprese* are recorded in Drummond's description of another set of hangings embroidered by her,[1] with another of her *imprese*, a loadstone turning towards the pole, with the anagram motto *Sa vertu m'attire*; her mother's device of a phoenix in flames, with the motto *En ma fin git mon commencement*; Henri II's crescents and Francis I's salamander; 'the Impresa of Godfrey of Bullogne, an Arrow passing throw Three Birds, the word *Dederitne viam casusve Deusve*. . . . The Impresa of the Cardinal of Lorrain, her uncle, a Pyramid overgrown with ivy, the vulgar word *Te stante virebo*. . . . The Impresa of King Henry VIII, a Portcullis, the word *Altera securitas*.'

6

Among all the symbols of the individual his cypher was not forgotten; his initial was considered worthy to figure even on the noblest Renaissance façade. The use of initials in decoration begins in the last quarter of the fourteenth century. Charles V of France used as his device the initial K of Karolus and a blue fleur-de-lis powdered with lesser golden lilies; his inventory of 1380 describes 'Une chambre de satanin blanc brodée de fleurs de lys azurées, et sur les dictes fleurs de lys autres petites fleur de lys d'or, et en chascune pièce cinq KK couronnéz de fleurs de lys comme dessus',[2] while much of his plate was similarly adorned.[3] Some of the Apocalypse tapestries at Angers made for Louis I of Anjou have their backgrounds powdered with LL and MM for him and Marie de Bretagne, and some with YY for Yolande of Aragon. In 1389 the Duke of Burgundy had a corselet of red velvet, lozenged with gold with PP and tufts of daisies in the lozenges, and six years later a book cover powdered with marguerites, MM and PP.[4] The fashion soon spread to England. The portrait of the young Richard II in the choir at Westminster shows his dress embroidered with golden flowers alternating with crowned RR. The EE of Edward Prince of Wales adorn his drinking-cup (fig. 152). Personal initials were used even on church vestments.[5] The 1388

i. 116). 'En pareilles tenebres sont comprises ces glorieux de court, et transporteurs de noms, lesquels, voulans en leur devises, signifier espoir, font pourtraire une sphere; des pennes d'oiseaux pour peines . . .'

[1] *Works*, Edinburgh, 1711, p. 137.

[2] Havard, *Dictionnaire de l'Ameublement*, s.v. Lettre.

[3] e.g. 'une tasse d'or . . . et ou fons a un esmail vert ront, ouquel a un K semé des armes de France . . .' Moranvillé, *Inventaires de Louis duc d'Anjou*, p. 81. His post-mortem inventory also describes girdles with MM and fleurs-de-lis, once belonging to Marie de France, and other with YY and fleurs-de-lis, belonging to Ysabel de Bavière. Labarte, *Inventaire du mobilier de Charles V*, p. 31. The inventory of Valentine de Milan drawn up in 1408 includes innumerable jewels and embroideries with her initials VVS. F. M. Graves, *Deux inventaires de la Maison d'Orléans*, p. 99 *et passim*.

[4] Laborde, *Glossaire des Émaux*, p. 213.

[5] The windows set up in the chapel of New College, Oxford, in 1385, show a curious development of the usage; St. Paulinus, St. Pelagius, St. Alphege, St. Bernard and Our Lady of Sorrows all have backgrounds powdered with the crowned initials of their names. The alb of some fourteenth-century vestments at St. Bernard de Comminges has letters arranged in vertical lines to indicate the names of the Apostles, Farcy, *La Broderie*, p. 45. Similarly the 'Founders Jewel' of New College is shaped as the M of its patron, the Virgin. Such MM, upheld by angels, appeared powdered on a cloth of gold cope described in the 1402 inventory of

173. Tomb of Charles the Bold, Church of Notre Dame, Bruges, 1559

174. Imprese of Anne de Bretagne, Claude de France, and Louis XII. Château de Blois

inventory of Westminster Abbey includes three new red copes damasked in gold with orphreys of black velvet embroidered with the letters T and A and swans of pearl, the gift of Thomas Duke of Gloucester and his wife Alianor Bohun.[1] With the fifteenth century the initials of living people[2] appeared in church architecture; Charles VII, when he rebuilt the balustrade of the Sainte Chapelle, had it carved with fleur-de-lis in quatrefoils with a crowned K held by two angels in the middle; and the balustrade of its oratory, built by Louis XI, has crowned LL against a background of fleur-de-lis.[3] Francis I glorified God less than himself in the decoration of the Chapel of Villers Cotterets; there are a few angels' heads, but crowned FF, his device of Salamanders and his armorial fleurs-de-lis play a far more important part in the scheme.

In the sixteenth century such initials were much used alike in the decoration of personal possessions and in secular architecture.[4] Anne of Brittany in 1498 had hangings of crimson velvet powdered with crowned AA for herself and KK for her husband;[5] Margaret of Austria an M of carved boxwood, hanging from a chain;[6] Caterina Jagellonica was buried with her pendant of a crowned C;[7] Henry VIII had to reset jewels with fresh initials with each new adventure in matrimony, and owned much plate decorated with 'H and R crownyd';[8] while endless embroideries and tapestries were ornamented with initials.[9]

On the façade of Blois the crowned L on a background of fleurs-de-lis, the crowned A on a background of ermine, the crossed CC, and the FF powdered with fleurs-de-lis, celebrate Louis XII, Anne of Brittany, Claude of Lorraine, and Francis I; at Chambord even the bolts of the doors are formed as a crowned F. On the Chateau de Chanteloup in Normandy, built about 1520, great panels

St. Paul's, as well as vestments powdered with the word 'Jhesu'. (*Archaeologia*, l. 501; cf. the 1471 inventory of Notre Dame de Lens, a cope of black damask embroidered 'Jhesu Maria'; the 1483 inventory of the Cathedral of Le Mans, a chasuble with 'Jhus' on the orphreys; and the 1521 inventory of Angers Cathedral, three crimson copes with 'Ihus Maria'. Farcy, *La Broderie*, p. 46.) The sacred monogram IHS appears everywhere; on vestments, as on a fine fifteenth-century chasuble in the Church of St. Nicholas at Namur; in architectural decoration, as in the choir at Albi; and worn, probably with prophylactic intent, as a jewel. See Joan Evans, *English jewellery*, p. 70, and *Proceedings of the Royal Institution*, vol. xxiv, 1923, p. 170.

[1] W. St. John Hope, *Heraldry for Craftsmen and Designers*, p. 323.

[2] And of those the building commemorated; the Tempio Malatestiano at Rimini has splendid chapel screens by Matteo de' Pasti with panels pierced with the monogram of Isotta.

[3] The balustrade of the Church of Josselin in the Morbihan is all of Anne of Brittany's crowned AA, some made of her knotted cordelière; Margaret of Austria jewelled the Church of Brou with the PP and MM of herself and her dead husband; and Ferdinand and Isabella set their crowned initials in their Chapel of San Juan de los Reyes at Toledo.

[4] By the time that Paradin wrote his *Devises héroiques* the briquet of Burgundy was supposed to have a double significance from its likeness to the letter B.

[5] Havard, *Dictionnaire de l'Ameublement*, s.v. Semé.

[6] Laborde, *Glossaire des Émaux*, ii. 358.

[7] Now in the Treasury of the Cathedral of Upsala.

[8] Palgrave, *Kalendars and Inventories*, ii. 278.

[9] e.g. Inventory of Lady Hungerford, 1523; 'four qushynges of russet damaske inbrodered with golde with E. C. A.'; one 'of blake velvett and white payned, inbrodered with A and E'; and a bed with its tester 'of whyte and blake damaske payned, inbrodered in golde with A and D'. *Archaeologia*, xxxviii, 1860, p. 360.

between the windows are filled with the knotted initials of its owner and his wife. The HH and CC of Henri II and Catherine de Médicis are reproduced more than two hundred times on the façade of the Louvre,[1] and reappear on the most varied objects, from the Resurrection reliquary given to Rheims by Henri at his coronation to his book-bindings. Anet, too, was fairly peppered with the Deltas and DD of Diane de Poitiers. With the growth of Hellenism, indeed, there was a fashion for Greek initials; Francis I sometimes used Φ instead of F for his cypher, and Louise de Lorraine, wife of Henri III, the double lambda. On the Chateau d'Oiron, built about 1545 by Claude Couffier and his wife Françoise, their initials appear as a monogram of the Greek X and Φ. Mary Queen of Scots, on the embroidered hangings now at Oxburgh, used a combined monogram of her own and her husband's initials, formed of MA and the Greek Φ; the same device appears on her signet ring[2] and on her book-stamp.[3]

Henri II used his initial as an integral part of his device, either combined with crowned crescents, as on the ceiling of the Salle des Caryatides of the Louvre,[4] or between two branches, one of oak and one of laurel, with the motto *Has dedit, his dabit ultra*. Whole names were anagrammatically turned into mottoes. The *Maria Stuart* of Mary Queen of Scots was transposed into *Sa vertu m'attire*, and *Veritas armata*.[5] A repertory of such anagrams—for instance *Elisabetha Steuarta —Has Artes beata valet*—appears in Henry Peacham's *Minerva Britanna* of 1612. But they did not remain long in fashion; Vauquelin de la Fresnaye's *Art Poétique*, begun in 1574 and published in 1605, holds them up to contempt.[6]

7

Such pretty fancies, indeed, were a sign that the golden days of heraldry were over. Men no longer went into battle wearing armorial bearings; tournaments were no more, and men sought distraction in academies rather than in the tiltyard. The art of swordsmanship had taken the place of earlier contests whether real or mimic; and whatever its influence upon manners, it had none upon the arts.

In Italian architecture the cartouche—said to be derived from the shield displayed upon a cartel of defiance—became the dominant ornamental motive of baroque art[7] and almost the only scheme of heraldic decoration. Occasionally, as on Bernini's Scala Regia at the Vatican, the cartouche is held by angels sailing in space; but ordinarily it is laid against wall, pilaster or pediment, or outlined

---

[1] Cf. the ceiling at Chenonceaux painted with interlaced CC's set in different directions, and the Palissy cup (in 1900 in the collection of Baron Gustave de Rothschild) pierced with HH and CC, and plates by the same maker with these initials.   [2] In the British Museum.

[3] Davenport, *English Heraldic book stamps*, p. 287. On the Oxburgh hangings she also uses a large monogram of 'Marie Stuart', while the names of Lord and Lady Shrewsbury, her gaolers, also appear in monogram.

[4] Painted in 1557–7; see M. Vachon, *Le Louvre et les Tuileries*, p. 74.

[5] See Drummond of Hawthornden, *Works*, Edinburgh, 1711, p. 137. *Sa vertu m'attire* appears also on the Oxburgh bed.   [6] Saintsbury, *History of Criticism*, ii. 130.   [7] See vol. II, p. 37.

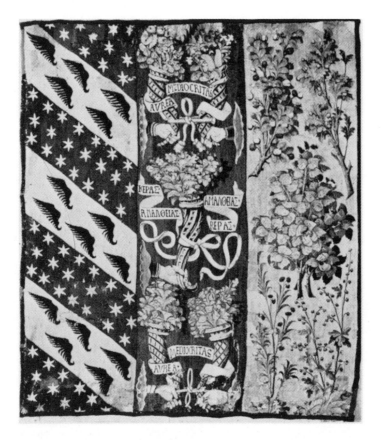

175. Tapestry, French or Flemish, *c.* 1560

176. Detail of the coffering of the ceiling of the Salle des Gardes. Château de Chambord, *c.* 1540

177. Initial and device of Henri II, designed by Philibert de l'Orme. Salle de Bal,
Palais de Fontainebleau, *c.* 1555

178. Cover of a crystal tazza, with the devices of Diane de Poitiers

FIG. 179. Baroque Cartouches by Federigo Zuccaro, c. 1590

against the sky as an acroterion.[1] The last great heraldic scheme of decoration invented in Italy is that devised by Pietro da Cortona in 1639 for the ceiling of the great hall of the Palazzo Barberini, where Pope Urban VIII could see the heavens opening to receive the shield of the Barberini, that, as it attained apotheosis, came to life, its outline dissolving into garlands of laurel held by floating genii and its three bees flying upwards into Heaven.

In countries where the hold of the classic convention was slighter, contemporary decoration made a freer use of heraldry. In 1633 the Saloon of the Kingdoms at Buen Retiro was decorated with shields of every state of the Spanish dominions. Even the mature classical style in Germany was not severe enough to eliminate heraldry; and such *ensembles* as the Rittersaal in the Royal Palace at Köpenick show how ill-assorted the result could be. Northern naturalism, too, could still include heraldry in its schemes. The Flemish tapestry weavers hung achievements of arms against a background of woodland landscape (fig. 180); and in England the restoration of Charles II was commemorated in a delightful design for iron fire-backs with the three crowns of the United Kingdom caught and held fast in an oak tree, with the royal initials on either side and the motto below.[2]

In France, heraldic decoration played a less and less important part. Its most important field was that of gold-work;[3] a French perfume burner of about 1640 in the collection of Viscount Lee of Fareham is decorated in pierced work of marvellous precision and delicacy with ciphers of the owner's initials, ensigned with a coronet and wreathed in palms, against a background of naturalistic flowers, while the whole is surmounted by a cover formed as an arched crown. Decoration of the sort was more rarely applied to architecture;[4] the mature French classic style was less enamoured of cartouche forms than Italian baroque.[5] Much ingenuity was shown in fusing heraldic elements into a classic scheme. On the stairs of Gaston d'Orleans' wing at Blois, built about 1638, his arms appear on one of the shields of a classic trophy (fig. 181). Le Brun included Fouquet's squirrel—*fouquet* in Angevin dialect—in the decoration of Vaux le Vicomte in 1658. A little later he designed basins for Louis XIV with the Seven Virtues and the Seven Liberal Arts

[1] For such cartouches engraved designs were published by many artists of the later Renaissance, from those published by Serlio in his *Architectura* published at Venice in 1566 to the rather heavy designs of the *Scudiero di varii designi d'arme e targhe* published by Bernardino Radi at Florence in 1636, and the cartouches of Stephano della Bella published in Paris about 1650.

[2] The design is in relation with that of two contemporary medals, one with the three crowns in a leafless tree, with the sun shining on it and the motto TANDEM REVIRESCET (*Medallic Illustrations*, Plate XLII, 3), and another of 1661 with the tree in full foliage and the motto IAM FLORESCIT (*ibid.*, Plate XLV, 13).

[3] It was also common on book-bindings—Mazarin, for instance, had his books powdered with his badges of star and fasces—but for such work design was simple.

[4] Lemercier, in 1653, designed ceiling panels for the small council chamber of the Louvre with crossed sceptres and *mains de justice*, centred with crowned LL. Hautecœur, *Le Louvre et les Tuileries de Louis XIV*, Plate VI.

[5] The Hôtel de Pierre at Toulouse and the Hôtel des Monnaies at Avignon afford good examples of their use in the more Italianate South.

with the royal arms in the middle, and on the sides eagles standing on swags of fruit, 'separez les uns par une fleur de lys couronnée, et les autres par un Caducée entre deux cornes d'abondance', and others with the twelve hours, six crowning globes charged with the royal arms and six holding flowers.[1] He even included the fleur-de-lis in the architectural decoration of Versailles; but heraldic decoration had become a mere survival in an epoch that had forgotten the Middle Ages and had created a mythological symbolism of its own. When the classical tyranny relaxed before the sentiment of the 'return to nature', heraldry still remained alien to the age. The fleurs-de-lis once more appeared as natural lilies,[2] or heraldic coronets were set not above achievements of arms but over branches of lilies, olives, juniper, and jasmine (fig. 183);[3] but heraldry played no living part in decoration. Since the beginning of the eighteenth century its uses have been confined to the commemoration of the dead and the indication of ownership on the portable possessions of the living.

[1] Guiffrey, *Inventaire général du Mobilier de la Couronne*, i. 70.
[2] See p. 107.
[3] As on carved oak panels of the time of Louis XVI in the Victoria and Albert Museum, 970–3. 1900.

IV

LITERATURE AND DECORATION

I

IN the early Middle Ages the written word was at once mysterious and sacred. Through it were the hoarded treasures of classic learning preserved; through it were the meditations and teaching of the Fathers perpetuated; through it were the feudal foundations of society assured. Even the national tradition of epic and romance was secure only thanks to its safeguard. The difficulty of reading, the rarity of literary knowledge, but served to emphasize the majesty of letters.

The chief literature of the early Middle Ages was Latin. It was studied and practised chiefly in monastic houses, and consequently its influence was chiefly upon work done either in monastic workshops or for religious foundations. Yet of the types created for Romanesque art and ecclesiastical use, some survived to be adapted to a Gothic style and secular employment. The Wheel of Fortune, that appeared as the frame of the wheel window of the north transept at Saint Étienne de Beauvais about 1130, was painted at the end of the Great Hall at Winchester Castle in 1238, and (together with a Tree of Jesse) over the fire-place of the Painted Chamber at Westminster a few years later. Similarly the occupations of the months, that appeared alike on calendars and on the façades of the cathedrals, were about the same time painted over the fire-place of the Queen's chamber at Westminster. They survived into the decoration of the fifteenth century alike on the plate of Charles the Bold,[1] the faience of the della Robbias,[2] and on English domestic painted glass.[3] The zodiac, represented in the sculpture and the stained glass of the cathedrals from Autun onwards, decorated an enamelled secular cup in 1377;[4] the stages of human life that adorn, for instance, the Psalter of Robert de Lyle[5] and a window at the Church of Saint Nizier at Troyes[6] were translated into tapestry for Charles VI.[7] Even the figures of the prophets with their scrolls of prophecies of the coming of Christ, and their parallels the apostles with the articles of the creed, found a place in secular decoration. Sauval records that in 1365 the kings' chamber at the Louvre had thirteen prophets standing on consoles, each prophet holding a scroll.[8] Louis d'Anjou in 1369 had six hanaps each with an apostle holding a

---

[1] Laborde, *Les Ducs de Bourgogne*, ii, p. 66.

[2] Medallions from a coved ceiling in the V. and A. M.

[3] Norbury Hall, Derbyshire, and Mayor's Parlour, Leicester; Westlake, *Design in Painted Glass*, iii. 144. The elaborate scheme of Calendar illustrations used by Jean Pucelle, 1325–53, does not seem to have found its way into decoration.

[4] Laborde, *Glossaire des Émaux*, ii. 301.   [5] B. M. Arundel MS. 83.

[6] See *Annales archéologiques*, i, 1844, p. 242.

[7] The set was mended in 1399; Guiffrey, *Histoire de la Tapisserie en France*, p. 22.

[8] *Histoire et antiquités de la ville de Paris*, ii. 279.

180. Panel of Heraldic tapestry. Audenarde, *c.* 1640

181. Panel of arms from the great staircase, Aile de Gaston d'Orléans,
Château de Blois, *c.* 1638

182. Shield crowning the grille of the entrance to the Cour d'Honneur,
Versailles, *c.* 1680

scroll of his clause of the creed,[1] and the Duke of Orleans in 1395 bought two tapestries with 'Histoire du Crédo à douze prophètes et à douze apôtres'.[2]

With the growth of the vernacular literature in the twelfth century a fresh literary influence was exerted upon art. Naturally in so far as it was a literature translated from the Latin, it only served to popularize and to modify the earlier patristic and ecclesiastical tradition; but the development of a truly vernacular literature, with a point of view, a style, and genres of its own did much to create a parallel tradition of ornament with its roots in civil rather than in ecclesiastical life. Such influence, however, was at first rarely exercised directly by literary tradition upon decorative art, but almost always indirectly through the miniatures which illustrated the manuscripts of the texts. The symbolic Bestiary of the Physiologus, and the early twelfth-century vernacular version of it by Philippe de Thaon, was one of the most common of illustrated books, and its influence on decoration is evident.

The margins of manuscript Psalters were adorned with such subjects as the panther, whose fragrance attracts the other animals; the tiger, who can be caught by the lure of a mirror; the water-snake, who eats his way through the body of the crocodile;[3] and the unicorn, who takes refuge in a maiden's lap.[4] The beasts of the Bestiary illustrations were also used in sculpture; the elephant, ostrich, griffin, and camel appear below the Sciences and Arts on the façade of Sens Cathedral; tigers being captured by means of mirrors are carved on Miserere seats at Chester Cathedral (fig. 184) and Boston Church; the Phœnix occurs at Westminster; the Elephant at Beverley, Gloucester, Exeter, and Ripon; the hyena at Carlisle and Alne, and the unicorn most often of all.[5] But the Bestiary tradition practically ended with Richard de Fournival's *Bestiaire d'Amour* about 1260, and the formal bestiary types with their symbolic significance began to fall into disuse, though as late as 1404 so courtly a personage as the Duc de Berry was given a salt-cellar decorated with four tigers lured by four sapphire mirrors.[6] Beasts continued to have some symbolic significance, but their symbolic use in decoration was rare and outside the general current of decorative art;[7] for in the meantime the animal stories of the *Isopet* and *Roman de Renart* cycles had endowed them with characters

[1] Moranvillé, *Inventaires de Louis, duc d'Anjou*, p. 326.

[2] Guiffrey, *Histoire de la Tapisserie en France*, p. 18.

[3] These appear among the earlier grotesques of 'Queen Mary's Psalter', B. M. Royal MS. 2 B VII.

[4] This occurs among the grotesques of the Ormesby Psalter.

[5] See F. Bond, *Wood-carvings in English Churches*, i, *Misericords*, p. 19 et seqq. Bestiary stories identifiable by their inscriptions are carved round the doorway of Alne Church, Yorks.

[6] Guiffrey, *Jean duc de Berry*, i. 176.

[7] A moralizing poet of the late thirteenth century bids his reader fly from the deadly sins:

Beaux fils, fui lion et dragon,
Ors, liépart et escorpion

and the paintings on a late fifteenth-century screen at Plolanff, Côtes-du-Nord, perpetuate the tradition; Pride appears as a peacock, Avarice as a frog, Lust as a goat, Envy as a viper, Greed as a pig, Anger as a lion, and Sloth as a snail. Lenient, *La Satire en France*, p. 108. See also Mâle, *L'Art religieux de la fin du moyen âge en France*, p. 354 et seqq.

and histories of their own, and they had become as real as men. The animal
stories were among the first manuscripts to be illustrated, and, since they belonged
to the clerical literature of the time, scenes from them appear among the fishes,
birds, and beasts of the Romanesque tradition in early twelfth-century illuminated
initials—Reynard the fox appears in the Silos manuscripts of Beatus on the
Apocalypse, written before 1109—and on Romanesque churches.[1] In England such
sculptures survived into the Gothic period. Aesop's Fox and Stork appear on the
north door of Holt, Worcestershire, and on a misericord at Chester, and his Fox
and Grapes on misericords at Chester and Faversham. The story of Reynard is
carved on the central pillar of Salisbury Chapter House, and a set of misericords
at Bristol Abbey are carved with Bruin caught in a cleft stick, Tybert the cat
caught in the gin; Isengrin and Bruin dancing with delight to hear of Reynard's
being condemned to death; and the gallows being erected for his benefit (fig. 187).

Besides such illustrations of well-known animal stories, the illuminators soon
produced little animal stories of their own, of which the text was never written or
is now lost. A late twelfth-century Psalter[2] has initials decorated with drawings
of a man with a dog and two apes, and an ass playing a harp while a goat sings; and
a thirteenth-century Psalter, probably from Chester,[3] has an initial B, decorated
with eight medallions of animal musicians; a donkey with a harp, a cat and fiddle,
and so on. Such subjects were soon transferred from the initials to the margin.
The Psalter of Edmund de Lacy, Earl of Lincoln,[4] who died in 1257, has marginal
grotesques of the Aesopic fox and crane, and of scenes of a warrior attacking
snails and mice hanging a cat; in the Ormesby Psalter[5] (fig. 188) written between
1290 and 1320, a fox, dressed in a capuchon and leaning on a crutch, comes to pay
a visit to a rather nervous rabbit, and a monkey on a hound pursues an owl on a
hare; in a Book of Hours of the Maestricht School of about 1300[6] the monkeys'
castle is besieged by the foxes with catapults and other engines of war. On the
margins of a manuscript executed for Joffroy d'Aspremont and his wife at about
the same date[7] there are monkeys begging and fishing; while on another Flemish
manuscript a little later in date[8] a rabbit plays the bagpipes, and a monkey a trumpet; a monkey goes out into the country with a hawk's lure; another tilts at a
rabbit, another falls off a horse, another bows before a bishop, and another reads
out of a horn-book to a bird, while a whole school of little monkeys plays in class
and has to be scolded by the master. In the Gorleston Psalter there is a funeral
procession of rabbits (fig. 189), and more rabbits watch round a bier, while a
monkey horseman goes rabbit hunting with a hound as big as himself, and a bear
teaches a pair of ducks to sing.

[1] Gautier de Coincy said in the thirteenth century that the clergy were less interested in statues of Our Lady
than in representations of Reynard the Fox. Didron, *Annales archéologiques*, ii. 169.
[2] Glasgow University, Hunterian Museum, MS. U. 32.   [3] B. M. MS. Lansdowne 420.
[4] Now in the collection of the Duke of Rutland.   [5] Bodleian MS. Douce, 366.
[6] B. M. Stowe MS. 17.   [7] Bodleian MS. Douce 118.   [8] Bodleian MS. Douce 5–6.

183. Panels of oak carved with jasmine and olive. French, *c.* 1775

184. Misericord with a knight luring tigers with a mirror. Chester Cathedral
c. 1380.

185. Misericord with cat playing the fiddle. Wells Cathedral. *c.* 1300

186. Misericord with Alexander borne by griffins. Wells Cathedral. *c.* 1300

From the manuscripts such scenes passed first into ecclesiastical decoration and then into secular ornament. Misereres in Beverley Minster have a pig playing the harp, a cat fiddling to dancing mice, and a monkey piping to a dancing bear; a cat fiddling appears again at Wells (fig. 185); a pig fiddling and another blowing a trumpet at Winchester; a pig playing the pipes at Durham Castle, and a pig and whistle at Westminster. Richard Tunnoc's window in York Minster, set up soon after 1320, has a border of monkeys playing wind instruments. Monkeys, indeed, had by the end of the fourteenth century become so much of a commonplace in decoration that the little French reliquary of the hair of St. Catherine, given to the Basilica of Assisi by Count Tommaso Orsini in 1381, could without impropriety be supported on the figures of four little apes.

From such fields animal decoration passed into secular use. Charles V in 1380 had a salt-cellar shaped like a ship, with dolphins at its prow and stern, and a crew of two monkeys,[1] while Louis of Anjou had plate decorated with monkeys mounted on donkeys, playing the bagpipes, carried in a litter borne by a lion and a bear, riding on horseback, eating apples, and fishing for barbel,[2] as well as an 'espreuve' with the foot adorned with a *carole* with a fox to bring up the rear.[3] In 1375 the hall of the castle of Valenciennes was decorated with a wall painting of monkeys pillaging the goods of a sleeping pedlar,[4] and a Flemish silver goblet in the Rütschi Collection at Zürich [5] shows the same scene. In the Renart cycle Bernart the ass is an arch-priest, and Primaut the wolf gets drunk and says mass before the altar; similarly Louis of Anjou had plate decorated with a monkey in a surplice bearing a crozier blessing a fox who hides two goslings in his hood, a fox with mitre and crozier, and another preaching to the geese.[6] Charles V in his study at the Hôtel Saint Pol had an ebony fox dressed as a friar, sitting upright to beg,[7] while among the plate in the Château de Pau was 'ung cinge d'argent qui dict ses heures dans ung parcq esmaillé de vert'.[8] Sometimes the moment of capture was shown, as on a ewer with a cock being seized by a fox;[9] sometimes the lesser beasts were allowed to get their revenge. At Malvern mice were carved hanging a cat at the gallows, and on bench ends at Beverley, Sherborne, and South Brent

---

[1] Labarte, *Inventaire du Mobilier de Charles V*, p. 62.

[2] Moranvillé, *Inventaire de Louis d'Anjou*, p. lxi. Among the plate at New College, Oxford, is a fifteenth-century cup, of which the crystal bowl is upheld by a monkey in silver gilt.

[3] Moranvillé, *Inventaire de Louis d'Anjou*, p. 57.

[4] Michel, *Histoire de l'Art*, iii. 893. Dr. R. W. Chambers tells me that the earliest illustration of the story that he knows occurs in the Smithfield Decretals, B.M. Royal MS. 10 E. IV f. 149 b, written in Italy, but considered to have been illuminated in England between c. 1300 and 1350. It belonged to the Priory of St. Bartholomew, Smithfields. The same subject is represented on misericords at Beverley and Manchester.

[5] Formerly in the Pierpont Morgan Collection.

[6] Moranvillé, *op. cit.*, p. lvi.

[7] Labarte, *Inventaire du Mobilier de Charles V*, p. 244.

[8] Molinier, *Inventaire des Meubles du Château de Pau*, 1561–2, p. 75. The figure was probably about a century earlier.

[9] Louis d'Anjou, 1368; Harvard, *Dictionnaire de l'Ameublement*, s.v. Aiguière.

two geese are hanging a fox.[1] The connexion between the illuminated manuscripts and such decoration is curiously close; the Gorleston Psalter[2] has a lively marginal picture of rabbits running through a hood to escape a hound (fig. 189), while in 1422 the King of France had three bankers of green tapestry, 'a chappeaulx, connins, et chiens dedens les chappeaulx.'[3]

The manuscript painters, however, were wearying of the style they had initiated,[4] and had developed it along new lines. On the one hand they filled their margins with scenes of everyday life, that might or might not have some literary reference; on the other they created hybrid monsters of their own imagining.[5] The Ormesby Psalter, for instance, has a rabbit-headed bird drawing a bow; a bird with the head of a horned man; a man with arms but no legs, and a tail between his shoulders; and a man-headed quadruped shooting an owl which has perched on his tail. Most often such grotesques are perfectly irrelevant in subject to the text and to the rest of the illustrations; a man-headed beast combing his hair before a mirror is set by an initial that enshrines a charming Virgin and Child. Occasionally one seems to be a comic prelude to a serious subject: a monster with his face on his breast being ejected from the jaws of two fishes is followed two pages later by an initial filled with a conventional representation of Jonah and the Whale. In some Flemish illustrations[6] each monster seems to be drawn from parts of at least three natural creatures—a woman's head, a bird's wings, a beast's legs, and a snake's tail is a typical creation—and it is a relief to come upon an ordinary monkey. A French fourteenth-century marriage casket in the Musée de Cluny shows a similar variety in its quatrefoil medallions (fig. 190); the three monsters repeated in its decoration all have human heads, bird wings, beast bodies, and tails. Similarly fantastic creatures decorate the foot and lid of the splendid fourteenth-century French enamelled ewer in the Copenhagen Museum.[7] Occasionally a satiric intention is evident: the early fourteenth-century Portail des Libraires and Portail de la Calende of Rouen Cathedral are adorned with little medallions of the doctor who is half a goose, of

[1] A late secular use of this subject occurs on a plaster overmantel of about 1610 at Westwood Manor House, Wilts.

[2] Fol. 202 verso.

[3] Guiffrey, *Histoire de la Tapisserie en France*, p. 29.

[4] The fourteenth-century Renard manuscripts (e. g. Bodleian MS. Douce 360, dated 1339) have miniatures neither so lively nor so well finished as the marginal grotesques.

[5] The Bestiary had included a certain number of monsters: Onoscentaurus, serra, manticore and basilisk, and sirens which might have bird, ass or bull bodies. In the time of Philippe le Bel even literature had its monsters, such as Fauvel, half man and half horse; St. Bernard compared Arnold of Brescia to a beast with a dove's head and scorpion's tail (Epist. cxcvi, ad Guidonem legatum), while fourteenth-century satire was always changing, or half changing, the Devil into man, bear, leopard, lion or other beast. Lenient, *La Satire en France au Moyen Âge*, p. 180.

[6] e. g. Psalter probably from Maestricht, Bodleian Canonici Liturg. 126.

[7] Rather similar monsters survive in a curiously episodic fashion on the Flamboyant organ stair of Saint Maclou. Such satirical grotesques were also fairly common in the Low Countries, as for instance in the churches of Saint Jean Baptiste, Liége, and Notre Dame, Courtrai, where a bishop is shown with a bat's wings and a monk with pig's legs.

187. Carvings of scenes from the story of Reynard the Fox. Bristol Abbey, *c.* 1450

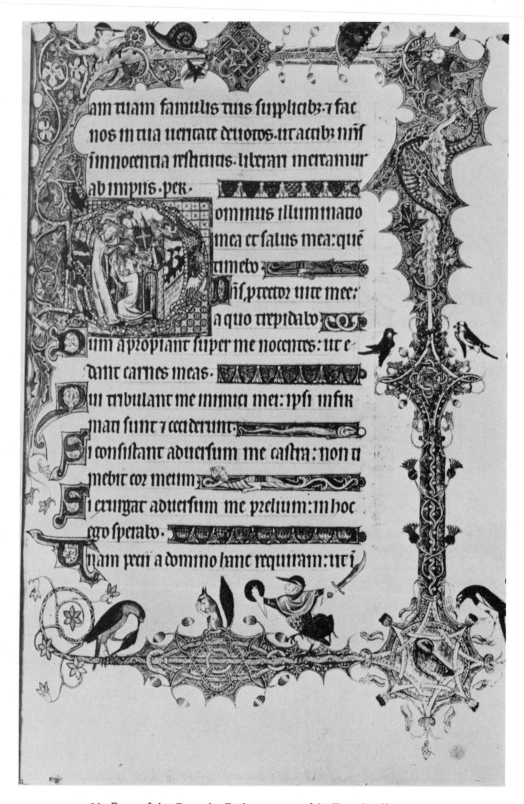

am tuam famulis tuis supplicib3 ⁊ fac
nos in tua ueritate deuotos. ut actib3 nisi
si innocentia restitutis. liberari mereamur
ab impiis. per.

Dominus illuminatio
mea et salus mea: que
timebo

His, pretector uite mee:
a quo trepidabo

Dum appropiant super me nocentes: ut e
dant carnes meas.

Qui tribulant me inimici mei: ipsi infir
mati sunt ⁊ ceciderunt.

Si consistant aduersum me castra: non ti
mebit cor meum.

Si exurgat aduersum me prelium: in hoc
ego sperabo.

Unam peti a domino hanc requiram: ut i

188. Page of the Ormesby Psalter, executed in East Anglia, *c.* 1295

the pig-headed philosopher, the cock-bodied musician, the calf-headed woman, the dog-man and the bird-lady [1] (fig. 191).

2

The influence of the 'genres nobles' of medieval literature upon decoration was naturally stronger and more direct than that of animal stories and satire. The Epics of Crusade, however, at first belonged to the category of sacred rather than of profane literature, and consequently influenced ecclesiastical rather than secular iconography. Monsieur Mâle has pointed out the representations of Roland on the pilgrimage route to Rome; he sounds his horn on the pavement of S. Maria Maggiore at Vercelli, and brandishes Durandel at Oliver's side on the portal of Verona.[2] In France he ranked as a saint and hardly appeared in secular decoration: it is on the windows of Chartres and not in castle halls that scenes from the *Chanson de Roland* are to be found.

The 'matter of Brittany', however, brought the heroes of chivalry into secular decoration. Arthur and his knights, it is true, were taken from the *Roman de Lancelot* to adorn the portal of Modena about 1160, but more usually they appeared in the paintings on castle walls, as in the Arthur's Hall and Guinevere's Room of Dover Castle, and on the decorative trifles of medieval courtly life. When in *L'Escoufle* (c. 1200) the hero dedicates a cup at the High Altar of Jerusalem, it is enamelled with the adventures of Tristan and Iseult. The Tristan story decorates the walls of the Castle of Saint Floret, near Issoire; according to the version of Thomas, it appears on some late twelfth-century Chertsey tiles, and according to the version written by Gottfried of Strasburg about 1210 is illustrated on a thirteenth-century woven table cover from Kloster Wienhausen near Celle, now in Erfurt Cathedral.[3] The whole story of the oppression of Cornwall by King Languis of Ireland and his champion the Morold and Sir Tristram's battle with the Morold on behalf of his uncle King Mark is elaborately stitched into a Sicilian linen quilt of about 1400 in the Victoria and Albert Museum (fig. 192). King Mark watching the lovers is a fairly common subject on

---

[1] For other examples see the cul-de-lampe of the tower staircase at Notre Dame de Dijon, and plate of the second half of the fourteenth century described in inventories. See Laborde, *Glossaire des Émaux*, ii. 503; Moranvillé, *op. cit.*, p. liii; Guiffrey, *Les Inventaires de Jean duc de Berry*, i. 169. Not even the Renaissance could altogether bring this tradition to an end; and the burlesque survived in literature also. All the beasts and birds and insects of the medieval illuminator reappear with a few classical accessories in such designs as those of anonymous German Master of 1527 (Guilmard, *Les Maîtres ornemanistes*, p. 537) with fantastic eagles, winged men and horses, horned lions, monstrous serpents and dolphins, satyrs, masks and chimeras, and in the slightly later arabesque panels of Virgil Solis of Nuremberg. Echoes of the same tradition add a strangely unclassical note to the *Disegni Varii* published by Polifilo Zancarli or Giancarli early in the seventeenth century, which appealed so strongly to the northern taste that they were exactly copied (without acknowledgement) by Nicholas Visscher of Nuremberg in 1617.

[2] 'L'Art du Moyen Âge et les Pèlerinages', *Revue de Paris*, Sept.–Oct. 1919, v. 717 et seq.

[3] See J. Lessing, *Wandteppiche und Decken des Mittelalters in Deutschland*, Berlin, 1901, figs. 11–13.

the domestic ivories of the fourteenth century; on an ivory casket from the Solty-koff Collection, now in the Victoria and Albert Museum, it is represented together with scenes of the siege of a Castle of Love, of Aristotle and Campaspe;[1] of the fountain of youth, of Galahad receiving the keys of the enchanted castle, of Gawain and the Lion, of Lancelot crossing the bridge of swords, of Gawain and the magic bed, and of the capture of the unicorn.[2] A silver fountain with Tristan and Yseult occurs in the royal accounts in 1353;[3] scenes from their story adorned the plate of Louis d'Anjou;[4] and King Mark watching them reflected in the fountain may still be seen on one of the bosses of the vaulting of Jacques Cœur's house at Bourges. The Chevalier au Cygne is represented on a misericord at Exeter, and his story is the theme of some fine Tournai tapestries of about 1460, now in St. Catherine's Church, Cracow. Scenes from *Perceval* and the poems of Chrétien de Troyes are carved on ivory caskets;[5] and scenes from the *Chatelaine de Vergi* appear alike on such caskets[6] and on the frescoes of the Palazzo Davanzati at Florence.[7] Guy of Warwick was the hero of an Anglo-Norman *roman d'aventure*,[8] and is represented slaying the dragon, with the legend

Gy de Warwyc ad a noun
Ke ci occis le dragoun

on the print of a mazer of Edward II's time at Harbledown Hospital, Kent.[9] Philippe le Bon in 1420 had tapestries with the stories of Percival, Garin le Lorrain, and Regnaut de Montaubon;[10] and Francesco Pesellino painted a chest with the story of patient Griselda.[11]

Classical romances, too, provided subjects for many such paintings.

La caumbre est painte tut entur;
Vénus la dieuesse d'amur
Fu très bien mis en la peinture,
Les traiz mustrez è la nature,
Cument hum deit amur tenir,
E léalment et bien servir,
Le livre Ovide u il enseigne
Coment cascuns s'amour tesmegne.[12]

[1] Cf. the fable *Aristote* by Henri d'Andely.   [2] One in the British Museum has the same subject.
[3] Doüet d'Arcq, *Comptes de l'argenterie du roi*, p. 312.
[4] Moranvillé, *op. cit.*, 276, 453, 494. Charles V had tapestries with the stories of the Holy Grail and of Ivinail and the Queen of Ireland. Michel, *Histoire de l'Art*, iii. 348.
[5] e.g. S. de Ricci, *Exposition d'Objets d'art à l'ancien hotel de Sagan*, mai–juin, 1913, no. xliv.
[6] Two in the Pierpont Morgan collection; others in the British Museum; Louvre; Imperial Museum, Vienna; and Museo Archeologico, Milan.
[7] These are based on an Italian version of the poem, and were painted by a pupil of Orcagna about 1395.
[8] *Early English Text Society*, Extra Series, xxv. 110.
[9] W. St. John Hope, 'On the English medieval drinking vessels called mazers', in *Archaeologia*, l, 1887, p. 139.
[10] Laborde, *Les Ducs de Bourgogne*, ii. 267.
[11] Schubring, *Cassoni, Truhen und Truhenbilder der Italienischen Frührenaissance*, Leipzig, 1915, figs. 268–9.
[12] Marie de France, *Lai de Gugemer*.

189. Animal grotesques from the Gorleston Psalter. *c.* 1305

190. Casket with grotesque medallions. French, *c.* 1340

191. Grotesque panels from the Portail des Libraires, Cathedral of Rouen, *c.* 1290

192. Linen coverlet, quilted with the story of Tristan. Italian, *c.* 1400

193. Ivory mirror case, carved with the Siege of the Castle of Love. French, *c.* 1360

The story of Helen according to the *Roman de Troie* of Benôit de Sainte More is represented on the mosaic pavement of Pesaro,[1] and the great washing basin of the monks of Saint Denis was carved in the time of Philip Augustus with figures of Paris and Helen, Venus, Pan and Jupiter.[2] A thirteenth century bronze bowl is engraved with scenes of the youth of Achilles.[3] When in *Galeran* Madame Gente leavesa piece of embroidery with the baby she abandons, in the hope of future identification, it is embroidered with scenes from the story of Flore and Blanche-flore, and with the rape of Helen, as well as with the traditional subjects of the twelve months and the four elements. The scene of Alexander's flight from the *Roman d'Alexandre* appears on misericords at Lincoln, Chester, Gloucester, Beverley St. Mary, Wells (fig. 186) and Darlington; while the *Lai d'Aristote* is illustrated at St. Pierre, Caen, the Cathedral of Lyons, the Portail de la Calende at Rouen, Verteuil, and many other·places in France; on Lausanne Cathedral; and on misericords at Exeter and Chichester in England. Innumerable ivories of about 1400 exist with the stories of Paris,[4] Jason, Pyramus and Thisbe, and the rest.[5]

The influence of literary *courtoisie* not only brought in countless scenes of love and chivalry—knights being armed by their ladies, receiving the crown of victory at their hands, knights beseiging a castle of love (fig. 193),[6] and so on, that are half *genre* scenes and half illustrations of romance—but even led to the pic-torial illustration of poetical metaphors. The aumonière of Thibaut de Champagne, now in the Treasury of Troyes Cathedral, is embroidered with Love, figured in angelic guise, looking at a sleeping girl; and with two ladies working with a saw upon a heart set upon an altar. Again in 1338 the Comte d'Eu was given two jerkins embroidered with ships bearing ladies fishing for hearts.[7] The influence of Romantic literature, too, created a hierarchy of unhappy lovers. In his *Temple of Glas* Lydgate records such a one:[8]

> I sauʒe depeynt opon euere wal,
> From est to west, ful many a faire Image
> Of sondri louers, lich as þei were of age
> I-sette in ordre, aftir þei were trwe,
> Wiþ lifli colours wondir fressh of hwe.
> And, as me þouʒt, I sauʒ somme sit & stonde,
> And some kneling wiþ billis in hir honde,
> And some with compleint woful & pitous . . .

---

[1] Mâle, 'L'Art du Moyen Age et les Pèlerinages', *Revue de Paris*, Sept.–Oct. 1919, v. 717.

[2] L. Palustre, *Renaissance en France*, ii. 25.   [3] Molinier, *Orfèvrerie religieuse et civile*, 173.

[4] Henry VIII had a golden cup with the Judgement of Paris, that was probably of fifteenth-century date. Palgrave, *Kalendars and Inventories*, ii. 276.

[5] Examples are in Victoria and Albert Museum. A fine late fifteenth-century Flemish tapestry of the Siege of Troy is in the Cathedral of Zamora.

[6] The Assault of the Castle of Love, included in the marginal decorations of the Peterborough Psalter, is found on many ivories, on the tapestries of the wife of Philippe le Hardi; and on a goblet of the Duke of Anjou's (Koechlin, *op. cit.* i. 403).

[7] Enlart, *Manuel d'Archéologie française*, iii. 420.   [8] l. 44; E.E.T.S., ed. Schick, p. 2.

Dido, Medea, Penelope, Alcestis, Griselda, Yseult, Thisbe, Phyllis, Helen, Polyxena, Philomela, and the rest. Literature, indeed, created as many hierarchies as the church. The inventory of 1379–80 of the plate of Louis d'Anjou describes two 'thiphenies' or large flat plates adorned with heroes of antiquity and of chivalry, arranged in a parallel that recalls the parallel between the prophets and apostles in Christian iconography.[1] Another hierarchy of valour was established early in the fourteenth century by Jacques de Longuyon's *Les Vœux du Paon*, with the nine worthies: three pagans, Hector, Caesar, and Alexander; three Jews, Joshua, David, and Judas Maccabaeus; and three Christians, Arthur, Charlemagne, and Godfrey of Bouillon.[2] Deschamps soon followed suit with the nine *Preuses*.[3] The nine worthies appear on the wall of the fourteenth century Hansa Saal at Cologne, and sets of both the Preux and the Preuses were among the tapestries of Philippe le Hardi in 1394,[4] and of Philippe le Bon in 1430.[5] Nor were these the only hierarchies; Louis d'Anjou had a flask with enamels of Paris, Hercules, Ulysses, Troilus, Hector, and Achilles, balanced by others of the Patience, Force, Justice, Temperance, Truth, and Wisdom that they were held to typify,[6] and the Duke of Burgundy in 1454–5 bought a hanging embroidered with 'trois sages, trois puissans et trois fors, chascun nommé par son nom.'[7] The capitals of the Loggia of the Ducal Palace at Venice[8] have the seven lawgivers, Solomon, Aristotle, Solon, Isidore, Numa, Moses, and Trajan;[9] and the twelve Paladins were represented on a set of tapestries belonging to Philippe le Bon in 1420.[10]

Nor were ancient heroes alone represented. It was enough for a man to have had his exploits commemorated in another literary *genre* than pure history for him to appear in other forms of art. A Close Roll of the thirty-fourth year of the reign of Henry III orders the Master of the Knights Templars in England, 'that

[1] The first was adorned with Hercules, Jason, Antenor, Troilus, Diomedes, Agamemnon, Patroclus, Telamon, Menelaus, Penthesilea, Ulysses, Hector, Achilles, Paris, Aeneas, and Priam; while the second bore the figures of Charlemagne, Renaud, Huon de Bordeaux, Geffroi, Roland, Astolf, Gualthier, Phebus, Gawain, Galéas, Lancelot, Tristan, Palamedes, Arthur, Percival, and Oliver. Further, the first had in the centre a scene with Priam, Hector, Andromache, and Polyxena, and the second a panel with a combat, 'comment Hercules ocist Antheo aus bras.' Moranvillé, *op. cit.*, p. 482. The 'thiphenies' were destined for use in the sacrament, and bore the inscriptions 'Verbum caro factum est et habitavit in nobis et vidimus gloriam' and 'Ejus gloriam quasi unigeniti a patre plenum gracie et veritatis. Amen.'

[2] These are to be found, with variations, on the façade of the Certosa of Pavia, and on the façade of Montacute.

[3] A late fifteenth-century inventory in the Milan archives records tapestries with scenes from Christine de Pisan's *Cité des dames*. E. Müntz, 'La tapisserie à l'epoque de Louis XII', in *Les Lettres et les Arts*, 1886, p. 213.

[4] Pinchart, *Histoire de la tapisserie dans les Flandres*, p. 13; Dehaisnes, *Art dans la Flandre*, p. 347.

[5] Laborde, *Les Ducs de Bourgogne*, ii. 267. A Paris tapestry of about 1390 of King Arthur from a set of the neuf Preuses is in the Clarence H. Mackay Collection. H. Goebel, *Wandteppiche. II Teil. Die Romanischen Länder*, Band 2, fig. 14, and a fifteenth-century tapestry of Penthesilea from a set of Preuses still survives at Angers.

[6] Moranvillé, *op. cit.*, p. lxix.   [7] Laborde, *Les Ducs de Bourgogne*, i, p. 440.

[8] Built between 1340–1404.

[9] They have also the seven virtues and the seven deadly sins, the seven wise men, the liberal arts, and the months.   [10] Laborde, *Les Ducs de Bourgogne*, ii. 267.

194. Ivory mirror case carved with man and woman playing
chess. French, *c.* 1320

195. Back of carved ivory casket, with scenes from *La Charette* by Chrestien de Troyes. On the
lid is the Siege of the Castle of Love, on the sides scenes from the Lai d'Aristote. French, *c.* 1400

196. Chest carved with scenes of the Battle of Courtrai. Flemish, c. 1420

he cause to be delivered to Henry of the Wardrobe, bearer of these presents, in aid of the Queen, a certain great book, which is in his house in London, written in the French language, in which are contained the gests of the King of Antioch and other matters.'[1] It was doubtless from the paintings of this book that the Antioch Chambers at Clarendon and in the Tower were painted. At the same time, perhaps from the Romance on the theme, Richard fighting with Saladin was painted on the walls of the Château de Pernes, Vaucluse,[2] and on Chertsey tiles. Joinville seems to have planned a whole scheme of decoration to illustrate his *Credo*, with some scenes of his own adventures, perhaps destined for the chapel he founded in the Maison Dieu of Joinville.[3] Guiart's rhyming Chronicle, *Branches des Royaux Lignages*, celebrated the battle of Courtrai, fought in 1302, that is carved on an early fourteenth-century Flemish chest now at New College, Oxford (fig. 196).[4] The *Geste de Liége* was followed by tapestries of the battles of Liége and Roosebek, such as Philippe le Bon owned in 1420.[5] The final triumph of the French in the Hundred Years War made Bertrand du Guesclin a national hero: Cuvelier celebrated him in a long poem; Louis d'Orléans set him beside the nine worthies in the great hall of Coucy[6] and Charles VI on a golden drageoir.[7] Jean de Berry had two silver basins, enamelled one with Hector of Troy and the other with Bertrand du Guesclin,[8] and Philippe le Bon had tapestries of his exploits.[9] Joan of Arc's exploits were celebrated in the *Mystere du siége d'Orléans*, and a hundred years later Florimond Robertet had a tapestry with 'les haults fais d'armes de la Pucelle d'Orléans'.[10] Moderns made their way even into the hierarchy of learning; Francis Bacon brought the Seven Arts up to date on the walls of his summerhouse at Old Gorhambury, setting Lilly between Donatus and Priscian for Grammar, Budé and Stifel with Pythagoras for Arithmetic, Rodolph and Seton with Aristotle for Logic, and Copernicus among the astronomers.[11]

3

After about 1375, the chief inspiration of tapestry design was literary;[12] the fourteenth-century style of illumination was perfectly fitted for reproduction in

[1] Walpole, *Anecdotes of Painting*, ed. Dallaway, i. 19.

[2] Michel, *Histoire de l'Art*, ii. 405. The 'Pas Saladin' was represented on the plate of Louis d'Anjou (Moranvillé, p. lxx) and on a seal of Charles V (Labarte, p. 88).

[3] H. F. Delaborde and P. Lauer, 'Un projet de décoration murale inspiré du Credo de Joinville', *Mon. Piot* xvi, 1909, p. 61.

[4] J. M. Richard, *Mahaut Comtesse d'Artois*, p. 356. In 1320 Pierre de Bruxelles painted the gallery at Conflans with the story of Robert d'Artois and the Sicilian Expedition.

[5] See Laborde, *Les Ducs de Bourgogne*, i. 5.

[6] Antoine Astesan, 1451, in Leroux de Lincy and Tisserand, *Paris et ses historiens*, p. 558.

[7] Laborde, *Glossaire des Émaux*, ii. 256.

[8] Guiffrey, *Les Inventaires du Duc de Berry*, i. 186.

[9] Laborde, *Les Ducs de Bourgogne*, ii. 267. Other tapestries of the same subject were woven by Pierre Baumetz and Nicolas Bataille. Michel, *Histoire de l'Art*, iii. 349.

[10] *Mémoires de la Société des Antiquaires de France*, 3rd series, x, 1868, pp. 38 and 39.

[11] Nichols, *Progresses of Elizabeth*, ii. 59.

[12] See Hagen, *Ueber die Gemälde in den Sammlungen der altdeutschen lyrischen Dichter*; von Schlosser, 'Ein

tapestry,[1] and it was almost enough for a story, whether fact or fiction, to be recorded in an illuminated manuscript for it to pass into the repertory of the tapestry weavers. Between 1375[2] and 1380 Jean de Bruges painted the miniatures of an illuminated manuscript of the Apocalypse for Charles V.[3] Louis I d'Anjou, his brother, borrowed the manuscript as a pattern for tapestry; Hennequin de Bruges, the King's painter, drew cartoons from the miniatures with some slight modifications, and Nicolas Bataille then wove them from the cartoons.[4]

The saints took on new interest in the age that produced the Golden Legend, when every individual and every corporation had its patron saint. Their statues were set to guard the gates and towers of the city and the houses and barns of its inhabitants,[5] and their legends were illustrated in both ecclesiastical and secular decoration. York Minster possesses a fine medieval chest carved with scenes from the life of St. George, while Queen Jeanne d'Évreux in 1372 owned a silver cup enamelled with the history of St. Louis,[6] and the gold cup made for the Duc de Berry about 1380, now one of the treasures of the British Museum, is enamelled with scenes of the life and miracles of St. Agnes (fig. 197).

At the same time didactic and moralizing literature of every kind assumed a new importance.[7] The *Dit des trois morts et des trois vifs* had been four times written in the thirteenth century. It was illustrated with miniatures as early as 1285,[8] and at a later date often served as a subject for wall paintings in church[9] and cemetery,[10] alike in France and England.[11] The *danse macabre*, that in a literary form was even

veronesiches Bilderbuch und die höfische Kunst des XIV Jahrhunderts', in *Jahrbuch der Kunsthistorische Sammlungen des A. H. Kaiserhauses*, 1895, pp. 166–76, 215 et seq; E. Molinier, in *Welt Post*, 1st April 1897, and in 'Tapisseries Allégoriques inédites ou peu connues' in *Mon. Piot*. ix, 1902, p. 95 et seq.

[1] e.g. the Bodleian MS. of the Alexander Romances, 1344, MS. Bodl. 264.

[2] When an illuminated manuscript did not exist a working substitute was made. In 1425 it was decided to make a set of tapestry of the story of its patron Saint for the Church of the Madeleine at Troyes. Brother Didier, a monk, read and wrote out the story, Jacquet the painter made a little sketch on paper, Poinsète the dressmaker and her apprentice sewed together large sheets on which Jacquet and Simon the illuminator painted the design from which the tapestry weavers worked.

[3] Now Cambrai MS. 422.   [4] The tapestries are now in the Musée de l'Evêché at Angers.

[5] See Mâle, *L'Art religieux en France*, ii. 158. Michael, Peter, Christopher, Sebastian, Barbara, Margaret, and Nicholas appear on the walls of Amiens; Peter, Anne, and Susanna at Chantelle; the Virgin, St. Geneviève, St. Christopher, and St. James on a house at Luynes; and the symbols of the Evangelists on the great barn at Glastonbury.

[6] Leber, *Collection des meilleures dissertations*, Paris, 1838, xix. 134.

[7] See Mâle, *op. cit.*, p. 316 et seq.

[8] For Marie de Brabant, second wife of Philippe le Hardi, H. Martin, *La miniature française*, p. 17. An instance of such miniatures being used to illustrate another devotional work is afforded by the Psalter of Robert de Lyle, c. 1320. B. M. Arundel MS. 83.

[9] e.g. in the churches of Ennezat, Puy de Dôme, Servigny, Meurthe et Moselle. For other instances see Mâle, *op. cit.*, p. 375.

[10] In 1408 Jean de Berry set up 'ymaiges des trois vifs et des trois morts' over the portal of the Cemetery of the Innocents in Paris.

[11] At Charlwood, Surrey; St. Martin's, Battle; and at Ditchingham and elsewhere in Norfolk. See W. F. Storck, 'Aspects of Death in English Art and Poetry', *Burlington Magazine*, Aug.-Sept. 1912, xxi. 249, 314. Before the end of the thirteenth century Amadeus V of Savoy bought in London two panels painted with the subject. Tristram and Borenius, *English Mediaeval Painting*, p. 37.

197. The Royal Gold Cup, enamelled with scenes of the life and miracles of St. Agnes. Made for the Duc de Berry, probably in Paris, c. 1380

198. Detail of the tomb of the Cardinal d'Amboise, 1520–5, Cathedral of Rouen

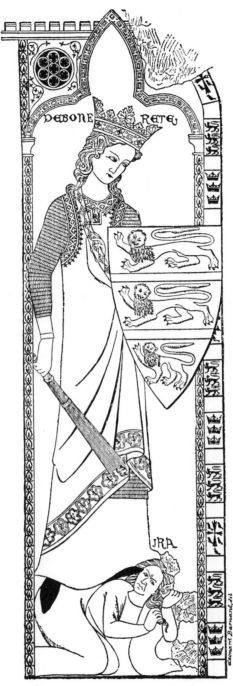

FIG. 199. Drawing from a painting by Stothard of the figure of Gentleness subduing Anger, formerly decorating the Painted Chamber in the Palace of Westminster. Painted in 1262, now destroyed

earlier in origin,[1] was made yet more horrible in imagery. The idea of Death was for a time omnipresent and unforgettable; René of Anjou, planning his tomb while he yet lived, set in a niche above it a figure of King Death enthroned.[2]

Such subjects were naturally better suited to church and cloister than to the home: a wall painting of the Danse Macabre may still be seen at La Chaise Dieu, while bas-reliefs of the subject appear on three galleries of the Aître Saint Maclou at Rouen;[3] but even on the chimney-piece of a house near Yvetot appears the legend 'Pensez à la mort. Mourir convient. Peu en souvient. Souvent avient. 1503.'[4] Didactic literature of a milder kind was more commonly reflected in secular decoration. In the fourteenth century Guillaume de Deguilleville's pious and allegorical romance of the *Pèlerinage de la vie humaine* had many readers, and the subject appears among the tapestries of the Duc de Berry in 1416.[5] In 1441 the Duke of Burgundy sent the Pope a tapestry 'de trois histoires morales du Pape, de l'Empereur, et de la noblesse'.[6] In several churches of Anjou[7] a procession of all sorts and conditions of men—the leper, the sick man, the prisoner, the pilgrim, the labourer, the mendicant, the widow, the orphan, and the 'mau maryé'—were painted helping to bear the Cross of Our Lord, according to a poem written by René of Anjou. In England the popularity of Langland's *Piers Plowman* was reflected all over England[8] in wall paintings of Christ surrounded by tools, as a symbol of the Labourer's Passion.

More fantastical literary subjects equally played a part in decoration; the 1386 inventory of the Duke of Burgundy includes a set of tapestries with 'l'istoire d'un roy qui s'en ala chacier et perdi en un bois ses gens et ses chevaux et y trouva une

---

[1] See C.V. Langlois, *Essai sur les danses des Morts*.

[2] See Bodley MS. 18346, Gaignières, p. 6.

[3] 1526–33. Palustre, *Renaissance en France*, ii. 196.

[4] Mâle, *L'Art religieux en France*, ii. 375. With the institution of the *Vigiles des Morts* funereal emblems become increasingly common. The Hours of Galeotto Pico della Mirandola (in the collection of Mr. Dyson Perrins) have the office of the dead bordered with bones, skulls, worms, and every charnel-house horror. *Memento mori* devices were in common decorative use in the sixteenth century. Brantôme speaks of the 'belles et honnestes dames' who lost their lovers in the wars, and wore, to show their 'regrets et lamentations', jewels in the shape of death's heads and other trophies of death. At Chenonceaux are the remains of panelling painted for the newly-widowed Louise de Lorraine, all in white on a black ground, with reversed and empty quivers, dropping tears, and mourning feathers entangled in crowns of thorns. It is refreshing to find in the Musée St. Jean at Angers a sixteenth-century chest carved with 'La Revanche de la danse macabre', with all its characters shooting at Death.

[5] Giovanni Bellini's allegorical picture in the Uffizi is based on this poem. Ludwig, *Jahrbuch der Kön. preuss. Kunsts.*, 1902, xxiii. 163, and R. E. Fry, *Giovanni Bellini*, p. 39.

[6] Guiffrey, *Histoire de la Tapisserie*, p. 71.

[7] At Montrion, Saint Aubin des Ponts de Cé, and Le Lion d'Angers. A linen hanging similarly painted was in the Castle of Angers, and may have been made for René himself. See C. Urseau, *La peinture décorative en Anjou*, Angers, 1920, p. 14. At Chauvigny, Vienne, the characters represented are Popes, Cardinals, Bishops, Franciscan and Dominican monks, and laymen. The painting is dated 1450.

[8] e.g. at Ampney St. Mary, Glos. See E. W. Tristram, 'Piers Plowman in English Wall Painting', in *Burlington Magazine*, xxxi, Oct. 1917, p. 135. The corresponding movement in France had less influence on decoration, though there is in the Musée de Dijon a fifteenth-century tile, with the labourer coming back from work, bearing a heavy hod, with the legend 'grant poine'.

200. Velvet panel, with appliqué work and embroidery. English, *c.* 1570. The Duke of Devonshire

201. The Studley Royal Bowl. English, *c.* 1385

marveilleuse aventure de fées qui le jugerent devenir cerf'.[1] It was, however, the allegories and personifications of the Middle Ages which had the strongest influence upon the decorative arts. Henry III had the chimney-hood of the Queen's Chamber at Westminster adorned with a figure of Winter 'which as well by its sad countenance as by other miserable distortions of the body may be deservedly likened to winter itself.'[2] The representations of the Virtues and Vices, that appear as personifications in thirteenth-century literature,[3] soon figured in decoration[4] in a form influenced by the usages of chivalry. On the great portal of Amiens, about 1225, the Christian Virtues appear as seated maidens each bearing a shield with her proper emblem, while at Chartres the Public Virtues—Libertas, Honor, Velocitas, Fortitudo, Concordia, Amicitia, Maiestas, Sanitas, and Securitas—are figured as women bearing shields. Soon after 1262 the Painted Chamber at Westminster was adorned with figures of Debonereté, bearing on a shield gules two bars and three lioncels or, overcoming Anger (fig. 199), and Largesse, bearing the King's shield, overcoming Avarice.[5] Louis d'Anjou had two silver-gilt jugs, the first enamelled with a medallion of *Liberalitas* distributing alms, surrounded by figures of the seven deadly sins and Vainglory, with a plate enamelled with *Theologia*, 'une dame ancienne séant en un grant chaiere', with figures of the seven Christian virtues and an eighth not named; the second with Fortune and her wheel, surrounded by eight more virtues and vices, with *Philosophia* on the plate surrounded by the seven Liberal Arts.[6]

Romance, too, had its personifications. The 'Dieu d'Amour' who in the twelfth century appears in *Le Fabel dou Dieu d'Amours*, in the thirteenth century in the *Roman de la Rose*, and in the fourteenth in the *Dit du Vergier* of Guillaume de Machaut and in the poems of Christine de Pisan, appeared first in the illuminations[7] and thence was transferred to the design of mirror cases and to

[1] Dehaisnes, *Histoire de l'Art dans la Flandre*, p. 346.

[2] H. Avray Tipping, *English Homes*, i, p. xxvi.

[3] Personifications of the Virtues and Vices (a type ultimately derived from Prudentius) appear in the thirteenth-century vernacular *Miserere* of the Recluse of Molliens, the *Besant* of Guillaume le Clerc, and in the *Songe d'Enfer* and *Voie de Paradis* of Raoul de Houdan. Jean de Meung brings in Reason and Nature and many of the abstractions of the schoolmen, and even the *Roman de Renart* has personifications of the vices.

[4] They are found in the twelfth century, for instance on a capital of Notre Dame du Port, Clermont Ferrand, and on the portal of Aulnay.

[5] Stothard's drawings of these are in the Library of the Society of Antiquaries. Other copies by Edward Crocker are in the University Galleries at Oxford. See W. R. Lethaby, 'The Painted Chamber', in *Burlington Magazine*, July 1905, vii. 257. On the early thirteenth-century font at Stanton Fitzwarren each Virtue appears in knightly guise, Largitas, Pietas, Misericordia, Modestia, Patientia, and Pudicitia armed with sword and shield, Humilitas with club and shield, and Temperantia with lance and banner, all overcoming their opposing vice. A combat of Virtues and Vices appears on an early fifteenth-century South German Tapestry in Regensburg Cathedral; and on a late fifteenth-century Flemish tapestry in the Cathedral of Burgos. A fifteenth-century painting in the Chapel of Kermaria, Côtes du Nord, shows the maiden Diligence, bearing a shield with the device of the swallow, pricking on the Ass of Laziness.

[6] Moranvillé, *op. cit.*, p. 450.

[7] e.g. the Roman de la Poire, B. N. fr. 2186, fol. 15, end of thirteenth century; Clé d'amours, B. N. nouv. acq. fr. 4531, fol. 63v, early fourteenth century; see R. Koechlin, *Les Ivoires Gothiques français*, i. 400.

tapestries.[1]   All the personifications of Love and its qualities had their decorative value:

> Plesaunce and hope, desyr, fool-hardinesse,
> Beautee and youthe, bauderie, richesse,
> Charmes and force, lesinges, flaterye,
> Dispense, busynesse and Jelousye,
> That wered of yelwe goldes a gerland,
> And had a cokkow sitting on hir hand,
> Festes, instruments, caroles, daunces,
> Lust and array, and all the circumstaunces
> Of love, whiche that I rekne and rekne shal,
> By ordre were peynted on the wal.[2]

The Fountain of Youth, that figures in the *Fabel dou Dieu d'Amours* and in *Huon de Bordeaux*, is found on ivory mirror cases, on a tapestry belonging to the Duke of Orleans in 1393[3] and on the frescoes of the Castle of Manta;[4] Louis d'Anjou had both a *nef* and a table fountain of silver gilt enamelled, each representing the fountain of Youth with men and women approaching it 'dont les uns sont portez en brouetes, les autres en litieres et sur mules, et aucuns vont à potences'. The fountain itself was guarded by two gates, each with a warder armed with mace and sword; and in the fountain were men and women bathing, and others dressing and undressing on its rim.[5]

The inventory of Charles V has tapestries with the story 'de Plaisance et de Leesse et de Oiseuse qui les introduit', and the 1388 inventory of Philippe le Hardi includes a tapestry with all the personifications of the *Roman de la Rose*. In 1420 Philippe le Bon had tapestries with the Church Militant and Youth[6] and 'une chambre vermeille ... ouvrée d'aournemens de Dames faisans personnages d'Onneur, de Noblesse, Largesse, Simplesse et autres', and tapestries 'du Corps et de l'Ame[7] et de l'arbre des vices et des vertus'.[8] The 1527 inventory of the goods of Thomas Cromwell includes 'a border of arras work with a picture of Occupation and Idleness'.[9] Such personifications were perpetuated by the 'imagini' of the engravers of the Renaissance.[10] Virtues were sculptured round many Italian tombs, as for

---

. [1] Such tapestries are recorded in the inventories of Charles V, and of the Dukes of Berry and Anjou; Koechlin, *loc. cit.* A fresco of the subject, dating from end of the fourteenth century, still exists in the castle of Avio. It shows Love, with eagle's wings and claws, mounted on a white horse, drawing his bow. He has just failed to transfix a lady with his arrow, but has pierced a youth through the heart. See A. Morassi, 'Una Camera d'Amore nel Castello di Avio', in *Festschrift für Julius Schlosser*, Vienna, 1927, p. 99.

[2] Chaucer, *Knight's Tale*, i. 1925.　　　[3] Guiffrey, *Histoire de la Tapisserie en France*, p. 18.
[4] See p. 149.　　　[5] Moranvillé, pp. 227 and 251.
[6] Laborde, *Les Ducs de Bourgogne*, ii. 267.

[7] *La Desputaison du Corps et de l'âme* was several times treated by French poets of the fourteenth and fifteenth centuries. See Petit de Julleville, *Littérature française*, ii. 209.

[8] The most splendid sixteenth-century Brussels tapestries of the Virtues and the Vices are in the Royal Collection at Madrid. See Mâle, *L'art religieux de la fin du Moyen Âge en France*, p. 307.

[9] Brewer, *Letters and Papers of Henry VIII*, iv, pt. 2, p. 1454.

[10] Others are to be found among Jost Amman's engravings in the *Perspectiva corporum regulorum* of Wenzel Jamnitzer, published at Nuremberg in 1568.

instance that at San Miniato of the Cardinal of Portugal who died in 1462; and such personifications as Glory crowning Merit, Time and History, Moderation, Industry, Vigilance, Abundance, Sweetness, Fidelity, Simplicity, and Fortune were represented in the frescoes of Veronese in the third quarter of the century. Personifications of the Virtues, stereotyped by the Italian engravers, appeared through their influence on the Choir Stalls of Gaillon and on the tomb of the Cardinal d'Amboise at Rouen (fig. 198) early in the sixteenth century. Many French and Netherlandish engravers—notably Etienne de Laune—provided further series of models of virtues, vices, arts, sciences and the rest for craftsmen in the various arts.[1] A sixteenth-century Brussels tapestry of Lot leaving the doomed city[2] has a border of such medallions, with figures labelled as *Discretio, Habondantia, Pax, Contentio, Invocatio, Requies, Divitiae, Separatio,* and *Concorde*: another of Abraham buying a sepulchre for Sarah[3] has similar medallions of *Iudicio, Immortalitas, Gloria, Spes, Querimonia, Atropos, Tempus, Senecta* and *Resurrectio*.[4]

Sometimes the personification was combined with its type or antitype; some embroidered hangings at Hardwick, dating from the end of the sixteenth century, show Faith with Mahomet, and Temperance with Sardanapalus, while a third (now lost) had Hope with Judas.[5] Another set at Hardwick combined in five panels Zenobia, Magnanimitas and Prudentia; Artemisia, Constantia and Pietas; Penelope, Prudentia and Sapientia; Cleopatra, Fortitudo and Justitia; and Lucretia, Castitas and Liberalitas.[6] As the century progressed such figures were used in more ambitious architectural schemes. On the balustrade of the Bailliage d'Aire, dated 1595, are large bas-reliefs of the four elements and the seven virtues. In 1609 Jacob Brunel decorated the Galerie des Antiques of the

[1] Cesare Ripa's *Iconologia* of 1593 is a good example, with figures of virtues, vices, arts, sciences, and the provinces and rivers of Italy, arranged alphabetically; and similar subjects, with nymphs, muses, seasons, months, Eternity, Hope, Victory, Piety and so on, appear in Pecham's *Graphice* of 1612. An account of Ripa's influence on the arts will be found in E. Mâle, 'La Clef des Allégories peintes et Sculptées au XVIIe et au XVIIIe siècle', in *Revue des Deux Mondes*, 1st and 15th May, 1927, pp. 106 and 375. Another type of such engravings was devoted to animals: e.g. the *Neu Thierbuechlein* of Martin Pleginck, 1594; the *Volatilium varii generis effigies* of C. Allard, Amsterdam, 1594, and the *Animalium quadrupedum variorum typi varii* of Isaac Brunn, 1621. Animals of this type are represented on the Oxburgh embroideries and on the ceiling of 1620 at Earlshall, Fife, which has medallions of the 'Nylghau', horse, cow, dromedary, wolf, &c. See *R.I.B.A. Journal*, 3rd series, iv, 1897, p. 271.

[2] Lent by the Austrian Government from the Kunsthistorisches Museum of Vienna to the Exhibition of Flemish and Belgian Art at Burlington House, 1927, No. 289.

[3] Woven in Brussels before 1548, lent by the First Commissioner of H.M. Office of Works to the Victoria and Albert Museum.

[4] Medallions of the Senses adorn a fine Barcheston tapestry table-cover, belonging to Mr. Leslie Urquhart. Grisaille paintings of the planets of about 1560, from a house at Stodmarsh, Kent, show how useful the imagini were to unskilled country workmen. They are now in the V. and A. M.: W. 28, 1913.

[5] The scheme is Italian in origin: Justice treading on Nero, Force on Holophernes, Temperance on Epicurus, Prudence on Sardanapalus, Charity on Herod, Hope on Judas, and Faith on Arius appear in two fourteenth-century Italian manuscripts studied by Dr. J. von Schlosser in *Jahrbuch der Kunsthistorischen Sammlungen des allerhöchsten Kaiserhauses*, 1896, p. 13 et seqq. See also Mâle, *L'art religieux de la fin du Moyen Âge en France*, p. 361.

[6] M. Jourdain, *English Secular Embroidery*, p. 49.

Louvre[1] with figures of the Four seasons, the four winds, the four elements, and the signs of the Zodiac—all medieval types redressed and perpetuated by the engravers, which academic France was a little later to admit into the decoration of Versailles.[2]

4

The Renaissance, too, brought its own literature into decoration; and the invention of engraved illustrations intensified its influence.

The first book to be so illustrated was the *Hypnerotomachia Poliphili* of Francesco Colonna, first issued in 1467, and republished by Aldus Manutius in 1499. These illustrations and those of the 1497 edition of Ovid's *Metamorphoses* inspired the design of a famous faience service of seventeen pieces ascribed to Nicolò da Urbino and painted about 1515.[3] Outside Italy artists in the Renaissance style were rare and its general principles little known, and such engravings therefore acquired a new value and importance. French design between 1520 and 1530 owes a good deal to the *Hypnerotomachia*. Panels with scenes copied or adapted from its engraved illustrations adorn a small staircase at Villers Cotterets[4] and the Hôtel d'Écoville at Caen.[5] Some of the culs-de-lampe of the printer's decoration of the *Hypnerotomachia* recall such medallions of classical heads as those used by Mantegra in the *Camera degli Sposi* in the castle of Mantua, by Antonio Filarete on the windows of the hospital at Milan, and by Caradosso at San Satiro, and they certainly helped to introduce such heads into French decoration. Another book similarly decorated is the illustrated edition of Petrarch's *Trionfi* published at Venice in 1500, 1523, and 1545; a set of heads on the 'Maison des Gendarmes' at Caen[6] shows by their inscriptions that they were drawn from this source.[7] Similar heads were drawn from the illustrations to Boccaccio's *De casibus virorum illustrium* and *De claris mulieribus*;[8] and the decorative tradition thus established was carried on by such books as Jacobus Philippus Bergomensis's *De plurimis selectisque*

---

[1] M. Vachon, *Le Louvre et les Tuileries*, p. 95. How late such types were perpetuated is shown by the figures of the Arts, Senses, Continents, Monarchies, and Virtues included in the 1765 price list of the Meissen China Factory; Hannover, *Pottery and Porcelain*, ed. Rackham III, p. 94.

[2] See vol. II, p. 44.

[3] Sixteen pieces are in the Museo Correr, Venice, and one in the Ashmolean Museum, Oxford.

[4] Palustre, *La Renaissance en France*, i. 132. For other instances of reliefs, &c., taken from its engravings see P. Marcel, *Un Vulgarisateur, Jean Martin*, p. 89.

[5] As late as the middle of the seventeenth century Le Sueur painted eight decorative pictures with subjects drawn from the *Hypnerotomachia*. Michel, *Histoire de l'Art*, vi. 229.

[6] *c.* 1520–30; Palustre, *op. cit.*, ii. 225.

[7] They are inscribed: *Amor vincit Mundum ; Pudicitia vincit Amorem ; Mors vincit Pudicitiam ; Fama vincit Mortem*. There must once have been two more with the inscriptions, *Tempus vincit Famam*, and *Eternitas* (or *Divinitas*) *omnia vincit*.

[8] Cf. the series of late fifteenth-century profile portraits of 'clare donne' by Bartolomeo degli Erri from a house in Modena, now in the Civic Museum. Venturi, *Storia dell' arte italiana*, vii, pt. 3, p. 1052.

202. Verdure tapestry with angels bearing the instruments of the Passion. Woven for the widow of Pierre de Rohan, c. 1515, in the valley of the Loire

203. Panel of allegorical tapestry. French, _c._ 1520

mulieribus of 1496, the *Illustrium imagines* published by Jacob Mazocchi and the pattern books published by Enea Vico [1] in 1517 and by Lucas van Leyden in 1527.

Petrarch's *Trionfi* had, however, a more important influence on decoration than that of helping to introduce head-medallions abroad.[2] As early as 1449 a Florentine *cassone* was painted with the Triumph of Fame,[3] and a little later the other Petrarchan Triumphs of Love, Chastity, and Death also appeared.[4] Thence they made their way into other decorative arts; the Cathedral of Graz possesses a fine Italian ivory casket with Petrarchan triumphs of Mantegna's type.[5] In Italy itself fresh subjects soon drove the *Trionfi* out,[6] but outside Italy they had a longer reign. The Hôtel de Bourgtheroulde at Rouen has panels taken from the illustrated edition of the *Triumphs*, published at Venice in 1545.[7] The tapestry weavers of Tours and Brussels wove splendid hangings of the Petrarchan Triumphs; a fine set is in the Imperial Collection at Vienna, and another, bought by Wolsey from Lord Durham's executors in 1523,[8] still hangs in his Guard-Chamber at Hampton Court. Fame triumphs over Death; bearing a many-mouthed trumpet and escorted by Virgil, Cicero, Homer, Aristotle, Alexander, Plato, and Charlemagne, she rides in her car over the bodies of the Three Fates.[9] The Petrarchan type of triumph was applied to other themes: Holbein painted a 'Triumph of Riches' and a 'Triumph of Poverty'[10] in tempera for the merchants of the Steelyard of London;[11] and about 1560 Delaune designed a dish with the Triumph of Spring, which Pierre Cortoys enamelled at Limoges.[12]

In Italy itself interest was soon centred not in Petrarch but in the writers of

[1] The *Primorum XII Caesarum verissimae effigies ; Ex libris XXIII commentariorum in vetera imperatorum Romanorum numismata ;* and *Omnium Caesarum verissimae imagines ex antiquis numismatis desumptae,* 1553. An early imitation outside Italy was A. Gessner's *Imperatorum Romanorum omnium orientalium et occidentalium verissimae imagines* published at Zurich in 1559.

[2] See Werner Weisbach, *Trionfi,* Berlin, 1919; and Prince d'Essling and E. Müntz, *Pétrarque,* chapter iv (p. 101) et seqq. A good example of an illuminated manuscript of the *Trionfi* is one of about 1485, now in the Seminario de San Carlos, Saragossa, and another, made for Federigo of Urbino, now in the Biblioteca Nacional of Madrid. (See E. Bertaux, *Exposition rétrospective de Saragosse,* 1908 p. 129.)

[3] In the collection of the New York Historical Society. P. Schubring, *Cassoni,* Leipzig, 1915, fig. 212.

[4] Example in the Victoria and Albert Museum.

[5] Venturi, *Storia dell' arte italiana,* vii, pt. 3, p. 215. A magnificent silver dish of about 1560 chased with Triumphs is in the Treasury of the Cathedral of Seville.

[6] The influence survives in such themes as Force conquered by Love, Virtue repelling Vice, and the triumph of conjugal love, painted by Veronese on the walls of the Barbarò Villa at Maser, near Treviso, in 1560.

[7] Palustre, *La Renaissance en France,* ii. 287. These again appear on the 'Maison d'Agnès Sorel' at Orleans, and once appeared on a balustrade (long since destroyed) in the Château de Madrid in the Bois de Boulogne.

[8] Law, *History of Hampton Court,* i. 63.

[9] As late as 1609 Brunel painted the ceiling of the Galerie des Antiques of the Louvre with 'La Renommée sur ung charriot, trayné par deux cerfs'. M. Vachon, *Le Louvre et les Tuileries,* p. 95.

[10] For a tapestry of about 1570 with this theme see Molinier in *Mon. Piot* ix, 1902, p. 117.

[11] Woltmann, *Holbein und seine Zeit,* 2nd ed., i. 380.

[12] Now in the Victoria and Albert Museum, Salting Bequest, C 2429, 1910. Even religious symbolism was affected; the 'Vitrail des Chars' of about 1515–20 in the Church of Saint Vincent at Rouen shows the Triumph of Adam and Eve in the Earthly Paradise, the Triumph of Sin after the Fall, and the Triumph of the Virgin, all figured in chariot-scenes of the most Petrarchan sort.

antiquity. Even Tasso, though he inspired a few schemes of decoration in France about 1600,[1] is hardly represented in Italian decoration.[2] Scenes from the *Aeneid*, the *Odyssey*, and the *Argonautica* appear on *cassoni* of the second half of the fifteenth century,[3] and were soon transferred to wall decoration. Scenes from the *Iliad* appear on the ceiling of the great hall of the Palazzo Doria Spinelli at Genoa, painted by Luca Cambiaso in 1535; the *Aeneid* is the theme of Nicolò dell'Abbate's frescoes in the villa of Count Boiardo at Scandiano about 1540;[4] Pellegrino Tibaldi uses the *Odyssey* some twenty years later for his paintings for the Palazzo Poggi, at Bologna; the *Argonautica* in 1584 furnishes a theme for the Carracci's frescoes in the Palazzo Fava in the same city. By this time, indeed, the classical repertory of story and legend had become so familiar that no special text had to be followed, and much Bolognese decoration of the end of the sixteenth century is simply a collection of mythological illustrations. Sometimes, if less familiar subjects were used, an explanation had to be provided; soon after 1587 the Carracci, in the great saloon of the Palazzo Magnani at Bologna, provided cartouches below with an explanation in Latin of the scenes of the history of Romulus and Remus illustrated in the medallions of the frieze.

Outside Italy it was longer before such subjects became common. The French humanists, it is true, dictated subjects to Il Rosso for the decoration of Fontainebleau, but the themes were varied to the point of confusion. Among those that can be identified are Venus chastizing Cupid for having loved Psyche; the education of Achilles; a shipwreck; Amphinomus and Anapicus bearing their parents out of the flames of Catania; Lapiths and Centaurs; the Fountain of Youth; Venus mourning for Adonis, and Cleobis and Biton, as well as many too recondite for modern identification. About 1600 Ambroise Dubois decorated the Grand Cabinet du Roi at Fontainebleau with scenes from the story of Theagenes and Chariclea, that Amyot's translation had brought into fashion; and some thirty years later Simon Vouet painted the gallery of the Hôtel de Bullion with thirty-two illustrations of the *Odyssey*; but such classical themes were soon turned to have a more national application.[5] It is chiefly in such minor work as French and Flemish ebony cabinets and in the painted enamels of Limoges and the school of Toutin that mythological scenes survive; and these are for the most part imitated from engraved compositions.[6]

[1] Scenes from his *Tancredo e Clorinda* were painted by Ambroise Dubois on the walls of the Queen's room at Fontainebleau (Michel, *Histoire de l'Art*, v. 781) and others from the *Gerusalemme Liberata* were used for one of her smaller rooms at the Louvre about 1609 (*ibid.*, p. 780).

[2] Nicolò dell'Abbate, however, painted some frescoes from Ariosto's *Orlando Furioso* about 1540 in the villa of Count Boiardo at Scandiano.

[3] See for example Schubring, *Cassoni*, figs. 245–55, and 296–7.

[4] It continued in fashion until the end of the century: see the Carracci's frescoes in the Palazzo Fava, Bologna, of 1584, and others in the same palace by Francesco Albani, 1598.

[5] See vol. II, p. 43. Seventeenth-century tapestries still occasionally drew their themes from contemporary literature; sets were woven at Aubusson, based on the illustrations of Chapelain's *Pucelle* and the *Grand Cyrus*.

[6] e. g. A Limoges dish of about 1560 with the Judgement of Paris from an engraving by Marcantonio

204. Carved walnut mirror frame with symbolical figures. Italian, *c.* 1560

205. Hanging embroidered with emblematic medallions by Mary, Queen of Scots, and Bess of Hardwick, c. 1570

5

In any age in which literacy is not a general privilege, but the mark of a lettered class, inscriptions are apt to have a place in decoration. The monastic literacy of the early Middle Ages is reflected in the religious inscriptions of Romanesque art; the knightly literacy of the late Middle Ages in all kinds of mottoes and legends in secular decoration. The scope of men's reading was governed only by their individual taste, and not only did literary influences of all kinds make themselves felt in decorative schemes, but they also brought with them an equal diversity of inscriptions.

The songs of *courtoisie* early played a part in decoration. The Chronicle of Saint Denis records that in 1235 Thibault de Champagne and Gaston Brulé composed 'les plus belles chansons, les plus delitables et les plus melodieuses qui oncques fussent oyes en chansons et en vielles; et le fist escripre en sa salle à Provins et en celle de Troyes'.[1] The thirteenth-century romance of *Cleomadès* describes an embroidered tester:

> De soie est ouvrez par maistrie,
> D'uevre cointe, noble et jolie.
> Par tout avoit chançons escrites
> Les meilleurs et les plus eslites
> C'on peust nule part trouver
> Au tans dont vous m'oez parler.[2]

About 1315 Mahaut, Countess of Artois, had a room in the château d'Hesdin painted with scenes of the 'chansons' of Robin and Marion, with the text of Adam de la Halle,[3] while Louis d'Anjou in 1379–80 had a belt of woven gold, 'et sur le tissu e escript un virelay qui se commence: "Se par fausse trayson."'[4] The poet Charles d'Orléans had in 1414 a dress sewn with pearls, which on the sleeves formed the words and music of the song: 'Madame, je suis plus joyeulx,'[5] and in 1455 gave to his duchess a golden ring, 'esmaillé à lermes auquel est escript une chançon, par lui fait.'[6] Even some of the angels in the windows of the Beauchamp Chapel at Warwick[7] hold scrolls inscribed with the words and music of antiphons from the Salisbury Gradual.

In the late fourteenth century the alphabet itself was felt to have beauty and

Raimondi after Raphael, with a Triumph of Diana on the cover adapted from an engraving by Jacques Androuet du Cerceau. Victoria and Albert Museum, Salting Bequest, C 2456, 1910.

[1] Laborde, *Glossaire des Émaux*, ii. 347.

[2] Quoted Michel, *Histoire du Commerce de la Soie*, ii. 110.

[3] J. M. Richard, *Mahaut, Comtesse d'Artois*, p. 324. The Collection Joseph Debrulle at Lille includes a fifteenth-century bronze brooch with a branch of wild rose and the line of a song: 'Par le joli bois s'an va Marion'; Enlart, *Manuel d'Archéologie française*, iii. 425.

[4] Moranvillé, *op. cit.*, p. 585.

[5] Laborde, *Les Ducs de Bourgogne*, iii. 267.   [6] *Ibid.*, iii. 352.

[7] The glass is of about 1447. See C. F. Hardy, 'On the Music in the painted glass of the windows in the Beauchamp Chapel at Warwick,' in *Archaeologia*, lxi, pt. 2, 1909, p. 583.

significance;[1] the Studley Royal bowl has the whole black-letter alphabet and five contractions for its decoration[2] (fig. 201). Magical inscriptions of all kinds were used on plate and personal adornments; Charles V in 1380 had two flasks shaped like fleur-de-lis, inscribed with the legend: 'Jasper fert myrram, thus Melchior, Balthazar aurum,' that preserved the user from the falling sickness,[3] and a pomander 'escript ou mylieu Jhesus autem transeans'[4]—a phrase that was commonly used as a protection against thieves.[5] Sometimes the inscription was conceived as a prayer like the 'God. help. at. ned.' on the stem of Dr. Richard Sokborn's standing cup of about 1450 at Pembroke College, Cambridge, or the 'Potum et nos benedicat Hagyos' on a mazer of about 1490 in the Franks Collection.[6] Occasionally it was simply convivial, like the 'Wacceyl' on the fourteenth-century horn at Queen's College, Oxford, the motto on the bowl of Dr. Richard Sokborn's cup, or the less explicit 'Let ye wynd blowe' on the mazer given to the Vicars' College at Wells by Canon John Lumbard about 1361.[7] More often the inscription was moral and didactic, like the English personal mottoes.[8] The romance of Flore and Blancheflore describes a roof painted with bands of angels holding scrolls of moral remarks; and Guillebert de Metz' description of the house of Maistre Jacques Duchié at Paris in 1407 includes a room 'embellie de divers tableaux et escriptures d'enseignement attachiés et pendus aux parois'.[9]

A bronze jug with the arms and badge of Richard II[10] has two such mottoes in Lombardic letters round its sides: 'He that wyl not spare when he may he schal not spend when he wold. Deme the best in every dowt til the trowthe be tryid out,' and another of about 1380 from a manor house in Norfolk[11] is inscribed: '✳ Goddes grace be in this place amen ✳ stond uttir from the fyre and lat ou lust come nere.'[12] A mazer of about 1420 in the British Museum has the legend:

> Hold youre tunge and sey the best
> And let youre neybore sitte in rest,
> Hoeso lustythe God to plese
> Let hys neybore lyve in ese.

---

[1] Huon le Roi wrote a little moralizing set of French verses on the A, B, C.

[2] Cf. the inventory of Jean, Duc de Berry, 1401: twenty-two silver gilt cups, 'esmaillées au fonds de A, B, C, D'. These, however, may each have borne only one letter. Guiffrey, i. 184. Similar letters are sometimes found on Italian plates and albarelli.

[3] Labarte, *Inventaire du Mobilier de Charles V*, p. 164. Late fifteenth-century mazers at Corpus College, Cambridge, and Holy Trinity Church, Colchester, have similar inscriptions. See W. St. John Hope, in *Archaeologia*, l. 155.

[4] Labarte, *op. cit.*, i. 246.   [5] See Joan Evans, *Magical Jewels*, p. 128.

[6] A pierced and chiselled fifteenth-century iron casket in the Salting Bequest in the Victoria and Albert Museum is inscribed on the cover with invocations to the Virgin: 'Ave gracie plena. O mater dey memento mei. O membra mea benedicat Virgo Maria. Regyna cely letare.'

[7] W. St. John Hope, 'On the medieval drinking bowls called mazers', in *Archaeologia*, l, 1887, p. 182.

[8] See p. 102.

[9] Leroux de Lincy and M. Tisserand, *Paris et ses historiens*, p. 199.

[10] Now in the British Museum; it was found among the possessions of King Prempeh at Kumasi, in Ashanti, in 1895.   [11] Now in the Victoria and Albert Museum, 217, 1879.

[12] 'Stand away from the fire and let who pleases come near.'

207. Brocade in silk and gold. Lucchese. First half of fourteenth century

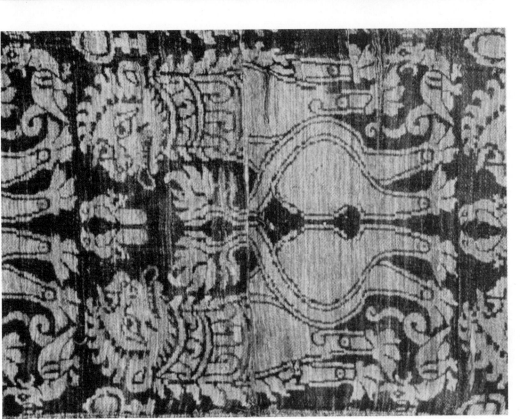

206. North Italian (? Lucchese) brocade. Thirteenth century

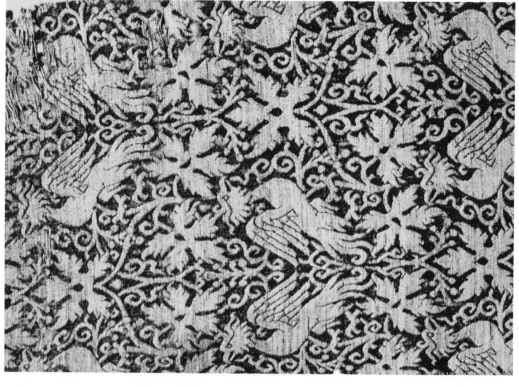

209. Brocade in blue and gold. North Italian (? Lucchese). Second half of fourteenth century

208. Part of a dalmatic in blue and gold brocade. North Italian (? Lucchese). Fourteenth century

Round the abbot's room at Clairvaux was painted a long set of verses:

> Plus est servy, et plus se plainct
> Plus est norry, et plus se fainct
> Plus est payé, pluy se demaine
> Plus est aymé, plus faict de peine,

and so on.[1] In 1481 Louis XI paid Jean Bourdichon for fifty great scrolls for his castle of Plessis-lez-Tours each inscribed: 'Misericordias Domini in aeternum cantabo,' and for three angels holding similar scrolls.[2]

In England, the fashion continued into the sixteenth century; the frieze of the dining-room at Brereton Hall, Cheshire,[3] is inscribed: 'Though thou be for thy pedegre accompted as ancient as Saturn, in wisdom as wise as Solomon, in power as mighty as Alexander, in wealthe as riche as Croesus, or for thy beautie as Flora, yet if thou be carrless of religion, and neglect the true service of the ever living God, thou art a caytife most vyle and miserable.' At Castle Inn, Earls Colne,[4] a rhymed inscription is combined with a simple pattern of hanging garlands. On a tablet are the lines:

> The hour runneth
> And time flyeth
> As flower fadeth
> So man dieth
> Sic transit gloria
> Mundi.[5]

In the sixteenth-century France humanism renewed the tradition of Latin inscriptions, and Montaigne had the rafters of his library painted with 'Fecit Deus hominem similem umbrae de qua post solis occasum judicabit' from Ecclesiastes, and with 'Nostra vagatur in tenebris nec caesa potest mens cernere verum', from a letter of Étienne Pasquier's. Such engravers as Pittoni produced many patterns of panels and cartouches to frame texts and moral remarks.[6] There was for a time a fashion for stone balustrades pierced with inscriptions; one in praise of the Virgin runs round the Church of La Ferté Bernard, while on such English houses as Levens and Felbrigg biblical texts crown the edifice.[7]

---

[1] *Annales archéologiques*, iii, 1845, p. 233.

[2] Havard, *Dictionnaire de l'Ameublement*, s.v. Papier peint. It is probably from the imitation of such scrolls that 'parchemin plié' panelling—anglice linenfold—is derived.

[3] Wall, *Medieval Wall paintings*, p. 122. Other inscriptions are given in Tusser's *Points of Husbandry* of 1573.

[4] *Ibid.*, p. 122. Equally gloomy inscriptions are to be found in the country parts of France. On a chimney-piece at Sonneville, in Normandy, is a portrait of the man who had the house built, with a skull to balance it and the legend: 'Il faut mourir. J'attends l'heure de la mort, 1533.' Another chimney-piece, in the Musée de Dôle, is inscribed: 'Hodie Mihi, Cras tibi,' and a cider-pot in the Musée de Rouen has: 'Pense à la mort, pauvre sot.' See Mâle, *op. cit.*, p. 381.

[5] A wall-painting from Campions, Essex, now in the Saffron Walden Museum, has a similar tablet inscribed; 'Gyve to the pore. Spende and be b[lest].'

[6] Cf. a French walnut coffer of about 1560 in the Salting Bequest, inscribed on the sides: 'Prudentia carnis mors. Prudentia spiritus vita,' and on the front: 'Jacta curam tuam in domino et ipse te enutriet.'

[7] At Oriel College, Oxford, a similar balustrade recalls the date: 'Regnante Carolo.'

6

Naturally inscriptions of all kinds were even more often used as a legend to amplify or elucidate some picture or device,[1] like the legend: 'Bon vent nous conduist' round a golden ship.[2] Sometimes, too, the decorative picture existed simply to illustrate a verbal allusion. A Flemish tapestry of the Perfections of Our Lady, given to Rheims Cathedral by Robert de Lenoncourt in 1530, and probably dating from 1509, has all the symbols of the Virgin's perfection represented and explained by Latin inscriptions on banderoles: *Lilium inter spinas, Plantacio rose, Ortus conclusus, Virga Jesse, Cedrus exaltata, Puteus aquarum,* and so on. Underneath they are all summed up in French verse:

> Marie vierge chaste, de mer estoille,
> Porte du ciel, comme soleil eslue,
> Puis de vive eaue, ainsi que lune belle,
> Tour de David, lis de noble value,
> Cité de Dieu, clair mirouer non pollue,
> Cèdre exalté, distillante fontaine,
> En ung jardin fermée, est résolue
> De besongnier, et de si grace pleine.[3]

Sometimes such devotional phrases were not illustrated, but were fitted into a decorative scheme. In the Church of Notre Dame de Nantilly, near Saumur, is a tapestry of the early years of the sixteenth century, with five angels playing musical instruments: the first has a banderole inscribed: *Ave est ista que ascendit sicut aurora diei,* the second one with *Pulchra ut luna, electa ut sol,* the third: *Ecce Stella maris,* the fourth: *O virgo Maria que genuisti lucem seculo,* and the last: *Viderunt eam filie Syon.* Another set in the same church has angels bearing the instruments of the Passion with panels inscribed with French verses on the Passion of Christ above. Even more beautiful are the verdure tapestries with angels bearing instruments of the Passion, woven about 1515 in the valley of the Loire for the widow of Pierre de Rohan, and now at Angers (fig. 202). Each angel half-kneels beside

---

[1] Curious early instances are the inscriptions of moral qualities on the seraph's wings in Robert de Lyle's Psalter of about 1320 (Bodley, Arundel MS. 83) and inscriptions on the fleurs-de-lis that powder the background of a portrait of Robert of Anjou in an address presented to him by the inhabitants of Prato, in Tuscany, about 1335–40. B. M. Royal MS. 6E. X, f. 10b. The inscriptions themselves were admired. When in 1332 the friars Simon and Hugh visited the Painted Chamber at Westminster, they recorded that the battle-scenes there portrayed were 'explained and completed by a regular series of texts beautifully written in French, to the great admiration of the beholder'. W. R. Lethaby, 'The Painted Chamber,' in *Burlington Magazine,* July, 1905, vii. 263.

[2] Molinier, *Inventaire des meubles du château de Pau,* 1561–2, p. 72.

[3] M. Sartor, *Les Tapisseries, toiles peintes et broderies de Reims,* Reims, 1912, p. 82. Cf. an embroidered antependium from the Church of Zudorf on the Lower Rhine in the Kunstgewerbe Museum at Cologne, and another in the Archiepiscopal Museum in the same city.

211. Brocade in green, yellow, and white on a red ground.
Hispano-Moresque. Fifteenth century

210. Brocade in gold and green. North Italian (? Venetian).
Early fifteenth century

213. Brocade in red, green, and yellow. Hispano-Moresque.
Fifteenth century

212. Brocade woven with gold thread and blue, green, and white
silk on a red ground. Hispano-Moresque. Fifteenth century

215. Brocade in green and gold. Italian, probably Florentine. End of the fifteenth century

214. Brocade in red and gold. Florentine. End of the fifteenth century

216. Lid of a covered bowl of carved mazer wood. Fifteenth century

a great scroll inscribed with a verse in honour of the Passion. A typical verse, that beside the angel with the Pillar and Scourge, runs:

> Regarde en pitié et voy comme
> Benignement par la doulceur
> Tresdure angoisse por toy homme
> Voulut souffrir ton Créateur.
> En ceste atache a grant douleur
> Ou son benoist corps longuement
> Si quoy repeult dire greigneur
> Endura non pareil torment.

Naturally some of the frescoes and tapestries with subjects derived from literary texts were accompanied by quotations. The figures of the Preux and the Preuses on the frescoes of the castle of Manta,[1] dating between 1411 and 1420, each have a painted tablet below with their names and feats and epoch described in verse, a little debased from the text of the *Chevalier Errant,* written about 1404.[2] Arthur's tablet, for instance, is inscribed:

> Je fui roy de Bertagne, d'Escose e d'Anglatere,
> Cinquante roy conquis qui de moy tregnen terre;
> J'ay tué VII grans Jehans, rust-ons en mi lour terre,
> Sus le munt Saint Michel un autre n'alay conquere.
> Vis le Seint Greal; puis moy fist Mordré goere;
> Qui moy ocist V.C. ans puis que Diu vint en tere.

The proverbial wisdom of the *Enseignement des Sages*[3] lent itself easily to such quotation. The castle of Fénis, in the Val d'Aosta, has three sides of its courtyard painted with twenty-five figures of philosophers and worthies—Boethius, Aristotle, Plato, and the rest—holding scrolls of quatrains from a version of the *Enseignement*;[4] and Louis of Anjou had a 'très grand et très noble tabernacle d'argent doré' similarly adorned.[5] Philippe le Bon had a set of tapestry hangings,

[1] See P. d'Ancona, 'Gli Affreschi del Castello di Manta nel Saluzzese,' in *L'Arte,* viii, 1905, pp. 94 and 183; Venturi, *Storia dell' arte italiana,* vii, pt. 1, p. 142.

[2] It is noteworthy that the figures show marked correspondences with the illuminations of the Paris manuscript of the poem—Bib. Nat. fonds français 12559—written before 1437.   [3] ed. Leroux de Lincy, ii. 99.

[4] The frescoes are of the early fifteenth century. See J. Boson, 'Proverbes en ancien français du château de Fénis,' in *Augusta Pretoria, Revue Valdôtaine,* Dec. 1919–Jan. 1920, and *L'Arte,* viii, 1905, p. 95; and A. Frizzi, *Il borgo e il castello medioevale di Torino,* Turin, 1894, pp. 215 and 263. Cf. the Philosophers who appear beside the Prophets and the Sibyls on the choir stalls at Ulm, carved by Jörg Syrlin between 1469 and 1474.

[5] Moranvillé, *op. cit.,* p. 122. It was borne by four kneeling prophets each holding a scroll. The first was inscribed:

> Qui riens commence il doit sentir
> A quelle fin il en puet venir.

The next bore the verse:

> Nul ne doit dire qu'ait rien fait
> De la chose, tant qu'il l'ait fait.

The next:

> N'est pas sire en son pays
> Qui de ses hommes est hays.

While on the fourth scroll was written:

> Bien doit estre sires clamez
> Qui de ses hommes est amez.

'appellée la Chambre de la Plaiderie d'amours, où il y a plusieurs personnages d'ommes et de femmes, et a plusieurs escriptures d'amours en rolleaux.'[1] Nicholas de la Chesnaye's 'Condamnation des Banquets, à la louange de Diepte et Sobriété', furnished the design of a set of tapestries belonging to Charles the Bold, and of another set now in the Musée Lorrain at Nancy,[2] with allegorical figures of Gourmandise, Friandise, Passe-temps, Je-bois-à-vous, and Bonne-compagnie, becoming the victims of Banquet and Souper with their allies Gravelle, Goutte, Colique, and Apoplexie. Souper and Banquet are finally led before the tribunal of the lady Experience, and Avicenna and the doctors condemn them to six hours digestion. All the story is told by inscriptions on 'Écriteaux' or panels. Many such 'tapisseries à écriteaux' are recorded in the 1420 inventory of Charles VI,[3] and in some instances the beginning of the inscription is given—'Povez regarder . . .', 'Droit cy a l'erbette jolie . . .' and others. Even when humanism brought in another and simpler literature some elucidation was needed; the hangings of brown velvet belonging to Louise de Savoie in 1525, with five medallions of scenes from Virgil's Bucolics, had above each 'ung épitaphe de toile d'argent à lectres et escripteaux de broderie'.[4] In such decoration a gradual development is evident from an illustrative type completed by a quotation to a type designed especially for tapestry, with verses written for the purpose. One of the most interesting of the transitional sort is a set of five early sixteenth-century[5] tapestries shown in Paris in 1900 and 1913[6] with an allegory of human life based on the ordinary type of stag-hunting scene. On the first Nature[7] (fig. 203) sends her tufter Jeunesse into cover.

Below are the verses:

> Cy voiez le buisson d'enfance
> Ou nature son chemin dresse
> Et le cerf fragille hors lance
> Avec son beau limyer Jeunesse.

[1] Pinchart, Histoire de la tapisserie dans les Flandres, p. 23.

[2] These have often been considered identical (see, for instance, Viollet le Duc, Dictionnaire du Mobilier, i, p. 277, s.v. Tapis), but the Nancy ones appear to be later in date.   [3] J. Guiffrey, La Tapisserie, p. 68.

[4] Havard, Dictionnaire de l'Ameublement, s.v. Chambre.

[5] The type was known earlier. The 1420 inventory of Charles VI includes a set of tapestries with the 'Histoire de la Jeunesse et Deduit, appelée la chasse au cerf' (E. Molinier, in Mon. Piot., ix, 1902, p. 95) which is probably that described in the inventory of his tapestries sold by the English in 1422 as 'ung autre tappiz de fil délyé, de volerie, sur champ noir, à plusieurs personnages à pié et à cheval, et a escrit dessus: Véez cy Jeunesse, etc.' (J. Guiffrey, Bibliothèque de l'École des Chartes, xlviii (1887), p. 108).

[6] S. de Ricci, Exposition d'objets d'art . . . à l'ancien hôtel de Sagan, Mai–Juin, 1913, Nos. lxxxiii and lxxiv; lent by M. de Kermalingant. See E. Picot, 'Le cerf allégorique dans les tapisseries et les miniatures,' in Bulletin de la Société française de reproductions de manuscrits à peintures, 3e année, 1913, no 1, p. 57. The tapestry was probably made at Tournai about 1520 for Guy de Baudreuil, abbé commendataire of the Abbey of Saint Martin du Bois. A set of similar but more elaborate designs of about 1544 is in the Bibliothèque Nationale, fonds français, 379.

[7] The personages and hounds all have their names writ large across them; cf. the tapestry with the four complexions 'with scriptures upon their bodies' in the 1530 inventory of Cardinal Wolsey. Brewer, Letters and Papers of Henry VIII, iv, pt. 3, p. 3045.

218. Brocade in red and gold. Italian, probably Florentine.
End of fifteenth century

217. Brocatelle in yellow, purple, and gold. Florentine.
End of fifteenth century

220. Brocade. Italian, probably Florentine. Middle of sixteenth century

219. Brocade in red, yellow, and gold. Florentine. First half of sixteenth century

(Q)ui le met sus et pas ne cesse
D'avoir et de l'approucher envie
(A)ffin (qu')en repos ne le laisse
Es bois de transitoire vie.

On the second tapestry *Ignorance* looses the hounds *Oultrecuidance, Haste* and *Vouloir,* and *Vanité* winds her horn.   The legend runs:

Les chiens que tenoit accouplez
Dedans le bois dame Ignorance
Après le cerf a descouplez
C'est Vouloir, Haste, Oultrecuidance,
Qui plains de mondaine plaisance,
Qui font maint sault de travers faire,
Et lors Vanité s'avance
De corner, comme elle scet faire.

On the third *Viellesse* hunts the stag with the hounds *Age, Doubtance, Pesanteur, Ennuy, Soucy, Chault, Froit,* and *Peine.*

Puis l'assault Viellesse a oultrance
Qui le fait hors du lac saillir,
Et luy lasche Peine et Dou(btance),
Chault et froit et fait venir
Soucy, Ennuy, pour le tenir.
Et Aage a la chere ridée,
Et Pesanteur le font fouyr
Devers Maladie le doubtée.

On the fourth tapestry *Maladie*, with the same hounds, brings the stag to bay and kills it with a hunting spear, while in the background Death sounds his horn for the kill.

Voy le Veneur espoventable
Qui la mort du cerf a emprise,
C'est Maladie la doubtable
De qui la charogne est surprise,
Elle lui fait forte entreprise,
Car de l'espieu le coup lui donne
Après la Mort vient corner prise
Ainsi que le temps ordonne.

The fifth tapestry sums up and emphasizes the moral.   The moralist, a bearded man in a long robe, stands by a large rectangular panel with these lines:

Gens de briefve durée mondaine
Qu(i a) chasse mortelle et soubdaine
Es(tes) comme cerf asservis,
Considérez la vie humaine.
Et la fin ou elle vous maine
Et les metz dont serez servis,

> A b(ien) que serez desservis
> De jeunesse et aurez advis
> Advisez a tels propos prendre
> Que quant serez de mort raviz,
> Et les vers seront au corps vifz
> Que puisssions à Dieu l'ame rendre.[1]

Soon, indeed, the poets of the time were writing specifically for the painters and tapestry-weavers. Martial d'Auvergne begins his *Dance des Femmes*:

> O vous, mes seigneurs et mes dames
> Qui contemplés ceste painture,
> Plaise vous prier pour les ames
> De ceulx qui sont en sepulture,

and such a beginning often betrays the origin of a poem when the picture it was intended to elucidate is destroyed and forgotten. Gradually such themes became more and more independent of the general current of literature. The *Dicts Moraulx pour mettre en tapisserie* written by Henri Baude towards the end of the fifteenth century[2] provide the craftsmen with an idea to illustrate and verses to append to his illustration. The first example is typical. 'Des pourceaulx qui ont répandu ung plain panier de fleurs' is the subject, with the motto

> Belles raisons qui sont mal entendues
> Ressemblent fleurs à pourceaulx estendues.

Some subjects are more complicated; in one a man presses stones in a wine press; in another a lighted candle is set between a courtier and a peasant; and in another a man moralizes to a friend on a spider's web spun between two trees.[3] In England such work was simpler in its type. William Billyng, for instance, between 1400 and 1430 wrote verses to illustrate devices of the Five Wounds of Christ, suitable for glass painting or embroidery.[4] The fourth Wound has for its device a wounded hand, rayed, on a scroll inscribed ' i h c the well of grace '. Below is the verse:

> Hayle welle of grace most precyouse in honoure
> In the Kynges left hande set of ierusalem
> Swettur thanne bawme is thy swete lycore

[1] This panel has at the top the arms of Baudreuil quartering Saint Martin. A rather similar figure, an astrologer, standing beside his desk, with book, astrolabe and armillary sphere, appears on a wall painting in the château of Villeneuve Lembron (Puy-de-Dôme) with a scroll labelled 'Le dit de l'astroloc' inscribed:

> Home vivant selon raison
> Considerent le temps qui court
> Est plus heureux en sa maison
> Que les grans qui vivent en court.

[2] *Les Vers*, ed. Quicherat, Paris, 1856, p. 95 et seqq.

[3] Cf. two early emblems on a window in the hotel of Jacques Cœur at Bourges, a man with donkey's ears and a scroll inscribed 'Taire' and another with padlocked mouth and a scroll inscribed 'En bouche close n'entre mouche'. Palliser, *Historical Devices, Badges, and War Cries*, p. 72.

[4] W. Billyng, *The Five Wounds of Christ*, ed. W. Bateman, Manchester, 1814. The five wounds, with short inscriptions, appear on a ring of about the same date found at Coventry Park, and now in the British Museum. See Joan Evans, *Magical Jewels*, p. 127, and *Archaeologia*, xviii, 1817, p. 307.

221. Brocade. Venetian. Early sixteenth century

222. Brass dish, engraved and damascened with silver, with an enamelled coat of arms of the Occhi di Cane family of Verona. Venetian-Saracenic, *c.* 1450

Whiche in largesse to us doth owt estreme
So precius a flode is in no Kinges reame
Of perfyte grece thow art restoratyfe
And in all vertu most preseruatyfe.

Thomas More in his early years 'devysed in hys father's house in London, a goodly hangyng of fyne paynted clothe, with nyne pageauntes, and verses over of euery of these pageauntes: which verses expressed and declared, what the ymages in those pageauntes represented, and also in those pageauntes were paynted, the thyngs that the verses ouer them dyd (in effecte) declare'. They represented the three Ages of Childhood, Manhood and Age, 'Venus and Cupyde . . . Fame, Tyme, Eternitee and the Poet'—probably the Petrarchan Triumphs [1] of Love, Fame, Death, Time and Eternity.

The Elizabethan Sheldon tapestry map of Worcestershire and the surrounding country [2] has on one side verses in praise of the western part:

Heare hills doo lift there heads aloft
From whence sweet springs doo flowe,
Whose moisture good doth fertil make
The valleis couchte belowe.
Hear goodly orchards planted are
In fruite which doo abounde,
Thine ey wolde make thin hart rejoice
To see so pleasant grounde.

On the bottom border the south is praised:

This sowthly part which hear below
Towards Glocester fall
Of corne and grasse great plentie yelds
But fruit excedith all.

More often in England the legends were on a much shorter scale. At West Stow in Suffolk, for instance,[3] the medieval types of 'esbattements' are moralized. The figure of a youth hawking has the inscription 'Thus doe I all the day'; another, making love to a girl, 'Thus doe I while I may'; a middle-aged man looking at the

---

[1] See p. 143. A typical extract is: 'In the sixt pageant was painted Lady Fame. And under her fete was the picture of Death that was in the fifth pageant. And over this sixt pageaunt the writyng was as foloweth:

FAME

Fame I am called, maruayle you nothing,
Though with tonges am compassed all rounde
For in voyce of people is my chiefe livyng.
O cruel death, thy power I confound,
When thou a noble man hath brought to grounde
Maugry thy teeth to lyve cause hym shall I,
Of people in perpetuall memory.'

Thomas More, *Workes*, London, 1557; quoted Dibdin, *Typographical Antiquities*, ii. 431.

[2] Belonging to the Bodleian Library; at present lent to the Victoria and Albert Museum. The verses on the north and east sides are missing.   [3] Wall, *Medieval Wall Paintings*, p. 117.

lovers, 'Thus did I while I might'; while an old cripple, too weary to keep rhythm, cries 'Good Lord, will this world last for ever?'

The invention of printing and engraving enormously intensified the influence of such inscriptions and pictures. A cut, with verses beneath, provided a model for the craftsman; and even if he omitted the verses familiarity with books made it easy for his lettered audience to supply the missing interpretation. Such publications, indeed, became numerous in the sixteenth century alike for the *impresa*, that was the device of an individual with a motto to complete and explain its significance,[1] and for the emblem, universal in its application, with verses appended that could be omitted or even used separately.[2] The earliest printed books definitely to exercise such influence were perhaps the *Dialogues of the Creatures*, published in 1481 by the Dutchman Gerard Leeu: a hundred and twenty-two dialogues, between sun and moon, wolf and ass, husband and wife, Man and Death, and so on, with illustrative woodcuts; and the German Sebastian Brant's famous *Ship of Fools* printed in 1494. The first book definitely of emblems, and the most important in its influence, was the *Emblematum libellus* of Alciatus, of which the earliest extant edition was printed at Milan in 1531.[3] This edition contains ninety-seven cuts, each accompanied by a set of verses: Insignia, God, the Virtues, the Vices, Nature, Astrology, Love, Fortune, the Prince, the Republic, Life, Death, Friendship, Hostility, Revenge, Peace, Science, Ignorance, Marriage, and fourteen trees: the medieval traditions of decorative personifications and of garden backgrounds simplified and revised for Renaissance use. But Renaissance Italy, fertile in the creation of pictorial decoration, made comparatively little use of emblems,[4] and always on a small scale. When good Italian decoration was emblematic it usually went back to a medieval tradition, and was independent of the engravers; a mirror frame, for instance (fig. 204), crowned with the flaming grenade of Alfonso d'Este, has at its base a Pythagorean Y, symbol of man's choice between good and evil. At the top on one side of the badge is a recording angel, and on the other a skeleton.

[1] See p. 117.
[2] In England the verses were often published separately without the cuts as 'naked emblems'.
[3] An earlier edition may have been printed there in 1522; see Elbert Thompson, *Literary By-paths of the Renaissance*, New Haven, 1924, p. 29.
[4] Vignola, it is true, has a metope and console frieze with emblems on the metopes (Gurlitt, *Geschichte des Barockstiles in Italian*, p. 41), but he had been subject to some northern influence. The Divine hand holding a grapnel, a common emblem type, appears in the border of a fifteenth-century Bolognese Book of Hours (Collection of Mr. Dyson Perrins); and the Italian vignettes and authors' and printers' devices, with such conceits as the triumphant owl standing on an overturned pitcher and hooting 'Kekrika' which adorns Castelvetro's *Poetics* of 1570, are in close connexion with the emblem books. When emblems are used in Italian decorative art the influence of foreign craftsmen may commonly be suspected. It is Karcher who designed his Ferrara tapestries of the middle of the century with emblems—a sphere in the middle of a countryside, a castle attacked by deformed men, a white eagle perching on ruins, and so on (Müntz, *Histoire de la tapisserie en Italie*, p. 58)—and it is French and Netherlandish workmen who set emblems on the bronze doors of Pisa Cathedral, made after the fire of 1575. The decorative side of emblems was sooner lost in Italy than was their symbolic significance. Picinelli's *Mondo Simbolco* published at Milan in 1680 has nearly 900 folio pages of small print on every conceivable emblem and impresa, but has only a few cuts, and Paolo Giovio's and Ruscelli's books on emblems are literary discussions without engravings.

223. Brass dish engraved and damascened with silver. Venetian-Saracenic, *c.* 1530

224. Writing-case of steel damascened with gold and silver. Milanese, *c.* 1520

Within the acanthus foliage down the sides are on the left a lion, a unicorn, an eagle, and other creatures symbolizing the virtues, while on the other side are a dog, an ape, a satyr, and other beasts for the vices. Beside each animal is a letter, spelling on the one side *Bonum*, on the other *Malum*.

Outside Italy, however, emblems helped to fulfil men's need of symbolic expression at a time when the Christian symbolism of the Middle Ages was being succeeded by the metaphors of the Renaissance. Emblem-books and the decorative use of their devices followed the Renaissance through Europe. Alciatus' *Emblematum libellus* had an international success; over a hundred and forty editions were published in Europe in the sixteenth century. Every succeeding version increased the number of the emblems given; the 1573 edition includes over a thousand, and is amplified by learned commentaries by Claude Mignault. An edition was printed by Wechel at Paris in 1534, and between 1544 and 1551 seven editions were printed at Lyons.[1] These helped to establish a French tradition of emblem books and emblem usage. Guillaume de la Perrière published his *Theatre des bons Engins* at Paris in 1539, and this was followed the next year by the *Hecatongraphie* of Gilles Corrozet. Each of its small cuts of an emblem in an engraved border is accompanied by a little motto of a proverbial type, two French poems, one short and pithy, and one drawing the moral at greater length. The subjects are varied and perpetuate the tradition of Baude rather than of Alciatus. One, for instance, has the motto 'Parler peu et venir au poinct', a cut of men shooting at a mark, and the quatrain:

> Celluy qui le mieulx tirera
> Droict au but, et plus pres du blanc,
> Son coup sera estimé franc
> Et la louange en recepvra.[2]

Similar emblems soon passed into French decoration. Jeanne de Vivonne, whose wit Brantôme extols, adorned the cofferings of the gallery ceiling of her Château de Dampierre with emblems: two monks walking together, rosary in hand, with the motto *Tropt tard cogneau, tropt tost laissé*; an open book, *En rien gist tout*; a hideous demon, *Mas perdido y menos arrepantido*; a tower beneath a rain of gold, *Auro clausa patent*; a stone rising from the waves, *Modice fidei quare dubitasti*; a snake cut in two, *Dum spiro sperabo*; a shield, *Aut hunc aut super hunc*; a dove and a branch, *Si te fata vocant*; and an urn of fate with human lots falling

---

[1] 1544: 109 emblems, by Jacob Moderne, and another edition by him with 113. 1547: 198 emblems, by Tornesius and Gazeius; 1548, the same in a French version; 1549, reprint of the Latin edition. 1549: 205 emblems and 161 devices by Roville, with French version by Bartholemy Aneau; 1550–1, Roville and Bonhommes, complete edition with 211 emblems.

[2] Corrozet's emblems were followed by Paradin's *Devises héroiques*, published at Lyons in 1557, which are rather *imprese* than emblems. Théodore de Bèze published 43 emblems of a religious sort, some very simple in form; the first is a plain circle, the second a circle divided into quadrants. J. Boissard's *Emblematum liber* published at Metz in 1588 has fairly long poems in Latin and French, each dedicated to some scholar, with elaborate pictorial engravings. Its influence on decoration was negligible.

out, *Que tegit sola fient manifesta ruina*.[1] A more bucolic wit is expressed in a panel of about 1550 over the chimney of the Salle des Peintures in the Château d'Oiron, with three peasants on three donkeys, and the legend *Nous sommes sept*. A French walnut cabinet[2] dated 1577 has two medallions framed in graceful strapwork: one of a dolphin and anchor, with the motto *Semper festina lente*, and the other of two jugs with flames issuing from them and tears dropping on them, with the legend *Probasti me et cognovisti me*.

Emblems likewise appeared on many French tapestries and embroideries; Louis XIV's inventory records a tapestry 'fort vielle et hors d'estat de servir . . . représentant un rocher au milieu d'une mer agitée de tempeste, auquel est attaché un ancre porté par une main qui sort des nues. Avec des escriteaux tout autour, et aux quatre coins les armes de Navarre'.[3] Even church embroideries were affected; the vestments given by Henri IV to St. François de Sales about 1585[4] have a little emblem of 'l'arbre de la vie et de la mort' and medallions of the brazen serpent and the tree of Jesse treated in the manner of the emblem-designers. With the creation of a mature French classic style emblems began to go out of use.[5] They do not appear at Versailles; it was only Bussy Rabutin, exiled into Burgundy, who about 1667 avenged himself upon his treacherous friend the Marquise de Monglat by decorating one of the rooms of his castle with emblems reflecting upon her character: a swallow with her face, *Fugit hiems*, a siren, also with her face, *Allicit ut perdat*, an urn spilling water upon lime, *E fredda m'accende*, and another, referring to Bussy himself, with a brazier *Splendescam, da materiam*, all set above views of the Royal castles from which he was exiled.

Emblems, like other forms of Renaissance decoration, passed from France into the Low Countries. Joannes Sambucus' *Emblemata*, published at Antwerp in 1564, has rather elaborate pictorial cuts with some dozen lines of Latin verse below each. It was followed by Hadrian Junius' *Emblemata* from Antwerp the next year, with homilies in a separate part of the book instead of moral poems.

England received a tradition of emblematic usage from France before she had emblem-books of her own. Spenser got his emblematic conceits from Du Bellay, and gave them poetic value; and Mary Queen of Scots likewise brought the fashion over from France and beguiled the long hours of her captivity with emblematic needlework.[6] Drummond of Hawthornden describes a State bed embroidered by her, with many imprese and emblems—'*Mercurius* charming *Argos*

[1] Palustre, *Renaissance en France*, iii. 292.

[2] In the Victoria and Albert Museum 2790. 1856.

[3] Guiffrey, *Inventaire général du Mobilier de la Couronne*, ii. 210.

[4] Preserved in the Church of Thonon, Savoie.

[5] They survived for a time in books: e.g. C. F. Menestrier, *La Philosophie des Images*, Paris, 1682, and in certain minor arts such as the engraving of sword-blades.

[6] See also M. Jourdain, 'Sixteenth-century embroidery with emblems,' in *Burlington Magazine*, xi, 1907, p. 326. For a description of the Lenox or Darnley jewel, a mine of emblematic decoration, see Fraser Tytler, *Historical Notes on the Lennox or Darnley Jewel*, and Joan Evans, *English Jewellery*, p. 88.

with his hundred Eyes expressed by his *Caduceus*, two flutes and a Peacock, the word *Eloquium tot lumina clausit* . . . a ship with her mast broken and fallen in the sea, the word *Nunquam nisi rectam.* . . . This for herself and her Son, a Big Lyon and a Young Whelp beside her, the word *unum quidem sed Leonem.* An emblem of a Lyon taken in a net, and Hares wantonly passing over him, the word *Et lepores devicto insultant leone.* Cammomel in a garden, the word *Fructus calcata dat amplos.* A Palm tree, the word *Ponderibus virtus innata resistit.* A Bird in a Cage and a Hawk flying with above, the word *Il mal me preme et me spaventa peggio.* A Triangle with a Sun in the middle of a Circle, the word *Trino non convenit Orbis.* A Porcupine amongst Sea Rocks, the word *ne volutetur.* . . . Flourishes of Arms, as Helms, Launces, Corslets, Pikes, Muskets, Cannons, . . . the word *Dabit Deus his quoque finem.*[1] A Tree planted in a churchyard environed with dead Men's Bones, the word *Pietas revocabit ab Orco.* Eclipses of the Sun and Moon, the word *Ipsa sibi lumen quod invidet aufert,* glancing, as may appear, at Queen Elizabeth. Brennus's Ballances, a Sword cast in to weigh gold, the word *Quid nisi victis dolor?* A Vine tree watered with Wine, which instead of making it spring and grow maketh it fade, the word *Mea sic mihi prosunt.* A wheel rolled from a Mountain into the Sea, *Piena di dolor voda de Speranza;* which appeareth to be her own, and it should be *Precipitio senza speranza.* A Heap of Wings and Feathers dispersed, the word *Magnatum Vicinitas.* A Trophie upon a Tree, with Mytres, Crowns, Hats, Masks, Swords, Books, and a Woman with a Vail about her Eyes or muffled, pointing to some about her, with this word, *Ut casus dederit.* Three Crowns, two opposite, and another above in the sky, *aliamque moratur.* The Sun in an Eclipse the word *Medio occidit die.'*[2] It will be seen how many of these emblems, though not adapted and recognized as formal *imprese*, have reference to the fortunes of Mary herself.

An important set of hangings, two embroidered by Bess of Hardwick and two hangings (one dismembered) and a valance worked by Mary Stuart and her ladies, came into the possession of the Bedingfields of Oxburgh after a fire at Cowdray in the middle of the eighteenth century, and are still at Oxburgh (fig. 205).[3] Like the hangings described by Drummond, those embroidered by Mary contain medallions of many imprese,[4] and also a certain number of emblems, for the most part with some personal reference: an apple tree, with the motto *Pulchriori detur,* presumably a hit at Queen Elizabeth; a rose, thistle, and lily, *Virtutis vincula sanguinis arctiora,* with a crowned monogram of Elizabeth and Mary; foliage,

---

[1] Cf. the Reliquary of Blessed Thomas More, now at Stonyhurst, which has on one side the emblems of the Passion and the figure of Christ by the open sepulchre, with the legend 'O passi graviora dabit his quoque finem'. Joan Evans, *op. cit.*, p. 73.

[2] W. Drummond of Hawthornden, *Works*, Edinburgh, 1711, p. 137.

[3] See F. de Zulueta, *Embroideries by Mary Stuart and Elizabeth Talbot at Oxburgh Hall, Norfolk.* Oxford (for private circulation) 1923. Other medallions apparently belonging to the same set are in the possession of the Duke of Devonshire.   [4] See p. 119.

with the motto *Anguis sub herba latet* (a device from Paradin's *Devises heroiques*), and apples, *Ne nimium crede colori*. There are besides some thirty medallions, mostly named, of birds, beasts, and fishes. Bess of Hardwick's hangings show similar medallions of animals; a large medallion with flames on which tears are dropping, with the motto *Extinctam lachrimae testantur vivere flammam*, with devices showing that it is her first husband, William Cavendish, who is commemorated; a tree, perhaps a chestnut, with the motto *Vera felicitas semper illaesa*; three flowering plants, *Vera virtus periculum affectat*; an oak, with the motto *Integritas vi robora perennis est* (probably meant for *Integritas vitae robore perennius est*); a cherry bush, *Fugacia sic speciosa*; flowers, *Fecem bibat qui vinum bibit*; and a large emblem of Paradin's, with a raven drinking out of a cup, and the motto *Ingenii largitor*.[1]

Bacon approved of emblems, as reducing intellectual conceptions to sensible images,[2] and decorated Old Gorhambury with 'curious pictures, all emblematical, with mottoes under each. . . . In the hall in the wall over the chimney is painted an oake, with akornes falling from it, with the words, *Nisi quid potius*, and on the wall over the table is painted Ceres teaching the soweing of corn, the words *Monita meliora*'.[3]

Elizabeth, too, had many emblems embroidered on her clothes; a picture of her at Hatfield shows her in a dress powdered with ears and eyes, and her inventories include dresses 'enbrodered all over with fountaines, snaikes, swordes and other devises', worked 'like rainebowes, cloudes, and droppes and flames of fire',[4] and 'enbrodered all over with black flies, with a border of fountaines and trees . . . and waves of the sea'.[5] Similar devices figured among the New Year's gifts offered her by her faithful courtiers; on New Year's Day, 1582, for instance, the Earl of Hertford gave her 'a paire of braceletts of golde, conteining seven peeces, three of the saide peeces having eies, thother having flyes in them, called lady-cowes'.[6]

Geffrey Whitney's *Choice of Emblems* was published in London in 1586. His preface declares 'Emblemes for the most parte, maie be reduced into these three kindes, which is Historicall, Naturall and Morall. Historicall, as representing the actes of some noble persons, being matter of history. Naturall, as in expressing the natures of creatures, for example, the love of the yonge storkes, to the oulde, or of suche like. Morall, pertaining to virtue and instruction of life, which is the chiefe of the three'. Of his 248 devices, only 23 are his own; the rest are derived from Alciatus, Paradin, Sambucus, Hadrian Junius, Gabriel Faerno, and the common stock. It is from Whitney's book that the designs of the verre-eglomisé

---

[1] Paradin explains 'il n'est que la necessité, pour faire inuenter les habilitez, et sutils moyens. Comme naturellement démontre le Corbeau . . . qui estant pressé de soif (et neanmoins de pouuant auenir à boire sus un monument, dans un seau, auquel residoit eau de pluie) porta, et getta tant ne pierres dans icelui, qu'en fin croissant le monceau, fit remonter de l'eau pour boire.'

[2] *De Augmentis Scientarum*, Bk. V, Ch. 5.   [3] Aubrey, quoted in Wall, *Medieval Wall Paintings*, p. 121.

[4] Nichols, *Progresses of Elizabeth*, iii. 503.

[5] *Ibid.*, iii. 508.   [6] *Ibid.*, ii. 396.

225. Brass lantern. Venetian, c. 1520

227. Panel of brocade. Italian, *c.* 1550

226. Lustred maiolica plate. Gubbio, 1537

panels of the Vyvyan Salt[1] are drawn; a vine trained up a tree, *Prudente vino absti-nent*; Tantalus, with the legend *Avaritiae stipendium*; a snake lying among straw-berry plants, *Latet anguis in herba*; and roses surrounded by a swarm of flies, *Vitae aut morti*. It is probably from Whitney that the emblems in the Jacobean painted chamber at Hawsted are derived.[2] Some twenty-nine of his emblems, together with many from Alciatus, are reproduced in the seventy emblematic medallions of the borders of the Hatfield tapestries of the Seasons, one of which is dated 1611.[3]

Emblems, indeed, like all 'conceits', were peculiarly congenial to the Elizabethan mind, which loved to exercise itself upon 'some wittie deuise expressed with cunning workemanship, something obscure to be perceiued at the first whereby, when with further consideration it is understood, it maie the greater delighte the behoulder'.[4] Whitney's book was followed in 1588 by Abraham Faunce's,[5] and about 1610 by Peacham's *Minerva Britanna, or Garden of Heroical Deuises*, with subjects treated in a naturalistic style suited to tapestry.[6] In 1646 appeared a trans-lation from Henri Estienne—Blount's *Art of Making Devices*. Even Cromwell had in 1659 a bed 'with a furniture of needlework of poeticall fancyes'.[7] But already religious moralizations were reducing the artistic element in emblems. The *Emblemes* of Francis Quarles, using the plates of Hugo's *Pia Desideria* of 1624 and 1628 and published in 1635, are admittedly 'but silent Parables' with no decorative intention. Fairlie's *Lychnocausia* of 1638, with its fifty engravings of candles, lanterns, beacons, and other illuminants, is moral rather than decorative in its intention; and by 1686 emblems had become fit only for peasants and children, and Bunyan published his as 'A Book for Boys and Girls, or, Country Rhymes for Children'.[8]

[1] Formerly in the possession of the Vyvyan family of Trelowarren, Cornwall, now in the Victoria and Albert Museum.

[2] Cullum, *History of Hawsted*, quoted Nichols, *Progresses of Elizabeth*, ii. 123.

[3] See A. F. Kendrick in *Walpole Society Annual*, ii. 89.

[4] Whitney's *Choice of Emblems*: Preface. A typical provincial use of emblems is provided by a carved stone chimney-piece of the end of the sixteenth century now in Saffron Walden Museum. It has a continuous frieze carved with the figure of a pack-mule, 'Aliis non nobis', men making ropes, 'nec aliis nec nobis', and a hive and bees 'Aliis et nobis.' Below is the inscription: 'Nostri placent[es] [s]unt labor[es]'

[5] *Insignium Armorum, Emblematum, Hieroglyphicorum et Symbolorum . . . explicatio.*

[6] Some panels in a plaster ceiling at Blickling are based upon his engravings. M. Jourdain, *English Decora-tive Plasterwork of the Renaissance*, p. 12.

[7] Law, *History of Hampton Court*, ii. 282.

[8] In England political circumstances occasionally revived emblematic usage. At Wynnstay, the centre of the White Rose faction in Wales, a ceiling was in the first half of the eighteenth century decorated with a rose and the legend 'Under the rose be it spoken' (*Apollo*, Jan.–June, 1926, iii. 21). An extraordinary survival of the use of emblems in Germany is the decoration of the obelisk of the Neuer Brunnen at Mainz, erected in 1726 in honour of the Bishop of Bamberg. The whole obelisk is covered with emblems carved in low relief: horns of fame, Janus, Man-headed birds, every kind of trophy, sphinxes, pelicans, storks, cocks, porcupines, lyres, &c.

V

THE ROMANCE OF DISTANCE

I

EDGAR ALLAN POE was the first to define Romance as the expression of Man's desire 'to enwrap himself in an exquisite sense of the strange'. Medieval Europe found this alien charm in the productions of Asia, of Byzantium, and of Moslem Sicily and Spain. Relations between western Europe and the powers that ruled these lands might be friendly or hostile, but they were on an equal footing; even the Crusader, once he reached Arab Spain or Asia Minor, recognized a kindred chivalry to his own among his heathen enemies. In another sphere, too, Europe recognized an Arab equality or supremacy; it was the Arabs that held the traditions of Aristotelian philosophy and Greek mathematics and medicine, the re-acquisition of which was the task of the medieval universities. Consequently whatever contempt or disdain the Christians of the West might feel for the religion of Islam, for the peoples of Islam they could feel nothing but an unwilling respect. Their artistic productions held all the glamour of unfamiliarity with none of the taint of inferiority. When Saladin in 1192 sent Henry of Champagne an arab tunic and turban, he received the reply: 'You know that robes and turbans are far from being held in scorn among us. I will certainly wear your gifts.'

Nor were such oriental manufactures so rarely seen in the Christian West as to be uncomfortably strange. Whatever the political relations between East and West, commercial relations were maintained. Not only were Byzantium, Damascus, Jaffa, and Beirut centres whence the fabrics of the East were dispatched to all the ports of the North-Western Mediterranean, but the half-Arab kingdom of Sicily, where East and West were merged and eastern art flourished under Norman protection, became in the twelfth century an important centre of oriental influence.[1] Roger Guiscard, when he captured Athens, Thebes, and Corinth in 1147, carried off Byzantine weavers among his prisoners, and set them to work in his silk factory at Palermo. Saracenic and Byzantine influences were there combined; and the Palermitan factory produced silks with roundels of animals, sometimes bordered with cufic inscriptions,[2] animal and palmette designs in the Spanish-

[1] The mantle of Roger II of Sicily, preserved in the National Treasury of Vienna, is of oriental purple, with a border worked with an Arabic inscription that records its weaving in Sicily. 'Woven at the Royal manufactory, the seat of happiness and honour, where prosperity and perfection, merit and distinction abound; which boasts of progress, glorious good fortune, wonderful splendour, and munificent endowment; which rejoices in the fulfilment of hopes and wishes; where days and nights glide by in continual pleasures without end or change; which is animated by feelings of honour and attachment; in promoting happiness, maintaining prosperity and encouraging activity. In the capital of Sicily, in the year of the Hegira, 528' (A.D. 1133).

[2] A magnificent example is the twelfth-century brocade with double eagles and the Arabic inscription 'Praised be Allah!' now at Siegburg.

228. Designs for details of jewels by Daniel Hailler, *c.* 1605

229. Design for a jewelled pendant by Hans Holbein, *c.* 1540

230. Pendant mirror case of enamelled gold. English, *c.* 1600

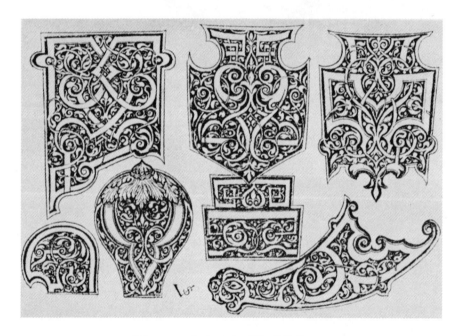

231. Moresque designs by Virgil Solis, *c.* 1550

Arab style as well as brocades with a chequer work of conventional patterns and inscribed borders, like that made about 1190 for the Imperial robe of the Emperor Henry VI.[1]

Meanwhile eastern merchants were themselves settled in most of the important trading centres of Italy and France. In the twelfth century Montpelier, according to Benjamin of Tudela, was a city to which Christians and Mahommedans alike came from all quarters to trade; from Pisa, that had its own oriental quarter, from Genoa, Lombardy, Rome, Greece, Syria, Egypt, Portugal, and Spain. The fairs of Champagne held at Troyes, Provins, Bar-sur-Aube, and Lagny, at the junction of trade routes from the north and south, brought together fresh companies of merchants, which included Italianate Arabs from Pisa, Ferrara, Amalfi, Genoa, and Florence, as well as traders from all Christendom. Consequently the number of surviving examples of eastern silks used for vestments or wrappings for the dead in the eleventh or twelfth centuries is not surprising.[2]

The great inventory of the vestments of St. Paul's Cathedral, drawn up in 1245,[3] includes silks of all the familiar oriental patterns: white damask, with spread eagles, red, with little circles in which were kings seated on lions, red, with pine trees and birds (a Persian pattern), and others with griffins, elephants, lions[4] and parrots,[5] stags and winged dragons. Even greater riches, with a certain preponderance of purely Byzantine silks, are evident in the inventories of St. Peter's at Rome.[6]

The influence of such textiles on Romanesque art was widespread; their motives reappear in almost all the arts of the tenth to the twelfth centuries.[7] It is, however, curious and interesting to see how soon their influence was lessened with the development of European art in the thirteenth century. The great style of Gothic architecture influenced every field of decoration and greatly restricted the sphere in which oriental influences could have free play. At Rheims the winged dragons and lions of the Romanesque tradition lurk among the foliage of the naturalistic capitals, like the monsters of a past age surviving in the remoter forests of a new civilization.[8]

[1] Now in the Cathedral of Regensburg. Its inscription states that it was woven for Master Abd-el-Aziz, on behalf of William II of Sicily.

[2] For a short account of them see Dalton, *Byzantine Art and Archaeology* pp. 593 et seqq. For the most recent general account of oriental and occidental silks see O. von Falke, *Decorative Silks*, Berlin and London, 1922.

[3] *Archaeologia*, l. 477 et seqq.

[4] Cf. a fine thirteenth-century dalmatic with roundels of lions in the Treasury of Halberstadt Cathedral.

[5] Cf. the thirteenth-century Persian brocade in green and red with parrots in ogee medallions now at Krauth College, Frankfurt.

[6] See E. Müntz and A. L. Frothingham, *Il Tesoro della Basilica di S. Pietro*, pp. 19 et seqq. It has been suggested (Dalton, *Byzantine Art and Archaeology*, p. 588) that Rome was an important distributing centre for such silks.

[7] See J. J. Marquet de Vasselot, 'Les Influences orientales', in Michel, *Histoire de l'art*, i. 882 et seqq, and J. Ebersolt, *Orient et Occident*, Paris, 1928.

[8] The same type appears in England on the Easter Sepulchre at Lincoln, *c.* 1300.

Further, the sack of Constantinople by the Crusaders in 1204 helped to change the balance of riches between east and west. Villehardouin tells us:[1] 'les gens qui furent espandu parmi la vile gaignièrent assez; et fu si granz li gaaienz faiz, que nus de vos en saurait dire la fin d'or et d'argent et de vaiselemente, et de pierres précieuses, et de samez, et de dras de soie, et de robes vaires et grises et hermines, et toz les chiers avoirs qui onques furent trové en terre.' For a moment there was an enormous influx of oriental and Byzantine wares into Europe, but it was followed by an ebb of commerce from which Constantinople took nearly three centuries to recover. Instead of Byzantium and Cairo being the twin centres of the Eastern Mediterranean, the death of Saladin in 1193, the consequent division of his empire, and the sack of Constantinople, left the Near East with so unstable a political balance that its wealth was dissipated, and its manufactures restricted by the general diminution of luxury. By the middle of the thirteenth century the Mongol invasion added a further menace to the civilization of the Near East, and under its shadow the Crusading impulse came to an end. In 1291 Saint Jean d'Acre, the last remaining Christian possession in the east, fell into Saracen hands. The Ottoman invasions of the fourteenth century added a new element to the complex of eastern politics; by 1390 the Turks held the Balkans and by 1453 Byzantium itself. Until Suleiman the Magnificent revived the glories of Constantinople, eastern influence on Europe was diffused and weakened. In 1282 the 'Sicilian Vespers' drove out the Arab weavers from the Palermitan silk factories, and there was a consequent decline of the importance of the Sicilian manufactures.[2]

From Sicily the practice of silk-weaving passed to the mainland of Italy, and took its place among the other industrial arts. Oriental tradition, though strong, was less dominant, and fresh impulses came to change the direction of its influence. Lucca was for a time the most important centre; and at Lucca the oriental traditions of Palermitan design were considerably modified. The roundel frames of the oriental type were generally omitted, and many of the animals of the oriental tradition were modified into heraldic forms, lions in all the heraldic positions, uncrowned, crowned, and gorged with crowns; unicorns, stags, and eagles. The most characteristic scheme is a series of affronted beasts arranged in horizontal lines (fig. 206), like the crowned gazelles with cockatrices on their backs alternating with lines of snake-tailed birds on a brocade in the treasury of Sens Cathedral.[3] After the beginning of the thirteenth century designs became lighter and much less symmetrical; and Persian influence[4] combined with Gothic naturalism to

[1] *Conquête de Constantinople*, ed. de Wailly, Paris, 1874, p. 146.

[2] O. von Falke notes (*op. cit.*, p. 21) that there is no mention of Sicilian silks in the Roman inventories of the Papal treasures after 1295, their place being taken by textiles from Spain, Lucca, Venice, and Genoa.

[3] The same brocade is used for the liturgical shoes of Cardinal Arnaud de la Vie (d. 1333) in the Musée de Cluny.

[4] A fine Lucchese brocade of the early fourteenth century in the treasury of Aix-la-Chapelle has a pattern of affronted griffins and birds with 'pine' motives between, that is very Persian in character. Cf. a similar brocade in Orcagna's painting of the Coronation of the Virgin in the National Gallery. For reproductions of

232. Front of a coffer with marquetry panels. French, c. 1540

233. Tazza of Saint Porchaire pottery, *c.* 1540

achieve more varied motives and a more naturalistic treatment.[1] It is almost certainly from Persian sources that certain Chinese motives appear on Lucchese silks; flying birds, dragons, stylized cloud forms, the lotus vine, all treated with the vigour and asymmetry of the Chinese style (figs. 207, 208).

Arabic inscriptions gradually passed into disuse; for a short time Italian inscriptions were used instead. A brocade in the Brussels collection has peacocks, and griffins with *grifone* on their wings.[2] This brocade is also interesting for the increasing naturalism of the vine sprays between the creatures; their use, derived from the east, is characteristic of the North Italian brocades of the later fourteenth century, and served to link the oriental tradition with medieval naturalism, and thus to bring about its modification (fig. 209). The inventory of the Duke of Normandy's possessions in 1363 includes Lucchese silks of this kind—blue with red vine leaves, green with birds, violet with yellow birds, white with green birds, 'blondet' with red and green leaves, and green with leaves of the colour of peach-blossom.[3]

From Lucca, especially after the capture of the city by Uguccione della Fagiuola in 1310, colonies of weavers passed to all the great cities of North Italy, Florence, Milan, Genoa, and Venice.[4] In Venice, always half-oriental in taste, eastern influences were strong. A group of early fourteenth-century Venetian brocades shows Chinese influence,[5] not only in scheme, but also in the dragon-headed horses,

this and other such patterns see S. Vacher, *Fifteenth-century Italian Ornament chiefly taken from brocades and stuffs found in pictures in the National Gallery*, 1886.

[1] At the same time it must be remembered that Italy had contacts even with the Far East. Marco Polo mentions silk-weaving as being practised at many of the cities he visited.

[2] The so-called chasuble of St. Dominic in the treasury of Saint Sernin at Toulouse is brocaded with rows of pelicans and peacocks in gold and green. Beside each peacock is the inscription PAONE, while on the wing of each pelican is HELICE (for *Pelice*). I. Errera, *Catalogue d'etoffes anciennes*, p. 58, no. 56.

[3] L. Doüet d'Arcq, *Comptes de l'argenterie des rois de France au XIVᵉ siècle*, 1851, p. xxvii.

[4] More than thirty-one families went to Venice alone after the capture of the city. O. von Falke, *op. cit.*, p. 35. At the same time orders drawn up by the authorities in Paris in 1260 to regulate the silk-weaving carried on by foreigners within their boundaries show that such colonies were not confined to Italy; and silk-weaving was certainly carried on at Ratisbon and perhaps in other centres. See O. von Falke, *op. cit.*, p. 28. A distinction can be made between North Italian brocades that perpetuate the Lucchese tradition of all-over bird and vine patterns, and others with a slighter powdering of detached alternating motives, that seem more characteristic of the northern countries, and follow an occidental rather than an oriental tradition. In 1317 there were bought for the Queen of France four pieces of blue silk brocaded with golden fishes, to make a surcoat and a mantle to wear when she went to mass, as well as five pieces with fishes and birds for a wedding dress (L. Douet d'Arcq, *Nouveau Recueil de Comptes de l'argenterie des rois de France*, 1874, pp. 9 and 11). These recall the brocades with rather thin powderings of stars and fishes, birds and leaves, in the treasury of Klosterneuburg. A late fourteenth-century camocas in the treasury of Troyes is similarly brocaded with green parrots and golden griffins and lions' heads on a white ground, panelled with gold lines and studded with golden stars. It is probably from such silks that parrots were introduced into general decoration; Clemence of Hungary, for instance, in 1328 had tapestries 'ouvrés de papegais et de compas' (Michel, *Histoire de l'art*, iii. 348) and a brooch 'à deux papegais' (J. Doüet d'Arcq, *Nouveau Recueil des comptes de l'argenterie des rois de France*, p. 43) and Louis d'Anjou a goblet enamelled with parrots holding butterflies (Laborde, *Glossaire des Émaux*, p. 22). A green corded silk in the Victoria and Albert Museum is brocaded in gold with a powdering of single vine leaves, griffins, and fleurs-de-lis. See also von Falke, *op. cit.*, p. 28.

[5] See von Falke, *op. cit.*, p. 34. As early as 1442 the Doge Foscari received a gift of Chinese porcelain from the Sultan of Egypt (H. Belevitch Stankevitch, *Le Goût chinois en France au temps de Louis XIV*, p. xxi) and

turtles, Khilins, and *Fong hoang* which appear in their designs. The bird motives are the commonest; the date of their use is roughly fixed by their presence in a design of Jacopo Bellini's for a brocade,[1] and on the brocade worn by God the Father and the Virgin in Orcagna's painting of the Coronation of the Virgin.[2] Yet even these motives were soon Europeanized into basilisks, pheasants, and other European beasts, treated with Gothic vigour and naturalism (fig. 210). The inventory of the possessions of Valentine de Milan and her husband drawn up in 1408 includes silks brocaded with lions and hawks among leafage, with a stag standing against a tree with a paling, with gerfalcons with thistles, one 'chevronné d'or à violetes d'or et vermeilles', and another brocaded with little feathers of gold.

Hunting scenes, castles of all kinds, naturalistic subjects such as swallows catching butterflies,[3] Christian themes and symbols, gradually drove out the alien subjects acquired with the tradition of silk-weaving. The first wave of oriental influence in a medieval Italy had exhausted itself, and had become merged in a national style.

2

Medieval Spain, with its large Moslem population, was in even closer touch with oriental art than was Italy. But since it had not so early to resolve the discord between eastern style and another national tradition in the minor arts, it was less progressive and less creative. Silk weaving, and especially the weaving of silks brocaded with the honorific titles of their wearers, had been carried on there since the ninth century. Almeria is recorded by Almakkari to have manufactured the *dibaj*, brocade of many colours, the *tiraz*, woven with the names of Sultans, *holol* or striped silk, and other brocades as well as robes, curtains and turban silks, while Malaga, Grenada[4] and Seville were also centres of the weaving industry.[5]

The use of oriental fabrics was also general. In February 1391, John of Aragon wrote from Saragossa to the Duke of Montblanch that he had heard that ships were coming from Alexandria 'bringing cloths of gold and silver and velvets; I beg that such things may be brought by them to you and that you will choose some of them that seem suitable in your opinion and are of the newest fashions and make'.[6]

In the course of the Middle Ages, however, a gradual change is evident. The

---

by the end of the fifteenth century 'Maestro Antuonio Archimista' was imitating porcelain there. Another kiln was set up there by Leonardo Peringer.

[1] See G. M. de Geltof in 'Bollettino d'arte e curiosità Veneziane' quoted in *L'Art Ancien à l'Exposition de 1878*, p. 476. The Venetian city accounts for 1508 include an entry of payment for seven bowls of 'porcellana contrafacta'. Hannover, *Pottery and Porcelain*, ed. Rackham, iii. 7.

[2] Now in the National Gallery.

[3] On an early fifteenth-century north Italian brocade in the Kunstgewerbe Museum at Berlin.

[4] Even in 1502 the *Voyage de Philippe le Beau* records: 'Auprès de ce lieu est une place apellée l'Allecasserie, où on vendt les draps de soyes ouvrés à la Moresque, qui sont moult beaus pour la multitude des couleurs et le diversité des ouvrages, et en font une grande marchandise.' Quoted, Riano, *Spanish Industrial Art*, p. 256.

[5] See O. von Falke, *Decorative Silks*, 1922, p. 19.

[6] Lady Evans, *Lustre Pottery*, p. 416.

234. Design for an Ionic Order. By Vredeman de Vries, 1563

235. Detail of a plaster ceiling in Broughton Castle, Oxon., *c.* 1600

236. Stucco decoration from the Escalier du Roi, Palais de Fontainebleau.
By Il Rosso, *c.* 1535

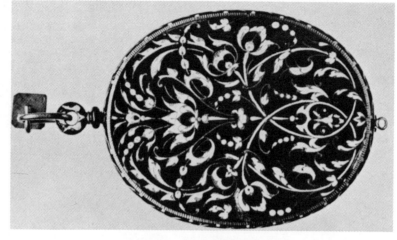

239. Miniature case of enamelled gold in the style of Jean Toutin of Château-dun, c. 1620

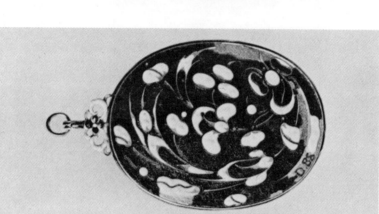

238. Miniature case enamelled after a design by Pierre Firens, c. 1625

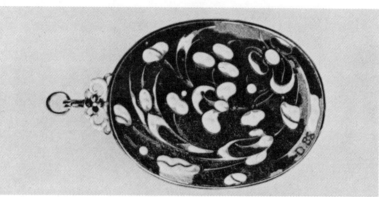

237. Design in peapod style by Lemersier, 1626

bands of inscriptions or of conventional strapwork tended to give place to all-over patterns, whether of strapwork (fig. 212) or of foliate (fig. 211) and animal forms (fig. 213). These, however, are always more formal and more traditional than the Italian models. The hand of Islam still lay heavy on Spanish art. Even when the Moslem power had been forced back till it held nothing but the Sultanate of Grenada, Aragon, and Castille, its conquerors, if in religious work they followed a style Flemish in origin and largely practised by northern artists,[1] in secular work perpetuated a Moslem style practised by the 'mudejars' or subject Moors. This latter reached its apogee in the fourteenth century. In its purely Moslem form it lies outside the scope of this book; but it combined with influences from Asia Minor to exercise a considerable influence on the European arts. The Moslem painted and lustred tiles and pottery were freely used outside Spain; Moslem brocades were familiar in all the greater trading centres of Europe;[2] Moslem glass was exported even to England[3] and was imitated at Venice; and Moslem goldwork and damascening, whether of Asiatic or Spanish origin, found a place in the great medieval treasure hoards. Cybo of Hyères painted a miniature definitely oriental in style and in the dress of its personages in a manuscript illuminated about 1390.[4] René of Anjou, patron of all the arts, did not neglect those of Moorish Spain; he had his Moors to tend his dromedaries, to weave him silken robes, and to dance the 'morisque'[5] before him. The fine manuscript known as his Book of Hours[6] has vignettes with meaningless Arab characters painted on a blue ground after the manner of Moorish tiles.

Inscriptions imitated from oriental work were reproduced on much European fourteenth-century goldwork; Louis of Anjou had at least a hundred and sixteen pieces of plate decorated with 'lettres de Damas', 'lettres Moresques', or 'lettres sarrasines'.[7] That those objects were not oriental in origin is shown by the other elements of their decoration; one goblet had a border of Moorish letters, leaves, stars, and hearts pierced by arrows;[8] a goblet and ewer of gold, engraved with 'lettres de Damas', had four roundels, two with the arms of Étampes and two with the device of an ermine chained to a tree;[9] while a pot of silver gilt was 'hachié à

[1] Yet Moorish work was far from being excluded from the churches. The cupola of the chapel of the Concepción convent at Toledo is lined with Manises tiles, some with I.H.S. and some with the Islamic 'Hand of Glory'. Font y Guma, *Rajolas Valencianas y Catalanas*, chap. vii.

[2] In 1389 Clement VII had gold brocades made to his order in Damascus, through the mediation of the Grand Master of Rhodes. *Gazette des Beaux Arts*, viii, 1892, p. 276.

[3] e.g. the 'Luck of Edenhall', dating from the fourteenth century. Flasks, glasses, lamps, plates, and bowls of painted Damascus glass are included in the inventories of Louis d'Anjou, Charles V, and of the Louvre in 1418. See Havard, *Dictionnaire de l'Ameublement*, s.v. Damas.

[4] B.M. Add. MS. 27695, fol. 13.

[5] Such Moorish dances were enamelled on two salt-cellars and a mirror belonging to Charles the Bold in 1467. Laborde, *Les Ducs de Bourgogne*, ii. 84.

[6] In the Bibliothèque Nationale, Paris.

[7] H. Moranvillé, *op. cit.*, p. xxxi.

[8] *Ibid.*, p. 344.

[9] *Ibid.*, pp. 90 and 113.

ceintures montans et avalans, dont l'une des parties sont à rosiers et l'autre à lettres moresques; et entre lesdites ceintures à plusieurs rainceaus de lis, plantez parmi grans couronnes; en l'une partie et en l'autre sont griffons'.[1]

The plate 'à lettres moresques' of the fourteenth and fifteenth centuries has perished, but a reproduction of it in less precious material has survived. A covered bowl of carved 'mazer'—root of box or maple wood—in the Victoria and Albert Museum[2] (fig. 216) has its lid carved with a meaningless inscription in Arabic letters, set as a border to little naturalistic sprays of violet, pea, daisy, pink, pimpernel and corncockle.

The European use of such Arab inscriptions, however, gradually declined as the Moorish artificers of Spain adopted European motives at the expense of oriental.[3] The fall of Malaga in 1487 and that of Granada five years later struck a death blow to the oriental tradition in Spain; and it came to an end with the persecution of the Moriscos, that began in 1499 and ended in their expulsion from the country in 1610.

3

Meanwhile the Ottoman Sultans were restoring the glories of the Eastern Empire. The European appreciation of eastern splendour was renewed, when an eastern power was once more a dominating factor in European politics. Ariosto in the *Orlando Furioso* has as much sympathy for the Saracens as for the Christians. By the beginning of the sixteenth century eastern figures were beginning to appear alike in European pageantry and decoration. An early sixteenth-century tapestry of Tournai manufacture[4] is woven with figures of a Turk and his wife and children, based on an engraving by Dürer, set against a verdure background; while in 1510 Henry VIII and the Earl of Essex appeared at a Shrove Tuesday banquet dressed 'after the Turkey fashion'.[5]

The Ottoman dynasty had re-established not only the political power of Turkey, but also the arts of Asia Minor. The oriental tradition had been once more modified and transformed to meet Turkish needs and to satisfy Turkish tastes. One of the most important developments of decorative tradition was the use of ogival forms in tile and brocade patterns. These, that had appeared as early as the end of the tenth century in Byzantine silk fabrics, had not dominated the line of oriental

[1] *Ibid.*, p. 363. Two similar goblets with roundels enamelled with the arms of France belonged to Charles V in 1380. Labarte, *Inventaire du mobilier de Charles V*, p. 73. The 1402 inventory of Jean, Duc de Berry, includes many pieces of plate 'à lettres grecques'. The general descriptions suggest that these too may have been Arabic characters.

[2] V. and A.M. 221. 66. See Joan Evans in *Burlington Magazine*, liii, 1928, p. 32.

[3] The process is clearly seen alike in architecture and in the minor arts. By the end of the fifteenth century the Moorish workmen had appropriated flamboyant tracery for stucco architectural decoration (for example, on the 'House of Pilate' at Seville) and for wall tiles. (Examples in the Osma collection at Madrid). The decoration of Hispano-Moresque pottery shows a steady and gradual transition from oriental to occidental motives.

[4] In the Museum of Fine Arts, Boston.   [5] Hall, *Chronicle*, 1809 ed., p. 513.

240. Panel of the door of St. Maclou, Rouen, 1557

241. Back of a dish, Limoges enamel in grisaille. By Pierre Reymond, *c.* 1560

silk design in the earlier middle ages,[1] but after the middle of the fifteenth century they take an increasingly important place in Anatolian silk design.[2]

Political and commercial relations between Turkey and the trading centres of North Italy were close; Venice held Dalmatia, Istria, Cyprus, Chios and Crete; the Florentine Acciajuoli still held Athens; and Italian colonies were established at Constantinople, Pera, Adrianople, Gallipoli, Broussa, Trebizond, Beyrout and Aleppo.[3] During the fifteenth and sixteenth centuries there were constant embassies between Constantinople and Venice, Milan, Genoa, Florence, Rome and Naples. Oriental weavers were employed in Italy (especially at Venice) and Italians were engaged in the textile trade at Constantinople.[4]

By this time the centre of silk-weaving in Italy had shifted to Florence; early in the fifteenth century Benedetto Dei recorded that Florence made as much silk and gold brocade as Venice, Genoa and Lucca put together. The Florentine designers were quick to realize the beauty of the Turkish ogival scheme, and the harmony that existed between its curves and the Gothic line of Europe. A similar scheme was quickly adapted for their silks: an ogival trellis enclosing a pine form, endlessly elaborated, is the base of the great majority of Florentine silks of the late fifteenth and early sixteenth centuries (figs. 215, 217). Such a brocade appears in Crivelli's picture of the Virgin enthroned, dated 1476;[5] and a similar fabric is used for the binding of Ferdinand and Isabella's copy of the *Partidas*, now in the National Library at Madrid. Other fine examples are to be found among the plunder taken from the field of Granson in 1476, now in the Museum of Berne.

The chief rivals to the patterns based on such ogival compartments were those which were indirectly derived from them: the patterns with great pines growing from a waved stem (fig. 218) such as appear on pictures of the middle of the century,[6] and others in which the pines are arranged on an ogival plan, but the actual framing is modified or omitted (fig. 215).

It was not long before the ogival framing and the pines became modified by the changing currents of Italian decoration. In the roundel Madonna painted by

[1] They occur to frame pine-patterns on some Arab textiles of the thirteenth–fourteenth centuries: e.g. I. Errera, *Catalogue d'Etoffes anciennes*, p. 37, no. 26. A very simple ogival pattern is used for one of the brocade dresses in Orcagna's Coronation of the Virgin in the National Gallery. For other fourteenth-century instances see O. von Falke, *op. cit.*, p. 40. The pall of Mary of Mangop, second wife of Stephen the Great, d. 1476, is of a brocade with ogives with a pine in the middle, and little pines on the ground. O. Tafrali, *Le Trésor Byzantin et Roumain du monastère de Poutna*, Plate XLIII.

[2] For a bibliography and brief account of the subject, see Victoria and Albert Museum, Department of Textiles, *Brief Guide to the Turkish Woven Fabrics* (Stationery Office, 1923). The question whether it appears in Italy as a result of Turkish influence, or vice versa, remains uncertain; Mr. A. J. B. Wace tells me that he inclines to the former view, while Herr v. Falke favours the latter. I have taken the view that the ogival scheme reached Italy from the Turkish East.

[3] See E. Müntz, 'La Propagande de la Renaissance en Orient', in *Gazette des Beaux Arts*, 1892, p. 279.

[4] In 1553 Coeck d'Alost founded a manufactory of tapestries in Constantinople. Müntz, *Histoire de la tapisserie en Italie*, p. 30.

[5] In the National Gallery.

[6] Such a brocade is copied on a page of the Breviary of Isabella of Spain. B.M. Add. MS. 18851, fol. 297.

Bernardino Fungai[1] the Virgin wears a mantle of white silk brocaded in gold with ogival compartments filled with pines, each curiously classicized by the addition of an anthemion centre; in other brocades classical urns and vases, medieval crowns and badges, are added to the oriental scheme, while there is a whole series of brocades of the middle of the sixteenth century in which the ogival framing is treated as a knotted cord, with badges woven in the medallions (fig. 219). The general tendency was towards an increasing naturalism, in which only the memory of ogival line survives (fig. 220); but for some dress brocades a more formal but equally occidental style was employed on a much smaller scale.

With the decline of the ogival scheme the influence of other types of Turkish brocades continued to be felt. A sixteenth-century Venetian brocade (fig. 221) might be Turkish, but for the classical detail of its fountains; and its scheme was perpetuated in a simplified and naturalized form in Venetian velvets of the seventeenth century. Not until the centre of European silk-weaving shifted from Italy to France towards the end of the seventeenth century did silk design altogether free itself from oriental influences.

4

The splendid damascened metal-work of Mesopotamia, Syria, and Egypt had long been familiar to the parts of Europe that were in touch with the East. They seem always to have been especially appreciated in Venice. A fourteenth-century candlestick in the British Museum, apparently of Syrian manufacture, bears the arms of the Venetian family of Boldù.

The sack of Damascus by Timur in 1401 drove the industry farther east into Persia, Bokhara, and India; but some of the workmen turned west and established themselves at Venice. There they produced work oriental in form and style, but completed with Italian heraldry, and gradually adapting itself to Italian needs (figs. 222, 223).[2] The Greco-Italian[3] and Italian metal-workers soon set themselves to imitate the Saracenic style and technique; and from Venice the practice of damascening passed to all the chief metal-working cities of Italy. Milan, perhaps the most important of these, produced splendid work in oriental style (fig. 224) for caskets and boxes of all kinds, mirror-frames, weapons, and armour. The art was also practised at Rome; the inventory of the contents of the Château de Pau in 1561–2[4] includes 'ung estuy d'acier faict à la moresque d'or et d'argent, ouvrage

---

[1] d. 1516. The picture is in the National Gallery.

[2] For a summary account of their work see British Museum, *Guide to the Mediaeval Room*, p. 223.

[3] An admirable plate of copper in the Kunstgewerbemuseum at Vienna, damascened with an oriental interlaced pattern, is signed 'Nicolo Rugina Greco da Corfu, fecce 1550'. It must be remembered that oriental strapwork and 'moresques' had early influenced Greek manuscript illumination; e.g. Bodleian MS. Auct. T. *infra*, 2. 7, twelfth century. Such Greek style became familiar in Italy at the end of the fifteenth century; for instance the *Etymologicum Magnum*, by the Cretan Kallierges, published at Venice in 1499, has its initials and borders designed by a Greek in this Balkan style.

[4] E. Molinier, *Inventaire des meubles du Château de Pau*, 1561–2, p. 51.

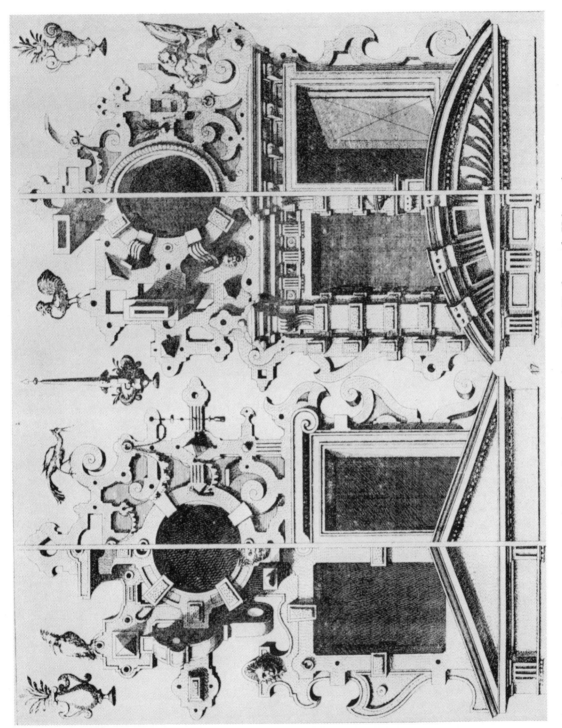

242. Designs for dormers in carved stone. By Vredeman de Vries, 1563

243. Carved oak mantelpiece in the house of Mr. E. R. Roberts Chanter, Barnstaple, 1617

de Romme'. Work in the Syrian style went by the name of damascening; that in
the Persian manner—especially used for armour—went by the name of *Algemina*
or *Azzimina*, from the Arab name of Persia, El Agem.[1]

The Italian workers, however, tended to modify the oriental designs into more
congenial forms even when practising the oriental technique. Benvenuto Cellini
himself tells us that in 1524:

'There fell into my hands certain little Turkish poniards, and the handle of each weapon was
of iron as well as the blade; the sheath was, moreover, of iron likewise. These said objects
were engraved by means of iron tools, with a quantity of very beautiful foliage after the
Turkish manner, and very delicately inlaid with gold: the which thing provoked greatly in
me a desire to experiment also with a view to labouring myself in that branch, so different
from the others, and when I saw that I succeeded very well, I made a number of articles.
These same objects were very much handsomer and much more durable than the Turkish
ones, for many different reasons. One of these was that in the case of my steel articles, I cut
very deeply beneath the surface,[2] which they are not accustomed to do in Turkish work.
Another was that the Turkish foliage is of no other species but arum leaves, with some
blossoms of the sunflower; and although they have a certain amount of elegance, they do
not continue to satisfy as does our foliage. For in Italy there are various methods of designing foliage . . . and in among this said foliage there are charmingly introduced some little
birds and divers animals, from which may be discovered the good taste of the artist.'[3]

Similarly the Milanese workers applied damascening to the decorative scrolls and
cartouches of the mature Renaissance style; and its designs were further influenced by the engraved *imagini*, since its lines and dots could exactly reproduce
their effects.

But if the patterns of damascening itself were Europeanized, the oriental patterns
that it had earlier introduced to Europe had a longer history when turned to the
use of other crafts. Such moresques[4] were welcome to the craftsmen of the
Renaissance, not merely because of their extreme complexity and sophistication,
their beauty of line and flowing regularity of design, but also because they were
designed definitely as *surface* ornament, and were therefore doubly welcome at a
time when decoration was apt to suffer from the domination of representational
painting and sculpture in the round. They offered a delightful diversification of
surface that did not impair the pure line of the whole; and there were many forms
of Renaissance ornament of which as much could not be said.

Moresque strapwork and leafage were early adapted to the repoussé decoration
of Venetian metal lanterns (fig. 225), and from such work they spread to metal-
work of a finer kind. On such work moresques were commonly treated in niello;

[1] H. Lavoix, in *Gazette des Beaux Arts*, vol. xii, 1862, p. 64, describes a casket decorated with such work,
signed 'Paulus. Ageminius. faciebat'.
[2] *Intagliare a sottosquadro*: to hollow out more deeply beneath than on the surface, in order to key in the
metal inlay securely.
[3] *The Life of Benvenuto Cellini*, Bk. i, chap. 6, trans. R. H. Hobart Cust, p. 112.
[4] I make no apology for reviving this word to designate such patterns, since the usage of the eighteenth
century has turned the more obvious 'arabesque' to connote patterns of quite another kind.

the oriental damascening tradition of colour-contrast was maintained, but was treated in a different technique. Such surface ornament was of a type that could be represented and transmitted by engravings without flattening or distortion, and consequently it early spread beyond Italy to the Northern countries. It was diffused not only by engraved patterns definitely intended for craftsmen, but also by the borders and adornments of printed books.[1] The German designers soon followed suit. Hans Holbein designed moresques,[2] and introduced them to England; Peter Flötner published in 1546 a good and well-drawn set of moresque designs; Virgil Solis published patterns for cups ornamented with medallions of such patterns and details for armourers. Ducerceau included such a pattern among his jewel designs,[3] and in the middle of the century others were produced in France,[4] Germany, and the Netherlands.[5] The first engraved pattern book ever published in England was a reprint of an Italian repertory of such designs.[6] That such patterns were freely applied to nielloed metal work is evident alike from contemporary inventories[7] and from surviving examples (figs. 229–30). A design by Hans Holbein[8] for a magnificent cup, with the initials of Jane Seymour as Queen, and therefore dating from 1536, has a wide band of moresque above one of classical foliage; a rose-water dish and ewer at Corpus Christi College, Cambridge, with the London hall-mark for 1545, have bands of delicate outlined moresques; as has another rose-water dish dated 1556, belonging to Lord Newton of Lyme. Such decoration was commonly used on English silver in the decade between 1560 and 1570.[9]

Moresque patterns gradually spread from metal-work into other arts. They appear on Venetian and Gubbio faience of the middle of the sixteenth century

[1] For instance the *Psalterium polyglottum*, printed at Genoa in 1516, has borders of moresque strapwork, and is but one of a great number of Renaissance printed books to be so decorated.

[2] See for instance his designs in the British Museum and Hollar's engravings of others. (Victoria and Albert Museum, Dept. of Engraved Ornament, EO22, 27381–2, 14112, 14107–9.)

[3] Ducerceau's *Suite de moresques et damasquines* are modelled on, if not copied from, those of Peter Flötner.

[4] e.g. *La Fleur de la Science de Portraiture et Patrons de Broderie façon arabicque et Italique*, by 'Messir Francisque Pelegrin de Florence', published at Paris in 1530.

[5] By Balthasar Sylvius (*Variorum protractionum quas vulgo maurusias vocant . . . libellus*, 1554) (Plate 178 with the devices of Diane de Poitiers is designed in his style), the German Master F.B. (Victoria and Albert Museum EO16, E80, A91); the Master of 1551 (Victoria and Albert Museum EO30, 21270; E1743, 1907; E2239, 1910) and the Master GI, finished by Reynard (EO19, 799, 1912). Before 1555 Heinrich Aldegrever published designs in the manner of Cellini's Turkish leafage.

[6] *Morysse and Damashin renewed and increased, very profitable for goldsmythes and embroderers* by Thomas Geminus, at London, anno. 1543. See Campbell Dodgson in *Proc. Soc. Ant.*, 1917 (June 28), p. 210. Copies of the Plates are in the Victoria and Albert Museum; a copy of the title-page is at Münster. I am inclined to think that 'Geminus' represents 'Algeminus', and that he was a maker of *Algemina* (see p. 169).

[7] e.g. in 1534 the Queen of Navarre had 'ung coffre d'or esmaillé de noir à la moresque'—Havard, *Dictionnaire de l'Ameublement*, s.v. More; while the 1561–2 inventory of the Château de Pau includes poignards and cases decorated 'à la moresque'.   [8] In the Ashmolean Museum.

[9] See for instance the standing cup of the Armourers and Braziers' Company, London, 1562; Communion cup at Hothfield, Kent, London, 1562; rose-water dish and ewer at Winchester College, London, 1562; silver tazza in St. Michael's Church, Southampton, 1567; and Communion cups at St. Mary's Coslany and St. Peter's Mancroft, Norwich, both Norwich 1567.

FIG. 244. Knotwork panel, designed and engraved by Albert Dürer, *c.* 1506

(fig. 226),[1] and on Italian and Spanish brocade[2] (fig. 227); they adorn Venetian marquetry[3] and lacquer[4] that imitate damascening, and their French and German imitations (fig. 232). The doors of Écouen, made about 1542, were inlaid with moresques in gold to imitate damascening,[5] and similar moresque inlays are common on South German coffers of the middle of the sixteenth century. From metal-work they easily passed to the bookbinders' metal stamps,[6] and thence to the decoration of Saint Porchaire faience (fig. 233).

Albert Dürer, who twice visited Venice, published a series of knot-work panels (fig. 244), that find their prototype in fifteenth-century Persian engraved metal-work;[7] and Giovanni di Michele's marquetry in Santa Croce at Florence shows a simpler form of such knot-work made angular to fit it for the technique of grained wood. In carved stone work it tended to a certain shapelessness, and was rarely happy in its application. It appears as a moulding on the porch of the Chapel of the Holy Blood at Bruges, built between 1529 and 1533, and inappropriately adorns the frieze of the Ionic order designed by Vredeman de Vries in 1565 (fig. 235). Even in its most successful application, in the piercing of the stair-balustrades on the rood-loft of Saint Étienne du Mont at Paris, designed by Pierre Biard in 1600, it is not really congruous with the architectural quality of the whole.

Gradually moresque patterns were modified by the influence of naturalism. A new and sometimes grotesque vigour was added to the foliage, and moresques were designed not as formal patterns usually combined with strapwork, but as a kind of bouquet with curving stems. This style, commonly called pea-pod or *cosse de pois* ornament, had its variations; it could be adapted to the flowing lines of enamel (fig. 238) or to a more clearcut and symmetrical scheme (fig. 239). The style was essentially one for jewellers and enamellers, but it was extraordinarily popular,[8] and might well have influenced other arts if it had had a living interest

---

[1] See Victoria and Albert Museum, Salting Bequest, no. 763.

[2] See a cope with a diminishing moresque pattern in the Musée historique des Tissus at Lyons. A typical moresque brocade is used for the dress of Eleanora da Toledo in her picture (*c.* 1555) by Bronzino in the Uffizi.

[3] e.g. a sixteenth-century clavecin in the Musée de Cluny. Cf. Depenses secrètes of Francis I, 1538; a crystal mirror in a frame of ebony, 'taillé à la damasquyne'. Havard, *Dictionnaire de l'Ameublement*, s.v. Damasquine.   [4] e.g. two mirror frames in the Victoria and Albert Museum, 218, 1866 and 1880, 1861.

[5] Palustre, *Renaissance en France*, ii. 61.

[6] See bindings made for Catherine de Médicis. An almost identical cover, with the cipher, arms, and name of George, Lord Seton, is in the Röhsska Konstslöjd Museum at Göteborg.

[7] Cf. a bowl cover in the Victoria and Albert Museum, 373A, 1897. Similar designs were produced by artists of the School of Leonardo da Vinci.

[8] The more important of the designs published in the style were:

1614. W. Dietterlin (Lyons).	1627. Jacques Caillart.
1619. Toutin (Chateaudun); Jacques Hurtu.	1630. Pierre de la Barre.
1621. P. Symony (Strasbourg).	1632. P. Firens.
1623. Pierre Marchant (Paris); Antoine Hedonyns, Paris; Vivot.	1635–6. F. Le Febvre.
1625. Le Mersier, Gilles Légaré (Paris); Honervogt (Holland).	1638. Jacques Caillart reprinted.
	1647. Le Mersier reprinted.
1626. Le Mersier; Hans Georg Mosbach; Bruckh.	1661. Le Febvre reprinted.
	No date: The Master IM (perhaps Jean Morien) and Assuerus van Londerseel.

FIG. 245. Strapwork panel by Cornelis Bos, 1546

behind it. As it was, however, it became gradually merged in the ordinary flower patterns of the seventeenth-century enamellers.

Meanwhile the other element in moresque decoration—interlaced strapwork[1]— was being developed on lines of its own. It had early been applied to the decoration of ceilings in Mudejar work in Spain; it appears combined with the emblems of Ferdinand and Isabella on the ceiling of the Aljaferia, near Saragossa, decorated about 1492. Thence it was transferred to the plaster ceilings of northern Europe, and its angular lines—found in England as early as 1521, in the plaster ceilings of Wolsey's Rooms at Hampton Court—continued to dominate such design until the middle of the seventeenth century (fig. 235).[2]

Such strapwork was, however, far from being confined to a single technique, or to a single use. The Renaissance feeling for plastic quality in design gradually transformed it for use in relief until it was changed out of all recognition. From paintings[3] and engravings on which its curves and relief were intensified it was soon transferred to sculptured decoration.[4] Such a use was not altogether happy; the strap-scrolls of Il Rosso's stucchi at Fontainebleau (fig. 236) are curiously meaningless in effect.[5] The results were on the whole more successful when such motives were less naturalistically treated in work on a smaller scale, but even so they were of a kind of which men soon tired. In their place designers such as René Boyvin and Etienne de Laune developed the style along more conventional lines (fig. 246), and their patterns were soon transferred to metal,[6] wood (fig. 240),[7] plaster,[8] and stone.[9] Benedetto Battini's engraved cartouches of about 1553 show this style represented in yet higher relief, and it was thus depicted in painting, enamel (fig. 241), and metal-work in low relief (fig. 247), though not in sculptured decoration on a larger scale. Indeed, when Vredeman de Vries finally applied it to architectural decoration (fig. 242),[10] it was reduced to little more than a fret of pierced stone; and it was in this form that strapwork appeared in English architecture, though on a smaller scale a more plastic treatment was attempted (fig. 243).

[1] Such strapwork was much used in fifteenth-century Moslem art, for instance in the funerary mosque of Kait Bey at Cairo, begun in 1483.

[2] For English examples see M. Jourdain, *English Decorative Plasterwork of the Renaissance*, pp. 1–39.

[3] e.g. on the triumphal arches set up for the entry of Philip of Spain into Antwerp in 1541.

[4] e.g. the borders of the Psalter of Pope Paul II, painted by Vincenzo Raymondi of Lodève in 1542. (Bibl. Nat. Lat. 8880).

[5] A tapestry of Danae from Fontainebleau shows Il Rosso's plastic scheme once more flattened into surface decoration. It is now in the Austrian State Collection at Vienna. H. Goebel, *Wandteppiche, II Teil. Die Romanischen Länder*, Band II, fig. 21.

[6] e.g. the Goldsmiths' Company's Bowes cup of 1554, and Gibbon salt-cellar of 1576. On plate there is a decided tendency towards an increasing simplicity and breadth of scale.

[7] See the 'Maison des fours-banaux' at Rouen.

[8] e.g. on the ceiling of the Church of Tillières sur Avre.

[9] See the dormer of a house at Poitiers, dated 1547; a house at 10 rue Noel Bellay, Chartres; houses at Orleans known as the 'Maison de Jean d'Alibert' and the 'Maison de Diane de Poitiers'; and stone panels on the exterior of the Church of Grand Andely. Rather similar ornament is used for chimney-pieces in Ducerceau's *Second livre d'Architecture*, 1559.

[10] Cf. the engraved designs of J. Marcucci, Assuerus van Londerseel, and Hans Jacob Edelmann (1609).

FIG. 246. Design for metalwork, by René Boyvin, *c.* 1560

FIG. 247. Design for a tankard, by Georg Wechter of Augsburg, 1579

For goldsmiths and enamellers the style was further developed definitely *en silhouette* with the same liveliness of outline that marks the human silhouettes of Jacques Callot (1592–1635). At the first the style shared in the tradition of the earlier moresque, but independence was soon achieved (fig. 248). Many engraved patterns were produced for this kind of design and for variations of it.[1] Sometimes it was combined with flowers and fruit (fig. 251), but more often silhouette scroll work was used alone in well-balanced frets of broken outline (fig. 252), achieving a curious effect of strength and grace from a discontinuity that does not impair the main lines of the pattern.[2] In spite of this air of vitality, the strapwork style of ornament had almost run its course; and when the more classic styles of the Renaissance tardily reached their climax in North-Western Europe it passed gradually into disuse.

5

It is evident that no eastern style was able to influence European art for long without being assimilated to it and modified out of all recognition. At the end of the Middle Ages, however, the great voyagers brought strange parts of the world into fresh connexion with Europe and endowed them with new romance. Sir Thomas More set Utopia in the new Continent; men of action—the Conquistadores, Raleigh, Hawkins, Drake—brought it into that relation with the everyday world which makes the wonderful convincing. But it was the voyages performed and not the countries discovered that fired men's imaginations and passed into art. Maps, even of familiar countries, came to have a new significance; a *Galleria delle Carte* was a worthy adjunct to a Palace, and those who paced there on a wet afternoon could enjoy the pleasures of the newly-discovered romance of distance.[3] America appears as a dusky goddess with horn of plenty and macaw in the

[1] 1585, Hans van Ghemert; 1590, Daniel Mignot and Hans de Bull; 1591 and 1593, Corvinianus Saur; 1592, Hieronymus Berkhausen; 1598, German Master A.C.; 1599, Hans Hensel; 1602, Jean Vovert; 1604, Daniel Hailler; 1605, Michel le Blon; 1607 and 1614, Nicholas Drusse; 1608, anonymous French master; 1609, P.R.K.; 1610, Sordot, Van Ryssen and N. Rouillart; 1614 and 1619, Hurtu; 1615, Carteron; 1617, M. Grundler; 1620, P. Nolin; 1621, Symony; 1622, G. B. Constantino; 1635, De la Queuellerie.

[2] e.g. in the designs published by Michael le Blon at Amsterdam in 1626, and in the *Newe Gradisco Buech* published by Lucas Kilian in 1632.

[3] The earliest decorative use of maps I have come across is the painting of a map of the world on a wall of the hall in Winchester Castle in 1256. The Inventory of Charles V of France includes two hangings of yellow cendal, 'de quoy l'un est paint a chasteaulx, à rivières et à gens par manière de mappemonde.' (Michel, *Recherches sur le commerce des étoffes de soie*, i. 207). In 1418 there was at the Castle of Vincennes a 'mappemonde' of gold, shaped like half an apple (Havard, *Dictionnaire de l'ameublement*, s.v. Mappemonde); in 1479 Anne of Brittany had nine maps (*ibid.*, s.v. Cartes). In the second half of the sixteenth century the decorative use of maps became fairly common in Italy: the 'Galleria delle Carte Geografiche' of the Vatican was painted at the order of Gregory XIII. A tapestry map of Paris was woven about 1555, and Sheldon wove maps of the English counties about 1588; an embroidered map of the world is recorded in Louis XIV's inventory of 1673 (Guiffrey, *Inventaire général du mobilier de la couronne*, ii, p. 212). On the front of S. Maria Zobenigo at Venice, designed by Sardi in 1683, are plans in relief of Rome, Candia, Padua, Corfu, Spalato and Pavia.

248. Silhouette design by Étienne Carteron, 1615

249. The Lyte Jewel, given to Mr. Thomas
Lyte by James I, *c.* 1610

250. Silver salt-cellar. Probably Venetian, *c.* 1550

FIG. 251. Design for the rim of a cup. By P. R. K., Dutch, *c.* 1617

FIG. 252. Fret by Michael le Blon, 1626

spandrel of the map at Caprarola, and complete with feathers and bow to accompany the other continents on Leonard Gauthier's emblem of Peace, engraved about 1606.[1]

In the maritime countries the symbols of the ocean and navigation gained a new significance. First Jacques Coeur, the greatest merchant of the fifteenth century, had a room in his house at Bourges painted with his trading galleys.[2] Then Portugal reflected its sea-going interests in decorative form at the end of the fifteenth century, in mysterious marine foliage, like seaweed under water, in coral forms, in the decorative use of fishnets and sails, all set in decadent flamboyant tracery of extreme richness. At Belem, whence Vasco de Gama sailed, the cloister was thus decorated about 1520 with cables, instruments of navigation, astrolabes, armillary spheres, and a strange vegetation that is half marine and half tropical. Then Venice used the nereids and tritons of her Bride in decoration; and her printers' use of them, as in the Terence of 1499, helped to diffuse and perpetuate the scheme.[3] It is probably for Venice that Marco Dente of Ravenna designed the frieze of *putti* with shells and tridents, topped by a dolphin and trident cornice, that he published in 1527.[4] Genoa next took up the theme; the great hall of the Palazzo Doria was about 1530 adorned with fine *stucchi* of marine deities, and plate and tapestries were decorated with the subject of Columbus starting upon his Atlantic voyage.[5]

France inherited such ornament as a part of Renaissance art; Jean Goujon used nereids and tritons upon his Fontaine des Innocents, finished in 1549. The silver-smiths had used them even a little earlier; the 1532 inventory of Florimond Robertet includes three round basins, one with Neptune and Amphitrite, one with the triumph of Neptune, and one with the great rivers, Ganges, Nile, Euphrates, Jordan, Danube and Rhïne, 'qui rendent le tribut de leurs eaux a ce dieu Neptune qui est au fond du bassin dans une coquille attelée de six chevaux marins, qui en nageans font des vagues les plus esmues que l'on puisse voir ny peindre'.

About 1540 Brussels was weaving tapestries with marine divinities for the Spanish market. Then the style passed almost simultaneously to the rival mari-

---

[1] See also J. H. Hyde, 'L'iconographie des quatre parties du monde dans les tapisseries', in *Gazette des Beaux Arts*, 1924, 5th series x, p. 253, and *Bulletin de la Société des Antiquaires de France*, 1927, p. 237.

[2] Havard, *Dictionnaire de l'ameublement*, s.v. Chambre.

[3] Cf. the printers' ornaments used by Jean Granjon at Paris about 1517. Victoria and Albert Museum, Dept. of Engraved Ornament, EO 15, 28193.

[4] Cf. some of the capitals on the pilaster-columns of the Court of the Doge's Palace. Such subjects long remained popular there; even towards the middle of the eighteenth century Tiepolo decorated the Hall of the Four Doors in the Ducal Palace with Venus and Neptune and their attendants.

[5] A plate with a medallion of this subject, surrounded by lesser medallions with genii of plenty, and a border of amorini playing with fruit, is in the collection of the Marchese Spinola at Genoa. The inventory of Florimond Robertet in 1532 (*Mémoires de la Société des Antiquaires de France*, 3rd series, x, 1868, p. 39) includes a tapestry with 'Les embarquements de Christophe Coulomb pour aller aux Indes'.

time powers of England[1] and Holland,[2] until, with the first dawn of French maritime ambition, dolphins, nereids, tritons and marine deities appeared with fresh significance on the ceiling of the long gallery of the Hôtel de la Vrillière and on ivory and ebony cabinets of the time of Louis XIII.[3] Soon, however, the riches of the Far East were imported in such quantities that they could serve as a more living symbol of maritime enterprise; and as the divinities of classical mythology went out of fashion, images of Chinese idols took their place.[4]

[1] See Jackson, *English Plate*, i, p. 198; Maye rose-water dish, 1583, and Swaythling ewer, 1596. See also Founder's Cup of Emmanuel College, Cambridge, *c.* 1580; Rose-water dish at Queen's College, Oxford, 1605; Flagons at Trinity College, Cambridge, 1607; Rose-water dish and ewer at Sidney Sussex College, Cambridge, 1606; Flagons at Queen's College, Oxford, 1616. In 1585 Lord Burghley gave the Queen a basin of Mother of pearl, the back silver-gilt, 'enamyled with skriptures and devyses of cosmogerefy'. Nichols, *Progresses of Elizabeth*, ii, 427. In 1600 she had the 'fore parte' of a dress of white satin 'embroidered all over verie faire like seas, with dyvers devyses of rockes, shippes and fishes'. *Ibid.*, ii, p. 508. About 1616, dolphins, mermaids and sea-monsters appear in the plasterwork at Audley End. M. Jourdain, *English Decorative Plasterwork of the Renaissance*, p. 30.

[2] See the engraved designs of the 'Master of 1551' (Victoria and Albert Museum, Dept. of Engraved Ornament, EO 30, E 1742–1907), Jakob Floris of Antwerp, 1567; Hans Hirtz, *c.* 1590; Paul Flindt, 1594; Jacob de Gheyn, *c.* 1600; Theodor de Bry, *c.* 1600; Adriaen Collaert, *c.* 1600; and Henri de Caiser, *c.* 1630. Tritons and nereids appear on the reliefs of the Rathaus of Bremen, 1612.

[3] See Guiffrey, *Inventaire général du mobilier de la couronne*, i. 54.   [4] See Chapter VII.

INDEX

Related Paperback Books from Da Capo Press

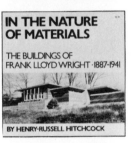